21st Century Guitar

21st Century Guitar

Evolutions and Augmentations

Edited by
Richard Perks and John McGrath

BLOOMSBURY ACADEMIC
NEW YORK • LONDON • OXFORD • NEW DELHI • SYDNEY

BLOOMSBURY ACADEMIC
Bloomsbury Publishing Inc
1385 Broadway, New York, NY 10018, USA
50 Bedford Square, London, WC1B 3DP, UK
29 Earlsfort Terrace, Dublin 2, Ireland

BLOOMSBURY, BLOOMSBURY ACADEMIC and the Diana logo are trademarks of
Bloomsbury Publishing Plc

First published in the United States of America 2023
Paperback edition published 2024

Copyright © Richard Perks and John McGrath, 2023

Each chapter copyright © by the contributor, 2023

For legal purposes the Acknowledgements on p. xii constitute an extension
of this copyright page.

Cover design: Louise Dugdale
Cover image © Milton Mermikides, 2023

All rights reserved. No part of this publication may be reproduced or transmitted
in any form or by any means, electronic or mechanical, including photocopying,
recording, or any information storage or retrieval system, without prior
permission in writing from the publishers.

Bloomsbury Publishing Inc does not have any control over, or responsibility for, any
third-party websites referred to or in this book. All internet addresses given in this
book were correct at the time of going to press. The author and publisher regret
any inconvenience caused if addresses have changed or sites have ceased
to exist, but can accept no responsibility for any such changes.

A catalog record for this book is available from the Library of Congress

ISBN: HB: 978-1-5013-7329-9
PB: 978-1-5013-7333-6
ePDF: 978-1-5013-7331-2
eBook: 978-1-5013-7330-5

Typeset by Deanta Global Publishing Services, Chennai, India

To find out more about our authors and books visit www.bloomsbury.com and
sign up for our newsletters.

Contents

List of figures	vi
List of contributors	x
Acknowledgements	xii
Introduction *Richard Perks and John McGrath*	1
1 The well-tuned guitar *John Schneider*	9
2 Transforming the microtonal fingerboard: 'Small' frets, LEGO and robots: Interview with Tolgahan Çoğulu *Richard Perks*	25
3 The expanding fretless guitarscape: Practice and progress *Richard Perks*	37
4 Touching the apple without gloves: Interview with Cenk Erdoğan *Richard Perks*	67
5 Extended range instruments: Towards a new organology of the guitar *Tom Williams*	77
6 I should have just learned how to play the organ: Interview with Charlie Hunter *Richard Perks*	101
7 The transformed space of the 'Ligeti Guitar' *Katalin Koltai*	111
8 Grains, glitches and infinite space: Guitar effects pedals, digitization and textural guitar aesthetics *Robert Strachan*	153
9 The sonic maelstrom: Interview with Nels Cline *John McGrath*	173
10 'Something seems wrong, should that be happening?': Avantfolk guitar and glitch aesthetics, a practice-based perspective *John McGrath*	185
11 A field of reactivity: Moog guitar and experimental systems: Interview with Bill Thompson *John McGrath*	205
12 The digital fretboard: Remapping and relearning the guitar's pitch matrix with MIDI and Max/MSP *Milton Mermikides*	215
13 Augmented reality guitars: Extended instruments and notation for a 21st-century practice *Amy Brandon*	239
Index	263

Figures

1.1	Intonation Systems sales brochure (1977)	10
1.2	Mode, lattice and fretting for *Serenade* (1978)	12
1.3	Tuning, lattice and fretting for *Ditone Set* (1978)	13
1.4	Guitar with interchangeable fingerboards	14
1.5	Vogt Fine-Tunable Precision Fretboard fretted in a baroque well temperament	15
1.6	Adapted Guitar I: (a) Harry Partch (1941) (b) Author (1993)	15
1.7	Partch's 1945 (fretless electric) Adapted Guitar I	16
1.8	Author's copy of Adapted Guitar II	17
1.9	Author's copy of Adapted Guitar III	17
1.10	PARTCH Ensemble	17
1.11	Fifteen-note Just tuning, fretting and scale for *The Tavern* (1998)	18
1.12	Tuning, mode, lattice and fretting for Harrison's *Scenes from Nek Chand* (2002)	21
2.1	Tolgahan Çoğulu playing his Adjustable Microtonal Guitar	27
2.2	Ruşen Can Acet (L), Atlas Çoğulu (C) and Tolgahan Çoğulu (R) with LEGO Microtonal Guitars	33
2.3	Tolgahan Çoğulu testing the Automatic Microtonal Guitar prototype	34
3.1	Ned Evett (with his glass fingerboard fretless Peavey Ripslide and glass-slide capo)	42
3.2	Buzz Gravelle (with his first fretless classical guitar)	49
3.3	Richard Perks (with fretless Fender Stratocaster) and Faraz Minooei (Santur), *Strung Together*, Buriel Clay Theatre, San Francisco, 2017	59
3.4	Interconnectivity between fretlessness, creative processes and musical outcomes	61
4.1	Cenk Erdoğan with his Marchione fretless classical guitar	68
6.1	Charlie Hunter playing his Hybrid Guitars long-scale Big 6 live	102
7.1	Sagreras, *El Colibri*, mm. 1–3	114
7.2	Kurtág, *Grabstein für Stephan*, op. 15/c, guitar part, mm. 1–4	115
7.3	Chopin, *Valse* op. 69, No. 2, piano, mm. 1–5	118
7.4	Chopin, *Valse* op. 69, No. 2, arranged for guitar by Dyens, mm. 1–4	118

Figures vii

7.5	Galbraith and the Brahms Guitar	119
7.6	Yepes and the ten-string guitar	120
7.7	Scordatura used by Hoppstock	121
7.8	Three capo models of the magnet capo system	122
7.9	Ligeti Guitar	122
7.10	Magnet capo placeholders on the Ligeti Guitar	123
7.11	Fretboard diagram with different string lengths	124
7.12	Bartók, *Im Freien* [*Out of Doors*], Sz.81, 'The Night's Music', mm. 1–2	126
7.13	Nature nocturnal sounds Bartók, 'The Night's Music', mm. 7–9	126
7.14	Lament song Bartók, 'The Night's Music', mm. 26–28	127
7.15	Wedding dance Bartók, 'The Night's Music', mm. 49–50	127
7.16	Open-string set and fretboard diagram for Bartók, 'The Night's Music'	128
7.17	Bartók, 'The Night's Music', mm. 1–2	128
7.18	Bartók, 'The Night's Music', Instrumental mapping of the first bar	129
7.19	Bartók, 'The Night's Music', nocturnal sounds on the piano and the guitar, mm. 9–11	130
7.20	Mapping of the nocturnal sounds of Bartók, 'The Night's Music', mm. 9–11	131
7.21	Bartók, 'The Night's Music', mm. 7–9	132
7.22	Open-string set and fretboard diagram for Ligeti, *Musica ricercata*, I	133
7.23	Ligeti, *Musica ricercata*, I, opening chord	133
7.24	Ligeti, *Musica ricercata*, I, mm. 1–4	134
7.25	Ligeti, *Musica ricercata*, I, mm. 14–17	134
7.26	*Klangfarbenmelodie* and different strumming techniques in the guitar arrangement of Ligeti's *Musica ricercata*, I, mm. 56–59	135
7.27	Ligeti, *Musica ricercata*, I, mm. 77–80	135
7.28	Demonstrating the spatial distances of the climax of Ligeti, *Musica ricercata*, no.2	136
7.29	Open-string set and fretboard diagram for Ligeti, *Musica ricercata*, II	137
7.30	Ligeti, *Musica ricercata*, II, mm. 24–26	138
7.31	Fretboard diagrams of three different open-string sets of the arrangement of Chopin, *Berceuse*	139
7.32	Chopin, *Berceuse* mm. 1–9	140

7.33	Chopin, *Berceuse* mm. 30–31	141
7.34	Chopin, *Berceuse* mm. 47–48	141
7.35	Chopin, *Berceuse* mm. 88–89	142
7.36	Microtonal tuning of Gorton, *Six Miniatures*	143
7.37	Open-string sets of Gorton, *Six Miniatures*	144
7.38	Gorton, *Six Miniatures* I. mm. 1–3	144
7.39	Gorton, *Six Miniatures* II. mm. 1–6	144
7.40	Gorton, *Six Miniatures* III. mm. 1–4	145
7.41	Gorton, *Six Miniatures* IV. mm. 1–8	145
7.42	Gorton, *Six Miniatures* V. mm. 36–38	146
7.43	Gorton, *Six Miniatures* VI. mm. 25–28	146
8.1	Time-based DSP and glitch effects pedals	154
8.2	Red Panda Particle Mk I	162
9.1	Nels Cline with pedal rig, taken on tour with Wilco 2022	175
10.1	Still from Adam Scovell's video for 'Four Hills'	196
10.2	Transcribed excerpt of BOSS DD6 hold function glitch effect in 'Four Hills'	197
11.1	Bill Thompson, Cafe Oto, London 2022	211
11.2	Bill Thompson's Moog guitar setup	211
12.1	Some fretboard 'stem cells'	218
12.2	Four spaces or 'ways of knowing' the guitar and their interactions	220
12.3	Three representations of the pitch repetition profile of a twenty-four-fret guitar in standard tuning	224
12.4	M-Space versus F-Space	226
12.5	An illustration of Pat Martino's concept (Martino 2016) of linking the *I Ching* hexagrams to the sixty-four possible combinations of string use	229
12.6	The *Fretboard Remapper* built in Max/MSP allowing the visualization and manipulation of real-time fretboard data	231
12.7	A sample of tuning systems with their characteristics	236
13.1	Performance of *flesh projektor II* at Winnipeg New Music Festival, 26 January 2020	240
13.2	Kristina Warren performing *Hidden Motive III* in NYC, 29 September 2018	240
13.3	Table of XR works 2017–21 by Amy Brandon	242
13.4	Amy Brandon – improvised performance in Halifax, May 2019	244

13.5	Emma Rush performing *7 Malagueña Fragments for Augmented Guitar* at the SMC Conference, 28 May 2019 in Málaga, Spain	245
13.6	Kristina Warren performing *Hidden Motive II* at the TENOR Conference, Montreal, 2018	246
13.7	Amy Brandon with *flesh projektor I* at New Music Edmonton in Edmonton, Alberta, 4 May 2019	247
13.8	Image of the field-of-view and performative space using the Metavision headset	248
13.9	Custom image-tracking fretboard	249
13.10	Improvised performance with 360 video score	250
13.11	Projected 360 graphic score at Nocturne Festival, Halifax NS, 14 October 2017	251
13.12	Amy Brandon experimenting with split video capture using HTC Vive, Halifax 2018	252
13.13	Amy Brandon performing using the Metavision headset, Winnipeg New Music Festival, 26 January 2020	252
13.14	Example of guitar scale charts	254

Contributors

Amy Brandon is a composer and guitarist. Her pieces have been described as 'gut wrenching and horrific' (Critipeg) and 'otherworldly, a clashing of bleakness with beauty' (Minor Seventh). Her performances, installations and acoustic works have been presented at the Gaudeamus Festival (Screen Dive), National Sawdust (NYC), Trinity College (Dublin), the mise-en Festival and the Winnipeg New Music Festival. In addition to performance and composition, she is completing an interdisciplinary PhD examining augmented reality, motor control and guitar performance at Dalhousie University in Halifax, Nova Scotia, Canada, and is the founder/director of the 21st Century Guitar Conference (21cguitar.com).

Katalin Koltai is a guitarist and researcher completing her PhD at the IGRC (University of Surrey, UK). Her research expands the boundaries of the guitar's idiom through arrangements, new music and inventing a new magnet capo system and guitar prototype, the 'Ligeti Guitar'. She champions new works and has collaborated with many composers, including György Kurtág, David Gorton, Gráinne Mulvey and Benjamin Dwyer. She has previously performed at the Royal Festival Hall, King's Place, Kuhmo Festival, London Guitar Festival and Haydn Festival. She has written for the *Lute Society of America Quarterly* and *Soundboard Scholar*, has presented conference papers internationally, her arrangements have been published by Doblinger and CDs by Hungaroton, Genuine, North South Recordings and Naxos.

John McGrath is senior lecturer of music at the University of Surrey, UK. His monograph, *Samuel Beckett, Repetition and Modern Music* (2018), has received positive reviews from *Music & Letters*, *Wire Magazine*, *Psychology of Music* and the *Irish Studies Review*. McGrath is also an active guitarist; recent appearances include a solo set at King's Place, London, while his compositions have been aired and screened internationally. He is Deputy Director of the International Guitar Research Centre (IGRC).

Milton Mermikides is a composer, guitarist, electronicist, academic, illustrator and unapologetic nerd. His writing is published in academic and popular journals; he delivers keynote talks on a range of disciplines, and his music (ranging from jazz, electronic, classical to data-based forms) is broadcast to millions of listeners. He is associate professor of music at the University of Surrey, UK, professor of guitar at the Royal College of Music and deputy director of the International Guitar Research Centre. His first monograph, *Hidden Music*, will be published by Cambridge University Press in 2023 (www.miltonline.com).

Richard Perks is senior lecturer in music performance at the University of Kent, UK, and Associate Professor of music at the Institute of Contemporary Music Performance, UK. He is one of Europe's leading exponents of the fretless electric guitar, has extensive experience as a session musician and has performed all over the world. Recent publications have explored the extended performance possibilities of the fretless electric guitar, guitar-focused musicology/analysis, the combination of composition with improvisation and intercultural collaboration. In 2021 he received funding to conduct independent field research and survey the fretless guitar scene in West Asia.

John Schneider is the Grammy Award-winning guitarist, author and broadcaster who has released over twenty records and is the founding artistic director of MicroFest, MicroFest Records and the contemporary music ensembles Just Strings and the PARTCH Ensemble. He is the author of the critically acclaimed volume *The Contemporary Guitar* and can be heard weekly on Pacifica Radio's The Global Village [www.KPFK.org].

Robert Strachan is senior lecturer of music at the University of Liverpool, UK. He has published numerous articles on a variety of aspects of popular music, including DIY music cultures, electronic music and creativity, sound art, audiovisual media and the history of British Black music. He is the author of *Sonic Technologies: Popular Music, Digital Culture and the Creative Process* (2017). He is also an active musician and sound artist. His audiovisual installations have been exhibited internationally and his experimental/psychedelic rock band Bonnacons of Doom have played at numerous festivals in the UK and Europe.

Tom Williams is a jazz guitarist, lecturer and musicologist specializing in improvisation, cognition, jazz and pedagogy. His PhD thesis 'Strategy in Contemporary Jazz Improvisation' (2017) created a detailed cognitive and contextual model of how expert-level improvisers develop and use their craft. Other related research areas include jazz guitar and distortion, gender and guitar, and nostalgia in guitar practice. He is head of Curriculum at the Academy of Contemporary Music in Guildford, UK.

Acknowledgements

The idea of a book on the manifold physicalities and related performance practices of the guitar in the 21st century, from the emic perspective of the performer, emerged from two directions: from thoughts Richard Perks developed while exploring performance techniques specific to the fretless electric guitar; and from a discussion between both editors at a conference entitled 'Improvisation and the Guitar', held in 2019 by the International Guitar Research Centre at the Hong Kong Academy of Performing Arts, Hong Kong. We would like to thank Steve Goss, Stanley Yates, Jonathan Leathwood, Milton Mermikides and everyone at the IGRC for organizing the conference, which, among its especially broad scope, highlighted to us the need for further investigation into, and the wider exposure of, a good deal of the themes and practices considered in this collection. Over the next year or so we established a pool of potential contributors and sent the book proposal to Bloomsbury Academic, which was gratefully approved. Thanks must go to Leah Babb-Rosenfeld and the team at Bloomsbury Academic for their support and enthusiasm for this project.

We would like to express our heartfelt thanks to everyone who has directly contributed to this volume as author, interviewee or otherwise, in particular John Schneider, Tolgahan Çoğulu, Ned Evett, Buzz Gravelle, Cenk Erdoğan, Tom Williams, Ant Law, Charlie Hunter, Katalin Koltai, Robert Strachan, Nels Cline, Bill Thompson, Milton Mermikides, Regan Bowering and Amy Brandon. We would also like to thank our colleagues at the Department of Music and Audio Technology, University of Kent, and the Department of Music and Media and the International Guitar Research Centre, University of Surrey, for their continued support in our research activities.

Rich would especially like to thank his partner Debbie for her support, the multitude of wonderful musicians he has been privileged to meet, perform and collaborate with over the years, and his parents for their sustained interest in his musical endeavours.

John would especially like to thank Holly, Daisy and all the Rogers/McGraths.

Rich and John

Introduction

Richard Perks and John McGrath

In the 21st century, the guitar, as both a material object and tool for artistic expression, continues to be reimagined and reinvented. From simple adaptations or modifications made by performers themselves, to custom-made instruments commissioned to fulfil very specific creative needs, to the mass production of new lines of commercially available instruments, the extant and emergent forms of this much-loved musical instrument vary perhaps more than ever before. Such diversity in physicality reignites the longstanding ontological question: What is a guitar? On the surface this may seem like a relatively simple, perhaps even facetious question, however, it is one that has consistently prompted further consideration by musicologists, ethnomusicologists, organologists and anthropologists alike. Indeed, while the guitar remains a staple instrument amidst a range of music traditions from around the world – and as such traditions progress from one generation to the next – this question takes on increasingly complex and nuanced meanings. As guitars sporting multiple necks, a greater number of strings and/or additional frets become increasingly common, so too do those with reduced registers, fewer strings and fretless fingerboards. Furthermore, as we approach the mark of the first quarter-century, the role of technology in relation to the guitar's ever-changing identity is proving key. On-board processing units, external synergies with computers and the use of ultra-modern peripheral musical devices – ranging from EBow and effects processing, to engagement with laptops, robots and AR headsets – are allowing players to augment their performance setup and, in doing so, exponentially expand the guitar's corporeal and timbral functionality. Such wide-ranging 'transmutations' of the guitar reflect the advancing performative and expressive needs of the modern guitarist and simultaneously afford them new creative potentialities; ultimately creating a feedback loop between artist and object, which further propels the guitar in fresh directions. Instruments and technological devices might be seen as more than inanimate objects, however, acting instead as agents themselves, with creative inputs of their own.

Engagement with such agents may be more of an artistic collaboration than a one-way, more servile utilization of objects.

The history of the guitar as a musical instrument, including developments in terms of design and innovation, has been well documented (Bellow 1970; Evans and Evans 1977; Grunfeld 1969; Ingram 2001; Landman and Hopkin 2012; Schneider 2015; Turnbull 1974, Wade 2001) as have the differences between its role and usage within various performance traditions and styles, together with multifarious associated sociocultural aspects (Bennett and Dawe 2001; Coelho 2003; Dawe 2010; Dawe and Eroğlu 2013; Millard 2004; Waksman 1999). To expand upon this significant body of work, this book seeks to question our understanding of what a guitar is, but to do so by focusing specifically on the myriad innovative approaches to guitar performance that are emerging now, in the 21st century. This book concentrates on the performative potentialities that physical, material or technological alterations may afford the player; and not on disparate guitar-based performance techniques that abound without a direct engagement with these tangible distinctions. Such an inquiry prompts further questions: What are the catalysts for different physical evolutions and augmentations? Is musicianship at the epicentre of these developments? Do trends in fashions, idiomatic or cultural conventions, or performative 'gimmicks' have a role to play? Are there wider considerations surrounding quiddity (the 'whatness' of a certain guitar 'type') versus haecceity (the 'thisness' of a specific artist's unique, perhaps self-built instrument)? How do each of these aspects inform a player's individual style, or vice versa? Crucially, this collection explores modern physicalities of the guitar in relation to the performative approaches and artistic goals of the player. Accordingly, rather than forming conclusions based on an observational style of musicology, each chapter here presents a different model of – or approach to performing with – the guitar from the emic perspective of the performing musician/s. To fortify this position and thus recognize the importance of the guitarist's first-hand insights, this book is presented in a novel and distinctive format. First, all academic chapters are written by dual-practitioners, each of whom has had a distinguished career as a performing guitarist. Next, to ensure a suitable degree of comprehensiveness, most chapters are followed by a special feature-length interview with a world-leading artist, best known for working in a closely related area of music or style of guitar performance. Contributions span diverse backgrounds and locations, including viewpoints from both established scholars and PhD students. The aim is that the reader can immerse themselves in various paradigms of guitar playing from multiple perspectives.

The volume is broadly arranged into two sections: namely evolutions and augmentations. Evolutions here refer to cases where the guitar has been physically adapted or developed in such a way that its timbral qualities, expressive potentials and/or affordances have been significantly advanced, but corporeal engagement with the instrument – in the most fundamental sense – remains unchanged. Augmentations refer to instances where comparable developments in sounds and performance techniques occur; however, they are primarily a consequence of the use, application or integration of additional technology, equipment, devices, tools, periphery objects and so forth. Of course, evolutions and augmentations are not mutually exclusive, and it is because of the possibility for them to coexist or combine that many chapters in this collection consider both themes. It is important to stress also that this book is concerned with different forms of the guitar and not any 'guitar-like' instrument belonging to the broader lute family (e.g. bağlama, banjo, bouzouki, guembri, oud, pipa, sarod, sitar and so on). To be clear, we shall only be dealing here with instruments that might be ontologically observed as, or are consistently referred to as, types of 'guitar'. Various relatives of the guitar will inevitably be included as part of wider discussions, but the emphasis throughout is on all things guitar.

In Chapter 1, 'The Well-Tuned Guitar', John Schneider despatches any notion that standardized or fixed fret positioning, based on twelve-tone equal temperament (12-TET), is an indispensable characteristic of the guitar in the 21st century. By interweaving a comprehensive overview of various microtonal fretting systems – Pythagorean, Meantone, Just (pure) intonation, different equal divisions of the octave (EDOs), Adjustable and so forth – with his lifetime experience of exploring and performing microtonal musics, Schneider provides significant insights into the guitar's role and future potential in this ever-growing area of music-making. Chapter 2, 'Transforming the Microtonal Fingerboard: "Small" Frets, LEGO and Robots' comprises an in-depth interview with Tolgahan Çoğulu, an internationally revered classical guitarist and inventor of the Adjustable Microtonal Guitar, the LEGO Microtonal Guitar and (at the time of writing) the world's first Automatic Microtonal Guitar. In this discussion, Çoğulu reveals his passion for – and fascination with – microtonal guitar playing, from his initial attraction to performing using Just intonation, to the incorporation of Turkish/Anatolian *makam* into classical guitar performance, to employing movable LEGO frets as a potential pedagogical device to teach students about microtonality. Throughout this piece Çoğulu divulges his thoughts, plans and predictions regarding the future of the (fretted) microtonal guitar. In Chapter 3, 'The Expanding Fretless Guitarscape: Practice and Progress', Richard Perks contextualizes manifold fretless guitar practices from around the world. By examining the fretless guitar in relation to different performance environments – from concentrated idiomatic, cultural and/or geographic locales to global interconnectivity realized primarily via online dissemination, social media and virtual networks – Perks considers a diverse array of playing approaches and techniques, highlights any recent developments and offers possible explanations for the instrument's increased pervasiveness of late. In addition, using 'affordance' (Gibson 1966; 1977; 1979) as a critical lens, the author presents an autoethnographic account of his experiences of working with the fretless electric guitar across a wide range of creative settings and provides insights into the ways in which 'fretlessness' – when viewed as a 'state of practice' – might benefit the modern guitarist. Chapter 4, 'Touching the Apple without Gloves', presents an intimate conversation with Turkish multi-instrumentalist, composer and fretless guitar virtuoso, Cenk Erdoğan. In this interview, Erdoğan discusses his fretless guitar journey to date – from his initial pursuit and study of the instrument, influenced by master Erkan Oğur, to the development of his own highly distinctive approach and style – and articulates his feelings about how the fretless guitar allows him to reflect and emphasize his identity as a Turkish musician on the international stage. In Chapter 5, 'Extended Range Instruments: Towards a New Organology of the Guitar', Tom Williams starts by establishing the historical background that led to a 'standardized' taxonomic qualification of the guitar (i.e. as the standard-tuned, six-string, *c.* four-octave range instrument), as well as a consideration of extant organological frameworks. Williams then identifies four primary musical 'communities' that regularly adopt extended register guitars and uses them as a means to distinguish between, assess and evaluate the manifold application(s) of extended register guitars in the 21st century. In addition, this chapter draws from an interview with innovative British jazz guitarist Ant Law to provide first-hand insights into his application of the eight-string guitar in a modern jazz context. Williams concludes the chapter by inviting the reader to consider a 'new organology' of the guitar: one that might sufficiently accommodate the many variations in instrumental range and the fresh performative potentialities they afford. Chapter 6, 'I Should Have Just Learned How to Play the Organ', is an interview with Charlie Hunter. Hunter is broadly considered to be the pioneer of six-, seven- and eight-string 'hybrid' guitar playing in a jazz/funk/popular music context. His hybrid guitars consist of three 'bass' strings, with the rest regular guitar strings (the exact number of which depends on the model being used at the time), and often have independent signal outputs to allow him to separate 'bass' from 'guitar' parts. Using this novel instrument, Hunter has established a truly innovative playing style whereby he simultaneously performs bass lines, chords (comps) and lead lines (solos), such that he can emulate an entire rhythm section. This interview unpacks Hunter's general philosophy on music-making and discusses the development of his distinctive technique. Jonathan De Souza's theory of 'guitar thinking' (2021), space, embodiment and cognition (2017), based on the phenomenological writings of Maurice Merleau-Ponty, provides the basis for Katalin Koltai's exploration of transformed guitar spaces, including new instruments and extensive scordatura in classical guitar arrangement and new music. In Chapter 7, 'The Transformed Space of the "Ligeti Guitar"', she discusses her innovative magnet capo system in practice. In particular, Koltai focuses on new applications for the music of György Ligeti, Béla Bartók, Frédéric Chopin and György Kurtág (who she also interviews) and explores a recent collaboration with the composer David Gorton.

Opening the more augmentation-focused part of the book, Chapter 8, 'Grains, Glitches and Infinite Space', provides an overview of the boutique guitar-pedal boom. Robert Strachan examines technological, cultural and aesthetic convergency in current guitar aesthetics by way of industrial manufacturing and Bruno Latour's concept of actor network theory (2005). Chapter 9, 'The Sonic Maelstrom', is an interview with Nels Cline (Wilco) and provides rich insights into the innovations of the trailblazing guitarist's approach to guitar augmentation. Cline has appeared on over 200 albums and successfully straddles both experimental and stadium alternative rock world-tour spheres. Recognizing the current climate as particular vibrant for sonic experimentation via technological augmentation of the instrument, Cline sees great potential for the future of guitar music. Chapter 10, '"Something seems wrong, should that be happening?": Avantfolk Guitar and Glitch Aesthetics, a Practice–Based Perspective', provides a specific case study of the author's multimodal 'avantfolk' guitar project utilizing the glitch affordances of pedal technology. John McGrath contextualizes the practice in terms of folk horror, hauntology and Mark Fisher's concept of 'the weird'. Chapter 11, 'A Field of Reactivity: Moog Guitar and Experimental Systems', explores via interview Bill Thompson's unique approach to tabletop Moog Guitar. This new evolution of the instrument affords unique possibilities for improvised drone experimentation, particularly when augmented with outboard gear. Milton Mermikides introduces us to the expanded digital fretboard in Chapter 12, 'The Digital Fretboard: Remapping and Relearning the Guitar's Pitch Matrix with MIDI and Max/MSP', providing new technologically afforded trajectories for guitar notation, composition and performance. Mermikides shows how this virtual reconfiguration of the guitar might disrupt, challenge and develop existing fretboard cognition and habits. In Chapter 13, 'Augmented Reality Guitars: Extended Instruments and Notation for a 21st-Century Practice', Amy Brandon examines another exciting avenue for 21st-century guitar, virtual spaces. Reflecting on her own XR compositional/performative projects Brandon explores how the guitar can operate in both real and digital worlds concurrently via technological augmentation.

Overall, the contributions offer fresh perspectives on how the 'new guitarscape' (Dawe 2010) continues to expand as the ontology of the instrument itself does. Together, the chapters in this volume highlight the ways in which the guitar's role in music-making and society grows as it evolves and augments. Through its form, content, scope and perspective, we hope that this book will provide significant insights into the rich array of guitar-based performance practices emerging and thriving in the 21st century, and in doing so invite the reader to reassess the guitar in terms of its identity, physicality and sound creating potentialities.

References

Bellow, A. (1970), *The Illustrated History of the Guitar*, New York: Franco Colombo (Belwin-Mills).

Bennett, A. and K. Dawe (eds) (2001), *Guitar Cultures*, Oxford: Berg.

Coelho, V.A. (eds) (2003), *The Cambridge Companion to the Guitar*, Cambridge: Cambridge University Press.

Dawe, K. (2010), *The New Guitarscape in Critical Theory, Cultural Practice and Musical Performance*, London: Routledge.

Dawe, K. and S.C. Eroğlu (2013), 'The Guitar in Turkey: Erkan Oğur and the Istanbul Guitarscape', *Ethnomusicology Forum*, 22 (1): 49–70.

De Souza, J. (2017), *Music at Hand: Instruments, Bodies, and Cognition*, Oxford Studies in Music Theory, New York: Oxford University Press.

De Souza, J. (2021), 'Guitar Thinking', *Soundboard Scholar*, 7(1): 1–23, https://digitalcommons.du.edu/sbs/vol7/iss1/1/ (accessed 5 Sep 2022).

Evans, T. and M. Evans (1977), *Guitars: Music, History, Construction and Players from Renaissance to Rock*, London: Paddington Press.

Fisher, M. (2016), *The Weird and the Eerie*, London: Repeater Books.
Gibson, J.J. (1966), *The Senses Considered as Perceptual Systems*, Boston, MA: Houghton Mifflin.
Gibson, J.J. (1977), 'The Theory of Affordances', in R. Shaw, and J. Bransford (eds), *Perceiving, Acting, and Knowing: Toward an Ecological Psychology*, 67–82, Hillsdale, NJ: Lawrence Erlbaum Associates.
Gibson, J.J. (1979), *The Ecological Approach to Visual Perception*, Hillsdale, Boston, MA: Houghton Mifflin.
Grunfeld, F. (1969), *The Art and Times of the Guitar*, New York: Collier-Macmillan.
Ingram, A. (2001), *A Concise History of the Electric Guitar*, Missouri: Mel Bay Publications, Incorporated.
Landman, Y. and B. Hopkin (2012), *Nice Noise: Modifications and Preparations for Guitar*, California: Experimental Musical Instruments.
Latour, B. (2005), *Reassembling the Social: An Introduction to Actor Network*, Oxford: Oxford University Press.
Millard, A. (ed.) (2004), *The Electric Guitar: A History of an American Icon*, Baltimore: The Johns Hopkins University Press.
Schneider, J.O. (2015), *The Contemporary Guitar*, Revised and Enlarged ed., Lanham, MD: Rowman & Littlefield.
Turnbull, H. (1974), *The Guitar: From Renaissance to the Present Day*, London: Batsford.
Wade, G. (2001), *A Concise History of the Classic Guitar*, Missouri: Mel Bay Publications, Incorporated.
Waksman, S. (1999), *Instruments of Desire: The Electric Guitar and the Shaping of Musical Experience*, Cambridge, MA: Harvard University Press.

1

The well-tuned guitar

John Schneider

20th-century Western art music famously reconsidered every aspect of musical composition, from its tools and timbres to the very language itself. While the addition of electricity to this process of reevaluation was a considerable game-changer – revealing unimagined vistas of an already profoundly expanded aesthetic landscape – traditional music instruments were certainly not immune to the feverish exploration and expansion of sonic possibilities that dominated much mid-century music-making. But where was the guitar? Still considered a second-class citizen in grand traditions of European concert music, surely the guitar must have had some role to play in the evolution of 'new music'. After all, hadn't Schoenberg's earliest serial experiments included the instrument in his *Serenade* back in 1923? As a young recently Stravinsky-smitten 'classical' guitarist, I had to find out.

My search for the 'contemporary guitar' eventually led to a 1977 PhD thesis of the same name, accomplished in the physics department of Cardiff University (UK) where the first half of my research was devoted to the exploration of *timbre*. Analysis of the actual physical processes that differentiate a *ponticello* tone from *sul tasto*, for example, was codified in a 'Rational Method of Tone Production' that enabled players to clarify lines of a Bach fugue, or colour the sonic textures in their 'Miniature Orchestra', as the guitar was sometimes known as far back as the early 19th century. The other half of the volume dealt with how new generations had expanded the instrument's performance possibilities in their compositions to embrace all aspects of tone production, from percussion and electronics to the scraping of strings, use of slide bars, exaggerated *scordatura*, and even the so-called microtones of Julián Carrillo and Maurice Ohana. There was also, as in so many history books, even a passing mention of Harry Partch, but nothing more.

On my way back to California, I gave a conference paper on my newly minted 'Rational Method', following someone who presented a demonstration of a 'Meantone' guitar (Orr 1977). I was stunned to see a fingerboard with a completely different fretting pattern than the usual twelve-tone equal temperament. Still reeling, the second revelation of the day was delivered by a gentleman called Tom Stone, who had recently invented a guitar with *interchangeable fingerboards*. He spent that life-changing afternoon introducing me to the charms of many fingerboards, including the 'Classic Series' (several varieties of meantone and Pythagorean), an 'Ethnic Series' (Indian, Arabian, Indonesian, and Chinese scales), the 'Experimental Series' (19, 24, and 31 equal temperaments), and 'Pure Intonation of scales tuned to the Harmonic Series', playing examples on each (Figure 1.1).

Figure 1.1 Intonation Systems sales brochure (1977).

Anyone who has seen the 1939 classic movie *The Wizard of Oz* will remember the moment when, after her tornado-tossed house is ripped from her previous black-and-white life in Depression-era Kansas and finally lands, Dorothy opens her front door to reveal a new world of spectacular Technicolor. Musically, I had just walked through that door, leaving what Lou Harrison would call the 'industrial gray of equal temperament' to enter the infinitely variegated world of *un*equal tunings. I had just spent years in a physics lab studying the minute variations of harmonic amplitudes in guitar tones to map their subtle timbral contrasts but had never considered the profound influence of the Harmonic Series on both pitch and harmony, let alone musical style.

I obtained what I later called a Switchboard guitar from Stone's company Intonation Systems and revelled in hearing my beloved Bach newly enhanced by tensions and resolutions possible only in the unequal tunings of the era. Dowland changed dramatically as well, since the virtually pure 'tritone' found in meantone's dominant seventh chord was far more dissonant than the modern equal-tempered version and its resolution to the tonic's pure major third profoundly consonant. While revisiting a familiar repertoire was a revelation, I learned that there was also an original repertoire for refretted instruments. Back in 1952, Lou Harrison had written his Esperanto-titled *Serenado por Gitaro* with the following instructions:

> Anyone who just might own a guitar with movable frets should arrange these to play the 'Intense Diatonic' (Syntonon Diatonic), which is the 'vocal' major scale. The piece will sound lovely in that tuning. (Harrison 1952)

Though no such instrument existed in 1952, when I asked him years later what in the world he was thinking, he replied that it seemed logical since 'lutes and gambas have movable frets, so why not guitars!'[1]

The following year, an invitation from the University of California Press to add my thesis to *The New Instrumentation* series gave me an opportunity to make amends for missing this vital aspect of the guitar development, which initiated an intense period of research that included a trip to San Diego to visit the extraordinary instruments of Harry Partch. The resulting volume gained twelve pages on tuning, intonation and microtonality, and I soon gave dozens of recitals and wrote articles about 'The Microtonal Guitar' in various publications.[2]

---

[1] Personal interview with Schneider, J. (1981, Valencia, California).
[2] Available online at https://johnschneider.la/Writings.html (accessed 23 February 2021).

I found that Tom Stone had also shared his invention with Lou Harrison, who was so inspired that he immediately began writing for the instrument, beginning with his *Serenade for Guitar (with optional percussion)* [1978] – a five movement suite composed in a Just (pure) intonation – and two movements of a second suite tuned in Pythagorean tuning. The *Serenade* is composed in an octatonic mode that alternates whole steps and half-steps, using both large and small Just sizes for each: semitones are diatonic 16/15 (112¢) or chromatic 25/24 (71¢), with major 9/8 (204¢) and minor 10/9 (182¢) whole tones (Figure 1.2).

The lattice shows the harmonic relationships inherent in this Just intonation scale. The horizontally connected notes ----- describe the acoustically pure perfect fifths that are slightly wide, while vertical relationships | | | are tuned in pure major thirds that are flatter than in modern equal temperament.

The composer's embrace of world music is abundantly apparent, as the suite is a global village of musical styles, including a North Indian *jahla* called 'Round', a Turkish *usul*, an 'Infinite Canon' and a baroque binary 'Sonata'.

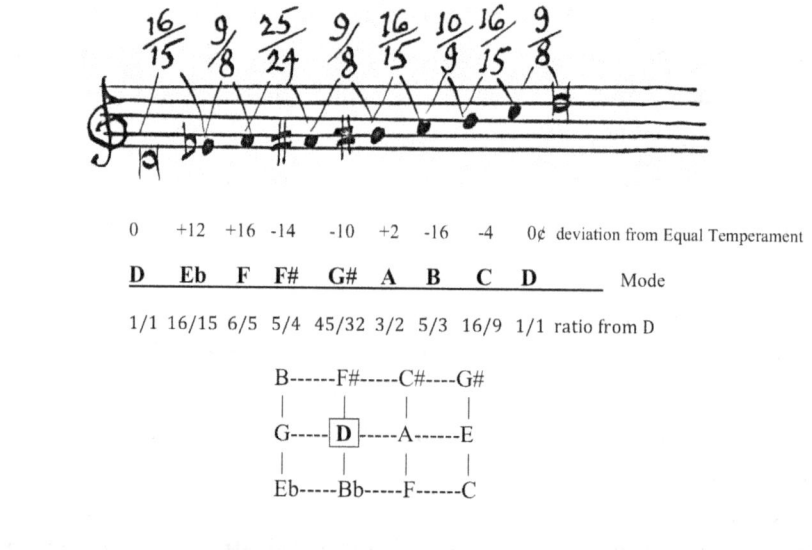

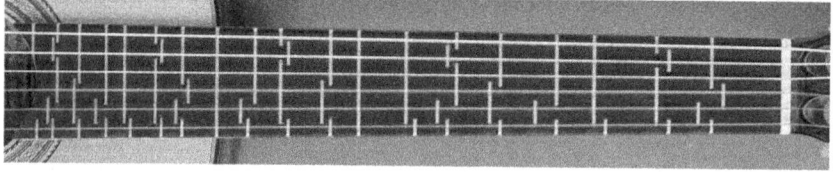

Figure 1.2 Mode, lattice and fretting for *Serenade* (1978). (Top image [notation]: used by permission of Peer International Corp.). (Photo: Author, 2002).

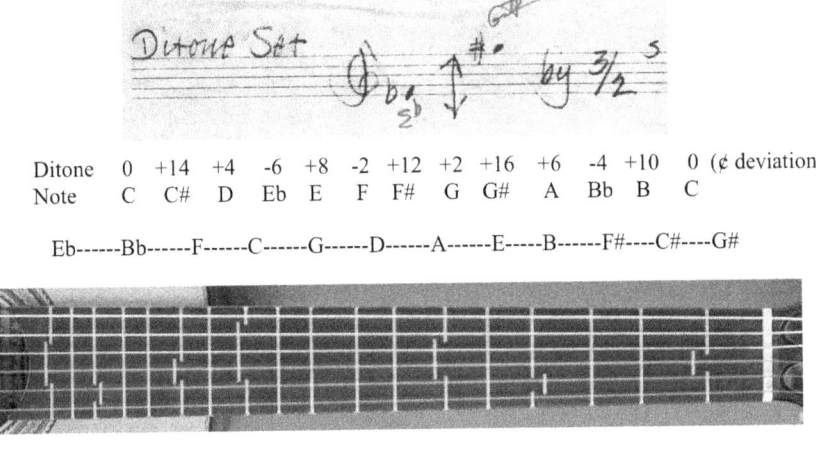

Figure 1.3 Tuning, lattice and fretting for *Ditone Set* (1978). (Top image [notation]: used by permission of Peer International Corp.). (Photo: Author, 2002).

In contrast, the second set of pieces from what became his *Ditone Set* (1978) is tuned in the medieval manner of eleven sequential pure fifths (ratio 3/2), a scale whose major thirds were so much wider than acceptable that they were classed as 'dissonant' during that era (Figure 1.3).

Harrison pays tribute to both Western and Middle Eastern medieval styles that shared this tuning, writing a *Variations* on the German *Minnesang* 'Palästinalied' in quintal harmony, an *Estampie* ('A medieval peasant's stamping dance, roughneck, and Brueghelish'), as well as a *taksim*-like *Plaint*, and another Turkish *usul*.

These pieces became the mainstay of my performance programmes and were the subject of my first CD,[3] though it turned out that Harrison had actually planned many more:

> I am engaged in what I hope will be five Suites in five different intonations, composed in such a way that the performer may, in fact, scramble movements, thus creating a number of Suites in which the possibility exists of a variety of intonation within each Suite.[4]

The project was never finished as such, but with the composer's assistance and blessing, over the next decade I arranged the remaining four suites from various harp and keyboard pieces for the premiere recording.[5]

---

[3] See: *Lou Harrison: Music for Guitar & Percussion* (1991), John Schneider, Etcetera KTC 1071.
[4] Personal correspondence with author (1978).
[5] See: *POR GITARO: Suites for Tuned Guitars* (2008), John Schneider, Mode Records 195.

Figure 1.4 Guitar with interchangeable fingerboards. (Photo: Author, 2002).

That project, however, would never have been possible without a new instrument. Sadly, though Intonation Systems (aka Novatone) had changed both their technology and name since my purchase, the company went out of business in 1985, limiting my repertoire to the fingerboards already in my possession (Figure 1.4).

The company did make precious few DIY kits available, but certainly not enough for a lifetime of music-making.

Luckily, the German luthier Walter Vogt (1935–90) had recently invented The Fine-Tunable Precision Fretboard system of sliding frets that solved the interminable problems of intonation on the standard equally tempered guitar. U-shaped channels run the entire fingerboard length under each string, gripping the 'fretlets' that precisely determine the tuning of each individual note (Figure 1.5).

I was able to find one of these rare instruments and could finally tune *any* scale, with the first results recorded in a CD of guitar and harp arrangements of music by John Cage, LaMonte Young, Lou Harrison and Harry Partch.[6]

I had also planned to arrange the original solo guitar/voice version of Partch's famous *Barstow: 8 Hitchhiker's Inscriptions* (1941) for this guitar, but after months of working on the score, I came to realize that it simply wouldn't

---

[6] See: *Just West Coast* (1993), John Schneider, Bridge Records 9041.

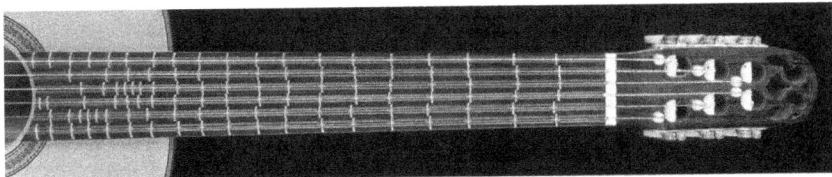

Figure 1.5 Vogt Fine-Tunable Precision Fretboard fretted in a baroque well temperament. (Photo: Salazar, F., 2017, used with permission).

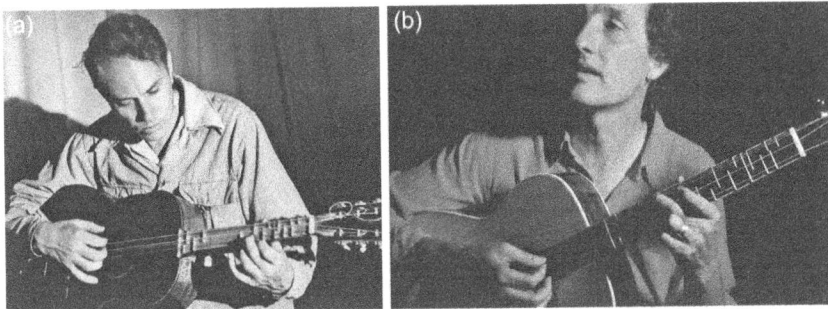

Figure 1.6 Adapted Guitar I: (a) Harry Partch (1941) (b) Author (1993). (Photos: (a) photographer unknown, used with permission: Harry Partch Archive; (b) Alancraig, D., 1993, used with permission).

work. After all, the Partch Adapted Guitar I was not only refretted but restrung as well, with three pairs of octave-doubled strings tuned E♭2–E♭3–G2–G3–B2–B3. It was either give up or do the unthinkable: make a copy of the original instrument. The problem was there were no available photos of the instrument and, therefore, no way to know which frets from his forty-three-tones/octave scale to install. So instead, I reverse-engineered the fingerboard by fretting only the notes found in the score, and nothing more. It made for a very strange fingerboard, but I was able to record the song for the album, not knowing if I was right or not (Schneider 1993). It would take years to find out that it was exactly how Partch had handled the problem, as his guitar had removable frets that slid into a brass fingerboard with pre-cut slots for his famed scale, though mine were permanently hammered in. For other pieces, he would change the fretting (Figure 1.6).

Partch had also adapted three other instruments in which he abandoned frets altogether (Schneider 2015a). In 1945, he reconceived his Guitar I by de-fretting an arch top National 'New Yorker' Electric Spanish Guitar, narrowing the neck and installing pinheads and brass rivets in the newly smooth fingerboard as note

Figure 1.7 Partch's 1945 (fretless electric) Adapted Guitar I (Partch 1949). (Photo: photographer unknown; from Partch, H. *Genesis of a Music*. Madison: University of Wisconsin Press, 1949, used with permission).

markers, visually connecting the notes that produced pure major thirds with lines of coloured plastic. He also made a walnut floating pick guard that was amplified, so the tapping that was an integral part of his music could be heard. It was the first-ever fingered-fretless electric guitar (Figure 1.7).

He also created the ten-string Adapted Guitar II (1945) by adding four strings to a square-neck Oahu Hawaiian guitar, removing the frets and playing it lap-style with a sliding plexiglass rod. The open tuning usually toggles between either a justly tuned **Fm**^{6} chord: C2-F2-C3-F3-A♭3-C4-D4-F4-F♯4-G♭4 or an **F**^{7}: C2-F2-C3-F3-A3-C4-E♭4-F4-F♯4-G4, though I have used other tunings for new compositions (Figure 1.8).

In 1950, he removed the high frets from his original Guitar and restrung it with six identical G-strings, overlaid the slotted brass with a paper fingerboard bearing the twelve standard note names – fine-tuned with forty-three fretlines to the octave – and played it on his lap with a weighted plastic rod, a virtual six-string monochord (Figure 1.9).

It soon became clear that I had started down a slippery and very expensive slope, since Partch's irresistible music demands multiple instruments, all of his own design and construction. As of this writing, I have recreated twenty-one of his over two dozen instruments and formed an ensemble to perform and record his extraordinary music, as well as newly commissioned pieces (see Schneider 2014)[7] (Figure 1.10).

The versatility of the Vogt guitar also instigated a crop of new compositions. Among others, John Luther Adams's *Yup'ik Dances* and *Athabascan Dances* were commissioned for my guitar/harp/percussion trio Just Strings,[8] while for his

---

[7] For audio examples, see: PARTCH Ensemble CDs: *Bitter Music* (2011), Bridge 9349A/C; *Plectra & Percussion Dances* (2014), Bridge 9432; *Sonata Dementia* (2019), Bridge 9525.
[8] See: *Just Strings* (2015), John Schneider, MicroFest Records M•F7.

Figure 1.8 Author's copy of Adapted Guitar II. (Photo: Kat Nockels, 2017, used with permission).

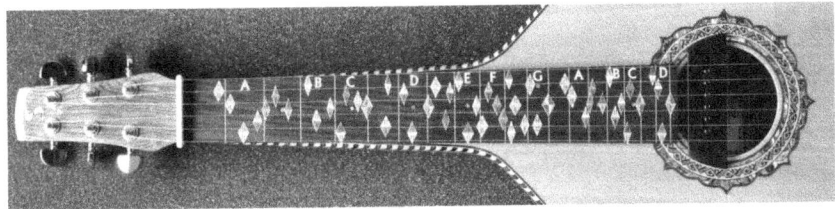

Figure 1.9 Author's copy of Adapted Guitar III. (Photo: Author, 2014).

Figure 1.10 PARTCH Ensemble. (Photo: Schneider, E., 2008, used with permission).

Concerto for Guitar & American Gamelan (2007), Bill Alves requested that the frets match the Just intonation seven-tone *pelog* to which his gamelan was tuned, creating the first work for that combination.[9]

When commissioning a solo work from Ben Johnston – whose towering cycle of Just intonation string quartets has become the gold standard of modern microtonality – I was able to give him *carte blanche* to choose any pitches he liked. The resulting song cycle *The Tavern* (1998) was composed in a fifteen-note/octave of thirteen-limit Just intonation. Training both the fingers and the voice to find these pitches was quite a challenge, too. While Partch's music always had strong vocal cues baked into the instrumental parts, Johnston's vocal writing was much more independent, often working in counterpoint to the guitar. Johnston's incredibly demanding *Quartet #7* (1984) had to famously wait over three decades for its premiere; it took me 'only' twelve years before I could perform both parts of *The Tavern* simultaneously due in part to its difficulty but also the fact that the instrument had to be refretted many times for other projects (Figure 1.11).

In his programme notes, the composer wrote:

> I was long ago convinced that the fingerboard, which is based on deciding upon a set of pitches needed for each particular tuning, ought if possible to become the next step in the history of the guitar in performance. Our work to make *The Tavern* is a major step toward this goal.[10]

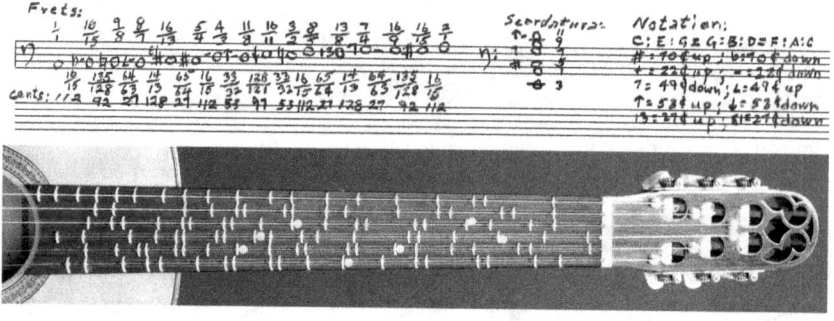

Figure 1.11 Fifteen-note Just tuning, fretting and scale for *The Tavern* (1998). (Top Image [notation]: From *The Tavern* by Ben Johnston. Copyright Smith Publications. Used by permission.) (Photo: Author, 2009).

---

[9] See: *Guitars & Gamelan* (2015), John Schneider, MicroFest Records M•F8.
[10] See 'The Tavern', *Ben Johnston: Ruminations* (2014), John Schneider, MicroFest Records M•F5.

You will have noticed that I prefer Just intonations for my instruments, but there is also a whole world of EDO (equal divisions of the octave) instruments and repertoire. That trend began last century with the creation of quartertone instruments and repertoire by Julian Carrillo and Alois Hába – who both wrote for acoustic instruments – and the equally productive though prolix Norwegian composer Bjørn Fongaard who used a solid-body electric guitar for his reverb-drenched 'space-age' music. Quartertones were an easy gateway to microtonality, since luthiers need only place new frets exactly between those already resident, though even in Carrillo's day, his theoretician compatriot Augusto Novaro commissioned instruments fretted in 15, 29, 31, 53 and 72 frets per octave (Novaro 1951).

In 1978, Ivor Darreg published a provocative call to arms in *Guitar Player Magazine* (Darreg 1978) to 'De-Twelvulate' in which he challenged players to explore the *xenharmonic* world, a term which he coined (Greek *xenos* = strange).

His re-frettings included 14-through-18/octave, as well as 19, 22, 24, and 31 EDOs, and he was surprised to find that each created its own unique mood, exclaiming, 'These moods were a complete surprise to me – almost a shock. Subtle difference one might expect – but these are astonishing differences' (Darreg 1975). He published a few short pieces, but it must be emphasized that with the creation of any new 'experimental' instrument, improvisation always precedes composition and most EDO players have yet to progress to that second stage, let alone attack the thorniest problem of notation.

In this century, electric guitarists have embraced EDO far more quickly than acoustic players, and it turns out that rock, and so-called metal music – in all its manifestations – provides a receptive platform for these new scales. It also helps that many production guitars have interchangeable necks, making experimentation far less intimidating. But these microtones are stubbornly style-neutral, ranging from the 15-EDO academic *Suite* of Easley Blackwood (1987), through rock and metal, to the swinging 31-EDO jazz of the young Austrian trio Dsilton that performs with a thirty-one-tone seven-string electric guitar and thirty-one-tone clavinet keyboard. Guitar legend Steve Vai uses a 16-EDO solid body, as does guitarist/luthier/author Ron Sword's metal band Last Testament that shreds in 16-EDO. He also makes replacement necks for equal temperaments thirteen through forty-one, Just intonation and non-octave frettings, and has published MicroGuitar scale books with hundreds of pages of scale charts and theory for numerous EDOs.[11]

---

[11] Available online: http://metatonalmusic.com/ (accessed 23 February 2021).

In fact, one such instrument actually started a festival. The Southern Californian theorist Larry Hanson had a Fender Telecaster refretted in 34 EDO and this interested the prolific guitarist Neil Haverstick to explore its capabilities. Already conversant in 19-, 22-, 24- and 31-EDO frettings and the creator of Denver's *MicroStock* festival, he found it very stimulating and, wanting to give a public display of its virtues in the creator's home town, asked me to produce a microtonal concert. What was supposed to be a one-off concert featuring the SoCal microtonal community turned out to be a huge over three-hour event featuring all sorts of refretted guitars, tuned percussion and even traditional koto. The next year I produced two completely different concerts, and it grew from there. Now in its twenty-third year, *MicroFest* has presented over 160 concerts in multiple Southern California venues and has premiered works by Ben Johnston, Lou Harrison, Terry Riley, James Tenney and Harry Partch, and featured world music microtonal traditions from India, Indonesia, Vietnam and the Middle East, while also presenting the newest generation of composers exploring this brave new world with both traditional and invented instruments.[12] I also started a record label to document these presentations of rare repertoire, but producing new projects seems to have taken priority. The Grammy-nominated label MicroFest Records just released their sixteenth studio recording, with a half-dozen more in the pipeline.[13]

The 21st century welcomed a new instrument that was created to perform Lou Harrison's last composition *Scenes from Nek Chand* (2002). Using the open tuning of D A D G A D (low to high), it is fretted with twelve notes/octave tuned to the first eleven harmonics of the keys of G and D, though the piece itself relies solely on the six-tone mode found between harmonics six and twelve of the fundamental G (Figure 1.12).

The composer specifically wrote for the National Tricone Resophonic guitar, a sound familiar from the Hawaiian music he heard in his youth. After I commissioned the instrument to perform the work, the National company made several more, including a 'loaner', which I have sent to various composers. Terry Riley, Larry Polansky, Toby Twining and many others have created over two dozen pieces for the guitar, yet another reminder that hardware does indeed stimulate software.[14]

---

[12] Available online: www.MicroFest.org (accessed 23 February 2021).
[13] Available online: www.MicroFestRecords.com (accessed 23 February 2021).
[14] See: *The Wayward Trail* (2015), Elliot Simpson, MicroFest Records M•F6; *the great hunt* (2017), Alex Wand, MicroFest Records M•F10; *Just National Guitar* (2018), John Schneider, MicroFest Records M•F12.

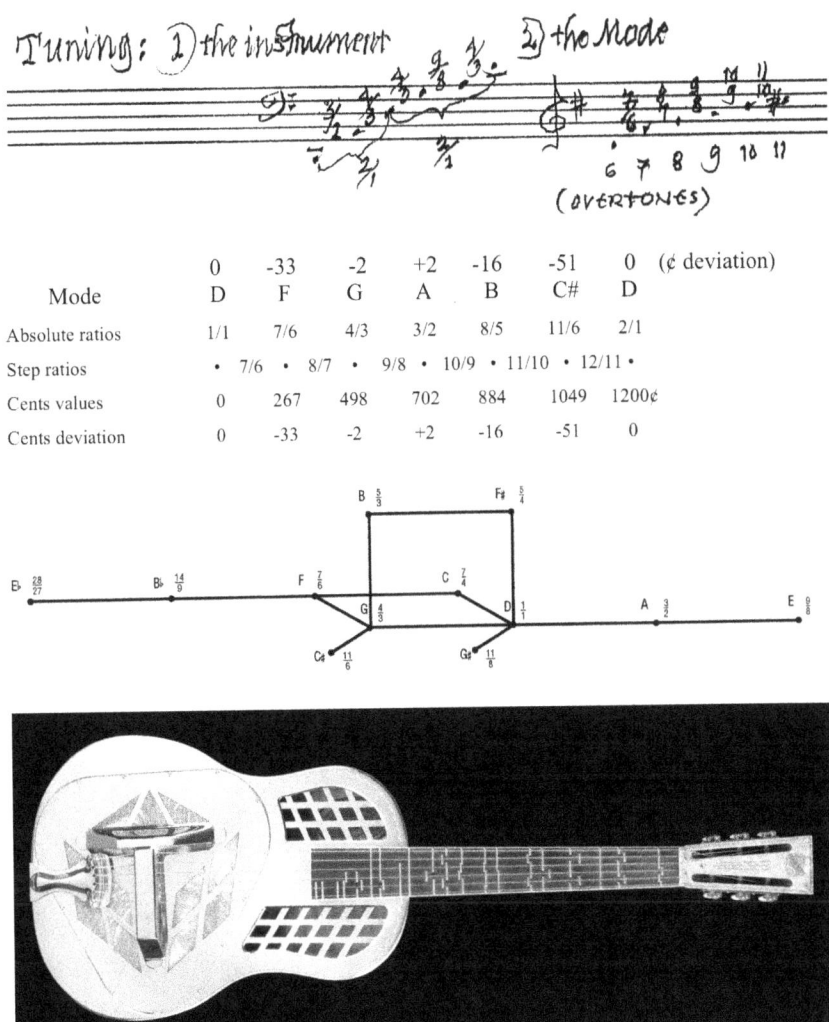

Figure 1.12 Tuning, mode, lattice and fretting for Harrison's *Scenes from Nek Chand* (2002). (Top Image [notation]: used with permission of Frog Peak Music.). (Middle Image: used with permission of David Doty). (Photo: Salazar, F., 2018, used with permission).

In 2008, Istanbul's Tolgahan Çoğulu invented an 'Adjustable Microtonal Guitar' which he has used to perform and record traditional *makam* as well as many new works.[15] He has since initiated the world's first Microtonal Guitar Competition for composers and players and the first-ever International

---

[15] See Chapter 2 of this volume for an in-depth interview with Tolgahan Çoğulu.

Microtonal Guitar Festival (2019). And as of this writing, the American company Microtone Guitars is once again producing a cornucopia of interchangeable fingerboards for nylon and steel-string guitars.[16]

In 2015, the publisher Rowman & Littlefield released a new expanded second edition of *The Contemporary Guitar* (Schneider 2015b). This time around, the ensuing thirty years of research, performing and recording have generated a brand new seventy-four-page chapter called 'Microtones: The Well-Tuned Guitar', with audio examples, of course.[17] Almost a century ago, Harry Partch declared,

> There can be no growth in musical art with the present worn-out system of music, limited to twelve tones to the octave . . . for that is what the piano is – twelve black and white bars in front of musical freedom. Twelve black and white stiflers. (Partch 1991)

He found the guitar's twelve shiny prison bars no better, suggesting that they not only robbed music of true consonance but slammed the door on any kind of new dissonance as well. These days, more and more performers, composers and listeners are happily going 'off the grid' of twelve-tone equal temperament.

The adventure continues.

References

Blackwood, E. (1987), *Suite for Guitar in 15–note Equal Tuning, Op.33* (1983), Chicago: Blackwood Enterprises.
Darreg, I. (1975), 'New Moods', Xenharmonic Bulletin No. 5, May.
Darreg, I. (1978), 'Non-12-Tone Guitar: Refretting Instruments for Unusual Harmonic Possibilities', *Guitar Player Magazine*, February: 24–5, 82–94.
Harrison, L. (1952), 'Serenado por Gitaro', in J. Schneider (ed.), *Por Gitaro: Works for Solo Guitar*, 8, New York: Peermusic.
Novaro, A. (1951), *Sistema Natural de la Música*, Mexico, D.F., 87, 163, 165, 174, 207, Available online: http://anaphoria.com/novaro51.pdf (accessed 16 July 2011).
Orr, R. (1977), *The Application of Quarter Comma Meantone Temperament to the Guitar*, M.A. thesis, San Jose State University.
Partch, H. (1949), *Genesis of a Music*, Madison: University of Wisconsin Press, 196.

---

[16] Available online: https://www.microtoneguitars.com/ (accessed 23 February 2021).
[17] Available online: https://soundcloud.com/contemporary-guitar (accessed 23 February 2021).

Partch, H. (1991), 'Bitter Music', in T. McGeary (ed.), *Bitter Music: Collected Journals, Essays, Introductions, and Librettos*, 12, Chicago: University of Illinois Press.

Schneider, J. (1993), 'Bringing Back Barstow', *Guitar Review*, 95: 1–13.

Schneider, J. (2014), 'Partch: Re-Genesis of a Music', in C. Pätzold and C.J. Walter (eds), *Mikrotonalität: Praxis und Utopie*, 176–91, Mainz: Schott.

Schneider, J. (2015a), 'The Microtonal Guitars of Harry Partch', *Soundboard Scholar*, 1: 1–15.

Schneider, J. (2015b), *The Contemporary Guitar*, Revised and Enlarged ed., London: Rowman & Littlefield.

2

Transforming the microtonal fingerboard: 'Small' frets, LEGO and robots

Interview with Tolgahan Çoğulu

Richard Perks

Tolgahan Çoğulu is a virtuosic classical guitarist and professor at Istanbul Technical University (Turkish Music State Conservatory), where he founded the world's first microtonal guitar department. He designed the Adjustable Microtonal Guitar in 2008[1] and has since helped build a significant repertoire of works for the instrument by collaborating with composers from all over the world. More recently, his work has taken the microtonal guitar into exciting and novel territories with his invention of the LEGO Microtonal Guitar,[2] and he is (at the time of writing) working towards creating the world's first Automatic Microtonal Guitar.[3]

RP: You once said that your interest in microtonal classical guitar began with 'an urge to play or arrange the *makam*-based music of the geography you live in' (Çoğulu 2010). How has your approach to microtonality progressed since then?

TC: When I was doing my PhD, I was so lucky because my first professor was Mark Lindley, who is the author of the *Temperament* and *Microtone* sections in Grove/Oxford Music Online. Then, after Mark, it was Michael Ellison who gave

---

[1] The Adjustable Microtonal Guitar won first place in the highly prestigious Guthman Musical Instrument Competition, 2014. See https://arts.gatech.edu/content/2014-guthman-competition-winners-announced (accessed 24 March 2021).
[2] The LEGO Microtonal Guitar won the People's Choice Award in the Guthman Musical Instrument Competition, 2021. See www.guthman.gatech.edu/winners (accessed 24 March 2021).
[3] The 1-string prototype Automatic Microtonal Guitar was publically revealed on 24 May 2021, several weeks after conducting this interview.

me John Schneider's [book] *The Contemporary Guitar*.[4] So, the PhD department was very much into new music, and for my first CD, by my duo Duoist, the commissions went to our friends. So, you know, in one song we used tools, for example pestles, to create interesting effects on our standard instruments... many different extended techniques, so I was already interested in contemporary music. But, of course, my main motivation was playing my own music. William Allaudin Mathieu wrote me a three-movement suite called *Lattice İşi*, in five-limit Just intonation, with some septimal tones. So, thanks to that piece, I was really interested in Just intonation from the beginning. So, I was already into new music, but *makam* music was my main motivation... then of course, since then, I became interested in the tunings of Renaissance and Baroque. And then I made some Bach and Renaissance experiments with several well-temperaments and meantone temperaments. So yes, my interest in the different tuning systems, since 2008, grew bigger and bigger, and it's *still* growing! For example, I've recently recorded a piece by Nicola Vicentino on the microtonal guitar, and I'm reading his treatise from 1555,[5] which uses thirty-one-tone equal temperament, and it's my first performance using 31-TET tuning. And this December I have a concert at The Huygens-Fokker Foundation in Amsterdam, where they have the Fokker organ in thirty-one-tone,[6] and an original piece has now been written for Fokker organ and microtonal guitar duo. So, I can say that, for me, 2021 is the year of thirty-one-tone equal temperament. So, it's growing bigger and bigger, and, you know, I'm open to all different genres of microtonal music.

RP: What inspired you to design the Adjustable Microtonal Guitar?

TC: Twenty-one years ago, in Boğaziçi University, where I was studying business administration, we organized a panel [competition] called 'arranging Anatolian traditional music with the classical guitar', and we invited Erkan Oğur [as a special guest]. I was the moderator of that panel and, during the break I showed Erkan Oğur my bağlama-fretted microtonal guitar – I had a fretless guitar, which I was experimenting with, but I wanted to preserve the timbre of the classical guitar, so had tied frets onto the neck – and he played it, and he said 'it doesn't work so much', and it was already buzzing because the bağlama frets were too low. And then, I waited eight more years for the [Adjustable] Microtonal Guitar

---

[4] See Schneider (1985).
[5] See Vicentino (1555).
[6] Due to the 2020–1 global pandemic, this concert was rescheduled, and took place on 13 March 2022.

Figure 2.1 Tolgahan Çoğulu playing his Adjustable Microtonal Guitar. (Photo: Tolgahan Çoğulu, used with permission).

[idea] to come (see Figure 2.1). Maybe, if I had persisted more with my earlier experiments, my Adjustable Microtonal Guitar journey would have begun sooner, and I would have gained eight years!

RP: Why was the Adjustable Microtonal Guitar a better option for you, compared to using Tom Stone's interchangeable fretboards or Lacôte's Movable-fretted Guitar?

TC: Of course, yeah, I like Tom Stone's interchangeable fretboards. First of all, there wasn't any luthier I could order [something like that] from in 2008 and I knew that Lacôte's and Vogt's design/s, was the ideal path I should follow, but I had to improve the design by opening the channels [in the fingerboard], and by inserting or removing the additional 'small' frets; so, that was an improvement in the mobile-fretted microtonal guitar's history. You know, I am still not playing interchangeable fretboards. Although Michael Kudirka is now producing amazing, high-quality, interchangeable fingerboards, which are available to everyone. So maybe, in the future, it will be a good option for my international concerts. My ideal guitar setup for concerts should be: interchangeable fingerboards, but where one of the fingerboards is the one from my Adjustable Microtonal Guitar, and the others, practical designs for certain *makams*, Just intonation and so on. I think that would be ideal. Or maybe, the Automatic

Microtonal Guitar – in two months we will release the one-string prototype, finally, after seven years! – of course, if this happens, and once it's been improved technologically to the max, I won't need interchangeable fingerboards. I only need to bring my Automatic Microtonal Guitar and I can change all the tunings by pressing a button or a pedal.

RP: With the Adjustable Microtonal Guitar, compared to fretless for example, you can play very exact and consistently accurate microtones. Is this precision, and the exploration of microtonal harmonization, the major driving force behind your work?

TC: Yes, because I'm a classical guitarist. You know, I want that sustain. I want that sound, and I want polyphony and homophony. . . . Of course, having learned a little oud, fretless guitar is the ideal design to play the *makam* – you can imitate the voice, kemençe or the ney, one-to-one, like Erkan Oğur, and it's awesome. But the Adjustable Microtonal Guitar can imitate bağlama, tanbur and kanun. So, for example, from the second degree in *Uşşâk makam*, when you are going to the tonic, you need a *gliss*, from a range of 35 to 60 cents. And on tanbur, there are two or three frets on that path, so you can have a little bit of a fretless feeling, also, the frets are very low, so it somehow sounds a little bit fretless; with kanun, with the mandals (levers), it sounds a bit further away from the fretless feeling. . . . So, with the Adjustable [Microtonal Guitar], I'm trying to imitate the tanbur by adding more frets in that glissando area.

RP: Your main guitar has eight strings; how does this help with the music you play?

TC: Well, it's a very funny story. I never thought that the Adjustable Microtonal Guitar would be a huge success. It was [just] one of my projects, you know? During that time, I also had a guitar–flute duo project, I had a guitar duo project, so it was one of my projects that I was trying; and I also got a twelve-string grand Chapman Stick during that time. So, I was planning a Chapman Stick career, because I like the tapping things; I was thinking, okay, bağlama tappings can be put on the Chapman Stick. . . . and I was so interested in nine-string, ten-string, twelve-string guitars, because the Chapman Stick was twelve-string . . . I was visiting the guitar festivals in Europe and in Cologne, Germany, there was an amazing guitar shop, and I tried a ten-string Ramirez.

I was so interested, and was thinking, how can I challenge myself and create new stuff? So, my luthier for this project starts building this [microtonal] guitar. One night I was thinking of combining ideas, and called him and said, 'let's have eight-string microtonal guitar' and he said, 'okay, I can do it'. And then, for the first few months [after it was finished] I was a little regretful. Because, you know, it was already working as a fretboard, and I'd sensed the potential that it could change my life. But, because it was eight-string, I lost my control in my right hand. My thumb couldn't find the sixth [string] as usual, as always; sometimes it finds seven, sometimes five – my mind blew up! . . . [at first] I just tuned DDD – so [strings] six, seven and eight, all D. And when you do this, [gestures right-hand finger pattern] it kind of gives you a feeling of the harp. So, it offers more than the six. Then, having the additional seventh and eighth strings, allowed Allaudin Mathieu to compose his Just intonation piece in three modes. So, because in Just intonation you need many different frets, for the different modes, the seven and eight strings helped a lot. Since then, over the last thirteen years, I always change them. For example, in my latest arrangements that I did, I notice that dropping the C [eighth string] to A is fantastic! And seventh is usually D. Because, you know, on the classical guitar, if it's not drop D, a D chord sounds very weak, too weak. So, my favourite is A, D, E [8, 7, 6] or C, D, E [8, 7, 6].

RP: In Microtonal Guitar Duo, you work with a fretless guitarist. How do the different approaches to microtonality complement one another?

TC: Sinan [Cem Eroğlu] knows the *makams* very well and he approves my frets. We mostly play Anatolian folk music, and some Erkan Oğur – And Charlie Haden, Erik Satie and Chopin as well; the solos are a little bit *makam* in those, but all the other stuff is 12-TET – so we never had an issue with the microtones. Sinan approves them and plays them accordingly [as appropriate to *makam*], and plays the glissandos in his solos or sometimes in his melodic lines, to give more 'taste' of *makam*. And with Bağlama–Guitar Duo, before our concerts, backstage, Sinan [Ayyıldız] is arranging his frets according to mine or I am arranging my frets according to his . . . and I like that he is very careful about it. Because I am a bit lazy about it. You know, for me, it doesn't matter, like five cents or so, because Turkish music ensembles create heterophony, and this comes from these cent deviations – they are not precise. So maybe that's why I don't care so much, because it's already in the tradition.

RP: Do you ever use amplification or effects pedals at all, or is it always acoustic?

TC: It's always acoustic. But, soon, when I get my electric [Adjustable Microtonal Guitar] my plan is . . . to use my old Line 6 Pod for the effects. But I always like the natural tone of the classical guitar. You know, actually, I used to be an electric guitar player at high school and as an undergrad, but the reason I went back to classical and flamenco was that I always failed to get nice tones [on electric], perhaps again it's a motivation thing. . . . Also, you need money to have a nice amplifier, with tubes and everything, so that's why I came back to the natural sound.

RP: To what extent does the microtonal guitar reflect, or contribute to, your identity as an artist?

TC: Microtonal guitar changed my artistic life completely, and I let it change. As I mentioned, during the early days of the Adjustable Microtonal Guitar project I had various other projects. And I gradually abandoned everything, all my previous 'ex-duos' [laughs] – the flute duo, guitar duo, violin duo – and simplified my life more and more, gradually, to leave only microtonal guitar, and classical guitar to some extent. But, for example, three months ago, my composer friend asked me to play in his opera in Istanbul. And I said, 'if you write it for microtonal guitar, I will of course play' – because that would be the first Adjustable Microtonal Guitar part in an opera for me, it's a first – 'but if you write for classical guitar I won't play, and I can find you great players for it'. Because, it doesn't matter if I play; my colleagues can play [it] better than me even, by giving more. So, I deliberately decided that I'll leave the classical 12-TET to my colleagues, the experts, who are doing great. And I'll just concentrate on, especially over the last six or seven years, it's been *only* microtonal.

RP: You're now on the fifth annual iteration of the International Microtonal Guitar Competition.[7] Is it gaining increasing momentum/participation?

TC: Yeah, it [first] happened in 2017, after I returned from Bristol, and the objective was very clear: to develop repertoire. So, really, the competition is the excuse to create and enrich the repertoire, and it's a good way for spreading

---

[7] The International Microtonal Guitar Competition was established by Çoğulu in 2017 and is now held annually at Istanbul Technical University (Turkish Music State Conservatory).

the 'fretlets'.[8] I send them to more than 500 people, so more than 3,000 free fretlets since 2017. . . . Each year I modify the content a little. The first one was centred around the arrangement of traditional Turkish/Anatolian folk music, and then I thought, oh, why not accept Arabic, Persian, Indian, Balinese? Because that is the traditional [microtonal] music of the world. And then I thought, what about adding chamber music? – but, so far, no applications for it [laughs]. Then in the fourth one I included the composition category. . . . And I hope it will continue with two categories, because now every year, it yields around twelve pieces – six performance, six composition; so, twelve new pieces every year, with the scores, is a big contribution.

RP: Who are your favourite microtonal guitarists at the moment, and why?

TC: Of course, John Schneider is our God. He is the pioneer, and thanks to him I owe my career, and thanks to him I owe my Adjustable [Microtonal Guitar], everything. So, John Schneider is our God. Then Jürgen Ruck is doing great things with Renaissance and Baroque tunings on his adjustable guitar. Mak Grgić, ooh, he's amazing, I'm looking forward to listening to his upcoming Bach album; Fernando Perez is doing crazy things about world music guitar traditions; Stefan Gerritsen is using 31-TET. The winners of the competitions, Emre Ünlenen, Ali Han, Marek Pasieczny, they all play microtonal guitar in a great way. And, of course, Stu Mackenzie from King Gizzard on the electric microtonal guitar. I am also a fan of Brendan Byrnes, The Mercury Tree, Dave Fiuczynski, Dsilton, among many others. I mean, I haven't mentioned any fretless players – and the fretless is like the 'God' of microtonal guitars – but I guess I'm thinking specifically about fretted microtonal guitarists here.

RP: You have your own adjustable microtonal fretboard company, what are you currently working on there?

TC: We are planning to start selling, I hope, in four or five months, an electric neck with adjustable fretboard, for Stratocaster-type guitars, and classical guitar [adjustable] fretboards. Right now though, our destiny depends on the Turkish Scientific Council. Because we applied to fund the company and we are in the final stage. In June, they will announce the winners, and if we win, it [production]

---

[8] Small adhesive frets, sent out to International Microtonal Guitar Competition entrants for free.

will be faster. We will invest these funds for all the machinery we need to have the standards production in a high-quality way.

RP: Tell me about the LEGO Microtonal Guitar.

TC: That was such a big surprise! After the Adjustable Microtonal Guitar, in my mind I thought the [next] big breakthrough would be the Automatic Microtonal Guitar, which in my opinion is the *ultimate* design for movable-fret guitar history. I'm always imagining that we could even have Automatic Microtonal Guitar design competitions – in an ideal world, you know? – with Harvard, Cambridge, Istanbul Technical University each contributing with their designs, with the new 3D design, and nanotechnologies, you know this is the ideal. If I ever won the lottery, I would invest 20 per cent in this Automatic Microtonal Guitar design competition. Anyway, coming back to LEGO. Atlas's idea,[9] and it came in the middle of Adjustable and Automatic, in 2018. And when the idea came, I was already overwhelmed with the automatic guitar project. I was working with the mechanical engineers, with the mechatronics engineers, and I saw that funding is not enough, people are not motivated, and I saw my own mistakes as well. My problem is, I always want the ideal. The perfect breakthrough design: You press a button and it's *Hüseynî* in A, you press a button and it's G♯ in seven-limit Just intonation; you press a button, it's Renaissance quarter-comma meantone in D♭, or Balinese tuning you, know? . . . So, LEGO 'pops up'. First, I took the idea to my luthier, and I took him a rubbish guitar, and I took Atlas's toys [laughs], and I said, 'OK, let's remove the fretboard, glue the LEGO frets, cut them if you need to, level them with the strings and the 12-TET ratios etc. and we can make a guitar'. But something was wrong. It was too primitive. So, after seven months, I decided to take back the guitar and my LEGO bricks. And I thought, okay, this is a big failure. *Then,* destiny took me to the right person, Ruşen Can Acet. Ruşen said 'let's design 3D-printed base-plates, and if the pieces don't fit, we can print them out as well'. And it happened, we finally made it (see Figure 2.2). Wait, I will show you something! – I *must*! Hang on! [briefly leaves, then returns with LEGO Microtonal Guitar] Okay, I'm so excited. Now you are seeing the first-ever marriage of fretless guitar and microtonal guitar. So, what do I mean? So, this is a very smooth surface piece of LEGO [holds up piece]. Let's say my tonic is E, with F♯ the second degree, I'm attaching this [quickly attaches smooth piece of

---

[9] Tolgahan's son, Atlas, first suggested the idea of a LEGO fretboard.

Figure 2.2 Ruşen Can Acet (L), Atlas Çoğulu (C) and Tolgahan Çoğulu (R) with LEGO Microtonal Guitars. (Photo: Tolgahan Çoğulu, used with permission).

LEGO to fingerboard]. Now as you can see, my F♯ has that special LEGO now, okay? Check it out [plays section of *Uşşâk makam*, demonstrating *gliss* from second to tonic]. The first marriage of fretless and microtonal guitar ever, and you can make any specific 'fret', fretless! And this happened on the LEGO Guitar, which I could *never* have predicted!

RP: How would you like to see the LEGO Microtonal Guitar used in future – in education, in performance?

TC: First of all, I would like to see it in education in Turkey. We have great music centres that can use this. We realized it was a good tool to teach music theory – both standard *and* microtonal – to guitar students, of any standard, by playing games.... We've made a second guitar for Kaki King, and now it's in New York with her. The third went to Lucas Brar, an amazing Swedish guy; he's a YouTuber with 500,000 subscribers, and he loves it. Winning the Guthman People's Choice

Award has helped too, we're so happy. It's gained a lot of press coverage here in Turkey and was even featured in the *New York Times*. So, I don't know, in fifteen years' time, I guess we will see!

RP: What's next for you in your microtonal guitar journey?

TC: There're infinite projects, you know? Of course, the next big thing is the Automatic Microtonal Guitar. We are nearly ready to release the prototype (see Figure 2.3), but soon I have to find sponsors as we will need money to develop the six-string, 'perfect', version. In terms of playing, microtonal guitar in popular music. Thanks to King Gizzard, we are seeing it in the electric guitar world lots now . . . so, I'm now working on classical microtonal guitar, in a popular music context, with a singer, where the guitar is not just strumming chords, it's combining counter melodies, bass lines etc., in an interactive way. I realized, I've never played with the voice – for the last thirteen years, I've only played instrumental music, and that's crazy! So, this is now my motivation, to play something like Anatolian Rock, Anatolian Pop, *makam*-rock pieces, and arrange them for microtonal guitar and voice. Also, in April, Sinan and I are releasing an

Figure 2.3 Tolgahan Çoğulu testing the Automatic Microtonal Guitar prototype. (Photo: Tolgahan Çoğulu, used with permission).

EP with the Bağlama–Guitar Duo[10] – we will apply to WOMEX too – and in May I will release my first single. So, you know, endless playing projects.

RP: How do you envisage the future of microtonal guitar playing?

TC: I see *huge* potential. Like last week, at the 21st Century Guitar Conference,[11] I chaired the microtonal roundtable and asked 'what's going to happen in the 22nd Century Guitar Conference?' And Mike [Kudirka] said, 'it's gonna be mostly microtonal' [laughs]. No, seriously, I agree, it's going to be a huge part. Both fretless guitar and microtonal guitar family members are going to be very important, I think, for the future of music – in rock, jazz, classical and, of course, traditional music as well. It's growing crazily already so, yeah, it's gonna be huge!

Editors' Choice – Recommended Listening:

Amorphous (2021), Tolgahan Çoğulu & Sinan Ayyıldız, Ahenk Müzik Yapım.
Microtonal (2018), Tolgahan Çoğulu, Ahenk Music.
Microtonal Guitar Duo (2015), Tolgahan Çoğulu and Sinan Cem Eroğlu, Kalan Music.
Atlas (2012), Tolgahan Çoğulu, Kalan Music.
Artist Website: www.tolgahancogulu.com

References

Çoğulu, T. (2010), 'Tolgahan Çoğulu', Interview by Jerfi Aji, *Soundboard: The Journal of the Guitar Foundation of America*, 36(3): 80–1, 101.
Schneider, J.O. (1985), *The Contemporary Guitar*, Berkeley: University of California Press.
Vicentino, N. (1555), *L'antica Musica Ridotta alla Moderna Prattica* [Ancient Music Adapted to Modern Practice], Rome: Antonio Barre.

---

[10] *Amorphous* (2021), Tolgahan Çoğulu & Sinan Ayyıldız, Ahenk Müzik Yapım.
[11] *The 21st Century Guitar – Unconventional Approaches to Performance, Composition and Research*, University NOVA de Lisbona, Portugal (2021).

3

The expanding fretless guitarscape

Practice and progress

Richard Perks

Introduction

Though less commonplace than its fretted cousin, the fretless guitar inhabits a range of musical genres and cultures around the world. Research addressing the fretless guitar and its practice has so far been limited, however. While it has been considered in various discussions about global guitar cultures (Dawe 2010; Bates 2011; Dawe and Eroğlu 2013; Arın 2014; Önder 2015), as well as in relation to innovations and developments in instrument design (Partch 1949; Schneider 2015; Brett 2021), specific and detailed examinations of the fretless guitar from a performative perspective (Berg 2014; Perks 2019) remain scarce. In *The New Guitarscape in Critical Theory, Cultural Practice and Musical Performance*, Kevin Dawe (2010) introduced the term 'new guitarscape' to conceptually frame the wide-spanning, varied and progressive international guitar landscape. He suggests:

> The new guitarscape is made up of the myriad and changing cultures of the guitar: cultures of the new guitarscape that merge and diverge as part of broader musical, social and cultural developments. . . . It connects up musics and cultures, individuals and communities, economics and politics, in various ways. (2010: 43–4)

The fretless guitar,[1] and its practice, represents a microcosm of Dawe's new guitarscape: smaller in terms of incidence, yet similarly diverse with respect

---

[1] Unless significant to the performance context, no distinction will be made between 'de-fretted' guitars (instruments that originally had frets, which have subsequently been removed) and those that have been purpose-built without frets; both types will simply be referred to as *fretless*.

to performance styles, expressive techniques, timbres, instrument types and so forth. Application ranges from sonic or aesthetic novelty, to 'serious' artistic experimentation, to routine engagement (where the instrument has become a standard feature within a specialist idiom). It seems apposite therefore to define the multiplex musical genres, cultures, settings and performance practices surrounding the fretless guitar as the *fretless guitarscape*.

It is important to first acknowledge the existence and significance of different fretless guitar communities in and of themselves. Take, for example, the use of fretless electric guitar in commercial rock music. In this context, any fretless-specific techniques or articulations are typically used to emphasize or augment the musical vocabulary already associated with rock electric guitar playing (wide-ranging slides, pinched-harmonic 'squeals', extra-wide vibrato and so forth).[2] Players may well convey a distinctive fretless voice, but their overall approach usually remains authentic to the aesthetic expectations of the commercial rock genre. By contrast, many 'neo-traditional' musicians from Turkey use fretless classical (and sometimes electric) guitars to incorporate the performance techniques, timbres and microtonal inflections associated with local traditional instruments, such as bağlama, oud and tanbur, into their playing styles. Here, the physical and sonic potentials of the fretless guitar help the performer to realize and expand upon the expressive devices found in both Turkish art and regional Anatolian folk musics and map them into more modern or eclectic performance environments (see Bates 2011; Dawe and Eroğlu 2013). Interestingly, there are two sides to this story: one of guitarists wishing to assimilate customary instrumental techniques and the other of traditional instrumentalists (oud players, for example) adopting a more 'guitaristic' approach, taking advantage of the technical and timbral benefits that the fretless (often electric, or amplified acoustic) guitar provides. In short, there are different groups of musicians using fretless guitars, in different ways, for different reasons.

At the same time, we are witnessing an eruption of networks of, and resources for, fretless guitar enthusiasts, including international fretless guitar festivals, special guitar magazine features, online forums and dedicated websites. This is generating an increasingly interconnected, globally unified stratum within the fretless guitarscape where the focus is on the instrument itself, irrespective of genre, locale or performance style. By facilitating the sharing of abundant

---

[2] See Perks (2019) for a comprehensive overview of fretless electric guitar techniques, including notations and audio examples.

and diverse musical material, social media is unsurprisingly at the forefront of such developments (see Mjos 2013), with platforms like YouTube, Facebook and Instagram generating a surge in readily accessible fretless guitar resources. These include virtuosic displays, equipment demonstrations, tutorials, personal-progress video diaries and so on. This 'virtual scene' (Bennett and Peterson 2004) constitutes a kind of online support network, linking together aspiring, amateur and professional fretless guitarists alike.

The intention here is not to attempt a 'complete history of the fretless guitar'.[3] Rather, it is to contextualize the present-day fretless guitarscape by providing the reader with insights into the manifold performance practices associated with the instrument, highlighting any recent developments. Furthermore, whether situated at the epicentre of a localized hotbed or viewing from a global perspective, it seems the fretless guitar has become noticeably more prevalent of late, and this work offers possible explanations for this phenomenon. To examine the fretless guitarscape in detail, this chapter is divided into three main sections. The first, 'Genre, Idiom and Culture', presents a synopsis of key practitioners from around the world, and considers their distinctive approaches to playing the fretless guitar. The second, 'Public Exposure, Online Media and Virtual Networks', provides a comprehensive review of recent and ongoing forms of community interaction in which the fretless guitar acts as the primary focus. The third, 'Affordance and Creativity: A Personal Perspective', comprises an autoethnographic account of my own experience of working with the fretless electric guitar across a range of creative contexts. This last section draws upon James J. Gibson's notion of 'affordance' (1966; 1977; [1979] 1986) to establish a theoretical framework, which is used to both critique my artistic practice and provide insights into the ways in which 'fretlessness' – when viewed as a 'state of practice' – might benefit the modern guitarist.

Genre, idiom and culture

Pop, rock and beyond

The fretless guitar has featured sporadically in commercial pop and rock music since the mid-1960s.[4] In 1967, George Harrison was gifted a prototype Bartell

---

[3] For a comprehensive account of the history, chronology and performance lineage of the fretless guitar, see Berg (2014).
[4] The earliest commercial pop recording featuring fretless guitar is believed to be 'Stainless Steel Gamelan' by John Cale and Sterling Morrison (see Berg 2014); the track is listed in the album notes

fretless electric guitar that both he and John Lennon experimented with at different points.[5] Frank Zappa used a similar model on various recordings some years later, most discernibly on 'The Torture Never Stops',[6] where his anarchic slides reflect the song's dystopian narrative throughout. He once gave a brief insight into his fretless playing, stating '[on fretless] you don't push the strings to bend them, you move them back and forth like violin-type vibrato, which is a funny movement to get used to' (Zappa 1977: 46). Towards the end of the 20th century, more well-known pop, rock and progressive-rock guitarists had started to explore the fretless electric guitar, including Andy Summers, Adrian Belew and John Frusciante,[7] to name a few. In 1993, rock guitarist Steve Vai used a fretless electric guitar on the opening track to *Sex and Religion*,[8] 'An Earth Dweller's Return', in which he combines smooth slides with whammy-bar expression over alternating drones. Almost a decade later, on the 2004 G3 tour, he played a standout solo improvisation at the beginning of 'I Know You're Here' in which he used fretless to layer continual ambient, textural glissandi over a looped backing;[9] this performance has since become one of the most celebrated among Vai fans.[10] In 2010, Matt Bellamy used a fretless to create styth-esque lead lines when performing 'Resistance' and 'Uprising' throughout MUSE's epic *The Resistance* world tour.[11] More recently, extraordinary up-and-coming guitarists in the progressive-rock scene, such as Tom Monda from Thank You Scientist, have employed the fretless electric guitar to great effect.[12]

---

as being recorded in the 'mid 60s', though it was not officially released until 2001. See: *Stainless Gamelan: Inside the Dream Syndicate Volume III* (2001), John Cale, Table of the Elements.

[5] The Bartell fretless electric guitar prototype was housed at Abbey Road Studios (London). There has been much speculation that it was used during several overdub sessions throughout the recording of *The Beatles* ('White Album', 1968), however, whether any fretless takes made the final cut remains uncertain. The guitar was auctioned at Bonhams auction house (London, 2020), where it sold for a staggering £190,000; making it one of the most significant finds in electric guitar history (see Brett 2021).

[6] See: *Zoot Allures* (1976), Frank Zappa, UMC.

[7] See: 'Driven to Tears' from *Zenyattà Mondatta* (1980), The Police, A&M; *Three of a Perfect Pair* (1984), King Crimson, E.G./Warner Brothers; 'Mellowship Slinky in B Major' from *Blood Sugar Sex Magik* (1991), Red Hot Chilli Peppers, Warner Brothers.

[8] See: *Sex and Religion* (1993), Vai, Relativity (Sony/Columbia).

[9] For this performance Vai used his triple-neck Ibanez Jem, on which the bottom neck is fretless, fitted with a Fernandes Sustainer pickup; this pickup facilitates continual sustain (much like an EBow). Incidentally, at the time of writing, Vai used his new triple-necked Ibanez 'Hydra' guitar (which has a twelve-string, partially fretless fingerboard on the upper neck) to record the track 'Teeth of the Hydra' from *Inviolate* (2022), Steve Vai, Favoured Nations. See: www.Vai.com

[10] See: 'I Know You're Here' from *G3 Live in Denver* (2004), Steve Vai, Joe Satriani and Yngwie Malmsteen, Epic Records.

[11] Bellamy's Manson Doubleneck has a fretless neck, with Sustainer pickup. See: www.musewiki.org/Manson_Doubleneck (accessed 12 April 2022).

[12] Monda was recently recognized by Guitar Player magazine in an article entitled *10 Future Prog Legends* (April 2021, 60). His fretless playing can be heard on the title track from *Terraformer* (2019),

While many famous rock-oriented guitarists may have used a fretless guitar, relatively few are famous *for* using it. An exception to this trend is Ron 'Bumblefoot' Thal, who – though admittedly already hailed by many as a guitar hero prior to adopting the fretless guitar – has made fretless an integral part of his playing style over the last two decades, gaining an unparalleled reputation among rock music fans and fretless guitar aficionados alike. Thal incorporates distinctive fretless electric guitar techniques to expand his already experimental rock-based vocabulary (a typical Thal fretless solo might include 'slid' pinched-harmonics in conjunction with his innovative use of a thimble).[13] In his current prog-rock outfit, Sons of Apollo, he predominantly uses his custom Vigier 'DoubleBfoot' signature model – a double-necked guitar, the fretless of which has a metal fingerboard.[14] Discussing his creative role in the band, he explains that 'with the fretless, you can get some interesting, dragging, low, growly things. The fretless can lead you into different riffs that you wouldn't necessarily come up with on the fretted. It's not just a gimmick. It's half my playing' (Thal 2020). In a similar vein, progressive-rock/fusion virtuoso Guthrie Govan is widely recognized for playing fretless electric guitar, as further testament to his consummate versatility.[15] He has used fretless across a variety of musical styles ranging from intimate jazz-fusion gigs with The Fellowship, to UK-grime sessions accompanying Dizzee Rascal,[16] to large-scale progressive-rock concerts with his power trio The Aristocrats.[17] Curiously, despite employing fretless in an array of performance contexts, Govan's prowess on the instrument is probably more widely known due to his appearance in several online Vigier product demonstration videos that went viral (this will be revisited later in the second section).

Another artist exhibiting a highly individual approach in this territory is Ned Evett, who invented the glass fingerboard in 1997 and has added them to

---

Thank You Scientist, New York: Evil Ink Records.

[13] Thal is renowned for placing a thimble on the little finger of his plucking hand to execute notes higher than those available on the fingerboard; extending the 'playable' range of each string. The fretless solo from *God of the Sun* by Sons of Apollo contains both slid pinched-harmonics and use of thimble to expand register (see: *Psychotic Symphony* (2017), Sons of Apollo, Inside Out Music/Sony).

[14] Vigier fretless electric guitars have metal-alloy fingerboards (originally 'Delta Metal' (1980); 'I-Metal' since 2012). A metal fingerboard enables greater sustain and is preferred by many rock-oriented fretless players. See: www.vigier.com

[15] Govan plays Vigier Excalibur Surfreter fretless electric guitars, which he has used since 2008.

[16] See: *Live Large 'N' In Charge* from: BBC Electric Proms with Dizzee Rascal. Available online: https://www.youtube.com/watch?v=l_ZHn4GyARg (accessed 12 April 2022)

[17] See: 'Erotic Cakes' (live) from, *Boing, We'll Do It Live!* (2013), The Aristocrats, Boing! B00AL0PW48

Figure 3.1 Ned Evett (with his glass fingerboard fretless Peavey Ripslide and glass-slide capo). (Photo: Ned Evett, used with permission.)

a variety of guitars since (see Figure 3.1).[18] He won the North American Rock Guitar Competition (2003) and has been described as 'the world's first fretless guitar rock star'.[19] Evett's style blends blues expression, country finger-picking and rock timbres, with the occasional articulatory nod towards Indian *raga*. He regularly uses a 'glass-slide capo' – made by combining a glass-slide and a capo (see Figure 3.1) – which allows him to strum, slide and add vibrato to open-tuned chords in real time, while leaving his 'fretting' hand free to embellish (with conventional fingering). In an interview, I asked him to elaborate on his approach to the instrument.[20]

RP: What does the fretless guitar facilitate or prompt, creatively, compared to fretted? Do you feel liberated, limited or both?

---

[18] Evett plays a range of fretless guitars, including a converted Fender Stratocaster, a custom 'Globro' steel resonator and a Fernandes Native Pro (with built-in sustainer pickup). See: *An Introduction to Fretless Guitar* (2000), Ned Evett, Altered Eg. B00004LN2U.

[19] See: Guitar Player Magazine (2007), 'Review of 2006 Fretless Guitar Festival', 41 (7), New York: Future US.

[20] Ned Evett, interview by Richard Perks. Conducted on 4 August 2020.

NE: Fretless guitar imparts certain technical challenges, and interesting constraints compared to playing with frets. I am able to play and record at a high enough level to not need a fretted guitar for my compositions. I should add that I don't find fretted guitar lacking, and I avoid switching between the two purely for conceptual reasons. My basic concept being: I am a fretless guitarist; what does that mean musically to me as an artist? I would say the constraints, once thoroughly explored, lead to an idiomatic method that would qualify fretless guitar as a true instrument, as opposed to pure novelty.

RP: How did you discover the glass-slide capo technique?

NE: While on tour for *Treehouse* in 2012,[21] I strummed a chord and grabbed the capo at the third position marker to readjust the tuning of the treble strings. I was telling a story to the crowd and grabbed a little too hard, pushing the capo from the third position to the first, and the open chord beautifully slid down a whole step from Gmaj to Fmaj. It was a sonic epiphany! I began working with the Dunlop capo to improve the technique, ultimately taking a Dunlop glass-slide and inserting the drum into it, which is the setup I use now.

RP: What things do you like to do/play on fretless that would be impossible on a fretted guitar?

NE: Movable artificial harmonics, slide-capo effects and faux-tenor-fretless bass lines.

Evett's insights here not only suggest a commitment to the creative pursuit and mastery of any expressive or technical benefits the fretless guitar may afford but also reveal a strong sense of artistic identity that is inextricably linked to the instrument itself – he *is* a 'fretless guitarist'.

More than ever, modern rock guitarists – in collaboration with dedicated luthiers, guitar manufacturers and so forth – are utilizing the fretless guitar in innovative ways to explore its creative potential. When high-profile rock guitarists adopt the fretless guitar, they propel it to the forefront of the commercial industry – highlighting its novel character in one sense, while simultaneously 'normalizing' its presence in another.

---

[21] See: *Treehouse* (2012), Ned Evett, Import. B006Z94JG6.

West Asia, fusions and eclecticism

Erkan Oğur is a Turkish multi-instrumentalist and composer, widely revered throughout West Asia as the pioneer of the fretless classical guitar. He made his first fretless guitar in 1976 to facilitate the microtonal inflections found in traditional Anatolian folk musics.[22] Subsequently, he developed a distinctive performing style that 'draws more on Turkish classical *tanbur* and oud technique and ornamentation than on any Western guitar picking or strumming technique' (Bates 2011: 96). Oğur achieved international recognition after the release of *Fretless* in 1993[23] and has produced many albums since, using a variety of fretless guitars.[24] He exhibits a versatile and eclectic approach, and his compositions 'combine a range of techniques and styles, including the microtonal scales and melodies of Turkish *makam* music, jazz harmony and free improvisation' (Dawe and Eroğlu 2013: 62). Stressing the impact of fretless on his career, he says that 'fretless guitar was an opening for me after regular guitar, there's no limit after you open that door. It was a real turning point in my life' (Oğur 2001). Owing in large part to Erkan Oğur's influence, a new wave of remarkable fretless guitarists has emerged from Turkey in recent years, including Cenk Erdoğan,[25] Sinan Cem Eroğlu[26] and Salih Korkut Peker,[27] to name but a few. Eliot Bates suggests that the '*perdesiz gitar* [fretless guitar] has practically become a new Anatolian folk instrument' (2011: 97). For this generation, the use of fretless guitars – alongside fretted – now appears to be 'par for the course', with players using a variety of guitar-types in conjunction with different technologies (amplifiers, effects pedals, EBow,[28] laptops and so forth) to continually straddle – or blur – the boundaries

---

[22] Both Anatolian folk music(s) and Turkish art music make use of *makam*, a centuries-old system of scales, melodic patterns, ornamentations and aesthetic conventions. The intervallic structures used within *makam* are not based around twelve-tone equal temperament; the fretless guitar therefore provides an advantage in performing the necessary microtonal pitches and inflections. For a detailed guide to Turkish traditional music see Aydemir (2010). Note that comparable systems are also found in Arabic traditional musics (*Maqām*) and Persian classical music (*Dastgāh*).

[23] See: *Fretless* (1993), Erkan Oğur, Feuer and Eis. FUEC 714.

[24] Oğur plays both nylon-string acoustic and electric fretless guitars. He also has a custom-build double-neck (fretless–fretted) electric guitar, enabling him to quickly switch between equal temperament and microtonal soundworlds when performing live.

[25] Erdoğan is a guitarist and composer based in Istanbul. He plays nylon-string, electric and baritone fretless guitars, as well as the *yaylı* tanbur. See Chapter 4.

[26] Eroğlu is a multi-instrumentalist (guitar, fretless guitar, saz/kopuz and kaval), producer and composer. He is a former lecturer of music at Istanbul Technical University (Turkish Music State Conservatory) and was actively involved in the setting up of the world's first fretless guitar department at Istanbul Medipol University.

[27] Peker performs using a variety of fretless instruments, including: six-string nylon, electric and harp guitars; the cümbüş and the 'efece'.

[28] The EBow enables guitarists to create 'infinite' sustain such that the legato techniques more commonly associated with wind instruments are made possible; fretless electric guitar players from

between Anatolian and Western expression. Of this movement, Cenk Erdoğan is arguably the most prolific, boasting an extensive international recording and touring profile as a soloist and session musician. An in-depth interview with Erdoğan can be found in Chapter 4, where he discusses his approach to playing the fretless guitar and explains how it reflects his identity as a Turkish musician (see pages 72–5).[29] In an earlier interview with *MAKAM* magazine, on the subject of teaching fretless, he conveys a similar sentiment, claiming 'this instrument was born in our territories and it belongs to our culture, so historically it is us who could teach this instrument better than anyone else' (Erdoğan 2020). Evidently, therefore, for Erdoğan, the fretless guitar not only forms part of his individual artistic voice but also carries cultural significance, about which he feels a great sense of pride and, to a certain extent, ownership.

Guitarists from different parts of West Asia have also started to take advantage of the fretless guitar's expressive potential, especially within World-fusion or 'cross-over' genres. Mahan Mirarab, for example, is a fretless guitarist originally from Tehran, whose work combines Persian articulations and modalities with contemporary Western jazz forms.[30] Similarly, Israeli guitarist Gilad Weiss uses the fretless guitar to incorporate aspects from *türkü* [Turkish folk song] when improvising.[31] Interestingly, some musicians are mirroring this process by augmenting West Asian performance traditions with Western guitar techniques, timbres and technologies. Tunisian oudist Amine Mraihi,[32] for instance, uses custom-built electric ouds, incorporating modern electric guitar techniques and an array of effects and sound sets, to blend Arabic traditional musics with jazz-rock fusion.[33] Although relatively localized, this groundswell of fretless guitar activity has resulted in many luthiers from the region offering fingerboard conversions, replacements, double-neck custom-builds and even interchangeable fingerboards, as standard services.

Turkey often use it to emulate the tone and articulations of traditional regional wind instruments (such as the kaval, ney and zurna).

[29] Cenk Erdoğan, interview by Richard Perks. Conducted on 4 August 2021.
[30] See: *The Persian Side of Jazz* (2010), Mahan Mirarab, Kamino Records; and *The Persian Side of Jazz, vol. 2* (2018), Mahan Mirarab, RHE Records.
[31] See: *Improvisations on Fretless Guitar, Vol. 1.* (2020), Gilad Weiss, independent release.
[32] Though not West Asian in the strictest sense, Mraihi's work and playing style is firmly rooted in Arabic classical music, so is pertinent here.
[33] Mraihi (known online as 'The Oud Dude') plays various electric ouds made by KOOL guitars. Several have only six strings, another has eight single strings and one is fitted with a tremolo arm (therefore, asides from scale-length, each closely resembles a fretless electric guitar). Furthermore, he often uses a guitar plectrum when playing.

Working laterally, numerous Western jazz, fusion and experimental guitarists are utilizing the fretless guitar to incorporate different techniques or articulations from around the world, as well as to explore diverse and complex microtonal aesthetics. Various jazz/fusion guitarists have been known to play fretless, including Pat Metheny,[34] Randy Roos,[35] John Stowell, Terje Rypdal and Michelle Webb, among others. More significant, however, are artists working in these spheres for whom the fretless guitar has become central to their practice. US-based guitarist and educator David 'Fuze' Fiuczynski, for example, uses the fretless electric guitar to integrate the melodic conventions found in different world musics into jazz-fusion contexts, through improvisation and microtonal harmonization (see Fiuczynski 2017: 106–7).[36] American fretless guitarist and multi-instrumentalist Gabriel Marin (from 'sci-fi'-fusion trio Consider the Source) innovatively combines modern technology (effects, on-board synth processing and so forth) with a variety of traditional South and West Asian expressive techniques, enabling him to readily access a wide range of sonorities, textual soundscapes and articulatory devices when improvising.[37] One of the most important figures in relation to performing with, and the development of, the fretless electric guitar is American guitarist Tim Donahue. Chiefly celebrated for playing his self-designed/built fretless harp guitars (with built-in MIDI/synth capabilities), Donahue has advanced a multiplicity of performance techniques and timbres, navigated manifold genres and revolutionized the instrument's design.[38] Italian acoustic guitar virtuoso Antonio Forcione is renowned for playing his 'oudan', a converted fretless nylon-string guitar with added sympathetic-string harp which he claims 'gives that kind of Middle Eastern feel', adding that 'a guitar without frets is like a world with no borders' (Forcione 2016: 69). By the same

---

[34] Metheny used a fretless nylon-string acoustic guitar on the title track of Grammy Award-Winning Album *Imaginary Day* (1997), Pat Metheny Group, Warner Bros; and a twelve-string nylon fretless acoustic on 'Counting Texas', from *Trio → Live* (2000), Pat Metheny, Warner Bros.

[35] See: *Mistral* (1978), Randy Roos, Spoon Fed Records, B008C1QN8C.

[36] Fiuczynski plays various custom-build double-neck (fretless–fretted) guitars. His 'Fuzeblaster' comprises a twelve-string fretless oud (on the upper neck) and a seven-string guitar, with a six-string tremolo and fixed low-B string (on the lower). He is professor of guitar at Berklee College of Music, Boston. See: *Planet Microjam* (2012), David Fiuczynski, Rare Noise RNR025.

[37] Marin predominantly plays a custom double-neck (fretless–fretted) Vigier fitted with Vo-96 synthesizer pickups (which allow him to vary the 'harmonic palette' in real time using on-board touch pad controls). He also plays an assortment of stringed instruments from around the world (including dutar, dombra, tanbour, balta saz and kamancha). See: *Ruminate: Improvisations for Fretless Guitar and Dutar* (2021), Gabriel Akhmad Marin, Worlds Within Worlds Records.

[38] Donahue built his first fretless electric guitar in 1980; followed by two fretless harp guitars in 1984. In 1986 one of his designs was licenced by Ishibashi Music (Japan), and the 'Selva Tim Donahue Model' – one of the first production model fretless electric guitars – became commercially available; each guitar came with a free copy of Donahue's *Fretless 6-String Guitar Technique* booklet (the earliest known 'guide' to fretless electric guitar playing – archived at www.unfretted.com).

token, Canada-born multi-instrumentalist Edward Powell blends the systems of Indian *raga* with Arabic/Turkish *maqām/makam* using his self-crafted acoustic 'ragmakamtar', a twin-necked sarod/oud hybrid. Finally, ever since Harry Partch's pioneering microtonal explorations using his fretless electric 'Adapted Guitar I' (see Partch 1949; Schneider 2015),[39] the fretless guitar has appeared within Western contemporary classical, experimental and improvised musics. Working amidst these terrains today we find such distinguished artists as Neil Haverstick and Elliott Sharp.[40,41] Discussing his fretless guitar practice Haverstick claims, 'playing fretless presents many challenges, but allows me to find new horizons as a composer, including many subtle microtonal shades of color, unavailable on a tempered instrument' (Haverstick 2010).

It seems, therefore, that for guitarists working across specific musical cultures the fretless guitar enables creative 'bridges' to be built, which facilitate the sharing and/or combining of different performance techniques, expressive devices and idiomatic conventions. Similarly, for eclectic and experimental musicians looking to expand their improvisatory or compositional lexica, the attraction to fretless is clear; as Fiuczynski puts it: 'with fretless guitars and microtonal music, the slate is totally clean . . . You can be Captain Kirk and go where no one's gone before' (Fiuczynski 2008).

Public exposure, online media and virtual networks

Organized by French fretless guitarist Franck Vigroux, *La Nuit de la Fretless* (held once in 1999, and again in 2001) is widely accepted as being the first fretless guitar–specific concert series to showcase multiple artists (see Berg 2014: 20). Following the second event, Vigroux, in collaboration with Ned Evett, invited a series of fretless artists to contribute tracks to an album, *Fretless*

---

[39] Partch constructed his fretless electric 'Adapted Guitar I' in 1945 while exploring different ways of facilitating Just intonation. It is widely considered to be the first-ever fingered (and amplifiable) fretless guitar, and he used it to record the album *U.S. Highball* (1946), GME. See: Partch (1949: 196–9); Schneider (2015: 190–1); as well as pages 15–16 of this volume.
[40] Haverstick is a microtonal guitarist and composer. He is particularly well known for experimenting with alternate forms of equal temperament (using guitars fretted in 19, 22, 24, 31, 34 and 36 EDO) as well as playing fretless, see: *Fretless* (2010), Neil Haverstick, independent release. He has also self-published several books on microtonal theory and microtonal guitar playing (see, for example: *Hopelessly Microtonal – The Musical Instruments of Neil Haverstick*, 2018).
[41] Sharp is a composer, multi-instrumentalist and performer. He is a central figure in New York City's avant-garde and experimental music scene, and regularly plays fretless electric guitar, fretless baritone guitar and glissentar. See: *Kármán Lines* (2021), Elliott Sharp, independent release.

Guitar Masters.[42] Over the last two decades, however, few have done more to raise the profile of the fretless guitar in the public domain than British guitarist and author Jeff Berg. In 2003, Berg founded the website unfretted.com, through which he has devotedly published news, reviewed new works, promoted players via featured guest interviews and hosted interactive forums, keeping visitors/members continually abreast of any developments relating to the instrument. This site was the first of its kind and for years acted as the primary conduit for fretless guitarists around the world to connect, irrespective of musical ability, taste, genre or culture. In 2005, Berg curated and produced a double compilation album entitled *Village of the Unfretted*,[43] which featured a host of well-known fretless players. To celebrate the release of this album, US fretless guitarist Michael 'Atonal' Vick organized the NYC Fretless Guitar Festival (New York City), enabling many leading international fretless artists to meet in person for the first time. The success of this event spurred two further fretless guitar festivals in New York City,[44] as well as numerous others across Europe, most notably the Dutch Fretless Guitar Festival (DFGF), which at the time of writing has been held eight times.[45] In recent years, Berg's website has served more as an online archive – a significant portion of which he published as *Fretless Guitar: The Definitive Guide* (Berg 2014) – and interaction between artists, fans and enthusiasts now takes place primarily via the affiliated Facebook group, *Unfretted*.

In parallel to the increasing number of live events and archiving of information online, the growth and distribution power of social media platforms have prompted a radical boost in public awareness of, and exposure to, the fretless guitar. Take the following, for example: between 2010 and 2011, Guthrie Govan produced a series of short product demonstration videos for Vigier ('Excalibur Surfreter') fretless electric guitars, in association with LickLibrary and Guitar Interactive Magazine.[46] These videos have collectively accrued *millions* of views on YouTube and, as such, appear towards the very top of any Google search for

---

[42] *Fretless Guitar Masters* (2001), Various Artists, Fretlessguitar Recordings. This was the first commercially available fretless guitar compilation album.
[43] *Village of the Unfretted* (2005), Various Artists, Unfretted Records.
[44] All three NYC Fretless Guitar Festivals were organized by Michael Vick (2005, 2006, 2008). See: http://soundasmusic.com/fretless-guitar-festival.html (accessed 12 April 2022).
[45] Each of the Dutch Fretless Guitar Festivals have been curated and organized by Willem Niehorster; DFGF I–VII, Den Haag (2006–12); DFGF VIII, Amsterdam (2019). Albert Dambeck and Inge Habereder also organized two fretless guitar and Just intonation festivals in Austria (2013, 2014).
[46] See, for example: *Guthrie Govan Vigier Fretless Guitar Demo – Guitar Interactive Magazine* (2011), available online: https://www.youtube.com/watch?v=ZjEGtUXGWa0 (accessed 12 April 2022).

'fretless guitar'; ironically, they have amassed more attention (in terms of 'views' and 'likes') than any of Govan's artistic fretless guitar endeavours published online. Govan, in fact, claims he was approached by composer Hans Zimmer to join his band after Zimmer had seen him playing fretless guitar in one of these videos (see Govan 2016).[47] Viral videos of this sort invariably become a point of discussion or reference – especially within guitar-centric communities – and this instance has undeniably helped to promote, amplify and 'demystify' the fretless electric guitar among wider musical audiences.

Buzz Gravelle is a fretless classical guitarist, composer and music educator based in Los Angeles (see Figure 3.2). Both his YouTube channel and Instagram page, on which he frequently posts performances of original music composed specifically for fretless classical guitar (as well as tutorials addressing fretless technique), have accumulated a remarkable number of views/subscribers/followers in recent years.[48] I interviewed him about the impact of social media on his career and creative output.[49]

Figure 3.2 Buzz Gravelle (with his first fretless classical guitar). (Photo: Buzz Gravelle, used with permission.)

---

[47] Govan used fretless when performing 'Wonder Woman (Main Theme)' throughout the 2022 Hans Zimmer Live European tour.
[48] At the time of publication, Gravelle's piece *Proof of Existence* has had over 1.4 million views on YouTube and he has over 83,000 followers on Instagram.
[49] Buzz Gravelle, interview by Richard Perks. Conducted on 10 November 2020.

RP: To what extent have social media platforms boosted your artistic profile as a fretless guitarist?

BG: For me, Instagram made all the difference . . . around 2017, I started posting some fretless guitar videos to Instagram. I went from a handful of followers to over twenty thousand, very quickly. I believe it's because of the international reach of social media. When I started to gain followers, Turkey and Iran were the places where I gained the most. Turkey already has a fretless guitar tradition and the oud is foundational to many Middle Eastern cultures, including Iran. The 'oddity' of a fretless plucked string instrument wasn't there for these listeners; they accepted it. . . . From there I gained the attention of the Instagram guitar community and a lot of Western guitarists became interested – rock players, fingerstyle players, classical players.

RP: Has the growth of your online reputation and fan base directly inspired you to create more work?

BG: Absolutely. Until somewhat recently Instagram only allowed sixty-second videos. My regimen has been to consistently upload new videos of original fretless guitar music every week. I sometimes don't meet that goal, however, it's a good goal: one minute of new music per week. It's not paralysingly ambitious, but it's enough of a self-imposed expectation to keep me composing and practising daily.

RP: Does the work you produce for an online audience take a different shape, or is the process any different, to pieces you'd compose to perform at concerts/recitals?

BG: Absolutely, I compose for a sixty-second video clip. Miniatures. It tightens up my compositions. I need to make an impact on the listener immediately. I believe that has forced me to edit more rigorously. Or I might improvise for a few minutes and extract sixty seconds of it if I feel I captured a singular mood. Then I immediately post it online. After a few months, I review my favourites and note the ones that seem to resonate most with my followers. I select those and expand them out to full-length pieces. . . . I recorded my album of original fretless guitar music this way.[50]

---

[50] See: *The Realm of Endless Concepts* (2019), Buzz Gravelle, independent release.

Several months after this interview, in 2021, Gravelle established a partnership with Altamira Guitars to develop a range of commercially available, 'affordable', fretless classical guitars, which are now distributed exclusively through his company G&G Guitars.[51]

As these examples demonstrate, public interest surrounding the fretless guitar is clearly growing. More pertinent perhaps is that an array of online sources (dedicated websites, chat rooms, listervs, artist channels, social media platforms, 'followable' hashtags[52] and so forth) appear to be interconnecting across cyberspace, forming an interactive niche-network of fretless guitar–based performers, fans, students and educators. Discussing 'virtual scenes', Andy Bennett and Richard A. Peterson suggest that 'like the participants of translocal scenes, participants in virtual scenes are widely separated geographically, but unlike them, virtual scene participants around the world come together in a single scene-making conversation via the internet' (2004: 10). In this sense one can assert with some degree of confidence that there now exists an active, global, 'virtual fretless guitar scene'. Rather than being centred on a specific musical genre or group of artists, this scene has as its focus the fretless guitar itself, encompassing all its physical 'forms' (electric, nylon- and steel-string acoustic, double-neck, glissentar, customized/hybrid, electric oud, old-fashioned banjos and so on) and any related practices. This collective virtual medium further unites fretless guitarists, enabling them to traverse diverse (sometimes divisive) musical and cultural boundaries and engage in multi-directional exchange, influence and collaboration.

Affordance and creativity: A personal perspective

During a moment of creative spontaneity in 2008, I de-fretted one of my Fender Stratocasters.[53] Fortunately, the fingerboard survived the process, and I have continued to work extensively with the fretless electric guitar ever since. Projects have included long-term collaborations with composers (to establish new repertoire); working with different improvisatory ensembles (including my own band, vLookup Trio); the development of original techniques, timbres and

---

[51] See: www.2gguitars.com.
[52] Number of Instagram posts containing various fretless guitar-specific hashtags (at time of writing): #fretlessguitar (15k+); #perdesizgitar (5k+); #perdesiz (1k+); #fretlessguitars (256); #unfretted (223); #fretelsselectricguitar (135). [Note: 'Perdesiz' is Turkish for fretless.]
[53] This took place while writing and recording my debut solo album *Imposition*. See: *Imposition* (2009), Rich Perks, independent release (cat no. RP1982).

corresponding notation systems (Perks 2019); experimenting with technological augmentation (including effects pedals, loops, EBow and so forth); and numerous intercultural collaborations (see Perks 2013; 2021). By employing 'affordance' (Gibson 1966; 1977; [1979] 1986) as a critical lens, this section will examine my own use of the fretless electric guitar and assess the extent to which it has informed my perspective as a guitarist, performer and artist.

Affordance – A general overview

Gibson (1966; 1977; [1979] 1986) introduced the concept of 'affordance', suggesting that 'the affordance of anything is a specific combination of the properties of its substance and its surfaces taken with reference to an animal' (1977: 67). Essentially, affordances are possibilities for action provided to an organism by its environment (which is made up of all the substances, surfaces, objects, places, other living creatures and so forth that surround that organism, see Gibson 1977; [1979] 1986). For instance, a stone or ball may afford throwing; a large rock or chair may afford sitting. Furthermore, Gibson proposes that the ecological notion of a 'niche' (i.e. *how* an animal lives in its environment) can be considered in terms of affordances. He writes:

> I suggest that a niche is a set of affordances. The natural environment offers many ways of life and a way of life is a set of affordances that are utilized. (1977: 69)

Notably, Gibson claims that affordances are invariant; thus, implying that the identification or exploitation of an affordance is the consequence of perception on the part of the organism – the 'observer'. He writes:

> The affordance of something does *not change* as the need of the observer changes. The observer may or may not perceive or attend to the affordance, according to his needs, but the affordance, being invariant, is always there to be perceived. An affordance is not bestowed upon an object by a need of an observer and his act of perceiving it. The object offers what it does because it is what it is. ([1979] 1986: 138–9)

He suggests that 'the "values" and "meanings" of things in the environment can be directly perceived' (Gibson [1979] 1986: 127) and that this is due to the fact that 'the affordances of things for an observer are specified in stimulus information' ([1979] 1986: 140).[54] Building upon Gibson's work, Robert E. Shaw and Michael

---

[54] While Gibson's contribution has been highly influential, he has encountered criticism from some, particularly in response to the idea that animals perceive affordances directly and his denial of the role played by inference (see Fodor and Pylyshyn 1981).

T. Turvey (1981) introduced the concept of 'effectivity' to complement affordance, such that an 'effectivity of an animal (or human) is a specific combination of the functions of its tissues and organs taken with reference to an environment' (Shaw, Turvey and Mace 1982: 197). On this, W. Luke Windsor and Christophe De Bézenac explain:

> The mutual relation between organism and environment is encapsulated in the affordance in the following way. Affordances are dependent upon the structure of the organism. This structure has been referred to as the organism's effectivities; its size, shape, muscular structure, movement capacities, needs and sensitivities that make action in the environment possible. . . . A rock which afforded throwing to an adult might be too massive to do so for an infant who does not have the appropriate size and muscular strength . . . as a child grows and becomes stronger, a rock that may have previously been unliftable may now afford throwing. (2012: 104)

Similarly, Don Norman's (2013) revised definition of affordance emphasizes the role of the 'capabilities' of the agent:

> An affordance is a relationship between the properties of an object and the capabilities of the agent that determine just how the object could possibly be used. . . . The presence of an affordance is jointly determined by the qualities of the object and the abilities of the agent that is interacting. (2013: 11)

Erik Rietveld and Julian Kiverstein refer to the 'skill' of the individual, suggesting that 'what shows up as an affordance for one skilled agent may not do so for another agent belonging to the same form of life but lacking the relevant ability' (2014: 335). Outlining a conceptual framework for 'cultural affordances', Maxwell J.D. Ramstead, Samuel P.L. Veissière and Laurence J. Kirmayer (2016) distinguish two kinds of cultural affordances: 'Natural' affordances (the engagement with which depends on an agent's exploitation or leverage of reliable correlations in its environment using its set of phenotypical abilities) and 'Conventional' affordances (the engagement with which depends on agents skilfully leveraging expectations, norms, conventions and cooperative social practices). Of the latter, they suggest that '[e]ngagement with these affordances requires that agents have the ability to correctly infer (implicitly or explicitly) the culturally specific sets of expectations in which they are immersed – expectations about how to interpret other agents, and the symbolically and linguistically mediated social world' (2016: 2). Finally, it is important to mention Anthony Chemero's 'Affordances 2.0' (2009), which considers 'the interaction over time between an animal's sensorimotor abilities, that is, its embodied capacities for perception and action, and its niche, that is, the set of affordances available to it', and suggests that 'affordances and abilities are not just defined in terms of one another . . . but causally interact in real time and are causally dependent on one another' (Chemero 2009: 150–1). Let us now turn our attention back to music and, more specifically, the fretless electric guitar.

Affordances of musical instruments (and the fretless electric guitar)

We can define a musical instrument as an object that may, in the hands of an appropriate agent, function as a medium for sound-based expression and creativity. Whether separated by type or variant, one musical instrument – or any piece of music-making equipment for that matter – is distinguishable from the other in terms of its respective physical form, material properties and the sonic possibilities it facilitates. Windsor and De Bézenac suggest that musical instruments 'come to embody the effectivities of their users and possess inbuilt affordances' and that 'such affordances, in turn, may create selective pressure on the behaviour of individuals, inviting, sustaining and also restricting certain bodily actions and action consequences (sound in the case of music-making)' (2012: 109). Conversely, they remind us:

> Musicians often go to great lengths to overcome bodily and instrumental constraints in order to achieve particular aesthetic or functional goals. . . . In this process, musicians change their effectivities through the development of new perceptual sensitivities and levels of motor complexity. (2012: 109)

Most musical instruments exist as a product of careful design, that is, with the facilitation of specific functionalities in mind – we might call these intended affordances.[55] However, some action possibilities, while equally connected to the instrument's physicality, emerge via the inferences of the performer and may reveal potentialities for sound-creation that were unforeseen by the instrument's designers or original users (consider, for example, the application of 'extended techniques' in various Western music traditions) – we might call these interpretive affordances (see also Windsor and De Bézenac 2012; Rodger et al. 2020). For

---

[55] It is possible, of course, that similar physical attributes belonging to the same type of musical instrument, across different performative or social cultures, were 'built-in' initially with different functionalities in mind.

simplicity, I shall refer to any possibility for action that is directly and inextricably dependent upon an instrument's physical and/or material attributes, whether intended or interpretive, as an *inherent* affordance. It is important to note at this point too that performers may modify an instrument (changing the pickups in an electric guitar, for example), or make use of peripheral music-making devices (effects pedals, EBow, laptop and so on), to alter or augment its physicality and/or sonic potentialities; by doing so, musicians make available different inherent affordances.

By virtue of its characteristic physical form (i.e. the fingerboard has no frets), the fretless guitar must possess distinctive inherent affordances, separate from those of the fretted guitar. The fretless *electric* guitar adds further exploratory potential by allowing the player to combine any fretless-specific affordances with those of modern signal processing devices (such as effects pedals, synths, amplifiers and so forth). Indeed, as with any instrument, it is the relationship between these affordances and a player's individual approach to technical development, the performative environments/cultures in which they work, and the music-making methods they adopt or pursue, that ultimately determine the type and degree of artistic expression that transpires. As Anna Einarsson and Tom Ziemke conclude in relation to music performance, 'it is the situation as a whole that has affordances' (2017:10).

The fretless electric guitar in creative practice

By studying the guitar comprehensively (as many reading this volume likely have), the player develops a high level of technical facility which, in part, constitutes a hardwiring of various finger patterns, fret positions, chord shapes, string choices, articulations, actions, gestures and so forth. Whether conducted independently or via formal education, this process often yields a musician–instrument relationship that traverses multiple 'levels of embodiment' (Nijs 2017), through which 'the musician is able to spontaneously respond to the musical environment by outsourcing small adaptations of movement patterns . . . avoiding the explicit processing of handling the instrument' (Nijs 2017: 53).

Having graduated from music college some years earlier, I was working as a professional guitarist and instrumental tutor when I completed the conversion of my fretless electric guitar and first attempted to play it. The experience was instantly transformative. As I tried to 'recall' various fingerings, techniques and so forth, an entirely refreshed sense of discovery on my instrument – or at least one that very closely resembled it – emerged. Even when I tried something basic, I could not rely solely on habit; yet, at the same time, I knew where all the notes, sounds and articulatory ideas *should* 'live' on the fingerboard. The process of physical comprehension was unlike playing a completely different instrument (piano, for example) in that the general corporeal engagement (playing position, posture, hand-to-hand coordination and so forth) was identical, yet any sense of haptic feedback from the fingerboard, on which I would ordinarily 'rely for fine gestural control of the instrument' (Leman 2007: 163) had changed dramatically. I was experiencing the comfort of familiarity on the one hand (quite literally in this case) while negotiating substantial differences on the other.

Over the years, playing the fretless electric guitar has enabled me to acquire, hone and develop a variety of expressive techniques, sounds and 'noises', many of which are not replicable on the fretted guitar. It has also forced me to reevaluate my relationship with pitch, to the extent that certain intervals in twelve-tone equal temperament now sound decisively 'incorrect' to my ear. This, in turn, has inspired me to advance my knowledge of microtonality, tempered and non-tempered tuning systems, both theoretically and in practice. In addition, studying the fretless guitar has notably (re)informed my fretted guitar playing. For example, to initially overcome the ergonomic and physical limitations encountered when playing chords/double-stops on fretless,[56] I had to re-map the entire fingerboard, reassigning each finger to different positions. As well as instilling a fresh conception of the fingerboard in my mind (one much less reliant on memorized shapes), this process furnished me with a series of useful, 'unconventional' alternatives when voicing chords on the fretted guitar. Similarly, various fretless-specific vibrato and sliding actions have gradually emerged in my fretted guitar playing, albeit in transmuted form, suggesting that my general expressive/articulatory instinct (comprised of motor function, instrumental technique, aural comprehension and so forth) has been markedly influenced by my fretless technique.

Due to the lack of 'orthodox' playing method(s), the fretless guitar lends itself particularly well to artistic experimentation; my exploration (and application)

---

[56] Many 'standard' guitar chord shapes are reliant on fingers being placed in the area 'between' the frets and are therefore not possible to play accurately (in tune) on the fretless guitar; barring is also far less practical – see Perks (2019).

of the fretless electric guitar has spanned a broad range of collaborative projects and creative settings, a selection of which will be discussed next.

In 2014 I released an international call for scores (for pieces for solo fretless electric guitar) entitled *Fretless Architecture*. This project saw the evolution of five new works over a one-year period, through sustained collaboration with the composers; I premiered the final pieces at Colchester Arts Centre, UK, in 2015.[57] A collection of innovative fretless-specific techniques and timbres were developed during the process; one of which, 'screeching', involved using an EBow to create very slow slid-harmonics, with the addition of multi-directional delay effects to (at the request of the composer) emulate the reverberating sound of 'multiple trains' singing and screeching breaks in a station' (Perks 2019).[58] Subsequently, this technique/timbre has become a routine (and integral) part of my individual improvisatory lexicon on the fretless. Similarly, when working with improvisation-based group vLookup Trio,[59] I devised 'underwater', a sonic-texture comprising a series of layered slides, reverbs, delays and 'scratchy' noises, intended to resemble the sounds one experiences when submerged in water. This sound has since become a characteristic feature of my work, appearing in both compositions and improvisations alike. Further examples include an attempt to replicate the ultra-wide vibrato of a theremin player during a rehearsal session, which prompted the development of 'extreme' and 'variable' vibratos, and discovering 'fingertip muting' while mimicking the wooden/staccato timbre of a marimba during an improvised duo recording (see Perks 2019).

Each of these examples evidences a form of teleological creativity, in that an objective is intimated (or perceived) in advance and becomes realized through a series of actions, iterations and refinements. Berys Gaut suggests:

> a creative process can, and standardly does, have a partly indeterminate goal. . . . So the process is teleological, and deliberation about achieving the goal consists not only in considering instrumental means (those actions that will realise it) but also constitutive means (more precise specifications of the end). (2010: 1041)

---

[57] A complete archive of videos, audio recordings and scores from this project are available online: www.richperks.co.uk/fretlessarchitecture.html (accessed 12 April 2022).

[58] 'Screeching' emerged through workshopping and rehearsing *Turbulence, for Unfretted Guitar*, composed by Julia Usher (2014). See Perks (2019) for a full account of this process; including excerpts from the score, handwritten performance notes/directions, video links and so forth.

[59] vLookup Trio is an improvisation-based ensemble comprising Andy Hall (trumpet), Tom Atherton (percussion) and Richard Perks (fretless electric guitar), which explores the textural possibilities of such a limited instrumentation by combining the use of effects pedals, MIDI triggers, Max MSP and laptop integration, among other means.

In the examples outlined, it is important to stress that the 'end' is not determined by the achievement of the objective/goal as a singular event; instead, the creative processes have given rise to the discovery of various 'additional' – *repeatable* – fretless-specific techniques and timbres that may then be injected into future creative processes, and which, through reiteration and refinement, have the potential to generate 'new' archetypes.[60]

I have also used the fretless electric guitar in an array of intercultural settings, from performing modern hybrid-embodiments of musics based on non-tempered/microtonal tuning systems, to recording and touring globally with a commercial Persian pop-rock artist.[61] Some years ago, I composed and performed several pieces that combined aspects of Persian classical music (drawing from the forms, melodic sub-structures and intervallic conventions used throughout various dastgāh systems) with post-Cageian indeterminacy and free improvisation. These works were rehearsed and developed over a two-year period, with an ensemble comprising tar, daf, clarinet, live electronics and fretless electric guitar. The pieces were premiered in 2012 (see Perks 2013). In 2017, I was commissioned by Diaspora Arts Connection (San Francisco) to lead an intercultural collaboration entitled *Strung Together* (see Figure 3.3). The objective was for a small ensemble, here comprising saz, oud, santur, darbuka and fretless electric guitar, to collectively create a full performance programme of original music, drawing eclectically from Persian, Arabic, Kurdish and Western musical traditions, within the space of just one week; the final performance was broadcast live via social media and reached a worldwide audience (see Perks 2021). In each case, the fretless electric guitar has afforded me expeditious *access* to the alternative tuning systems, microtonal inflections, performance techniques and conventions fundamental to the relevant musical traditions, enabling me to not only expand my technical capabilities on the instrument but to contribute in a more meaningful way. Over time, this access has allowed me to discover and utilize a variety of affordances that were previously either unavailable or imperceptible, and in doing so, 'occupy' (Gibson [1979] 1986) different performative 'niches' (see Gibson 1977; [1979] 1986; Chemero 2009). Finally, working within diverse

---

[60] To showcase a selection of novel techniques and timbres specific to the fretless electric guitar, I composed *Improweb MMXIX* (for solo fretless electric guitar + effects). In 2019, I premiered the piece as part of the International Guitar Research Centre's conference 'Improvisation and the Guitar' (Hong Kong Academy for Performing Arts, Hong Kong).

[61] I recorded guitars on three studio albums and performed live throughout two world tours with Ali Azimi (between 2013 and 2019). For an example of fretless electric guitar in this context, see: 'Ahange Aroosi' from *Till Glory Finds Us* (2016), Ali Azimi, independent release.

Figure 3.3 Richard Perks (with fretless Fender Stratocaster) and Faraz Minooei (Santur), *Strung Together*, Buriel Clay Theatre, San Francisco, 2017. (Photo: Diaspora Arts Connection, used with permission.)

intercultural ensembles has urged me to acquire and use various 'types' of fretless guitar (steel-/nylon-string acoustic, glissentar) and has also inspired me to learn the oud, saz and setar – each of which (in terms of technique, timbre and musicianship) has re-informed both my fretless *and* fretted guitar playing.

This section has shown that by engaging in a wide range of creative processes my awareness of the affordances of the fretless electric guitar (as perceived through any modality, either directly or via various forms/levels of inference) has evolved. Furthermore, the continual development of my individual capabilities, effectivities and skills (in response to various changes in performative environments, needs or goals) has enabled me to both discover and take advantage of 'new' affordances. We have seen too that, through comparison and reflexivity, playing the fretless guitar has repeatedly nudged my fretted guitar playing in unexpected directions, suggesting that it influences my artistic identity on multiple levels.

Fretlessness

From the ideas considered so far, it follows that a performer's state of practice is determined, at any given time, by a combination of factors: the inherent affordances of their instrument (the possibilities for action that exist in relation to their instrument as a physical object), their perceived affordances (the possibilities for action they are aware of at the time), their capabilities in relation to the instrument (as informed by their effectivities, sensorimotor abilities, level of skill and so forth), the niche occupied (the offerings of the performance environment that are taken advantage of; that is, the set of affordances they utilize), their engagement with conventional affordances (the possibilities for action that depend on their ability to appropriately infer and exploit the expectations, norms and conventions of the performance culture(s) in which they are immersed), any instinctive expressive bias or conflict (convergences with, or divergences from, hardwired intuition, techniques, articulations and so forth connected with other instruments played), any creative needs or goals, the degree to which they value the instrument as part of their broader artistic identity and so on.

Most fretless guitarists have, at some point, transitioned from fretted guitar (or perhaps another similar stringed instrument, such as the oud or sarod); I am, in fact, yet to meet a fretless guitarist who *began* their musical journey on the fretless guitar (though that is not to say it is impossible). For clarity, therefore – to distinguish my engagement with the fretless electric guitar from any underlying system(s) of norms established by my experience playing fretted guitar – I shall use the term *fretlessness* from here on to refer to my fretless-specific state of practice at any given time. Figure 3.4 illustrates the interconnectivity between fretlessness, creative processes and musical outcomes in relation to my music-making endeavours (see section 'The fretless electric guitar in creative practice').

We can see from Figure 3.4 that, for me, fretlessness is both active (serving as a point of departure; a catalyst that stimulates creative activity) and reactive (continually changing in response to each creative process or musical outcome) – it is *dynamic*. Creative processes may lead to multiple musical outcomes, as well as interact with other processes, each of which feeds back into fretlessness. Furthermore, over time, aspects of musical outcomes start to inform one another directly, irrespective of the fact that they originally emanated from fretlessness (e.g. new works may be composed specifically to showcase new techniques or timbres; deeper knowledge of microtonality may be consciously applied to slide/whammy-bar techniques on fretted guitar and so on). Fretlessness, therefore, in and of itself, acts as a highly influential agent in the shaping of my wider creative practice and artistic values, allowing me to cultivate an increasingly distinctive voice as a guitarist.

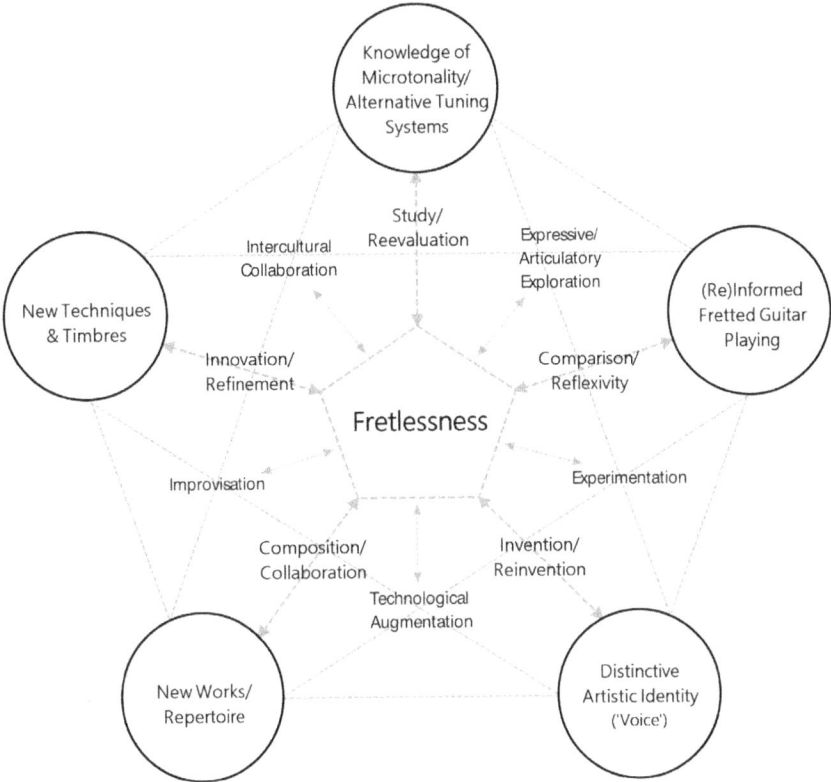

Figure 3.4 Interconnectivity between fretlessness, creative processes and musical outcomes.

Applying this to the general case, it seems reasonable to suggest that any guitarist who adopts the fretless guitar is likely to embody an equivalent form of fretlessness (though, of course, entirely subjective; in accordance with respective affordances, capabilities, goals and so forth), and so has the potential to generate a network of creative processes and musical outcomes that not only reflects but *enhances* their individuality as an artist.

Conclusion

We have seen that the fretless guitarscape is expanding on a global scale both in terms of diversity of performance practice and ubiquity of the instrument. What may once have been considered an 'unusual' or 'specialist' instrument – or by some perhaps, little more than a gimmick or fad – is emerging as a significant expressive force, providing the modern guitarist with new technical and timbral possibilities. In addition, these sounds are becoming increasingly familiar to the listener and are accepted – *expected* even – within an array of musical cultures and idioms. The adoption of fretless by well-known virtuosic performers, coupled with the fact that more and more manufacturers are producing fretless models, has fuelled worldwide exposure and access to the instrument in recent years. Furthermore, the growth of online dissemination, especially via social media, has spawned a vibrant virtual fretless guitar scene, which allows players, fans, luthiers, students and teachers from all over the world to regularly connect, regardless of stylistic preference, playing ability or musical/cultural background. Each of these factors contributes to a feedback loop which furthers the pervasiveness of the fretless guitar.

For some players, the fretless guitar is an important symbol of their artistic, idiomatic or cultural identity; for others, it serves as a vehicle for stylistic fusion or intercultural exchange. Importantly, such exchange appears to be multi-directional and is not overtly determined by hierarchical cultural positionings. The fretless guitar may provide a means to discover or facilitate fresh ideas and approaches (the execution of specific – 'new' – expressive techniques, access to microtonality/alternative tuning systems, and so forth), or perhaps instead, an opportunity to modernize or technologically augment more traditional performance styles (through electrification, amplification, the incorporation of effects/synths/MIDI/laptops and so on). It may act as a useful tool to explore more 'abstract' genres, such as noise music, contemporary classical or free improvisation, or simply stimulate play and intrigue, much like a new toy or puzzle.

Many guitarists, myself included, are drawn to the fretless guitar for a combination of these reasons. Through reflecting upon my own experience, it has been suggested here that fretlessness has the potential to significantly reshape a guitarist's creative practice. Notably, this condition is fluid, such that the player constantly reassesses their relationship with the fretless guitar in response to their creative needs or goals; their perception of the expressive possibilities available continually evolves not only in relation to the fretless guitar but the fretted guitar too, which in turn influences – and in some cases, *determines* – their individuality as an artist.

On contemplating the insights and examples presented throughout this chapter, one cannot help but wonder what lies ahead for the fretless guitar.

Will guitarists, in time, embrace fretless as standard practice? Will there be an expectation for professional players to double on both instruments (like many bassists do today, for example)? Or, might the fretless guitar evolve or diverge to such an extent that the instrument achieves autonomy and is considered separate from the fretted guitar entirely? Whatever the future holds, one thing is certain: *now* is a truly exciting time to be a part of the expanding fretless guitarscape.

Acknowledgements

Special thanks to Ned Evett, Cenk Erdoğan and Buzz Gravelle for their time and insights.

References

Arın, E. (2014), 'Yerelden Küresele Açılan Bir Model Olarak Perdesiz Gitar', *Karabük Üniversitesi Sosyal Bilimler Enstitüsü Dergisi*, 4 (1): 79–90.

Aydemir, M. (2010), *Turkish Music Makam Guide*, Istanbul: Pan Yayıncılık.

Bates, E. (2011), *Music in Turkey: Experiencing Music, Expressing Culture*, Oxford: Oxford University Press.

Bennett, A. and R.A. Peterson (2004), *Music Scenes: Local, Translocal and Virtual*, Nashville: Vanderbilt U P.

Berg, J. (2014), *Fretless Guitar – The Definitive Guide*, Self-published: Unfretted.com.

Brett, P. (2021), *Finding Fretless – The Story of George Harrison's 'Mad' Guitar*, Prestatyn: This Day In Music Books.

Chemero, A. (2009), *Radical Embodied Cognitive Science*, Cambridge, MA: MIT Press.

Dawe, K. (2010), *The New Guitarscape in Critical Theory, Cultural Practice and Musical Performance*, London: Routledge.

Dawe, K. and S.C. Eroğlu (2013), 'The Guitar in Turkey: Erkan Oğur and the Istanbul Guitarscape', *Ethnomusicology Forum*, 22 (1): 49–70.

Einarsson, A. and T. Ziemke (2017), 'Exploring the Multi-Layered Affordances of Composing and Performing Interactive Music with Responsive Technologies', *Frontiers in Psychology*, 8: 1701, Available online: https://www.frontiersin.org/article/10.3389/fpsyg.2017.01701 (accessed 5 January 2021), doi:10.3389/fpsyg.2017.01701.

Erdoğan, C. (2020), Interview by Reşad Çiçek, 'I am Still Looking For', *MAKAM Music Magazine*, 12 (Autumn): 50–60.

Fiuczynski, D. (2008), Interview by Anil Prasad, 'Global Microjamming', *Innerviews – Music without Borders*, Available online: https://www.innerviews.org/inner/fuze.html (accessed 30 September 2020).

Fiuczynski, D. (2017), 'Microtonality – New Directions for the Future and Past', in J. Zorn (ed.), *Arcana VIII – Musicians on Music*, 104–10, New York: Hips Road, Tzadik.

Fodor, J.A. and Z.W. Pylyshyn (1981), 'How Direct is Visual Perception?: Some Reflections on Gibson's "Ecological Approach"', *Cognition*, 9 (2): 139–96.

Forcione, A. (2016), Interview by David Mead, 'Interview – Antonio Forcione', *ACOUSTIC*, Spring: 64–70.

Gaut, B. (2010), 'The Philosophy of Creativity', *Philosophy Compass*, 5 (12): 1034–46.

Gibson, J.J. (1966), *The Senses Considered as Perceptual Systems*, Boston, MA: Houghton Mifflin.

Gibson, J.J. (1977), 'The Theory of Affordances', in R. Shaw and J. Bransford (eds), *Perceiving, Acting, and Knowing: Toward an Ecological Psychology*, 67–82, Hillsdale, NJ: Lawrence Erlbaum Associates.

Gibson, J.J. ([1979] 1986), *The Ecological Approach to Visual Perception*, Hillsdale, NJ: Lawrence Erlbaum Associates.

Govan, G. (2016), [Interview] Dir. Maxime Marion, *Hans Zimmer Live on Tour: 3M5 Guitars Echo In Eternity (feat. Johnny Marr)*, Available online: https://www.youtube.com/watch?v=-3W5DZd2vFo (accessed 10 November 2020).

Haverstick, N. ['Stickman'] (2010), [CD Liner Notes] *Fretless*, Independent release.

Leman, M. (2007), *Embodied Music Cognition and Mediation Technology*, Cambridge, MA: MIT Press.

Mjos, O.J. (2013), *Music, Social Media and Global Mobility: MySpace, Facebook, YouTube*, London: Routledge.

Nijs, L. (2017), 'The Merging of Musician and Musical Instrument: Incorporation, Presence, and Levels of Embodiment', in M. Lesaffre, P.J. Maes, and M. Leman (eds), *The Routledge Companion to Embodied Music Interaction*, 49–57, London: Routledge.

Norman, D.A. (2013), *The Design of Everyday Things*, Revised and Expanded ed., New York: Basic Books.

Oğur, E. (2001), Interview by Francesco Martinelli, *Roots World*, Available online: http://www.rootsworld.com/interview/ogur.html (accessed 26 September 2020).

Önder, T. (2015), 'An Instrument Emerged from East and West Interactions: Fretless Classical Guitar', *Musicology & Cultural Science*, 11: 25–30.

Partch, H. (1949), *Genesis of a Music*, Madison: University of Wisconsin Press.

Perks, R. (2013), *Combining Musical Identities through Composition and Improvisation*, PhD Thesis, Brunel University London, London.

Perks, R. (2019), 'Fretless Architecture: Towards the Development of Original Techniques and Musical Notation Specific to the Fretless Electric Guitar', *Music* and Practice, New Perspectives on Technique and Practice, 4, Available online: https://www.musicandpractice.org/volume-4/fretless-architecture-towards-the-development-of-original-techniques-and-musical-notation-specific-to-the-fretless-electric-guitar.

Perks, R. (2021), 'Strung Together: Realizing Music-cultural Hybridity within a Limited Time Frame', *Music and Practice*, 9, Available online: https://www.musicandpractice.org/strung-together-realizing-music-cultural-hybridity-within-a-limited-timeframe/.

Ramstead, M.J.D., S.P.L. Veissière and L.J. Kirmayer (2016), 'Cultural Affordances: Scaffolding Local Worlds through Shared Intentionality and Regimes of Attention', *Frontiers in Psychology*, 7: 1090.

Rietveld, E. and J. Kiverstein (2014), 'A Rich Landscape of Affordances', *Ecological Psychology*, 26 (4): 325–52.

Rodger, M., P. Stapleton, M. Van Walstijn, M. Ortiz and L. Pardue (2020), 'What Makes a Good Musical Instrument? A Matter of Processes, Ecologies and Specificities', in *Proceedings of the International Conference on New Interfaces for Musical Expression*, Birmingham City University: 484–90.

Schneider, J.O. (2015), *The Contemporary Guitar*, Revised and Enlarged Edition, Lanham, MD: Rowman & Littlefield.

Shaw, R. and M.T. Turvey (1981), 'Coalitions as Models for Ecosystems: A Realist Perspective on Perceptual Organization', in M. Kubovy and J. Pomerantz (eds), *Perceptual Organization*, 343–415, Hillsdale, NJ: Lawrence Erlbaum Associates, Inc.

Shaw, R.E., M.T. Turvey and W.M. Mace (1982), 'Ecological Psychology. The Consequence of a Commitment to Realism', in W. Weimer and D. Palermo (eds), *Cognition and the Symbolic Processes. Vol. 2I*, 159–226, Hillsdale, NJ: Lawrence Erlbaum Associates, Inc.

Thal, R. (2020), Interview by Tzvi Gluckin, '"It's Not Just a Gimmick." Bumblefoot Defends Fretless Guitar – and Billy Sheehan Backs Him Up', *Premier Guitar*, 11 February, Available online: https://www.premierguitar.com/articles/30053-sons-of-apollo_flame-on-sons-of-apollos-new-album-mmxx-Sons-of-Apollo-MMXX-Ron-Bumblefoot-Thal-Billy-Sheehan-Yamaha-Attitude-Bass-Vigier-DoubleBfoot (accessed 22 November 2020).

Windsor, W.L. and C. De Bézenac (2012), 'Music and Affordances', *Musicae Scientiae*, 16 (1): 102–20.

Zappa, F. (1977), Interview by Steve Rosen, 'Frank Zappa – A Talk with Rock's Premiere Iconoclast', *Guitar Player Magazine*, 11 (1), New York: Future US: 24–6, 42, 44, 46, 48, 50.

4

Touching the apple without gloves
Interview with Cenk Erdoğan
Richard Perks

Cenk Erdoğan is a multi-instrumentalist and composer based in Istanbul. He is celebrated for his virtuosity, playing nylon-string, electric and baritone *perdesiz* [fretless] guitars, and the *yaylı* [bowed] tanbur. As well as being a highly prolific recording artist, he has performed concerts and delivered masterclasses using fretless guitar all over the world. More recently, he has produced an extensive selection of online instructional videos, including some which focus on techniques specific to Turkish/Anatolian musics.

RP: Why did you start playing fretless guitar?

CE: When I was a kid I was very much into guitar, listening and playing. I was trying to play some chords and during these days I was in Antalya, which is in the south part of Turkey – it's a kind of vacation place – and there are not many record stores. A friend of mine went to visit his grandmother in Istanbul ... and I asked him to bring me [back] some guitar albums, and he brought me a cassette of Erkan Oğur's album, *Fretless*. I mean, *Bir Ömürlük Misafir*, but, *Fretless*.[1] ... I looked at the cover and I thought the pressing must be very bad, because I couldn't see the frets – the guitar should have frets?! So, then I started to read the text ... and there's a very big literature in that text, where Oğur says, 'this is a very emotional and expressive instrument, which is very close to the human voice; and it's my gift to all human beings ... to listen.' And then I realize this is something different, and I started to listen to the first

---

[1] *Fretless* was released in 1993 (Feuer und Eis FUEC 714); and later rereleased in Turkey (remastered and containing additional tracks), renamed as *Bir Ömürlük Misafir* (1996, Kalan Ses Görüntü).

Figure 4.1 Cenk Erdoğan with his Marchione fretless classical guitar. (Photo: Cenk Erdoğan, used with permission.)

piece and I was really mesmerized by the sound, because it is so warm, so soft. [For] a guy who is like eighteen years old, that music is so hard to understand, because it's very deep music, but it took me very much into its atmosphere. So, then I take the tools, you know? And then I take out my frets [laughs], and then I start that journey, like this – by chance.

RP: What does the fretless guitar offer you, that the fretted guitar does not?

CE: The sound. The warmth of the sound. Because frets give a little bit of artificial treble on guitar, artificial top-end, you know? It depends on the fret material also. If you have stainless steel frets, it gives much more presence and high pitch, like 10-kilohertz frequency; If you have aluminium frets, you have another frequency. But, on the fretless guitar, the wood gives its own voice to the string. I feel like when I play fretless guitar, I don't wear gloves, you know? Because touching an apple with a glove is one feeling and *touching* an apple [without gloves] is another feeling. So, I'm *touching* the apple with fretless guitar. I mean fretted guitar, it is an amazing instrument – I have a huge love for fretted guitars also – but, the sound and the quality of the sound [of the fretless] makes me feel like I'm playing something real, much more wood, you know? Fretless guitar gives me the real sound of the wood of my guitar. And, also, when you have frets, it puts you into certain [physical] spaces. . . . If you play this second fret on the lowest string, it is F♯. But who can say if it is the right F♯ for yourself, or the right F♯ for the harmony of the world, you know? I believe that yes, the harmonics and the notes are same all over the place, but the feelings are different. You know, for example, you can play an F♯ and you can hear something. But if a Spanish guy plays an F♯, same note, but different feelings.

RP: What are your favourite techniques, or sounds, to perform on the fretless guitar that are not possible on a guitar with frets?

CE: First, scales and microtones . . . sometimes [people] ask me about the scale playing, and how I learned the [Turkish] scales, and I say, 'man, we have five times of prayer every day, I'm forty-two years old, so imagine three-hundred-and-sixty-five, times forty-two, times five, of hearing those scales?!' – at least! . . . But in terms of techniques, of course, slides are the biggest difference. When you slide on fretted guitar, you hear all the notes separately. . . . But, [on fretless] it's like a ribbon. So, this gives a huge emotional, expressive, feeling to the instrument. I think the glissandos, the slides, are the biggest difference between both guitars. . . . Also, on fretless guitar, the string choice is very important, because you can play the same melodies with different timbres. And if you know the best parts of your instrument then you will sound better.

RP: You once taught me how to play *çarpma* technique.[2] Do these more traditional Turkish/Anatolian instrumental techniques work better on fretless?

CE: Yes, definitely. Because of the string height. Generally Turkish instruments – like tanbur, oud, bağlama – the string height above the fret is very low. So, it [these techniques] is really nice to play [on fretless guitar]. It is very easy to make those *çarpmas* also. Also, when you practise *çarpma* on fretless guitar, and you're using the nylon strings also, it gives a little bit of a 'ghost-note', like a snare. And we know that a snare with a ghost-note makes a groove, you know? So, that's

---

[2] *Çarpma* (which translates in English as 'bump' or 'hit') is an ornamentation common in traditional Anatolian musics. It is performed in a similar way to a hammer-on on the guitar, however, the note of decoration is slightly muted; it is used to accent or emphasize different notes within a melody.

why, when you play the *çarpma* in the right way, and in the right timing, then it means that your melody is grooving. It is so important to make a groove in the melody, not in the rhythm. In the rhythm, most of the people can play the groove, but in the melodies, if you can play groovy, that's another story.

RP: You also play *yaylı* tanbur. Do you ever use these techniques, or articulations on fretless guitar?

CE: No, I take the techniques from the normal tanbur, not the *yaylı* tanbur. Because with normal tanbur, you have *mizrap*, which is the name of the pic [plectrum], which is made from turtle shell and it is very thick and is long. So, I generate, most of the people in fact, especially Erkan Oğur, generate these *çarpma* techniques and phrases from tanbur techniques; because the tanbur is the master, the highlighted instrument of classical Turkish music. . . . But *yaylı* tanbur gives another feeling to my EBow playing. It helped [that] a lot because, I'm messing around with the bow, which is a very hard thing for a guitar player to do [gestures opposing directional hand movements] . . . so it helped me to play much more effectively with the EBow, phrasing, etc. But, actually, my *main* [fretless] technique comes from bağlama.

RP: You play both nylon-string acoustic and electric fretless guitars. Do you have a preference? And, if so, why?

CE: I think it is because of being Turkish . . . probably you will think it's funny, but if you want to survive in music scene in Turkey, you have to do many things. You know, you can't say 'I'm only a classical guitar player and I can only play classical music'. Then you can only teach music. You can't make music because we don't have churches. We don't have a history of European Classical music. So, because of that, in the orchestras in Turkey, you have to play electric guitars, classical guitar, steel-string guitars. Fretless is extraordinary, of course, it is not common, but if you want to be in the A-league, you have to play both of these instruments [electric and acoustic] here. . . . And also, when I look at my childhood, I was in the school band and we were playing like Toto, U2, whatever, all these old rock band tunes, and I had to play electric. I didn't have an electric guitar before 2000. . . . I was listening to Paco de Lucia on the school bus, and I'm going to the rehearsal to play U2 or Pearl Jam, you know? So, it's like mixed in my head? And then I come to fretless guitar, and then it's like three totally different worlds are inside my head, so I can't choose which one is better for me. *But*, I can say that I never play electric guitar at my studio. I never have the desire to say, 'okay, let's put all my pedals out and let's play an electric guitar', but I *do* have a desire to play nylon-string guitars (see Figure 4.1).

RP: So, the nylon-string is your 'go to' guitar?

CE: Yeah, definitely.

RP: How do you feel about players who 'cross over' to fretless guitar from more traditional instruments, like, for example, the oud? Do they approach the instrument in a different way, compared to players who started on guitar first?

CE: Yeah, they sound the same. They only change the instrument. . . . When they switch from oud to fretless guitar, they sound the same, and they play it like [an] oud. . . . They only play like the same melodic structures, same ornaments – like oud. So, what is the point? I mean, just play your instrument [laughs] . . . I believe that, if you didn't play guitar at all in your life, you can't have a sound. You can't take a sound out of fretless guitar. Guitar *has* to be your first instrument, because, this is fretless *guitar*.

RP: You also use a baritone fretless. How does it compare?

CE: Yeah, I have a baritone fretless, which is amazing. I've always liked baritone guitars, [but] there are no baritone guitars in Turkey. And when I first saw one in Musikmesse in Frankfurt, I played if for like four hours man, you know? It's much more deep than a guitar, the sound, the vibrations. . . . I've tried lots of lots of different tunings, and combinations of strings, and I find my way now, and I like three different combinations of tuning. But, there is one high string in the middle! It's a different combination, you know? The three bass strings are the same, and imagine that the top two strings are the same, but the third string sounds one octave higher.

RP: Do you find it takes time to adjust to the difference in scale-length?

CE: Definitely [smiles], because the measurements are different. So, for example, I can't play a recording just grabbing the guitar after one week. I have to play for like twenty to thirty minutes to get the angle of the fingers . . . but I learn it. [Now] it's very easy to make the switch. The main problem is, when you play baritone for a long time, you hate the normal guitar [laughs].

RP: How do you feel playing the fretless guitar reflects your identity, both as a guitarist and as someone who is Turkish?

CE: Oh, hard question. . . . You know, these microtones and these scales belong to my country, and, as a musician, I think that they belong to me too, you know? So, I have a huge respect to my roots. But I'm also open to any kind of music. But, I believe that, you know, because Erkan Oğur is still living – a *giant* musician – and he still produces [music], and *he* is the founder of this instrument – well, maybe not the 'founder', but the guy who took this instrument from the ground to the top – I think of the fretless guitar as Turkish. But, of course, you can't say that. You can't say 'this is a Turkish instrument'. Yes, the instrument comes from Turkish roots, it comes from the techniques, comes from the sounds – everything totally comes up like this, but nobody can say, for example, 'the classical guitar belongs to Spain!' . . . I think fretless guitar has an emotional sound which sounds better when you use the microtones, but, of course, there are some players around the world who play the fretless guitar and feel they have a certain communication with the instrument, and then I feel that, okay, this is your guitar too. So probably music is on top of identities. . . . But, to be honest, I do my works and compositions around these scales and these flavours to express that this [the fretless guitar] is coming from this land. I believe that, and I want people to understand that also – because Turkey is not a country that can show itself too much in the world, you know?

RP: Why do you think fretless guitar is becoming increasingly popular in Turkey?

CE: The fretless guitar is popular in Turkey because, I think . . . when people ask me how I get [international] gigs, I always say, 'Okay, do your own music. Do your compositions and put *your* flavour on it', as a Turkish musician, as an Anatolian guy, you know? If you don't put your flavour on that music, you can't survive in the world, because after the borders of Turkey, there are *amazing* guitar players. You can't go to Spain and say 'I'm a Flamenco player', they will take the guitar and put it in your mouth, and scratch at you. Or, when you go to New York City, you can't say 'I'm a straight ahead jazz player', it's like, 'okay let's play a standard', and then you're out. Or England, you can't say 'I'm a very good rock player', they say 'okay play', and then Guthrie [Govan] walks in, y'know? That's the thing. But fretless guitar is something that is unique, and in Turkey, you can find it, you can practise it, and if you can produce some music, it will open some doors to you . . . the younger generation now understands that playing flamenco is a very good thing, but it's not helpful for your career. Okay, it will help you to get better. But if you want to have a career in the world, an international career, you *have* to do something Turkish, because they [the audience] will buy [accept] that.

RP: How did you first meet Erkan Oğur?

CE: Maybe six months after hearing *Fretless*, my father had a birthday . . . I said, I want to record something for my dad, and I sent a track. And my father called me and said, 'there's a guy in my building, and he knows Erkan Oğur, and he thinks that you guys should meet'. And I was like dying on the phone! I said, 'are you serious?', and he [the friend] called Erkan Oğur, then he called me and gave me his phone [number], and I called him [Erkan Oğur], and we spoke from the direct phone, like from house to house. He invited me to a bar, to listen, and the first time we keep in touch [met] with the master was that night. I was sitting very, very close to him and looking always on the fingers like this [amazed expression] . . . around seven years later, we saw each other in the luthier place, he handed me his 'broken' fretless guitar – the signature one – the *first*, the very first fretless guitar I mean, he tuned it and gave it to me, and said 'play something'. And I was like, of course, really excited and shaking a little bit. I started to play and I remember that I played the B note on the high E string and I played a low B, and it was perfectly in tune, and he just turned to me and said, 'go on', and I started to play and then I began to feel relaxed a little bit. Then he started to ask some questions. He grabbed another guitar and he said, 'okay, play this interval' and I try to play the interval – for like two hours, you know? – a two-hour test! And then, and this point is very important, at the end the luthier asked 'hey master, do you see any future hope for him?' And he [Erkan Oğur] said 'you know, future hopes are always there'. Only these words. So, you understand? You know, either you don't have any future, or you have a chance to become something. So, I believed in the second, and I started to practise. And, I'm so very, very proud to have [had] this conversation with him as, maybe one year ago, we played together and he brought his fretless guitar, and I had my new Marchione; we put them both together and took a picture, and he said 'I want to share this picture' . . . he said 'share it like this: the left one (belonging to him) [label] "starting point" and [right] (under my guitar) "the future."'

RP: How is your approach different to Erkan Oğur?

CE: So, the thing is, let's speak about guitar. There are millions of guitar players, and they all sound different, and there are styles like tango, choro, steel-string, fingerstyle, rock, blues, fusions, straighter jazz, and there are many, many styles. But with fretless guitar, which is [only] like forty years old, there is only one star. One guy who made it. So, it's very hard to find another way from the master. But, after I started to compose my own pieces on fretless guitar, nowadays in Turkey, they say there are two styles: one is Erkan Oğur's style and one is my style. I use more chordal structures and I use flamenco technique . . . I take all these Flamingo techniques [gestures right thumb], all the down strokes and arpeggios, and hitting the guitar, and combine them with my composition ideas and jazz harmony, and then I take some of the phrases or vibes of tanbur playing and Anatolia, and then I come up with a different music. Also, he is using cedar guitars and I use cypress guitars, because cypress has much more attack, and you can play really fast and powerful. Also, a very big difference between me and the master is that he has a *very* low action. Believe me, when you take his guitar, it takes like one hour for you to get a sound, right? You can't play it because there's only buzz on that guitar. And my action is almost twice as [high as] his. Because, then I can make the flamenco techniques better. . . . When I played Erkan Oğur's guitar, I was like, 'Oh my God, I don't want to break the guitar, it is so gentle'. Only he can [make a] sound perfectly on that guitar. . . . So, our styles are now totally different. And the younger generation is now starting to practise like me, with more chords, funky grooves, and whatever. I think it's much more appropriate for this generation, that power. . . . So, nowadays there are two styles, my master's style and the one that I'm producing now, still producing; so, one and a half I guess [laughs].

RP: Tell me a little about your online fretless guitar video-lessons.

CE: Well, I used to have a website called fretlessguitarlessons.com . . . but, recently I thought, okay, nobody's going to visit my website, so let's make something on Instagram, which is much more popular and easy to spread out. And then I started to make some new lessons there . . . I thought, if you're interested in fretless guitar, learn from good direction, you know? It's my purpose. We are working on this instrument for around twenty years, I've made compositions, this is my life. It's my career, you know, and then I can teach something, and it's good.

RP: You're alone on a desert island, and you're allowed just one of your guitars, which do you take?

CE: [without hesitation] Classical fretless [smiles]. Easy!

Editors' Choice – Recommended Listening:

Ara Nağma (2021), Cenk Erdoğan, UND Records
Fermata (2018), Cenk Erdoğan, Lin Records
Kavis (Arc) (2011), Cenk Erdoğan, Baykus Kitap
Website: www.cenkerdogan.net
Instagram: prdszgitarist | fretlessguitarlessons

5

Extended range instruments
Towards a new organology of the guitar

Tom Williams

Introduction

Exploring ideas relating to scale length, number of strings, range, tuning systems, modes of tactility, affordance and utility, this chapter will discuss the physical boundaries of the guitar, as it stood and now stands at the turn of the 21st century. The historical development of the guitar's extended range will be considered in terms of Kevin Dawe's concept of the 'new guitarscape' (2010). The totemic imagery surrounding the guitar has changed significantly in recent years; the standard-tuned six-string instrument is no longer prime, and instead a multitude of interesting and eclectic instruments occupy distinct spaces of their own.

The choice was made to avoid any oversimplified binary distinctions that may exclude guitarists/guitars from this study (classical vs contemporary, acoustic vs electric, jazz vs rock and so forth). Instead, a range of eclectic examples will be given to motivate the enquiry behind extended range guitars – what they are, what they afford the player, how they have come to be, how they inform their associated musical idiolects and how they are developing among other points of inquiry. Spanning artists as diverse as Yamandu Costa, Charlie Hunter and Tosin Abasi, the following examples are representative of extended range guitar use in the 21st century.

Crucial to the discussion here is the field of organology. Research by Eliot Bates (2012), Jonathan De Souza (2017), Otso Lähdeoja et al. (2010) and Margaret J. Kartomi (1990) helps us to consider the guitar as an ever-changing instrument that should be considered in light of various 'scapes' (Dawe 2010) that surround it. Dawe reminds us, however, that 'organologists have mainly focused upon the investigation of the material and acoustic properties of musical instruments, the description of probable methods of construction, tuning systems, timbre, the techniques required to produce sounds from them, and an analysis of their repertoire' (2010: 51). It is important to consider the social and community aspects of the extended range guitar community. More generally, the organological discussion that surrounds this topic is best tempered with an understanding of the 'social life of the musical instruments' (Bates 2012) themselves, constituting the design, music, artistry, personalities, localities and communities that surround them. As Dawe encourages us, we must reconsider guitars not merely as familiar instruments of wood and metal but also as 'sites of meaning construction' (2010: 181) whose effects permeate social, cultural, political and economic domains.

This chapter will offer some new definitions of what the 'extended' guitar might be and how we might realign our perception of the guitar considering the many factional communities of the 21st century guitar landscape. In addition to highlighting key guitarists, artistic departures from six-string norms and providing some academic scaffolding to important events in the development of the extended guitar (such as the metal communities' seeming infatuation with adding additional strings to the point of novel effect), practicalities such as utility, affordance and creativity will be discussed. More specifically this will aim to challenge the idea of the six-string totem and alight on a new understanding of the developing world of extended range guitars and their place within the wider organology of the 21st-century guitar.

Fundamental to this study is a community perspective; an extended section highlighting existent and newly curated interview material leads to the apex of the chapter before a final summary. Crucially, this chapter invites the reader to reconsider the boundaries, definition and imagery typically associated with the guitar.

New organological frameworks

While it might seem counterintuitive to objectify the properties of an instrument as socially amorphous as the guitar, it is for this very reason we must try. Furthermore, it is the author's belief that at this point in the historical development of the guitar, never has such a broad term – guitar – been applied to so many different and nuanced iterations.

Guitar cultures are already deeply embedded with organological thinking at a user level. Guitarists are notorious for arguing the fine points of the instrument and craft. Debates revolve around every aspect of the instrument from larger considerations such as building materials and 'tone woods', years of vintage, neck shape, scale length, to minute details such as material properties of the strings, picks and even the audible difference between electrical conductor materials. Organological discussions can, as Kartomi explains, be pleasurable and create a sense of affinity or belonging within the community (1990: 4). Equally, factions may arise within communities, which can lead to dialogue that affects the direction of change for the development of the instrument. There is often a long lag between community discourse, and what we see formally written about cutting-edge developments in guitar cultures.

Of course, the guitar was focal throughout social-cultural change in the 20th century. It is a 'device used to explore, challenge, and compose the systems of order and disorder, sameness and difference that have constituted popular music in this century' (Waksman 1999: 294). The development of the guitar in the 21st century through emerging technologies, cross-cultural developments and globalization is effecting its design – physically, sonically and culturally – expanding the classificatory requirements for the instrument.

As Kartomi (1990: 273) states: '[c]lassification of instruments and ensembles, and their operative taxonomical concepts of instruments, are in a constant state of flux.' Prevailing organology classification systems tend to be centred on the properties of the sound-producing materials of the instruments. The Hornbostel–Sachs classification system (see Kartomi 1990) is the most widely used and discussed. It distinguishes musical instruments at its highest level into idiophones, membranophones, chordophones, aerophones and electrophones. It is particularly useful when identifying the physical commonalities of instruments from across the globe, although it lacks the ability to delineate between the specificity of inner species of instruments. Furthermore, no information about the sociocultural aspects of the instruments can be found within such a classification. Situated in opposition to traditional organology, some authors (see DeVale 1990; Kartomi 1990; Dawe 2010; Bates 2012) provide cogent arguments for classification systems to take account of not only the physical properties of the instrument but also the sound and the social function of the instrument in order to 'help explain society and culture' (DeVale 1990: 22). Many of the instruments discussed in this chapter have come into being as a result of social stimulus and are steeped in and driven by the stories, lore and communities surrounding them.

Kartomi states that 'a classification with a limited aim tends to come to an end when it has fulfilled the primary purpose for which it was intended' (1990: 4). This raises several questions in relation to this study, all of which will be explored throughout the chapter – What is the aim of classification here? What is the most appropriate way to explore the organology of the extended range guitar? What, even, is a guitar?

Care must be taken when considering the tacit social cultures that surround the definitions herein, alongside the developing canon of written discourse surrounding the guitar. We should certainly not neglect the former and be mindful of the goal of the latter. As Kartomi (1990: 13) states: 'artificial, or observer-imposed, schemes, on the other hand, are frequently based on the goals of an individual investigator.'

A combination of various methodologies will be used in this chapter to provoke many aspects of organizational understanding and codification of the guitar. Empirically, classification and discussion will move upwards from the individual examples presented (as is common in modern taxonomy). A blend of what Ernst Mayr discusses as 'microtaxonomy' or 'the methods and principles by which kinds of organisms (objects) are recognized and delimited', and 'macrotaxonomy', 'the methods and principles by which kinds of organisms (objects) are . . . arranged in the form of classifications' will be used to create a better framework to understand the extended range guitar in the 21st century (1982: 1327). Microtaxonomy focuses on the individual object initially, covering as many aspects as possible. Similar objects may then be grouped together into taxa of increasing generality. As the classification moves to higher levels of generality, macrotaxonomy allows us to complete the arrangement of the taxa to give a broader understanding of the groupings and their relationships. This will be interwoven with artistic account and conjecture to provide the reader with a better understanding of the communities these instruments exist within.

An understanding of the extended range guitar will therefore be built on the following criteria:

1. General separation by means of extensions (i.e. number of strings, tuning systems, physical augmentations, extension by device);
2. Hard properties:
    a. Physical attributes,
    b. Utility and affordance,
    c. Sonic characteristics.

3. Historical development of the instrument(s) and its relationship to the wider guitar community;
4. Folk taxonomies, comprising:
   a. The discussion of the instrument(s) within community,
   b. A discussion of the vernacular of community,
   c. Presence within community,
   d. Typical idiomatic uses,
   e. Artistic understanding.

In this chapter, the guitar will be viewed as an open-ended concept, whose definitions differ across a wide spectrum of contexts, as Kartomi suggests (1990: 272). Readers should also consider the rate of variance of instrument development, which is exponentially increasing. In addition, it must be stated that work herein is a composite of taxonomical organology, social survey and author perspective.

Physical range boundaries

We must first consider how we might frame the guitar in the 21st century. Systems of classification are useful in this aspect to take both a broad and nuanced look. The main concern here, of course, is guitars whose range has been extended physically, through new tuning systems, or by other means of augmentation. A complete history of the development of the extended range guitar lies outside the scope of this chapter; the focus here is on activity surrounding the extended range of guitar both in the 21st century and leading up to it.

Backgrounds

In comparison to the early Spanish origins of the guitar or 'guitarra', there is both a historical and musical chasm between the six-string instrument and its many iterations now. Accounts suggest that the first six-string guitar was produced in 1779 by Gaetano Vinaccia in Naples (see Turnbull 1974), though accounts vary, suggesting a more gradual process (Wade 2018: 96). The design development of the guitar continued exponentially for at least half a century, before normalization and homogenization created a more 'stable' instrument.

Players have little difficulty in identifying the mixed heritage of the guitar and the many instruments which inform the one we now know, although there is still significant contention concerning the genus of the six-string guitar. This is especially important to note, given the growing interest in developing the guitar to evoke older instruments such as the oud, cithara, lute and harp, for example.

Standard tuning (E A D G B E, for strings 6 to 1, respectively) is likely to have emerged as a result of its physical convenience in relation to Western harmonic practices and was certainly solidified by the body of repertoire that grew through the 19th century, and indeed luthier Antonio de Torres's paradigm-changing instrument which became the template for what we now call the 'classical' guitar (Wade 2018). Considering the development of contemporary popular guitar music, it is not surprising that standard tuning remained common, given the prevalence of classical guitar at the turn of the 20th century. Though, of course, aural traditions such as early blues and folk often rely on open tunings which are more idiomatically organized and easy to navigate musically, without any formal training. Rather than viewing these guitars as different instruments, their players as explorers of non-standard tunings, we must recognize that that was their 'standard' and the idea of playing in Western classical standard was as alienating as full fourths tuning may be for those finding it for the first time now.

None of this information will likely be new to the reader; however, the idea here is that open tunings and the systems of fingering afforded by them should not be thought of as departures but instead as 'arrivals' in terms of idiomatic realignment of the instrument. Older perceptions have remained because of the ubiquity of standard tuning and Western harmonic practices, which has come to dominate much of the contemporary popular guitar repertoire too. By contrast, guitar cultures in the 21st century now readily use non-standard tuning systems as the foundation for entire idioms. These rich and curious tunings, which have profound effects on the range afforded to their players, will be explored further in this chapter.

Extended range instruments are perhaps less revolutionary to classical guitarists. There is a rich history of development in the classical guitar world, ranging from instruments designed to enhance the sonority of the instrument such as Narciso Yepes's ten-string guitar (1963), which emphasizes sympathetic resonance through the use of its additional strings to instruments; to instruments which cater to specific repertoire such as Paul Galbraith's 'Brahms Guitar' (1994); and instruments that blur the definition of other stringed instruments such as Michael Thames's thirteen-string, which is designed to function as a baroque lute for guitarists.

There is a misconception, certainly among contemporary electric guitar players, that physically extended range guitars (such as the seven-string) are relatively new. This is not the case. Take, for example, the Russian 'gypsy' guitar, a seven-string guitar developed in the late 18th century. While physically and materially different from the seven-string electric guitars we see as foundational to many modern progressive metal styles, both instrument species share a number of identifying traits. For instance, open tuning systems like the Russian Guitar's Open G major (D G B D G B E: 7–1) allows it to fall into a similar category as Devin Townsend's industrious Open C tuning (G C G C G C E: 7–1). Arguably, there is perhaps more of a difference between the Russian Guitar and the Brazilian seven-string (tuned to standard with a low A, and popularized more recently by virtuosos like Yamandu Costa), than there is between the former and certain localities of contemporary metal guitar culture.

Jazz guitarists too have a rich history of extended range experimentation. Guitarist George Van Eps inspired a generation of seven-string jazz players, using his lower seventh string to extend his harmonic accessibility. Lenny Breau extended his instrument in the other direction, creating a high A above his E, allowing him to manipulate higher register voicings in much lower positions, maintaining a proximity to the lowest register of the standard six-string. And of course, extended range by means of fourths/fifths tuning systems, while still limited in use, matured roots in the 20th century.

Manipulation of the range of the guitar can happen in several ways. Number of strings, fretboard extensions, differential tuning systems, physical augmentation of the instrument, multi-neck composites and playing technique allow the player to change the range and navigational systems for the instrument. Even the smallest change can have the most profound change. For instance, British jazz guitarist Ant Law's fourths tuning system removes much of the typical physical motor schema that drives guitar-based popular music of the last century. The causal effect of extending the range of the instrument by any of the means listed must be considered when mapping the landscape of the extended guitar.

The landscape of the 21st-century extended guitar

In modern times, the exporting of culture is exponentially wider and far more rapid due to the internet, technologies, public understanding and appreciation, among other aspects, which all contribute to far more amorphous cultural landscapes, of which there are far more in number, constantly interacting with and affecting one another. In this sense, our modern-day musical 'scapes' may be considered generally less stable and more easily displaced or evolved.

Of course, academia is not the only way knowledge and dispersion of idioms have spread and developed. The YouTube revolution has given voice to many independent and amateur guitarists who have crafted careers and a large body of work online. Through companies such as LickLibrary, Jam Track Central, Truefire and others, guitarists have been exposed to music, pedagogical materials without the need to engage in a local music scenes or communities. The online communities are different. Saturated with guitarists, in pursuit of bettering themselves through the many online competitions, the communities are simultaneously isolated (in the sense of being self-contained, and operationally outside of the 'physical' music industry) and open (to anyone, irrespective of background).

There are many idiomatic guitar communities that use extended range. While it is perhaps counterintuitive to apply arbitrary boundaries here, some method of dissection is needed. It is problematic to use a single categorization system in this instance; therefore, a multimodal classification system has been used, at least initially, to best demarcate the *communities* built on extended range guitar. These will be split as follows:

1. Extended acoustic guitar
2. Extended jazz guitar
3. Extended rock/metal guitar
4. Extended abstract guitar

Extended acoustic guitar

While this category may seem overly broad and all-encompassing, it seeks to reflect the continual dissolution of smaller categories (such as classical guitar, folk guitar, percussive guitar) on the basis that there is clear evidence that these communities regularly mix with one another. In doing so, repertoire, technique, orchestration and tuning become part of a wider community vernacular. Developments in online guitar communities have, in part, helped to create a more open and less stylistically-defined community. Such a community focuses not on preserving artefacts of idiom but instead on developing innovation and broadening their field through fantastical developments in technique, orchestration and, as we will discuss, exploitation of range – both physically and artificially.

Defining the 21st-century extended acoustic guitar community is perhaps best done by looking at some of the key exponents. We might do this, initially, by using arbitrary categorization to create an initial separation, though the problems with such a categorization will be discussed herein too. Some of these might include folk guitar, classical guitar, South American jazz/classical crossover, instrumental revival and reinvention, for example. Within our larger category, extended acoustic guitar, we might see artists as diverse as Yamandu Costa, Pat Metheny, John McLaughlin, Andy Mckee, Michael Hedges and Antoine Dufour.

As we have already discussed, the acoustic guitar has a rich history of extended range properties that predate the popularization of extended range instruments in the electric guitar community. The classical guitar community is currently more open than ever to deviations from the dominance of the Torres guitar. Many classical guitarists engage with a range of instruments, which are extended by adding strings and frets, augmenting necks and incorporating drone strings (not to mention microtonal guitar practices, which extend the inner range opportunities afforded to the player).[1] As mentioned, some of these instruments came into existence to allow the guitar player a more effective and 'authentic' way of performing specific repertoire without reduction or transposition – the eight-string Brahms Guitar, the eleven-string alto guitar (used to play the music of Bach) and the thirteen-string Dresden (for emulating lute), for example. The demarcation of organological categories of guitar becomes murky when viewed through the lens of classical guitar, given the close proximity to other stringed instruments which may be viewed as part of the guitar family.

Not all extended instruments are built for physical manipulation, however. The Yepes ten-string, developed to improve the resonance and 'balance' of the guitar (Kozinn 1980) through sympathetic vibration of the four low strings, extends (and balances) the range of the guitar. Yepes discussed the deliberate nature of the design of his instrument often (Yepes 1989), stating that the extra strings, in addition to providing sympathetic resonance, are used appropriately in accordance with the demands of the music (Yepes 1973). Yepes's perspective aligns with that of this chapter, as he states: '[t]he guitar has been extended in its sonorous capacity and when I want sound without resonance, I only need to

---

[1] See also Schneider (Chapter 1 of this volume).

cover the four strings with the hand. Just as a pianist can lift a foot off the pedal because it has that pedal' (Rubio 1990).

Within what we might call the percussive guitar community, appropriate ranges and tuning systems are often applied song to song to allow a player to more easily align their instruments to the demands of the harmonic structures in each piece. There is now a firmly solidified group of players who embrace extended range approach not as curious or esoteric, but as necessity for their idiom – for example Andy Mckee, Antoine Dufour, Eric Roche, Mike Dawes, Erik Mongrain and Kaki King to name but a few; for these players, the concept of a 'standardized' tuning system becomes moot.[2] As mentioned in Dawe (2010), the contemporary percussive guitar community takes the ranged D A D G A D (6–1) open tuning (popularized by early 'traditional' folk guitarists such as Davy Graham) as a starting point and deviates from there. Dawe suggests that the nuanced exploitation of open tuning systems (and the idiosyncratic ranges they create) form part of the unique identity of a guitar player.

Multi-necked and non-parallel instruments are now common in the acoustic guitar community. These 'augmented' instruments have various functionalities and may afford the player more creative options than a single-neck instrument can. The harp guitar, for example, while developed and played by many virtuosos in the 19th century (Carulli, Coste, and Giuliani to name but a few), has seen a resurgence and reapplication in contemporary acoustic guitar communities. Andy Mckee, Don Ross, Pat Metheny and Antoine Dufour are among many who use and play a harp guitar. Harp guitar expert Gregg Miner created an organological framework for the harp guitar, which at its core defines it as a guitar-based instrument which must have at least one unfretted unstopped string off the fretboard.[3]

John McLaughlin famously used an augmented harp-like guitar with Shakti. The guitar, a Gibson J-2000, was fitted with a set of seven 'drone' strings, which run obliquely underneath the standard six, allowing the player to either play the strings or let them sympathetically resonate (Wheeler 1978). McLaughlin's Shakti guitar is perhaps not another world apart from the Yepes guitar in that both are designed with idiom and resonance in mind.

---

[2] See also McGrath (Chapter 10 of this volume).
[3] See Miner, G. (2021) Harpguitars.net. Available online: www.harpguitars.net (accessed 1 October 2021).

Extended jazz guitar

The role of the guitar in jazz has been developmental for as long as it has been present. While the dynamic and timbral affordance of the banjo dominated early jazz ensembles, the versatility of the amplified guitar ultimately led to widespread adoption. Curiously, early jazz guitar players were more open to experimentation and development, perhaps because the instrument/idiom was in its infancy and less well-defined.

Inspired by pivotal guitarist Eddie Lang, a guitar player by the name of George Van Eps (GVE) switched, as many players did, from banjo to guitar. GVE transitioned to the seven-string guitar in the 1930s, using a custom-made seven-string. Different from what we see as standard seven-string tuning now, Van Eps used, and popularized, a low A string. His 1968 signature Gretch model was the first production line signature seven-string guitar and became extremely popular and influential within the guitar community.

Low A tuning is particularly useful as it allows the player to simply mirror their fifth A string. This allowed players to quickly adapt to the instrument and delegate bass notes to a frequency range that crosses into the range of a double bass, freeing up the fifth string to either strengthen the octave or extend the harmony in lower frequencies, resulting in a much richer harmonic frequency spectrum. In ensembles that feature seven-string *and* double bass, antiphonal interplay appears frequently as the guitarist may emulate the role/range of the bass to create dialogue during improvisations (see Bucky Pizarelli in Arbogast and Del Mastro 2011).

GVE inspired a range of guitarists, including Bucky Pizzarelli, Ron Eschete and Howard Alden, to transition to the seven-string guitar. Not all seven-string guitars are the same of course. As we saw earlier, Lenny Breau used a high A string on his seven-string to add a richer palette of upper extensions fixed in relation to the familiar six-string fretboard schema. Interestingly, at the time of conception, no commercially available string could withstand the tension to reach the desired tuning for Breau's instrument. Until the LaBella company developed a string capable of this, Breau substituted a monofilament fishing line of approximate gauge.

Alden was instrumental in reintroducing the seven-string to straight-ahead jazz. Contrary to what might be perceived as introducing further complexity to the instrument, extending the range with additional strings can, as Alden states, provide 'a more complete picture of harmony. The way it's structured you're able to hear and see more harmonic possibilities, which makes everything clearer and easier to see' (qtd. in Gilbert 2015). Alden's perspective here is intriguing and must also be tempered with the idea that those likely to wish to explore extended range are perhaps more critically aware of the importance of having a robust and malleable understanding of fretboard navigation and orchestration. Alden's explorations into the 'rarified harmonies of Bill Evans' (ibid.) suggests extended range guitars can be more practical in exploring complex piano music. The curiosity of perception in Alden's understanding is echoed in his engagement with various styles of music. While we may situate him here under the larger grouping of jazz, Alden's work has led him to explore Brazilian choro styles too, another style synonymous with the seven-string.

Extended range jazz guitar in the 21st century continues to be developed. Most widely known, of course, is Charlie Hunter. A common thread among the players discussed herein is the exploratory nature that might lead one to engage with extended range instruments. Hunter has had a range of different instruments and configurations and has re-limited his range to a seven-string, following earlier experiments with an eight-string. Hunter discusses various perceptive shifts that influenced his change here – 'When I was playing eight-string on all those Blue Note records, I was really trying to be a bass and a guitar and cover all that ground, but there are some inherent issues with that' (Shadrick 2012). Hunter goes on to discuss these issues in relation to scale length, affordance and tactility. Hunter's tuning (and the range it affords him) is certainly unorthodox when compared to guitarists such as GVE. Now tuned G C F, C F B♭ D (7–1), he argues that this is the most effective for his scale length and analogizes it to being like having the lower three strings of a bass (tuned in strict fourths) and the middle four of a standard-tuned six-string guitar. Hunter sits on the far end of a prescriptive–exploratory continuum in relation to his perception and manipulation of range. In many ways, Hunter has eschewed the totemic 'guitar' entirely, and in interviews simply refers to his 'instrument' (see Chapter 6 of this volume for an in-depth interview with Charlie Hunter).

Another pioneering jazz player at the forefront of many interesting physical and musical innovations is British guitarist Ant Law. Widely known for his work with a customized Ibanez eight-string in his trio HLK, Law distinguishes and operates in specific cognitive areas of his guitar to separate the different 'voices' – low, middle, high – and engage different mind-sets. Concerning the lower two strings, Law thinks of these as separate yet connected areas of the extended range instrument, allowing him to occupy the space a bass player normally would in the context of his trio. While the lines demarcating the range areas of the instrument are separated, they can also blur. Interestingly, as Law explains, many idiomatic consonant structures common to the standard six-string become impractical at lower registers. Close tertial voicings for instance become muddy and lack clarity. This raises interesting questions about how we may exploit the utility of various range areas, re-organizing the way we are able to interact with overriding harmonies and tonal centres.

Curiously, extended range guitars fell into obscurity in the second half of the 20th century; and further to this, Gretch stopped production of its GVE signature model. Hunter and Law perhaps occupy an inter-idiomatic space here with their unique tunings and approaches, garnering interest from guitar players from unexpected backgrounds. As Law discusses, his fan base is eclectic drawing interest from not only jazz guitarists but those with affinities for rock and metal too. In a similar fashion, many online guitar communities share an appreciation for the instruments and their players regardless of idiomatic backgrounds.

Many central aspects of jazz practice, such as the harmonic complexity, now permeate a range of other styles without obstruction. In doing so, dialogues begin to emerge between these styles musically and also physically.

Extended range rock and metal guitar – A race to the bottom

Perhaps one of the largest areas of convergence with extended range practices in recent years is within the rock and metal communities. While altogether too vast to survey within the confines of this overview piece, many key exponents must be mentioned. Guitar virtuoso Steve Vai is often credited with laying down the first seven-string guitar parts within the rock idiom, on Whitesnake's *Slip of the Tongue* (1989). Vai's collaboration with Ibanez led to the introduction and popularity of seven-string instruments in the rock and metal community. Vai was unaware of the impact his evolved 'Jem' guitar had: '[l]ittle did I know this subculture that it was going to create, you know? [Chuckles] That was another one of those just simply innocent things where I didn't set out to . . . I wasn't sitting, going, "This is gonna change the world"' (qtd. in Laing, 2019). Despite this, Vai suggests that following the release of the album the guitar had the potential to inspire a new generation of guitarists.

Much like the life-cycle of the seven-string in jazz history, following Vai's initial experimentation, sales of the Ibanez Universe model were limited initially, and often considered obscure or novelty. Vai recalls that he convinced Ibanez to keep selling the instrument and give it time to gestate in the hands of young emerging musicians. He recollects listening to the radio and being stunned with the sound of an extended range instrument and refers to this, and the band in question, Korn, as the 'rebirth of the seven-string' (Kennelty 2020).

In the 1990s and early 2000s the popularity of the seven-string guitar grew, with many emblematic nu-metal artists exploiting the lower range to increase the 'heaviness' of their music. Korn set a precedent for many metal bands in the 1990s and created a clear sonic identity in doing so, with many other bands from similar and divergent streams of metal following suit: Deftones and Fear Factory, to name but two. An interesting distinction should be made here, in that these bands detune their instruments to create more idiosyncratic intervallic ranges. Both Korn and the Deftones drop the tuning further and start to merge into the range typically occupied by a bass guitar.

Devin Townsend, and others like him, take an even more angular approach by taking a six-string guitar and tuning it significantly lower (in his case, C G C G C E: 6–1), allowing them to create a rich two-octave fifth chord, simply by forming a barre. The tactility and ease of such motor schema makes such an extended tuning popular, as it enables those without knowledge of harmony or fretting hand conventions to navigate the instrument quickly.

Others opted for a more balanced approach, with many bands leading from Vai's examples and keeping the seven-string instrument in standard tuning with the addition of the low B. Incidentally, at the time of Korn's self-titled debut (1994), which Vai refers to, Dream Theater released *Awake* (1994) which features multiple tracks that exploit the low range of the seven-string. In truth, however, it is likely that the adoption of extended range instruments in rock and metal is perhaps, historically, not as linear as is described.

As metal cultures developed, with 'heaviness' becoming a more and more important facet of 'authenticity', this fundamentally became a 'race to the bottom' (at least in terms of register). Anyone remotely interested in the development of rock/metal idioms in the 21st century will be familiar with the musically analogous and onomatopoeically named 'djent'. While it is hard to pinpoint the catalyst for this development, many place the band Meshuggah at the nucleus.

'Djent', progressive metal and other recent deviations in metal culture have been heavily influenced and affected by extended range instruments.[4] Much like the way that Vai popularized the seven-string, the effect Meshuggah and

---

[4] An onomatopoetic term ascribed to music which has heavily palm-muted lower register riffs, which often focus on complex and irregular rhythmic placements.

their contemporaries have had on guitar cultures has led to many companies marketing entry-level eight-string instruments (e.g. the Ibanez RG2228).

Tosin Abasi of Animals as Leaders further blurs the lines between the guitar and bass and is in this sense an outlier in the world of eight-string metal guitarists. Abasi, for instance, tunes his eight-string so that the lowest string is the same pitch as the lowest of a standard-tuned four-string bass (E). Technically, Abasi's approach occupies a similar space to Charlie Hunter's, with Abasi incorporating common bass techniques (slap/pop) among many other contemporary techniques that both exploit and redefine the instrument's capabilities.

The metal communities' seeming 'obsession' with lower, heavier sound has irrevocably changed the boundaries of guitar and displaced the six-string as the most common instrument, at least in relation to this idiom.

Extended abstract guitar

Some instruments have carved out such a distinctive space that they have become almost completely separated from the indigeneity of the guitar. The following examples provide a spectrum of the different types of extreme extension, in one way or another.

One of the simplest ways of extending the range of a guitar is to extend the number of frets. While for many twenty-four is too many, Ibanez's RG 550XH sports thirty frets, and Washburn's EC36 has thirty-six. Perhaps most intriguing, though, is Uli Jon Roth's Sky Guitar range, of which the Infinity Sky model has seven strings and thirty-nine frets.[5] Roth's experimentation allowed him to extend an octave further than is conventional. He is one of the very few guitarists to use an extended fingerboard which allows him to take advantage of the higher octave register. At the extreme end of range extension lies Bill Delap and the guitars he built for Allan Holdsworth. Of these instruments, Holdsworth had a custom-made acoustic five-string acoustic, tuned in fifths (C G D A E: 5–1). Interestingly Holdsworth discussed how he would have preferred to have tuned strictly fourths (Resnicoff 1989) (as many players now do – Law, Tom Quayle, Stanley Jordan). More renowned, however, were the baritone guitars created for

---

[5] The Infinity Sky fingerboard is deep-scalloped from fret six onwards and, past fret 33 (as the space in-between frets becomes unusably small) the last 'six-fret'-section is fretted only as three whole-tone steps. For more information about this guitar, visit www.sky-guitars.com

Holdsworth – a thirty-four-inch scale length (tuned to C), a thirty-six-inch scale length (tuned to B♭) and a thirty-eight-inch scale length (tuned to A).[6] The largest of the three would be unwieldly to most, as Holdsworth suggests himself when he discusses the difficulty in having a 'first fret you can fit your whole hand in' (ibid). Expanding the pitch options available *within* the octave is also pertinent here; microtonal and fretless guitars in particular have become increasingly popular within the contemporary guitar world of late (see Chapters 1 to 4 of this volume).

Less frequently mentioned, though, are those which have created an entirely unique 'inner' extension. Vai's custom Steve Ripley 16-EDO guitar, which divides the octave equally across sixteen frets, is one such instrument. He refers to each of the divisions as 'fractals' (Di Perna 2011) and likens the idea of two of these divisions to that of a whole-step, calling them 'nova'. Vai's description and perception of this instrument is somewhat eccentric, and despite little discussion and use by Vai, it has become fable in the guitar community (though this may not have been considered especially ground-breaking by those already familiar with alternative equal divisions of the octave, such as 8-EDO, 24-EDO and so on). This instrument only features on one track in Vai's catalogue ('Deep Down Into the Pain'),[7] in which he creates a ten-note scale, drawn from the sixteen divisions, which he refers to as the 'Xavian scale', also referring to its qualities of 'divine dissonance' (ibid). Vai's understanding and perception align with eastern organology paradigms, with spirituality tied to the centre of meaning for the instrument.

Guitar cultures are self-aware and parodistic at times also. Following the metal guitar community's obsession with lower registers, Jared Dines (a well-known YouTuber) had a custom eighteen-string multi-scale guitar built for him by Ormsby guitars, aptly named 'Djent 2018'. The virtually unplayable instrument mocks the sometimes overly serious nature of the guitar community and at the same time became an excellent marketing gimmick for Ormsby. This chapter is altogether too small to cover the entire topography of the 21st-century guitarscape; however, it would be remiss to not at least mention a few more examples of instruments that radically challenge the guitar's range boundaries

---

[6] A baritone guitar, is a longer-scale instrument (typically up to 30.5 inches) with stronger bracing, which allows much lower tuning. The electric baritone guitar was first introduced by Danelectro in the 1950s and has been used across the history of contemporary popular music (e.g. the Beach Boys' 'Caroline No' (1966), Glen Campbell's 'Wichita Lineman' (1968)). More recently the baritone guitar has seen a surge in use in a range of areas – guitar sensation Mark Lettieri of Snarky Puppy has released two albums, *Deep: The Baritone Sessions, Vol 1 & 2* (2019/2021) on which he uses the baritone guitar as focal point throughout.

[7] See: *Sex and Religion* (1993), Vai, Relativity (Sony/Columbia).

– whether as a means to fulfil specific artistic or aesthetic needs, or for self-parody or 'gimmickry' – such as Michael Manring's 'Hyperbass', Manson Kaos Pad Augmented guitars, Michael Angelo Batio's X-shaped 'Quad Guitar', Gary Hutchins's sextuple-neck 'The Beast' guitar and Steve Vai's triple-necked Ibanez 'Hydra' guitar.[8]

The following section, based on an interview with guitarist Ant Law, provides a user perspective on many aspects of extended range guitar use.

Artist perspective – Ant Law

British jazz guitarist Ant Law was kind enough to discuss his relationship with extended instruments and approaches for this chapter.[9] Law's experimentation with application began subtly when he chose to tune his guitar exclusively in fourths. Unlike other players, Law tunes from the high E down, giving a relationship of (high to low; 1–6) E B G♭ D♭ A♭ E♭. While this may look like a negligible shift from standard tuning, it completely reorients the typical motor schema one must use to navigate the fretboard. Law acknowledges the usefulness of this tuning when considering typical jazz repertoire, aligning his open strings more effectively to the standard B♭/E♭ emphasis of the jazz canon, which is typically oriented towards brass instruments therein.

TW: How does your tuning affect your ability to interact with common repertoire?

AL: For me, those open strings, which I could drone, made far more sense in terms of the repertoire I was performing, which is organized around horns.

Considering organological approaches here, Law refers to Vai's 'Alien Love Secrets' website feature as pivotal. Vai mentions a 'Buddhist' approach which he linked to the idea of individuality and realization of self. Unlike many others, Law's relationship with the guitar allows him to see it as a malleable instrument,

---

[8] At the time of writing, Ibanez built a new guitar for Vai, aptly named the 'Hydra'. This instrument features three necks: a seven-string, a twelve-string (half fretted and half fretless) and a four-string (¾ scale length headless bass); it also includes an additional set of thirteen sympathetic resonance harp strings. Furthermore, it has configurable options for splitting pickups, controlling MIDI, sustainer and phase split. If anything, the development of extended range instruments is showing no signs of slowing down.

[9] Ant Law, interview by Tom Williams. Conducted on 14 December 2020.

which should be organized around the individual instead of the individual organizing around the instrument.

TW: How did your perception of the instrument change in light of the affordance of your tuning system?

AL: I'm not sure if this is relevant, but one thing that Vai mentions on his website, was this sort of Buddhist thing, which informed me a lot. I guess the message was: you are an individual and you should celebrate this. So, when I changed to fourths, I was thinking, why don't I do something individualistic that might make me do things in my own way instead of being led?

Law also states that fourth-based tuning is 'definitely not for someone who wants to perform music that's already been written, but for someone who wants to understand, comprehend, and manipulate'. Fourth-based tuning on the instrument allows for a more symmetrically driven approach which allows finger 'routes' and 'shapes' to be applied consistently across the fretboard, without being changed by the G–B string (major third) relationship as is typical in standard tuning. Pedagogically, he does not advocate any one tuning over another, despite extolling the efficacy of fourths-based tuning, and instead suggests that idiom is an important driver for range and tuning alignment.

Law goes on to suggest some innovative approaches which are generally not discussed as part of 'standard practice' in the guitar world, including tuning in fifths, thirds, and emulating other instrument ranges to exploit the instrument in different ways, advocating that everyone find their own tuning systems.

TW: The more I consider it, wouldn't it be excellent if pedagogy didn't revolve around tuning systems at all? While teaching a class of twenty guitarists, each with a unique tuning system, might be difficult, it would yield some very creative and innovative approaches. What do you think about this?

AL: I would advocate that everyone finds their own tuning. If you really love piano style voicings, why not tune in major or minor thirds? If you wanted to do wider interval voicings, not tune in fifths? Music, as we hear it, doesn't care what tuning we used, so try to exploit tuning systems that allow you to access the sounds you want.

Law references other experiments with diminishing inner register, splitting the instrument into an 8-EDO octatonic iteration which facilitated microtonal experimentation and Messiaen-inspired explorations.

AL: I even went down a little false alleyway where I thought, I wonder what it is about this symmetrical octatonic stuff?. Is it because I can hear there's a symmetry? I got a guitar and tried this, splitting first into minor thirds then half again. I tried to play some Messiaen and other piano music. . . . It sounded awful and I hated it! But I guess I've always been interested in exploring new ideas.

Law takes an experimental approach more generally, as many of the other artists referenced here do. Law's approach here speaks of not only the instrument design, function and malleability of the guitar but also the curiosity in those who play the instrument as often being a driver for the development of the instrument and its idioms.

Law is also well known for his use of an eight-string Ibanez electric guitar, which he has modified to gain further access to the higher registers. There is a similarity in design between his eight-string and Uli Jon Roth's Sky Guitar, at least in terms of the cutaway. Its use is inspired by utilitarian purposes, especially within a trio setting, allowing Law to 'produce complementary frequencies' considering how a piano player might split their approach between left and right hand. Law's perception of his instrument can shift in the lower registers, where he may adopt more of a bass player approach. Through experimentation he has also delineated clearly what works and what does not, citing normal tertiary intervallic relationships in the standard-six guitar's range as something to avoid.

TW: Do you find that you imitate things you would do in the higher register but in the lower register?

AL: Yeah, but they don't work. Sometimes you have to actively avoid intervallic relationships in certain registers. I don't know why, but intervallic leaps sound wider to me lower down. Even thirds can sound really off in lower registers, for example.

He also suggests that this is simply an extreme extension of what many experience on a standard-six, when considering the different 'areas' or ranges one might occupy. One of the most striking things mentioned when considering the low register afforded by the eight-string is that 'rhythm carries more weight' in those registers. This has profound implications for our understanding of the organization of tonal materials and rhythmic purpose. Furthermore, Law discussed how intervals, which may appear dissonant or jagged in closer proximity octaves, can become more acceptable and take on new colours and purpose when moved into more distant octaves.

The perception of harmony can be more challenged as frequency range increases and with this comes, as Law states, 'more harmonic responsibility'. Considering community, Law notes a range of aspects. When asked if he would take his eight-string on a jazz standards gig, there was some hesitancy and suggestion that appropriate practice would dictate not to, on the one hand, while, on the other hand, he considers the pull of his own exploratory approach and balances this with idiomatic convention. He goes on to discuss this in terms of a 'friction that is within all of us', which seeks to authenticate, balance and, at the same time, innovate and challenge. The guitar's range and aesthetic in Law's work also has an effect on the perception of his music and idiom too. Law also mentions that it is common for 'metal-heads' to attend his concerts and ask questions about his guitar and his music. Just as the definitions of the guitar continue to blur, so too do the idioms in which the guitar is placed centrally.

Law still firmly considers himself a guitarist, although he references times when he might wish to evoke or emulate another instrument, at least in terms of sonority. Tellingly, Law finishes our interview by discussing his perception of the guitar more generally, stating that 'in reality, the parameters of where the guitar starts and ends are not clear', though he acknowledges that this is a reflection of his character and 'the way he perceives the world'. I suspect Law's perception here is one shared by many of the guitarists discussed within this chapter.

Picking boundaries: A new organology of the guitar

This chapter has provided a range of examples, perspectives, theories, accounts and frameworks for how we might understand the definitions of a guitar in relation to where it begins and ends, when considering range.

It must also be noted that there are factors that ground the guitar in its most familiar guise. Were it not for the Western canon and repertoire, the fact that tuition (for those that could afford it) would be given by someone trained in Western classical practice, and various social class shifts, we may have a completely different history of popular music, and by extension, contemporary popular guitar. If classical music stayed the preserve of the bourgeois, then the gap between that and 'folk' music would have been wide enough for there to be a distinction and two divergent instrument sets. Instead, social movement has meant that we adopted 19th-century guitar with its standard range and tuning. It was then exploited by players to suit their own needs in contemporary styles with the tuning system unquestioned. The gravity and pull of the 19th-century guitar cannot be understated.

There are many important factors to consider, including utility, affordance, creativity, idiomatic vernacular and, of course, the central theme of exploration in the case of the guitarist. Several important areas converge here in relation to our understanding of how one might 'extend' the guitar both in terms of range but also definition:

1. What are we extending from? – the assumption that the guitar is a six-string instrument with a standard tuning is dissolving. There is now more of an equality between instrument variations than ever, though within some idioms certain aesthetic and sonic dogmas are still perpetuated. It is essential that organology is aware of this, given the importance of communities in the understanding and framing of the instrument.
2. Extension by string and fret number – range can be extended by string and fret number in higher and/or lower registers. Equally, in the globalized guitarscape we see more approaches to inner frequency manipulation, at times expanding, and also reducing the divisions of the octave – for example, Tolgahan Çoğulu's 'Adjustable Microtonal Guitar' (Dawe and Eroğlu 2013).[10]
3. Extension by tuning – altered tuning is perhaps the most widely used technique for extension. It allows any player to readily extend or diminish their range, creating environments for novel intervallic design, through using familiar motor schema on the instrument. With small variations, such as 'drop D', a player usually still has full awareness of the range manipulation, and in some cases (tuning in fourths, for example), this can lead to a more consistent organization of the fretboard. As consistency between strings is removed in tuning systems, as happens in more eclectic tunings, players are introduced to novel relationships of range on a string-to-string basis, which can be at once liberating, though potentially constrictive if interacting with others in 'standard' practice settings.
4. Extension by augmentation – larger physical changes to the instrument are now integral to the wider taxonomy of extended range guitars. Double-, triple-, harp-neck augmentations are less of a spectacle than they once were. The guitar community is far less exclusive than it once

---

[10] See also Chapter 2 of this volume for an in-depth interview with Tolgahan Çoğulu.

was. As organalogical boundaries between stringed instruments dissolve, many instruments become more akin to distant cousins than entirely alien. Take for instance the recent resurgence of the theorbo. In the world of extended range guitars, what is the theorbo, if not a site of exploration that resonates with the profiles of those extended range players discussed herein? Communities of guitarists might then be organized around range, be that ukulele, baritone, fretless, eight-string or otherwise.

While physical evolutions and augmentations are increasingly common, digital augmentations are becoming increasingly popular too and, while not within the scope of this chapter, as digital technologies develop in the coming years, the corporeal definition of the guitar should be informed by these (see Chapters 12 and 13 of this volume for more on digital augmentations).

5. Extension by device – while not discussed within this chapter, modalities of execution are also important to our understanding. Guitarists have used many tools – power drills, magnets, bows, EBows, fans, combs, dildos to name but a few – to create unique and varied ways of playing a guitar, regardless of the effect on range affordance.[11] While often this is for timbral effect, some tools acutely develop the range extension possibilities on the instrument. Perhaps one of the best examples here is Ron Thal's use of a thimble to create artificial pitch points beyond the end of the fretboard, much like a slide player can. Within this category we might also place the Digitech Whammy, Eventide Harmonizer and a range of other pitch manipulation devices. We must, therefore, consider that a guitar's range is not necessarily defined by the ends of the fretboard alone, and that the 'instrument' extends much further in some instances to the technologies that surround it.

Considering the above, I therefore call for a reevaluation of our perception of the standard six-string guitar. Rather than talking about the many eclectic and interesting instruments and approaches herein as *extended range*, I propose instead that we consider the standard-tuned six-string guitar as a *limited range* instrument; in doing so, we might reposition our understanding of the 'guitar' in the 21st century to view it as an instrument of vast spectral possibilities.

---

[11] See also interview with Bill Thompson (Chapter 11 of this volume).

References

Arbogast, L. and L. Del Mastro (2011), *The Seventh String: The Life and Tales of Bucky Pizzarelli*, Available online: https://www.youtube.com/watch?v=goDqtP4MtqQ (accessed 14 July 2021).

Bates, E. (2012), 'The Social Life of Musical Instruments', *Ethnomusicology*, 56 (3): 363–95.

Dawe, K. (2010), *The New Guitarscape in Critical Theory, Cultural Practice and Musical Performance*, London: Routledge.

Dawe, K. and S.C. Eroğlu (2013), 'The Guitar in Turkey: Erkan Oğur and the Istanbul Guitarscape', *Ethnomusicology Forum*, 22 (1): 49–70.

De Souza, J. (2017), *Music at Hand: Instruments, Bodies, and Cognition*, Oxford: Oxford University Press.

DeVale, S. (1990), 'Organizing Organology', *Selected Reports in Ethnomusicology*, 8: 1–34.

Di Perna, A. (2011), 'Steve Vai Discusses Devin Townsend and New Album, "Sex And Religion"', in 1993 Guitar World Interview, *Guitarworld*, Available online: https://www.guitarworld.com/gw-archive/steve-vai-discusses-devin-townsend-and-new-album-sex-and-religion-1993-guitar-world-interview (accessed 14 July 2021).

Gilbert, A. (2015), 'Howard Alden: Seven Strings, will Travel', *Berkeleyside*, Available online: https://www.berkeleyside.org/2015/08/06/howard-alden-seven-strings-will-travel (accessed 14 July 2021).

Kartomi, M. J. (1990), *On Concepts and Classifications of Musical Instruments*, Chicago, IL: The University of Chicago Press.

Kennelty, G. (2020), 'Steve Vai Credits KORN with Popularizing the Seven String Guitar', *Metalinjection.net*, Available online: https://metalinjection.net/news/steve-vai-credits-korn-with-popularizing-the-seven-string-guitar (accessed 14 July 2021).

Kozinn, A. (1980), 'Narciso Yepes: Classical Master of the 10-String Guitar', *Frets Magazine*, 39–42.

Lähdeoja, O., B. Navarret, S. Quintans and A. Sedes, (2010), 'The Electric Guitar: An Augmented Instrument and a Tool for Musical Composition', *Journal of Interdisciplinary Music Studies*, 4 (2): 37–54.

Laing, R. (2019), 'Steve Vai: Whitesnake's Slip Of The Tongue was "the first rock record that has a seven-string guitar throughout the whole thing"', *MusicRadar*, Available online: https://www.musicradar.com/news/steve-vai-whitesnakes-slip-of-the-tongue-was-the-first-rock-record-that-has-a-seven-string-guitar-throughout-the-whole-thing (accessed 14 July 2021).

Mayr, E. (1982), *The Growth of Biological Thought: Diversity, Evolution and Inheritance*, Cambridge, MA: Harvard University Press.

Resnicoff, M. (1989), 'The Unreachable Star', *Guitar World*, May.

Rubio, J.L. (1990), 'Entrevista a Narciso Yepes', Available online: http://club.telepolis.com/entrevistayepes (accessed 14 July 2021).

Shadrick, J. (2012), 'Charlie Hunter – Get Rhythm', *Premier Guitar*, Available online: https://www.premierguitar.com/artists/interview-charlie-hunter-get-rhythm?page=2 (accessed 14 July 2021).

Turnbull, H. (1974), *The Guitar from the Renaissance to the Present Day*, New York: Scribner's Sons.

Wade, G. (2018), *Traditions of the Classical Guitar*, Richmond: Alma Books.

Waksman, S. (1999), *Instruments of Desire: The Electric Guitar and the Shaping of Musical Experience*, Cambridge, MA: Harvard University Press.

Wheeler, T. (1978), 'Interview with John McLaughlin', *Guitar Player*, August.

Yepes, N. (1973), 'The Ten-String Guitar', trans. L. Salter, *La Cantarela*, July.

Yepes, N. (1989), '"Ser Instrumento" [To Be an Instrument], Speech of Ingression into the Real Academia de Bellas Artes de San Fernando', 30 April, Available online: http://www.narcisoyepes.org (accessed 21 September 2021).

6

I should have just learned how to play the organ

Interview with Charlie Hunter

Richard Perks

Charlie Hunter is widely considered the pioneer of six-, seven- and eight-string – 'hybrid' – guitar playing. His distinctive technique combines guitar parts with bass lines and percussive elements, allowing him to function as a complete rhythm section. He has worked alongside an array of celebrated artists, spanning jazz, funk, soul and fusion settings, and has fronted many successful solo, duo and trio projects of his own.

RP: Let's start with a controversial one: Are you a guitarist, bassist or drummer?

CH: Well, oddly enough, I'm kind of all three. And especially in this, Covid,[1] I've actually been playing more gigs on drums than anything else! But it all informs what I do, and I've been lucky enough to play with some of the greats in all those kinds of fields, and learned from some great people as well, so everything is informed from that, you know?

RP: What about when you're doing the seven- or eight-string 'thing'? What 'role' do you adopt then?

CH: Well I haven't done the eight-string thing in years, I just felt like that was more than I needed. And I just settled on that [then] because it, it was an easy way for me to get a guitar slash bass brain around that, but ultimately I felt like having that many strings wasn't really serving me. It was more work to

---

[1] Reference to lockdown during 2020 coronavirus pandemic.

deal with, the extra string. I realized, okay, I don't know if these extra strings are *really* giving me anything that I need more. And also, every time you add an extra string, you're increasing the tension on the neck of the guitar and the body of the guitar and you're changing the resonance and the dynamics. So, I switched to seven and I had a tuning with that that I liked, but I felt like, well, you're still sacrificing a little bit there. Especially because so much of what I do is about the bass and playing with the drummer, that's the big part of what I do. I found that it was just all about counterpoint, and how do I refine the concept so that it's all about counterpoint and rhythm? Now I play something that has only six strings, really – divided into three bass and three guitar [strings] (see Figure 6.1) . . . and I'll go back and play the seventh string too, just depending upon the gig, you know? If I'm playing with a drummer, it's gotta punch, and the time has got to be paramount, and the feel. All the rest is just frills. The groove is the foundation and everything else is secondary to it. You know what I mean? Unfortunately, that requires that you have an insane amount of technique – to be able to play the stuff that nobody notices, until you stop playing it.

RP: What does this type of guitar afford you that a regular six-string doesn't? And in what ways has your technique developed through playing hybrid guitar?

Figure 6.1 Charlie Hunter playing his Hybrid Guitars long-scale Big 6 live. (Photo: Ryan Bell, 2022, used with permission).

CH: Well, you can really be a presence with the drummer. *That* was the whole thing, to be a part of the rhythm section, and also, be able to play kind of guitar on top of it, you know? – biggest mistake I ever made in my life! [laughs] I made my life so difficult with that. And the technique is infinitely more involved and harder than playing a six-string guitar because you're taking on all this [extra] stuff . . . it's an entirely different technique. For instance, as you go lower, every note you go lower, you need exponentially more surface area and you have to strike it a little bit harder in a different way . . . my thing is, it's gotta be like a bass, it's gotta 'pop'! And when you're playing with a drummer, you really have to be rhythmically present all the time, you know? So, it's hard on the brain, and it's really hard on the technical aspects of it. I mean, what you say with the instrument is a whole other thing; once you go through what I've gone through with this instrument, going back to playing guitar, there's technically nothing difficult about it, you can put the heaviest strings on it and you can do it in your sleep!

RP: I noticed you said 'this instrument'. Does that mean you think of it as something quite separate from a regular guitar?

CH: *Absolutely.* It's different in the same way that Chinese is a different language and culture from Japanese, but they're related . . . If you deal with the history of the guitar, it's a folk instrument, going back as far as you want to go, to our ancestors . . . when they developed like a one-string or two-string instrument, that was essentially plucked. That was the beginnings of it, right? And we haven't come *that* far. We've just refined it and developed certain aspects of it, you know?

RP: You've spoken before about the importance of *interdependence*.[2] Could you explain what you mean by that idea?

CH: Sure. People are really enamoured of this idea that what's important is independence. But, it's really *interdependence*, and independence is a way that you get *to* interdependence. It's about the parts working together to create a more grooving whole. If you listen to Elvin Jones play, everyone gets like, 'Oh man, listen to the independence'. I'm like, 'it's interdependence!' Listen to his right hand, what his right hand is doing, and then relate that to what the other

[2] See: *Putting It Together*, Charlie Hunter Clinic (June 2011); available at https://www.youtube.com/watch?v=-JSBOQA5en8 (accessed 24 August 2020).

limbs are doing. And then relate that to the larger picture that he's painting, which doesn't have anything to do with any of that stuff.

RP: In the same way you might, for example, learn jazz progressions on a regular guitar, do you have a set of 'stock' patterns or movements that you've 'drilled in' over the years?

CH: Yeah, you're absolutely right. That's how we learn, right? Everything revolves around learning and a pattern, I think that's how our brains work. But the way I think about it with my weird instrument is, it comes down to a lot of different combinations. So, you want to learn as many combinations as possible. And you don't just have the combinations in your left hand. The way I break it down for people is like, generally you think of things as your right hand being the 'execution' hand and your left hand being the 'conception' hand. But, when you start to *really* deal with rhythm and time and rhythmic counterpoint, both hands have to incorporate [both aspects]. This [gestures to right hand] becomes execution *and* rhythmic conception, and this hand [gestures to left hand] no longer gets to just be a conception hand; it *has* to be rhythmic because every time you're starting to do something with the right [hand], you have to articulate every rest. You can't just *play* the rest. You have to be really rhythmically astute, and really be inside there so that you can articulate and manipulate those rests. So, you have to think like a drummer; all of that technical stuff, you're dealing with that all the time.

RP: Does it ever stop becoming a kind of 'layers' exercise, where you might have a rhythm and then a bass part, and then chords on top?

CH: Well, the longer answer would be that you have to develop as many combinations as possible. You have to internalize them. As many combinations as you can, rhythmically, harmonically, all of those things together. So, you instinctively know how to avoid bottlenecks, right? ... So when you're on the stage and you're improvising and with other people, you're almost not thinking about the instrument at all; you're not trying, not even to look at it; you're just trying to be in the moment and listen to the other people. You want to develop that to such a level that you can get to a point – and I haven't gotten there yet, it's a goal [laughs] – where you're not listening to yourself at all. You're listening to everybody else, and then you play. You're just part of them. You're part of their sound.

RP: What aspects of hybrid guitar do you find liberating, versus limiting that is? And how has that changed over time?

CH: It's all liberating when you come at it from a standpoint of music and how you can contribute to whatever situation you're in, it's about finding how you can make a contribution to the music you're playing and really get into that . . . When I first started on these kind of weird hybrid instruments, I was young and I had a lot of chops and was just like, 'I gotta show people that I can do all this shit.' It was a challenge. It was like, 'man, I need to learn how to play all this Larry Young shit, alright, I'm going to do that!' Or man, 'I need to learn how to put all of this montuno with a tumbao on the bottom, I'm going to do this shit!' . . . So, you know, I did a lot of that, and I think it's kind of impressive in its own way, but there's a lot of issues with it, that I feel, y'know, if you're going for that 'covert' vibe where everything is [really] about, 'Oh, let me show people all this fucking shit I can kinda do', then you're going to lose out on a lot of the other stuff. And you have to ask yourself, 'well, wait a minute, am I an asset to the other musicians? Or am I a liability?' And 'is the fact that I want to play a lot of stuff that is impressive to an audience? Is that really good for the other people I'm playing with right now, and for the music?' . . . It's just like anything else, you just go there and you figure it out, you know? Limitations are good man, everything has limitations . . . figure out what those are, work through them or work around them, but they're there, you know? You may be playing something very simply, but it may really add everything that the music needs . . . And putting yourself in these positions, with different instruments and weird tunings, I think is good for you. It's good for your brain. It puts you in a position where you're having to think of different things; it puts you out of your regular patterns that you fall into. I think that's really good. For instance, if I retune my instrument, I'm still bringing all the years. I learned how to groove and have a feel and my ideas of harmony or whatever. I'm still bringing it to that instrument. So, something's going to happen, but you never know what it's going to be.

RP: So you conceive entirely new musical ideas through playing this kind of guitar?

CH: Oh *yeah*! I mean, it'll *definitely* change your perspective, and it changes the way the music sounds. The music is going to sound different.

RP: If you ever use a regular six-string now, how would you say playing hybrid for so long has affected your technique/style?

CH: I mean everything influences everything else, you know? Technically when I play a regular six-string guitar, the strings have to be *super* heavy for me to be able to play it without kind of, I don't know, shredding it apart, you know?! [laughs] And a lot of times I'll play with a pick on those things, because it's just cool. Or, if I play acoustic guitar, I'll finger-pick, you know what I mean? And, and it influences everything because you can play all of that contrapuntal stuff on the [regular] guitar, it's just not going to be as dramatic, but it all works on the regular guitar.

RP: How do you approach different tunings? When you play the seven-string, for instance, you tune the bottom three strings to G C F, then the upper four C F B♭ D, right?

CH: Yeah. That's a tuning I used for a long time with the seven-string. I also did that same tuning [with] everything down a whole-step. When I was playing the eight-string originally, it was like E A D, A D G B E. So, most of those Blue Note records are with that.

RP: Does your sense of harmony or pitch get ever confused when switching between different tunings?

CH: Not really, you just get used to it, you know? And it's not a reading instrument. I mean, reading on the bass is fine, on drums, even regular guitar, but this instrument, honestly, it's just not a reading instrument so much. So, you know, you just kind of find which key you're in and go for it, you know?! The instrument I play now [six-string hybrid] (see Figure 6.1), sometimes I tune it like a G C F, C F B♭. Sometimes it's the same thing down a whole step. I've even been experimenting with tuning it weird, like G C F, B♭ D G, almost like a six, but up a minor third – because a friend of mine has one of these [six-string hybrid guitar] and he's been doing that, and it's pretty cool actually!

RP: As a guitar player, the fifth in the middle of those tunings would fry my brain.

CH: Yeah! That whole fifth thing came out of just like, well, 'where are these notes?' But in retrospect I think tuning it that way made my life a little harder. In terms of tone and intonation as well, because you're dealing with a lot of extreme gauges and all these things. But I felt like once I had learned that, it was what it was. But now I'm rethinking tuning and rethinking everything because so much of what I play is based around counterpoint. I'm not trying to play a lot of really frilly guitar stuff on the top, you know, I'm just trying to play good time with a good feel.

RP: Was having the duplicate of the lower strings an octave higher an ergonomic decision? So your fingers could reach certain things easier?

CH: Nah, it's actually worse that way to be totally honest, it was just for my brain. So, my brain could get around it, and I'd have something familiar, that was more guitar-based. But as it evolved away from the eight-string, it kind of made less and less sense, I guess, but I [still] go back and forth between different tunings.

RP: Those top four strings [on seven-string] are tuned relative to the middle four on a regular guitar. So, do you still use 'regular' chord shapes? Or are there not enough fingers left to do that?

CH: It all depends on what the bass is doing. If it's a simple bass line and you have room to play in a rhythmically astute way with the guitar on top of that, then it's okay. If you're moving bass lines, whether it's a swinging thing, shuffle, a funk thing, whatever it is, I find that it's nice to do a bass line with a two-note chord on top, kind of vibe. Our ears are hearing so much stuff that you're not really noticing that you don't have a three-note chord on top. And, in fact, there's so much you can do with that pivot finger, because if you have four fingers and you're always playing [only] three notes, there's always a finger open to get to the next thing, right? So, I find that to be kind of a good rule of thumb for doing that kind of thing. So, really you're not thinking of things 'guitaristically', you're just thinking of things musically. I don't need to have a seventh and a third on every chord I want; sometimes I'm playing the seventh and the root. Sometimes I'm going to play the third and the fourth and the seventh and resolve it. Sometimes I'm going to play the seventh and the ninth, sometimes who knows, just whatever makes sense and feels good at the time. It's the overall colour and harmony in relation to the group rather than prioritizing the functional harmony and those sorts of things.

RP: How does that change if you're playing with a larger rhythm section, for example with a bassist and a drummer?

CH: If I do that, I would just play regular guitar. It makes no sense to play this instrument with a bass player, not for me at least, I wouldn't want to do that. It would just be a waste of everyone's time I think.

RP: One of my favourite tunes of yours is 'Run For It' from the *Songs From The Analog Playground* album. You have a Hammond organ style/sound going on. Were you specifically trying to emulate the playing style of organists?

CH: Ha! In the early days of my instrument, I definitely referenced organ players a lot, because that was what I needed to do to learn how to get an idea of, well, how does this bass work with this chord? And really, in retrospect, I should have just learned how to play the organ. It would have been much easier . . . way, *way* easier than what I ended up doing! [laughs]

RP: Do you still use a separate line-out for the 'bass' strings and another for the 'guitar'?

CH: Yeah. Well, *now* I'm kind of a part of a guitar company Hybrid Guitars Co. here in North Carolina.[3] We're making really great instruments for actually really good prices. If they had been around, you know, ten, fifteen years ago, [it] would have been very different. But, we have a thing where, we use these Armstrong pickups and we have two outputs, but there's a switch, so you can make it mono. So, for instance, if you want to play seven-string with a low E, and you don't want to use two amps, you can just boom, go with it.

RP: Do you use different effects with each signal line too?

CH: Yeah. You can effect the guitar and the bass differently. I used to use a lot of effects, but I don't really do that anymore.

---

[3] See: www.hybrid-guitars.com.

RP: Do you have a 'preferred' line up in terms of instrumentation?

CH: Oh, trio is the best format for me and my weird little instrument. And duo is great, but I get tired of listening to myself play, you know? So, a trio with me, a drummer and singer, or me a percussionist and a singer, or me a drummer and a horn player, that works for me.

RP: Have you ever met any resistance from people to your instrument? I'm thinking 'jazz police', for example?

CH: Not really. I mean, I'm lucky I've played with some great musicians and most of them are just looking for a different sound or something that they're interested in. I don't think about music that way. I just really don't, it's much more of an open prospect for me . . . it's not an athletic event. It's foolish, and arrogant, to think that because we live in an era with unfettered access to all the information, that some among us can decide that they are the arbiters of how that information should be used. It's absurd. Music has been around for thousands of years. We have been evolving as humans, playing music for thousands of years, at best. And those that everyone thinks is the biggest deal are, at best, insignificant little chains, links in that chain, and I might not even be on it, you know?

RP: Lastly, how would you define a guitar?

CH: Oh, what a great idea! I mean, honestly, it's a folk instrument and every folk has a different version of it. But it's also the only instrument that really has elements of harmony, melody and rhythm in it, but doesn't own any of those things outright. You can hear a guitar playing like horn players; you can hear guitar players playing like Freddie Green; you can hear guitar players playing like Nile Rodgers; you can hear guitar players playing shred metal. You can hear guitar players playing Cuban music, and they would call that a tres; you could hear them playing Venezuelan music and they'd call it a cuatro. It goes on and on and on, but it's a folk instrument. And it can be adapted to any group of people's idea of what is important to them.

RP: So, is the instrument you play a guitar?

CH: [Laughs] I guess. Yeah. Sure. Perfect. That's great. Why not? *Why not?!*

Editors' Choice – Recommended Listening:

Voodoo (2000), D'Angelo, Virgin Records.

Solo Eight-String Guitar (2000), Charlie Hunter, Contra Punto Records, Independent Release.

Songs From The Analog Playground (2001), Charlie Hunter Quartet, Blue Note.

Dionne Dionne (2015), Dionne Farris and Charlie Hunter, Atlanta Records.

Music! Music! Music! (2019), Lucy Woodward and Charlie Hunter, Independent Release.

Artist Website: www.charliehunter.com

7

The transformed space of the 'Ligeti Guitar'

Katalin Koltai

The new is the longing for the new, not the new itself.

—Adorno (1997: 32)

Guitar space and guitar thinking: Tool or agency?

Discovering the driving forces behind organological innovation leads to interdisciplinary fields. The Ligeti Guitar, the central theme of this chapter, is an outcome of a journey in performance, arrangement, composition, technology and music cognition. Guitar idiom is often associated with limited use of keys, unbalanced resonances, idiosyncrasy and complexity. While Hector Berlioz (Berlioz 1948: 145) states that only a guitarist can write well for the instrument, Pierre Boulez (qtd. in 1976:20) accuses Berlioz's orchestration of 'clumsiness' coming from his guitar-based thinking. Although conventional music theory often represents instruments as 'transparent', which is in some way, a 'dream of science' (Tresch 2013: 290), current cutting-edge research explores the agency of musical instruments in music perception and cognition. Alexander Rehding (2016) explores how specific instruments serve as 'theoretical instruments', in other words, 'tools for musical thinking' (De Souza 2021: 3), and affect formulating music theory. Jonathan De Souza's (2017) research draws upon ecological psychology and relates key aspects of our perception of music to spaces and 'affordances' (see Gibson 1966; 1977; 1979). He integrates some of Maurice Merleau-Ponty's phenomenological observations and describes playing a musical instrument as acting in a specific space: '[the organist] "sizes up the instrument with his body, incorporates its directions and dimensions, and settles into the organ as one settles into a house"' (Merleau-Ponty 2012: 146 qtd. in De Souza 2017: 22).

For the sake of understanding and describing instrumental spaces, De Souza (2017) applies James J. Gibson's concept of 'affordance' (see Gibson 1966; 1977; 1979). In the context of ecological psychology, action and perception are just as bound together as environment and organism (De Souza 2017: 12). In his consideration of 'the cultural environment', Gibson argues against distinguishing '"material" culture' and '"non-material" culture' and refutes the notion that 'language, tradition, art, music, law, and religion are immaterial, insubstantial, or intangible, whereas tools, shelters, clothing, vehicles, and books are not' (Gibson 1966: 26). He states that there always have to be 'modes of stimulation, or ways of conveying information, for any individual to perceive anything, however abstract' (ibid). Therefore, we can see musical space as an environment where a musical work exists: it is bounded by the instrument's and the performer's physical affordances, as well as the affordances of the conceptual space (Shea 2020: 31) designed by the composer. A piece written for a musical instrument 'lives' in a space bounded by idiomatic affordances. For instance, a piece for Baroque flute is determined by the 'strong' and 'weak' notes of the instrument, creating an idiomatic space, where characters and timbres are tied to different keys. An instrumental piece efficiently using the instrumental space is considered idiomatic. The composer writing for a commission may also consider the performer's *bodily* affordances.[1] Maurice Ravel, when writing his left-hand concerto, considers that Paul Wittgenstein tragically lost his right arm during the First World War. Johann Adolf Hasse composed the role of Cleopatra based on the extremely wide vocal affordances of Farinelli.[2]

A sizeable majority of guitar music builds on favourite keys, offering the comprehensive utilization of open strings. De Souza connects this notion with the theories of Maurice Merleau-Ponty and Edmund Husserl (De Souza 2018: 11) and talks about open strings as the '*zero point* of embodied spatiality' determining musical features. De Souza, in the article 'Fretboard Transformations' (2018), examines the musical space of the guitar fretboard. He models different left-hand shapes based on Timothy Koozin's relative system of fret intervals (Koozin 2011)[3] and applies David Lewin's (Lewin 1987) transformational theory in his

---

[1] Gibson did not apply the term 'affordances' to one's own body. Although we may distinguish between objects' affordances and agents' abilities, I decided to extend the Gibsonian term here for the sake of this argument. For more on affordance, see Perks's Chapter 3 of this volume.

[2] Johann Adolf Hasse had written the roles of Cleopatra in *Marc'Antonio e Cleopatra* (Naples, 1725), Arbace in *Artaserse* (Venice, 1730) and Arbace *in Catone in Utica* (Turin, 1732) for Farinelli.

[3] In this system the finger stopping the string at the lowest fret is always marked as a 1, and all the strings are filled with numbers unless they are not stopped when they are marked with dashes.

analyses. Based on this theoretical accessory, he analyses Leo Brouwer's *Simple Studies*[4] (1972) in a later article (De Souza, 2021). Through his analyses, De Souza encounters an interesting dualism between the complexity of musical text and the simplicity of instrumental choreography: 'In these études, Brouwer's motifs combine both fingering patterns and sounding patterns. This can create a tension between performers' and listeners' experience, making the pieces sound more complex than they feel' (De Souza 2021: 17). We can see that De Souza's approach crucially confronts the Schenkerian mindset: 'tones mean nothing but themselves' (Treitler 1997: 43). Analysing how instrumental affordances influence key compositional choices creates a growing research field: Nicholas Shea talks about 'enactive landscapes' (Kirsh 2013: 3) and applies an affordance-based theory in analysing rock guitar works (Shea 2020), David Huron and Jonathon Berec (2009) study affordances and idiomaticism of trumpet works, while Ian Quinn and Christopher Wm. White (2017) examine piano repertoire.

The abovementioned authors explored 'extramusical contents', such as embodiment and sequences of movements, in other words, instrumental choreography[5] and their role in transforming the musical text (Clarke et al. 2017).[6] The cross-domain mappings[7] of instrumental space and pitch also connect us to the topic of analogical thinking: association and metaphor. Lawrence M. Zbikowski, in his *Foundations of Musical Grammar* (2017), demonstrates how our music perception is affected by instrumental choreography and bodily gestures. He examines Sagreras's famous virtuoso guitar piece, *El Colibrí*[8] (1954). Zbikowski states that despite the odd and idiosyncratic nature of the piece: 'Once the title is known, features that seemed odd quickly organize themselves into a coherent image' (Zbikowski 2017: 26). The somewhat idiosyncratic fingerings of the opening three bars, which would be much more convenient played on adjacent strings (Figure 7.1), serve a purpose. The choreography, rapid shifts along the length of the strings, creates an analogy for the hummingbird's flight,

---

[4] Leo Brouwer, *Estudios sencillos* (1972).
[5] The term 'instrumental choreography' is thoroughly discussed in the collaborative research of Gorton, Shaw-Miller and Heyde (2013). Another utilization of the term happens in the Kreutzer Quartet's DVD (2017) released on Métier called 'Quartet Choreography'.
[6] Clarke et al. (2017) define instrumental choreography as 'physical movements of the hands that can be built into the musical materials for dramatic effect'. However, I use the term in a wider context, stating that instrumental choreography is always there having or not a 'dramatic effect'.
[7] 'Cross-domain mapping is a process through which we structure our understanding of one domain (which is typically unfamiliar or abstract) in terms of another (which is most often familiar and concrete)' (Zbikowski 2017: 13).
[8] Julio Salvador Sagreras: *El Colibri* (1954).

Figure 7.1 Sagreras, *El Colibri*, mm. 1–3.

'for a brief moment, the guitarist's hand becomes the hummingbird flitting between flowers' (Zbikowski 2017: 43).

We have now explored some scholarly concepts and theories towards understanding the guitar as a space. However, a satisfying contextual background to my journey with the Ligeti Guitar must include an identification of influential artistic concepts in contemporary composition and guitar arrangement.

Artistic concepts towards the guitar space in contemporary music and arrangement

Three perspectives on the guitar space in contemporary music

In an interview, Julian Anderson (2016) describes his very first feelings when receiving the letter from Julian Bream commissioning a new guitar piece:[9]

> I was thrilled, but I immediately realized that this is going to be a very big challenge. . . . I tried writing just out of the blue a few sketches for guitar and found quite quickly that I hadn't a clue what I was doing. Eventually, I worked out that I was going to have to buy a guitar and learn it to some extent in order to write the piece.

Anderson then describes a process of searching cross-domain mapping between visual colours (inspired by Joan Miró's painting *Catalan Peasant with Guitar*)[10] and timbres:

> I wanted the piece to have very vivid colours like that [Miró's painting] . . . I was trying to find something that related to 'the blues' [blue colours] and therefore to

---

[9] As a result of this commission and a collaborative work between the composer and Laura Snowden, Julian Anderson composed his solo guitar piece, *Catalan Peasant with Guitar*, in 2015, published by Schott. See Anderson interview (2016).
[10] Joan Miró, *Catalan Peasant with a Guitar* 1924, Museo Nacional Thyssen-Bornemisza, Madrid.

Figure 7.2 Kurtág, *Grabstein für Stephan*, op. 15/c, guitar part, mm. 1–4.

notes that are pitch unstable, or differently tuned, and finally, that ended up with having one string, the G string retuned towards the middle of the piece. And when I started experimenting with that at home, the chords I could get suddenly sounded to me as they were coloured in different ways, and for me, that gave something like a blue atmosphere if I can put it like that.

We can see how Anderson decides to transform the guitar space to achieve the association of different colours. In the compositional process, he physically engages with the instrument and starts experimenting with its affordances of timbre and resonance. Resultingly, he creates a scordatura, which also serves as an analogue: strings represent different colours of a palette, and the whole soundscape represents the atmosphere of the colour blue.

As I am talking about a string of artistic concepts in composition underpinning the thought process behind my journey to the Ligeti Guitar, I cannot avoid talking about György Kurtág as one of the main inspirational figures in my Hungarian music education background. We will see from the few points I make in the following paragraphs that the composer takes a very different approach towards the instrumental space and formulates a somewhat resigned notion of the guitar idiom. *Grabstein für Stephan*,[11] one of Kurtág's most dramatic orchestral works, embraces a soloist guitar part. The dedication to Stephan Stein, husband of the Hungarian gestalt psychologist Marianne Stein leads us to autobiographical sources. The composer refers to the piece as a 'harrowing experience' (Varga 2009: 50) and also repeatedly talks about the therapeutic sessions with the psychologist Marianne Stein which involved 'painful acting-out of our most traumatic experiences through composition' (Hajdu 2008)[12] and helped him to resolve his compositional crisis between 1957 and 1958 in Paris. *Grabstein für Stephan* (Figure 7.2) has a dramatic contrast between two media: the guitar and

---

[11] György Kurtág, *Grabstein für Stephan*, op. 15/c. Budapest: Editio Musica Budapest, 1989.
[12] 'In 1959, Kurtág presented me to a rather exceptional person, Marianne Stein, a Hungarian Gestalt psychologist then living in Paris, who worked only with artists. Her influence on our lives was decisive. She suggested – and obtained – a strong and painful acting-out of our most traumatic experiences through composition. One can hardly understand Kurtag's *Játékok*, but also his Kafka, Beckett and Hölderlin pieces without the huge liberating effect of her method' (Hajdu 2008).

the orchestra. Although the setup is similar to a guitar concerto, the guitar part is restricted to the obsessive repetition of open strings and its minor modifications. One may feel that there is a lack of voice, a struggle of expression and a failure of it. These associations may get better understood by quoting Kurtág himself, who told me the following while working with him in 2021:

> What I attempted to accomplish is that [the guitar plays . . . only on the open strings]. . . . The guitar can become a tombstone this way, and all the rest of the music happens in the ensemble, which surrounds it. Yet this, on the other hand, is very little, when I tried to fill it out, it always broke down. The hand positions that resulted were so complicated, they would not sound. There is the guitarist, the soloist sitting there, perhaps in the spotlight, and it is all they have to play. They make it from e minor to c sharp minor, and never any further, anywhere else. And this is how it came to make sense. And then I composed it again at least three or four times, so it would have meaning, you know, so it would be a piece for the guitar, and [the instrument] is not suitable for that. (Kurtág 2021, own translation from Hungarian)

In a way, Kurtág creates a cross-domain mapping between the (in)ability of speech and instrumental affordances: the guitar's 'mutism' creates a metaphor for the tombstone. We can see how Kurtág and Anderson represent two thoroughly contrasting artistic approaches to the guitar idiom. We know that both composers compose at the piano in general, and they would probably accept the statement that it is the *music-theoretical instrument* or *compositional instrument* (De Souza 2017: 109–44) of their compositional thinking. Anderson picks up the guitar, experiments with it and transforms it. He accepts it as a tool for his composition. However, Kurtág considers both the guitar's 'positive and negative affordances' (see Gibson 1977; 1979) towards harmony progression and decides to create an artistic meaning through denial.

The third perspective that we'll consider here is that of the guitarist-composer Leo Brouwer. In an interview, Brouwer (2018) talks about how his music can sound virtuosic while it is based on the simplicity of instrumental technique elements:

> It's not the music, which is simple, . . . I always have a complicated harmony or meaning or lines or broken figures in the music, which is not simple. What is simple is the way to play. Simplicity for fingers; complexity for ear.

However, in another conversation, Brouwer raises the often-heard accusation that the composition choices of guitar composers are *corrupted* by their 'guitar thinking':

[Brouwer] talked about the importance of composing away from the guitar. He mimed picking up a guitar and fingering a chord: 'It sounds marvelous!' Then he mimed sliding the chord shape higher up the fingerboard: 'Marvelous again!' Then he mimed moving it again: 'Still marvelous!' Then came the critique: 'But who is composing? You or the guitar?' (Leathwood 2020)

De Souza gives us a commentary on Brouwer's rhetorical question:

You *or* the guitar? Why not both? Of course, the guitar doesn't compose independently. But, in a sense, neither does the composer. . . . The instrument might not be an autonomous agent – but, in a sense, neither am I. My own embodied agency is distributed; my actions respond to the instrument's call. (De Souza 2021: 18)

Discovering new affordances in guitar arrangement: Dyens and 'guitar lungs'

Although guitar arrangers may not directly apply any of the discussed theoretical frameworks in their work, it is quite straightforward to identify in the following examples the intense effort of pushing the boundaries through newly discovered affordances and the transformation of space. We have already looked at theories describing the importance of open strings and their transformation with scordatura, creating new compositional means (De Souza 2017: 88). Now I would like to look at Roland Dyens's work on guitar arrangement.

In an interview Dyens gives us a definition of a 'guitaristic' arrangement as 'an arrangement that uses . . . either open strings as guitar "lungs" or . . . scordatura which "enlarge" things in general' (Vincens 2009: 79). Indeed, Dyens's application of scordaturas in his arrangements enables the extensive use of open strings. In his arrangement of Chopin *Valse* op.69. no.2. (1829) (Figure 7.3) he keeps the original b-minor key (Figure 7.4), although the piece would offer many guitaristic solutions in a-minor. For this inconvenient key, he applies a scordatura of 5 = B, 6 = F♯. This unusual scordatura opens the space for new resonances and vertical structures and helps him to overstep the challenge of over-used guitar patterns tied to a-minor:

Most of the arrangements I know sound too 'guitar' to my ears. Arrangements obviously have to be guitaristic (besides it's the goal number one to reach) but they are too frequently stuffed with usual 'guitar habits' therefore limited in a way (guitar should 'obey' the music and not the contrary). (Vincens 2009: 78–83)

Figure 7.3 Chopin, *Valse* op. 69, No. 2, piano, mm. 1–5.

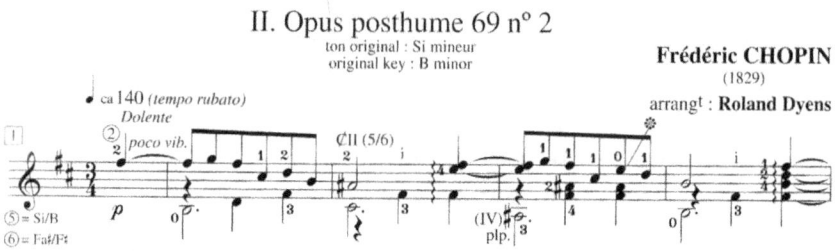

Figure 7.4 Chopin, *Valse* op. 69, No. 2, arranged for guitar by Dyens, mm. 1–4.

Stretching space with the 'Brahms Guitar'

'Enlarging' the space and the 'lungs' of the guitar also appears in an interview with one of the greatest pioneers of guitar transcription, Paul Galbraith explaining how his artistic path led him to the Brahms Guitar. Galbraith describes the musical and instrumental space in a Cartesian way linking it to three dimensions where the repertoire urged a wider space, the vertical guitar posture led to the open stretch that was combined with the conversion to eight strings, and then the vertical posture and a resonance box liberating the resonance:

> one day it really became inevitable for me that a guitar with a wider range would better cope with the entire repertoire. . . . I'd already previously played six-string guitar for years in a vertical position, which allowed for a wider range of technical options than those normally available in the standard guitar posture, using a footstool or equivalent. Things like a ready, open stretch available at any given moment to the left hand, and access to what Kreisler called 'the lungs of the string player – the free wrist' in the right hand. So, when the eight-string was finally ready, I dived straight in, feeling that I was still basically dealing with those same technical challenges that I had already been facing since I changed

The Transformed Space of the 'Ligeti Guitar' 119

Figure 7.5 Galbraith and the Brahms Guitar. (Galbraith, P., 2015).

> posture, only now extended to a wider set of coordinates. . . . Then I came to the idea that I could take advantage of my already cello-like vertical posture, and use a cello end-pin, whilst sitting up on a chair again, thus liberating the full resonance of the instrument.

Later on, a resonance box, designed to further enrich the sound and volume of the guitar, was to complete his stage equipment (Galbraith 2018) (Figure 7.5).

Yepes rebalancing resonances

Opening and supporting the resonance as a drive for changing the instrumental space appears in the case of Narciso Yepes too in his explanation for his decision to transfer to the ten-string guitar (Figure 7.6):

> A few years before 1964, I was unhappy with the six-string guitar because it is not a balanced instrument. As you know, there are only four tones on the six-string guitar, E, B, A and D, which have more resonance because of the basses, and eight tones which are sounding very dry. To make it more balanced, I decided that four extra bass strings would be all that was needed to make the difference so that all twelve tones will have similar resonance. You see, if I have one tone sounding, for example an A. We hear one A and one E sounding, we hear other tones also, but one A and one E are of course the strongest. And then, I imagined to have a guitar with four extra strings inside the guitar through the neck and inside

Figure 7.6 Yepes and the ten-string guitar. (Yepes, N., 1976).

the body, showing me with his hands]. These strings I wanted to control with a similar system that is used on the piano . . . the pedals.[13] (Kazandijan 1992: 233)

Although his plan for the inner strings and pedals was never realized, we can recognize how Yepes links musical challenges to the innovation of the instrumental space.

Hoppstock and imitating other instruments (or different timbre-worlds) through scordatura

Tilman Hoppstock explains his search for imitating the dark c-minor timbre world in Frohberger's *Suite No. 19* for harpsichord and Bach's *Cello Suite No. 5* BWV 1011[14] and how these soundscapes inspired him to transform the guitar's musical space through restringing and retuning the guitar as demonstrated in Figure 7.7:

> The music is very dark. In the cello version, there is a scordatura; the first string is tuned one note lower from A to G. This changes everything. The resonance

---

[13] 'Yepes . . . envisioned a guitar with four extra sympathetic strings, which would run through the centre of the neck, into the body of the guitar, much like the viola d'amore. These strings were to be controlled by a damper inside the body of the guitar. In turn, this damper would be linked to a radio transmitter placed in the footstool. He could therefore control the resonance of the guitar, in much the same way that a pianist does with the pedals. For practical reasons, this idea did not materialise. Instead, Yepes decided to place the additional strings on the neck of the guitar, as we have it today, and to control the resonance with his hands' (Kazandijan 1992: 142).

[14] Johann Jakob Frohberger: *Suite No. 19* for harpsichord and J. S. Bach: *Cello Suite No. 5* BWV 1011.

Figure 7.7 Scordatura used by Hoppstock.

is completely different. For the guitar I changed the strings to another position; therefore, it sounds like a lute a little bit. I thought this music needs more deep sound; how can I do that? The effect is really interesting because you have the feeling, not only that is to lower the sound but you think that there are two or three more strings at the bass. (Hoppstock 2021)[15]

The scholarly and artistic values discussed in this introduction give a contextual background to my arrangement practice and guitar research. In my further explorations, I introduce two of my inventions, a new magnet capo system and the Ligeti Guitar and demonstrate how this innovative journey provided a new (transformed) musical space for arrangements and collaborative work. In these observations I apply a mixed methodology based on reflexive ethnography (Davies 2007) and collaborative autoethnography (Chang, Ngunjiri and Hernandez 2013).

A transformed guitar landscape

A new magnet capo system and the Ligeti Guitar

To start the main body of this chapter, I would like to introduce the *tools* I have designed and their effect on instrumental affordances. Between 2018 and 2020, I developed a new magnet capo system (Figure 7.8) for the guitar. The adjustable single- and double-string capos consist of two main components; a thin steel plate fixed under the strings and neodymium magnets embedded in 3D printed cases. The magnets can be affixed and removed in two seconds, and the capos can be used on any fret between I-X and on the highest fret.

I demonstrated this system in a previous article (Koltai 2020) and explained the transformation of instrumental affordances by using the terminology of De Souza (2017). I started deploying the magnet capo system in new arrangements

---

[15] This quotation is from a personal interview with Tilman Hoppstock carried out on 16 November 2021.

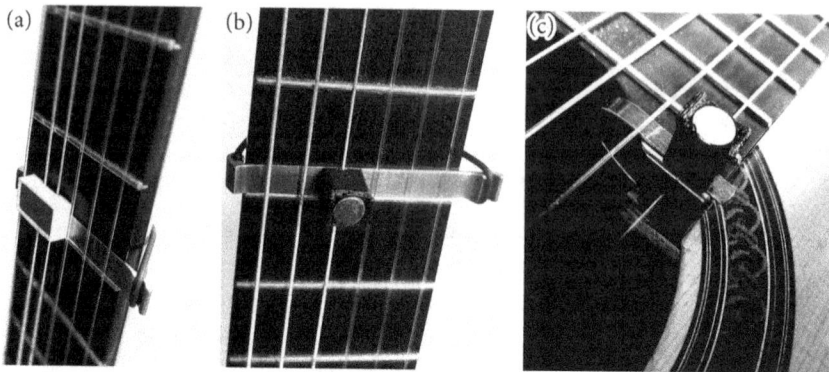

Figure 7.8 Three capo models of the magnet capo system. (Photo: Franciska Bethlenfalvy, used with permission).

Figure 7.9 Ligeti Guitar. (Photo: Author, 2022).

of Ligeti's *Musica ricercata*[16] and recognizing a method of translating certain pitch centres into open-string sets, to be discussed here later. I realized that the magnet capo system might radically redraw the guitar's idiomatic borders, especially if stretched further by integrating it into the whole guitar fretboard. In fact, the musical ideas of Ligeti's music and a possible (cross-domain) analogy between Ligeti's pitch sets and guitar scordaturas made such a prime effect that it directly led to designing a new guitar prototype; therefore, the name, Ligeti Guitar (Figure 7.9).

[16] Ligeti, György *Musica ricercata* (1951–53).

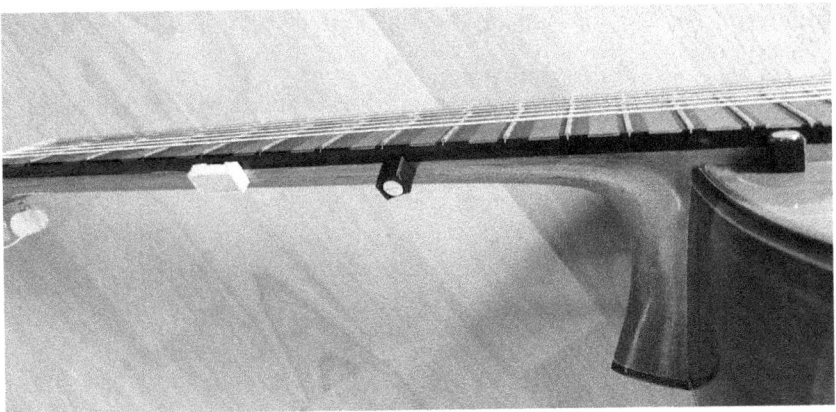

Figure 7.10 Magnet capo placeholders on the Ligeti Guitar. (Photo: Author, 2022).

The Ligeti Guitar has a transformed fretboard with embedded steel plates that enables the unlimited use of the magnet capo system. It also includes hidden magnetic placeholders under the neck and the soundboard where magnets can be placed while not in action (Figure 7.10). This new invention was supported by the Altamira Guitar Foundation and the International Guitar Research Centre through my PhD research. The transformed fretboard was manufactured by the luthier, Oren Myers.

Let us describe the space of the Ligeti Guitar in a theoretical way. Standard guitar space is determined by the six parallel strings, each of the same length. On the fretboard the nut is the zero point (marked as a zero on a standard guitar tablature, also called an open string); the instrumental space continues with the first fret, marked as 1, all the way to the bridge.[17] On the classical guitar the left hand typically has a stretch of five to seven frets, depending on the position along the fingerboard. Based on Koozin's (2011) terminology we shall call this span 'fret-interval'. Taking x to be the higher-numbered fret and y to be the lower-numbered fret, the fret-interval is given by x–y. Assuming a guitar with twenty frets, the fret-interval cannot be more than seven frets,[18] unless we use an open string, when the maximum fret-interval can be as large as the number of frets on the guitar.

---

[17] Although other plucked instruments – such as the lute – have different lengths of strings, the longer bass strings are only to be plucked and do not have frets below them, so the fretboard still starts at the same point at the nut. On the contrary, some banjos have a string with a shorter fretboard (the so-called thumb string).

[18] Standard 'chord-window' diagrams show a five-fret span, because mainstream guitar chords do not exceed a fret-interval of 5.

That is, either: x–y ≤ 7, if y ≠ 0; or, x–y ≤ 20, if y = 0

The Ligeti Guitar offers a new and expanded set of affordances by transforming the fretboard. With the capo or a set of capos positioned at any fret, all combinations of fret intervals become possible:

Such that: x–y ≤ 20

We can see this transformed new instrumental interface as a musical space where the strings start at different 'zero points' depending on the position of the capos. Figure 7.11 shows an example of the musical space where the magnet capos are positioned on the different strings and frets, therefore resulting in different string lengths.

In the discussion of new arrangements and compositions for the Ligeti Guitar that follows, I explore the ways in which these new affordances enhanced idiomatic elements. I also highlight and explain certain compositional aspects with autoethnographic perspectives.

Translating the conceptual space of 'The Night's Music' by Béla Bartók

Background and inspiration behind the creation of Béla Bartók's 'most personal genre' (Tallián 1981: 156), 'Night music', can be discovered in the memoires of family members, especially the composer's son Péter, who recounts his father's summertime stay with Elza (Bartók's sister) in Szőllőspuszta and how his father spent many nights outdoors listening to the sounds of nature and of the distant village:

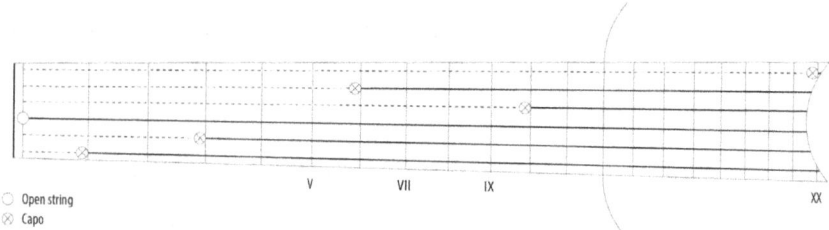

Figure 7.11 Fretboard diagram with different string lengths. This kind of diagram will be used throughout the ensuing discussion as an aid to visualize the interface.

In the front of the house we were surrounded by silence, except for distant dogs barking, crickets or similar pretty sounds, and frogs. Do not forget the frogs.... In the fourth movement [of *Out of Doors*] ... I recognized the frogs of Szöllös in an altogether reminiscent atmosphere. There were even those occasional jumps into the water. And in the distance sounded some faint music, the man-made kind, perhaps coming from the nearby village. (Bartók 2002: 161–4)

The multi-layered piece, the fourth movement of the piano cycle *Out of Doors* (1926), the first full work in 'Night music' style, builds on 'antihuman chords' (clusters), creating a vision of 'the secretive murmurs of cool, starry, demonic Night' (Schneider 2006: 85). Turning to the score, five-note clusters create an atmospheric background for the whole piece. Above this first layer, we find irregular intervals spread over a wide range, imitating the noises of nature, alongside other layers of nocturnal sounds, a lament and a wedding dance. Bartók, also an eminent pianist, creates a somewhat ecological system of instrumental choreography based on instrumental gestures and their mapping in the instrumental space, the piano keyboard. Based on the previously discussed theory of Zbikowski's (examining the instrumental choreography of a Sagreras guitar piece) describing how the left-hand movement creates the analogue of the hummingbird's flight; I would like to briefly describe the extramusical content of the instrumental choreography of the signature themes of Bartók's 'The Night's Music' (*Out of Doors*, movement IV).

The piece consists of four contrasting types of musical material expressed in parallelly contrasting instrumental choreography:

1. The atmospheric cluster layer played by the left hand is motionless, stays in the same hand position and is produced by the gentle movements of the left-hand fingers (Figure 7.12).
2. The randomness of nature noises spreads over the keyboard, played by sudden jumps of the right hand (Figure 7.13).
3. Lament song is played by slow and gracious parallel movements of both hands (Figure 7.14).
4. Wedding dance is played by complementary rhythmical movements of the two 'dancing hands' (Figure 7.15).

Bartók literature quite commonly describes elements of 'The Night's Music' on a metaphorical level. The motionless but ever-present clusters offer the association of the presence of an observer: watching, listening, perceiving. As András Schiff

Figure 7.12 Bartók, *Im Freien* [*Out of Doors*], Sz.81, 'The Night's Music', mm. 1–2.

Figure 7.13 Nature nocturnal sounds Bartók, 'The Night's Music', mm. 7–9.

puts it: 'In the middle of this there is a man, a single solitary man, probably Béla Bartók.'[19] The sonic landscape scattered by nocturnal noises has its three-dimensional equivalent: the irregular intervals embodied in diverse right-hand shapes are distributed all over the keyboard. Talking about the *lament* and its expansion to additional octaves, embodied in parallel movements of the two hands, Schiff associates this with 'even more voices of the women's choir' joining. Finally, in the *wedding dance*, the rhythmical interrelation between the two hands playing contrasting elements, an ornamented melodic line with broken chord shapes, brings a vivid image of a man and a woman dancing at a wedding feast.

---

[19] Schiff, https://youtu.be/Ibbkz2FxI74, accessed 23 April 2022.

Figure 7.14 Lament song Bartók, 'The Night's Music', mm. 26–28.

Figure 7.15 Wedding dance Bartók, 'The Night's Music', mm. 49–50.

Can one create a similarly associative choreographic system in the guitar space? Evidently, the described complexity of the material scarcely suggests the guitar, both the multi-layer nature and the cluster-based content conflict with the instrumental affordances. The solution is to create an open-string set integrating the cluster[20] by deploying the magnet capos. With the cluster thus assigned to 'open' strings, additional layers can be added – the capos function as a kind of pedal, leaving the left hand free to play other motives above that layer. Figure 7.16

---

[20] Transposing the whole piece a major third higher, in my arrangement, I reduced the five-note cluster to four notes.

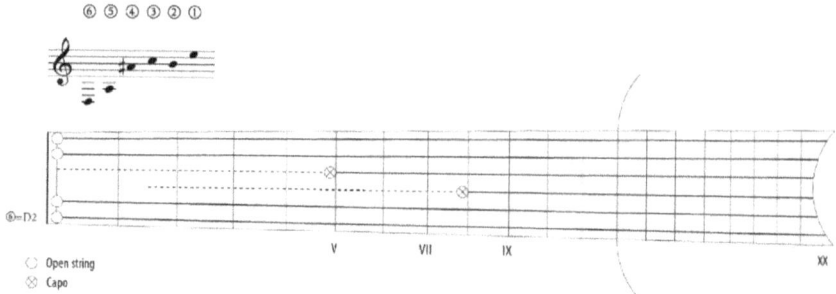

Figure 7.16 Open-string set and fretboard diagram for Bartók, 'The Night's Music'.

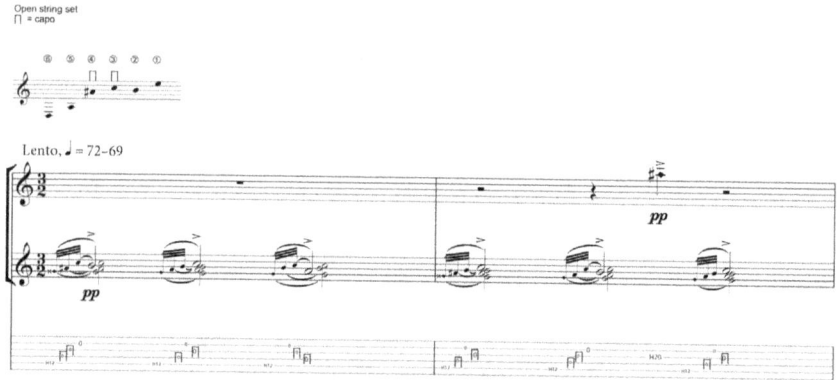

Figure 7.17 Bartók, 'The Night's Music', mm. 1–2 (transcription by the author).

shows the open-string set and the fretboard diagram of the instrumental space with the capos positioned at two of the frets.

As a result, we see a similar mapping of movements in the instrumental space. The notated score of the original two bars of Bartók's motionless clusters in Figure 7.12 can be put in comparison with the guitar transcription in Figure 7.17. Figure 7.18 compares the first bar as mapped in the instrumental space of the piano and the guitar.

Figure 7.19 compares the notation of the nocturnal sounds on the piano and the guitar. Figure 7.20 compares the spatial distribution of the scattered nocturnal sounds from bars 9 to 11 in the instrumental space of the piano and the guitar.

Although the multi-layer texture in Figure 7.13 might seem impossible to the guitarist's eye, Figure 7.21, with its clarifying annotations in tablature, shows how the instrumental landscape shifts with the new tools and transposition. In

The Transformed Space of the 'Ligeti Guitar' 129

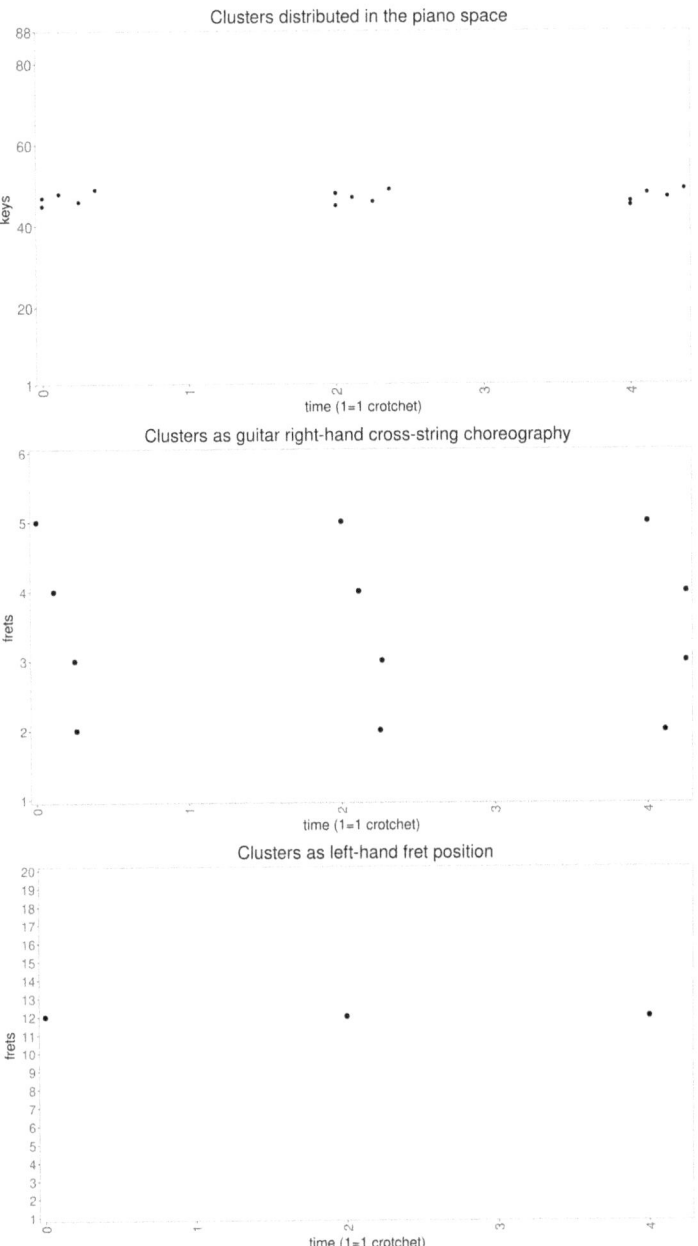

Figure 7.18 Bartók, 'The Night's Music', Instrumental mapping of the first bar.

Figure 7.19 Bartók, 'The Night's Music', nocturnal sounds on the piano and the guitar, mm. 9–11.

this example, I demonstrate how the transformable space of the Ligeti Guitar allowed embodying compositional features (a cluster shape) and, as a result, enabled a cluster-centred multi-layer texture.

Translating Ligeti's pitch sets to open-string sets

The 1950s saw the worst decade of Hungary's communist dictatorship. Between 1951 and 1953, Ligeti – isolated and censored – composed a set of eleven pieces for a secret 'bottom drawer': his *Musica ricercata*.

> I was twenty-seven years old and lived in Budapest completely isolated from all the ideas, trends, and techniques that had emerged in Western Europe after the war. In 1951 I began to experiment with very simple structures of rhythms and sonorities as if to build up a 'new music' from nothing. I regarded all the music I knew and loved as being, for my purpose, irrelevant. I asked myself: what can I do with a single note? With its octave? With an interval? With two intervals? With certain rhythmic relationships? In this way, several small pieces resulted, mostly for piano. (Ligeti qtd. in Kerékfy 2008: 3–4)

The composer builds eleven 'studies' on sets with an increasing number of pitch classes, meaning that the first movement consists of two pitch classes, the second three, the third four, the next five and so on until, finally, the eleventh has a full twelve-tone aggregate.

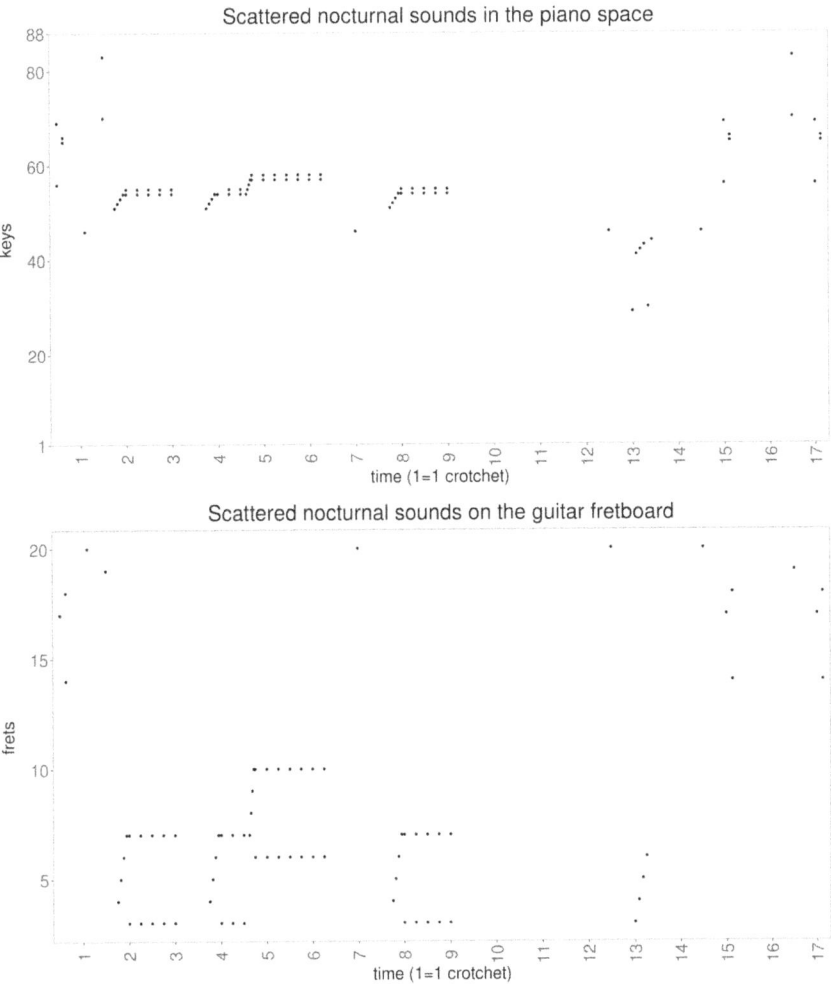

Figure 7.20 Mapping of the nocturnal sounds of Bartók, 'The Night's Music', mm. 9–11.

In my arrangement of selected movements of *Musica ricercata*, in a way I was seeking for the expression of the underpinning compositional concepts through translating and mapping Ligeti's musical 'research' onto the set of new affordances of the Ligeti Guitar, almost as though he was writing for them. In a way, I aimed to translate Ligeti's compositional simplicity into instrumental elements. In this chapter, I will consider two examples, my arrangement of *Musica ricercata* no.1 and no.2.

Figure 7.21 Bartók, 'The Night's Music', mm. 7–9 (transcription by the author).

Musica ricercata no.1., a composition on one note

The first movement of *Musica ricercata* is a composition on one note, A, repeated in all the octave ranges of the piano, which resolves itself to D in the last few bars. While Ligeti works with a very limited pitch content here, he uses a wide range of instrumental accessories. Ligeti explicitly composes with all registers of the piano, but on a conventionally strung and tuned guitar, only three octave spans can be played simultaneously. Combining the single-string capos with

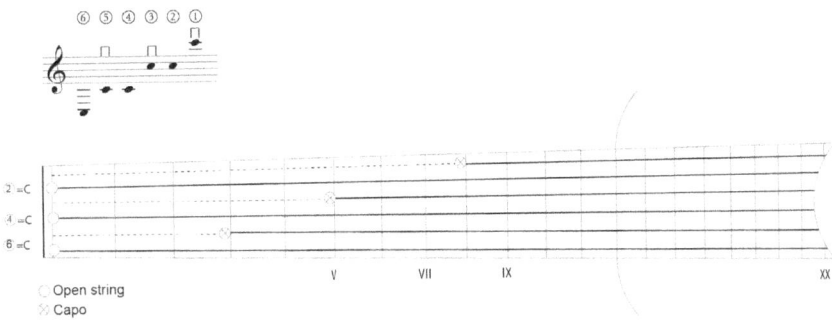

Figure 7.22 Open-string set and fretboard diagram for Ligeti, *Musica ricercata*, I.

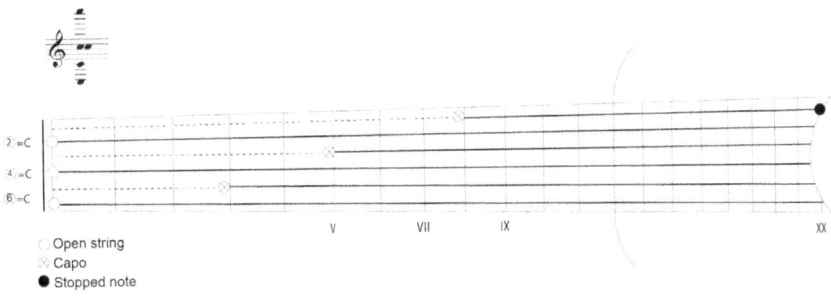

Figure 7.23 Ligeti, *Musica ricercata*, I, opening chord.

scordatura and substituting C for Ligeti's A, I created the set of open strings shown in Figure 7.22. Assuming that the guitar has an additional twentieth fret for string 1, and the sixth string is lowered to C2, it becomes possible to play seven different Cs – six of them simultaneously in four octaves. The diagram in Figure 7.23 shows the opening chord of the piece, which exploits the maximum range given by the alternations.

Now I am going to look at the instrumental *accessoire* and its translation between the piano and the guitar. The piece starts with a *tremolando* effect; on the guitar, I translated it to a *rasgueado* – an equivalent kind of vibration (Figure 7.24).

Later on, Ligeti uses the low register of the piano to create a rhythmical octave ostinato. This rough and suppressed voice becomes a damped *pizzicato* on the guitar's two lowest strings (Figure 7.25).

The piano possesses seven octaves to the guitar's four, but as a counterbalance, the guitar offers a wider scale of timbres and techniques. Not only is there the

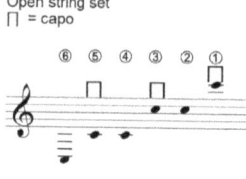

Figure 7.24 Ligeti, *Musica ricercata*, I, mm. 1–4 (transcription by the author).

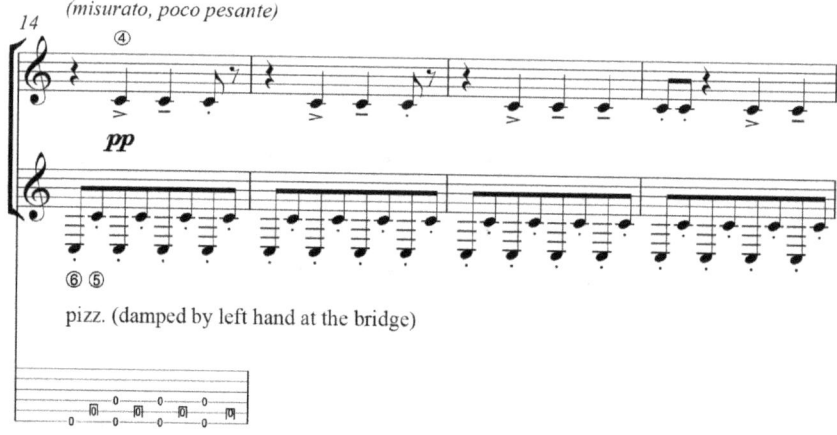

Figure 7.25 Ligeti, *Musica ricercata*, I, mm. 14–17 (transcription by the author).

scale of colours from *tasto* to *ponticello*, as well as *pizzicato* to *metallico*, but there is also the possibility of playing the same pitch on different strings. The set of three capos allows the guitarist to exploit different fingerings, thereby creating *Klangfarbenmelodie* (Figure 7.26) throughout the culmination of the

Figure 7.26 *Klangfarbenmelodie* and different strumming techniques in the guitar arrangement of Ligeti's *Musica ricercata*, I, mm. 56–59 (transcription by the author).

Figure 7.27 Ligeti, *Musica ricercata*, I, mm. 77–80 (transcription by the author).

motivic structure. Step by step, the composition escalates through the increasing frequency of motives, additional octaves, *stringendo* and *crescendo*. While the build-up in the piano version is achieved through an increase in tempo, octave range, volume and density of rhythm, the guitar version can offer a wider technical palette by using *Klangfarbenmelodie*, *campanellas* and different strumming techniques demonstrated in Figure 7.26.

At the climax, the pianist plays *tutta la forza* in four different octaves and accelerates. In the guitar version, six different Cs can be played together in four different octaves, accelerating into a strumming technique (Figure 7.27).

The last four bars of the piece are a resolution to D (to F in the transcription), sporting an extended technique on the piano: by holding the previously played D and depressing A keys without sounding, the natural harmonics ring on the depressed notes. This technique has an equivalent in the guitar arrangement, as the silently depressed notes are held by the capos. Playing the F creates the same sympathetic resonance.

Musica ricercata no.2, 'a knife through Stalin's heart.'

The second movement of *Musica ricercata* is well known from Stanley Kubrick's film *Eyes Wide Shut* (1999), where sections are repeated throughout the most

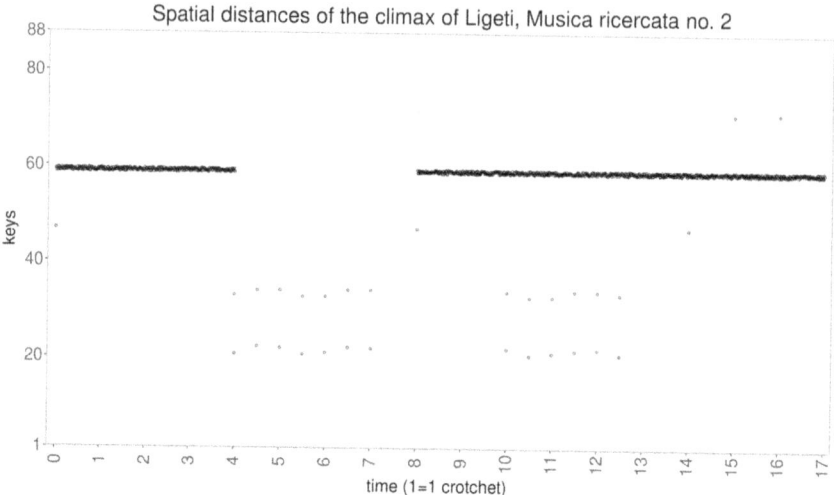

Figure 7.28 Demonstrating the spatial distances (on the piano) of the climax of Ligeti, *Musica ricercata* no.2.

disturbing scenes of the film. The movement consists of three pitch classes: E♯, F♯, and G. The principal theme of the piece, a varied, haunting melody on E♯ and F♯, is dramatically opposed by G. In an interview about the Kubrick film's production, Ligeti revealed that the 'reiterated Gs symbolized for him "a knife through Stalin's heart"' (Steinitz 2003: 57). The principal theme appears in a rather slow funeral type of motif in the middle and low register, while the 'knife' is expressed in a tremolo enforced with occasional octave jumps in the high register. At the climax of the piece, Ligeti juxtaposes the two contrasting themes, well separated in space, having four octaves and a major second between them. By intentionally putting aside the exact pitch classes of the original composition, Figure 7.28 demonstrates the piano mapping of the two contrasting themes.

We can easily answer the question as to whether this texture is idiomatic to the guitar. Obviously, it is impossible. A moving bass line with a high tremolo is only possible when the fretboard interval is no more than five to seven frets, resulting in a distance (with traditional tuning) of maximum of two octaves and a perfect fifth. Looking for the ideal open-string set or scordatura for this movement, my main aim was to stretch the range to the maximum limit of the instrument and to play the high-pitched 'knife' in the left hand as high as possible, independently from the theme. I transposed the piece a perfect fourth higher and created the

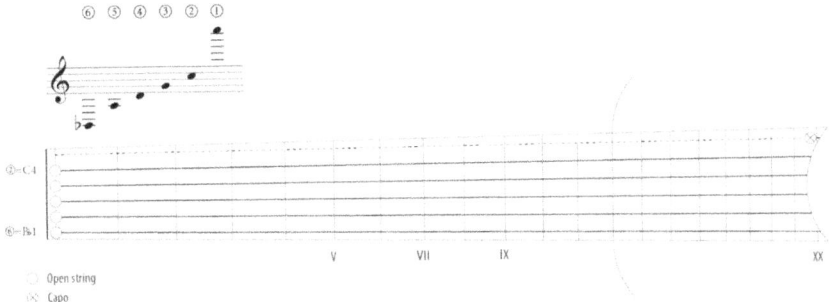

Figure 7.29 Open-string set and fretboard diagram for Ligeti, *Musica ricercata*, II.

open-string set shown in Figure 7.29, with string 6 tuned to B♭2, string 2 tuned to C4, and string 1 pressed down by a single-string capo on fret 20 to sound C6.

Figure 7.30 shows how the principal theme with the dissonant high tremolo becomes a tremolo on the high C, held by the capo at the twentieth fret. In idiomatic terms, I find this solution particularly exciting to perform: moving low bass lines with simultaneous high notes is not generally possible on the guitar. With the magnet capos, the fretboard's affordances are transformed almost to the extreme: the sixth string is tuned down to its practical limit, and the first string is stopped at the highest available fret.

Translating Chopin's pure tone colour

In this last discussed arrangement the magnet capos also serve as a sort of compositional tool. Some of the compositional features of Chopin's *Berceuse* (1844) led me to a freer arrangement approach. This is related to the historical background and the improvisatory features of the piece. The significance of improvisation in Chopin's compositional and performance practice can be discovered in contemporary reports, recounting how the composer 'never played his own compositions twice alike, but varied each according to the mood of the moment' (Hipkins 1937: 7), and passionately describing his concert recitals sometimes included 'improvisation in which he evoked all the sweet and sorrowful voices of the past' (Zaleski 1844). Some Chopin scholars even distinguish a category of his works as 'improvisatory compositions' (Rink 1989). Coming to Chopin's *Berceuse*, there is no doubt that its compositional features connect to keyboard improvisation practices, such as figured bass tradition and forms such as the ground bass or ostinato variation-based passacaglia or

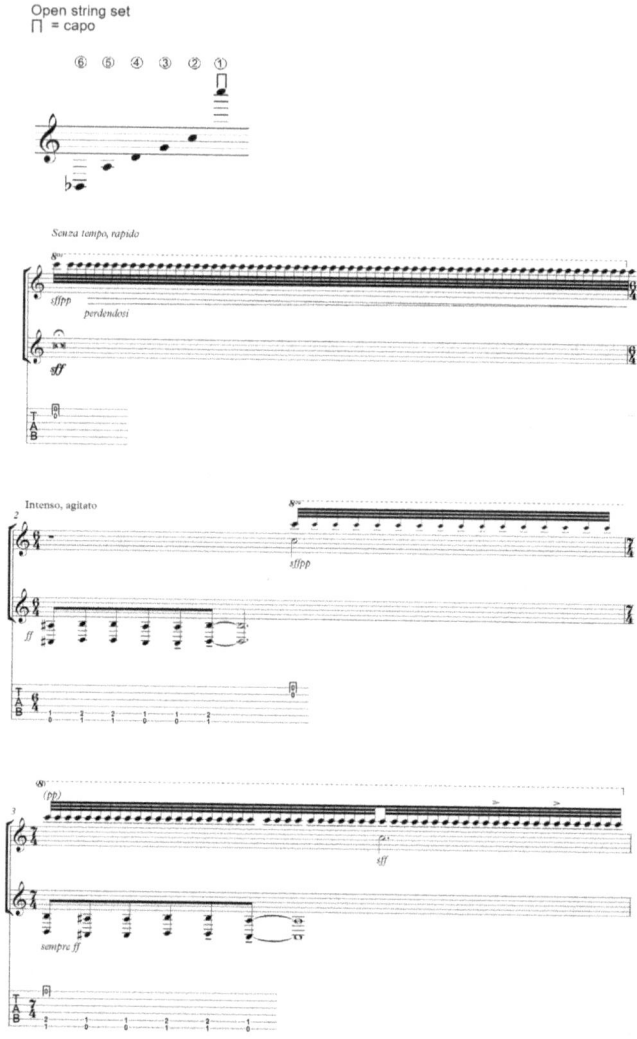

Figure 7.30 Ligeti, *Musica ricercata*, II, mm. 24–26 (transcription by the author).

chaconne. Chopin's piece may be described as an improvisatory flow of variations on a one-bar-long ostinato ground bass encompassing an oscillation between the tonic and its dominant seventh chords. In fact, Chopin first started the piece as a set of variations.[21] Some scholars suggest that *Berceuse* is a notated result of Chopin's various improvisations on the simple one-bar-long ostinato (Grunstein

---

[21] Nowik analysed Chopin's compositional process based on his markings on the sketch, and proved that *Berceuse* was originally structured as variations. Nowik, W., 1988. Fryderyk Chopin's op. 57: from Variantes to Berceuse. *Chopin Studies*, pp.25–40.

2005). Charles Rosen (1995: 395) describes the piece as 'a series of minuscule [right-hand] etudes' independent from the 'monotonous underpinning' basic harmony in the left hand. The earliest account of the performance of the piece appears in the diary entry in 1844 of the Polish poet Józef Bohdan Zaleski (1844), who visited Chopin and listened to *Berceuse* 'not once, but twice', again suggesting the possibility of different improvised versions.

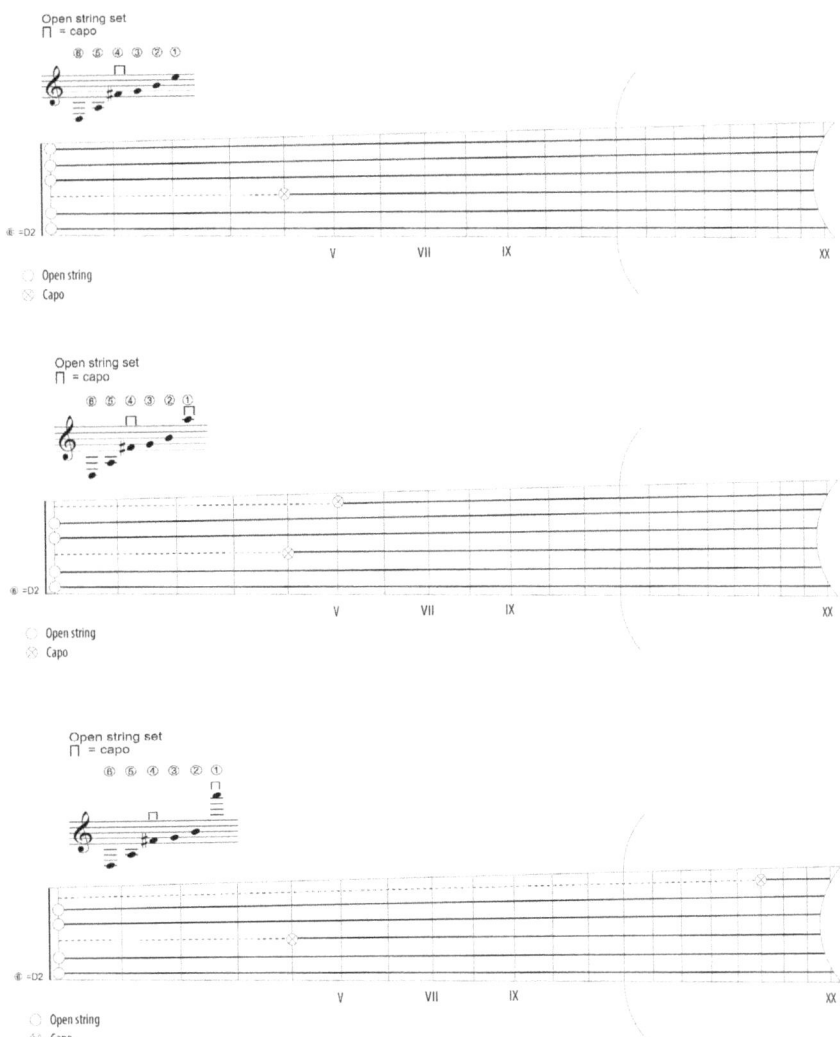

Figure 7.31 Fretboard diagrams of three different open-string sets of the arrangement of Chopin, *Berceuse*.

All this analytic and historical background led me to a free-arrangement approach. In many sections, I literally transcribed Chopin's original material, but I also wanted to create space for guitaristic patterns in other parts. In a way, my attempt was to translate, as Rosen puts it (Rosen 1995: 395), the 'metamorphosis of the finger exercise into a play of sound…, a pure tone color', bringing Chopin's soundworld to the guitar. I transposed the piece a minor step above, from D flat major to a D major. I created an open-string set (Figure 7.31a), which comprises the ostinato ground bass, therefore providing the independence between hands playing 'minuscules etudes' similarly to the original. I later transformed the original open-string set (Figure 7.31b and c) further into two different versions to enable high *campanella* notes used in the different sections of the piece.

The piece starts with an introduction with a melody line, later flourishing into a counterpoint. Figure 7.32 shows the open-string ostinato solution enabled a complex second layer with literal transcription of the counterpoint.

In Figure 7.33, I demonstrate a section that I composed to enable a guitaristic *tremolo* pattern based on the principal theme.

Figure 7.32 Chopin, *Berceuse* mm. 1–9 (transcription by the author).

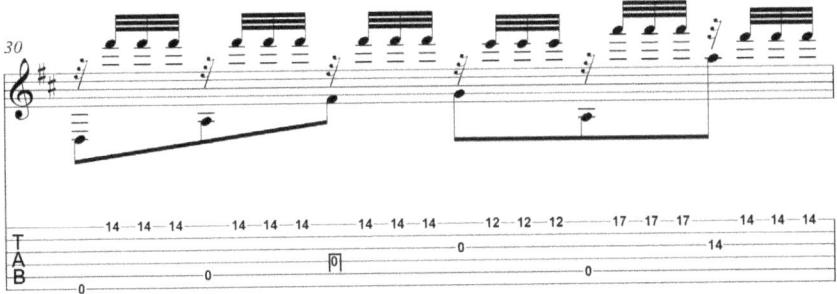

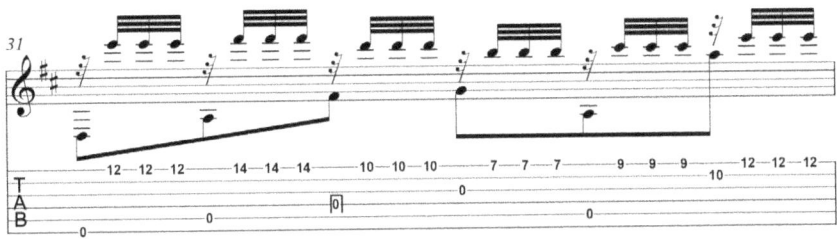

Figure 7.33 Chopin, *Berceuse* mm. 30–31. (transcription by the author).

Figure 7.34 Chopin, *Berceuse* mm. 47–48. (transcription by the author).

Figure 7.34 demonstrates the second open-string set allowing ringing *campanella* notes on A combined with a chromatic progression.

The final section on Figure 7.35 demonstrates the most radical utilization of space with maximalized fret intervals, where the principal theme is appearing

Figure 7.35 Chopin, *Berceuse* mm. 88–89. (transcription by the author).

as a bass line and accompanied by a high tremolando layer on the high A at the fifteenth position of the first string.

New affordances for the composer's mind: Collaboration with David Gorton

I have already explored in length how the transformed instrumental interface of the Ligeti Guitar provided new affordances and enabled idiomatically novel arrangements of piano pieces. As collaboration with composers has always been a prime element of my guitar journey, this innovation also led to new commissions and calls for scores with an international scope.[22] I started to collaborate with David Gorton after our acquaintance at the Doctoral Research Programme at the Royal Academy of Music. Gorton had previously created extensive work in the field of composition and research of radically novel guitar works, including his

---

[22] Together with Contemporary Music Center Ireland and Budapest Music Center we released a highly successful 'call for scores' in 2019, resulting in more than thirty submitted pieces. Due to the covid crisis however, the premieres only started to take place in 2022 in the framework of *Ulysses Journey* in Ireland, Hungary and France.

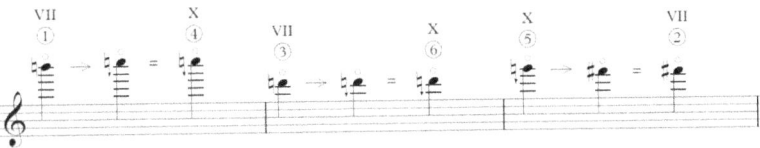

The following diagram represents the final tuning.

Figure 7.36 Microtonal tuning of D. Gorton's *Six Miniatures*. © Verlag Neue Musik, Berlin.

Forlorn Hope[23] (2011) composed for guitarist Stefan Östersjö, deploying a microtonally tuned eleven-string alto guitar. Gorton was very keen to experiment with the new instrumental features through the magnet capos and later the Ligeti Guitar, as a result of our collaboration, he composed the *Six Miniatures*[24] in 2021, published by Verlag Neue Musik. I interviewed David about the compositional process, and in the following section I aim to demonstrate the interrelation of the expanded instrumental affordances and composition. David decided to write a 'proof of concept' (Gorton 2022)[25] for the Ligeti Guitar, so that the patterns and contexts are actually impossible on a standard six-string guitar without the magnet capo system. He combined a microtonal scordatura with different open-string sets in each of the six movements. In Figure 7.36 you can see the tuning instructions and the resulted scordatura.

The scordatura is based on 'sixth or third tone alterations, which are found in relationship to the seventh harmonic sounds of another string'. So, the magnet capos provide an easy way to create a 'lot of different types of microtonal scordatura very quickly in the same piece' through moving the capos, in other words, an 'alternating up and down pattern of six tone alterations' (Gorton 2022).

In Figure 7.37 we can see the six different open-string sets of the *Miniatures*.

In the first movement (Figure 7.38) Gorton was experimenting with creating different *impossible* 'chord shapes defined by capos' and alternated by the left hand. The material is static as each section varies the resulting chord shapes, and throughout we experience beautiful new worlds of 'internal resonance'.

---

[23] Gorton ([2011] 2018).
[24] David Gorton, *Six Miniatures* Verlag Neue Musik 2021.
[25] The following quotations are from a personal interview with David Gorton carried out on 23 March 2022.

144   21st Century Guitar

Figure 7.37 Open-string sets of Gorton, *Six Miniatures*. © Verlag Neue Musik, Berlin.

Figure 7.38 Gorton, *Six Miniatures* I. mm. 1–3. © Verlag Neue Musik, Berlin.

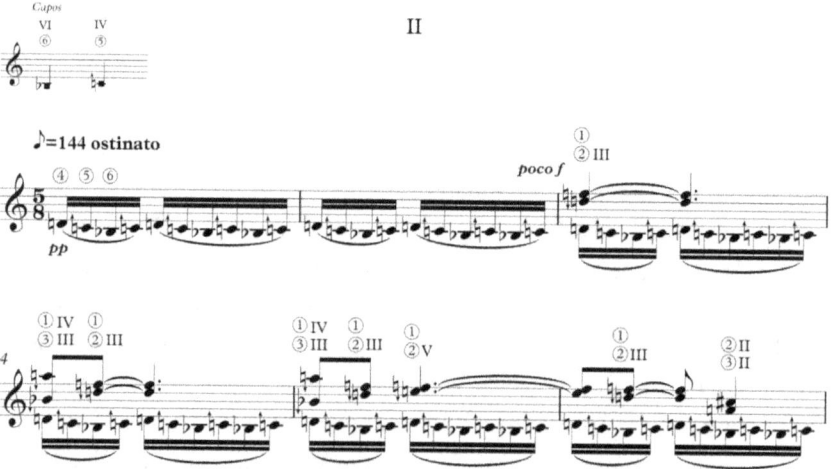

Figure 7.39 Gorton, *Six Miniatures* II. mm. 1–6. © Verlag Neue Musik, Berlin.

For the second movement (Figure 7.39) Gorton creates an ostinato incorporated in the open-string set. As the ostinatos are provided as open strings and the left hand is free, Gorton adds another *independent* layer. It creates counterpoint and the two worlds blend in a world of 'extended harmony'. However, the guitar as a compositional tool is seen here as a space separated

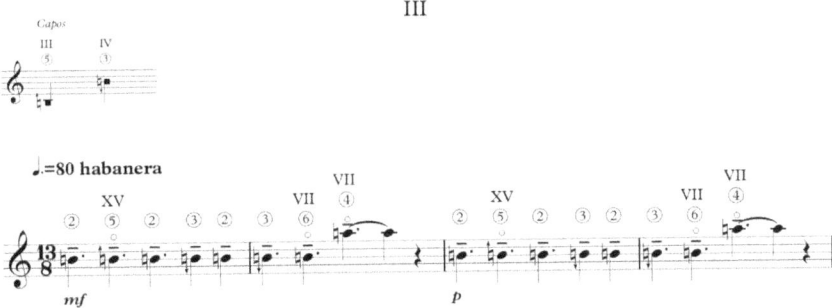

Figure 7.40 Gorton, *Six Miniatures* III. mm. 1–4. © Verlag Neue Musik, Berlin.

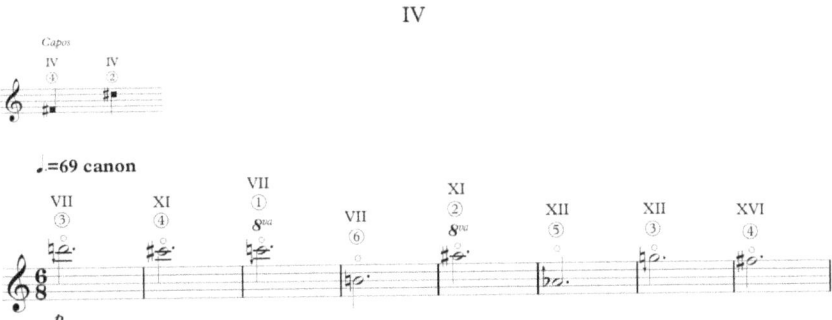

Figure 7.41 Gorton, *Six Miniatures* IV. mm. 1–8. © Verlag Neue Musik, Berlin.

in two: the bass 'ostinato' 6–4 strings with different string lengths and the 1–3 strings enabling a melodic second layer.

In the third movement (Figure 7.40) we listen to many differently tuned Bs across all the strings. The delicacy of all the timbres of this dense microtonal palette is quite extraordinary for the guitar.

For the fourth movement (Figure 7.41) Gorton uses the capos to create a setting that enables a 'weird kind of chromatically descending [harmonic] scale'. He describes a lengthy search for the ideal capo setting: '[it] took me ages to find the capo position that would then allow me, not all, but almost all of the semitones, even if they're a bit sharp or flat' (Gorton 2022).

Movement five comprises (Figure 7.42) clashes of differently tuned Gs and G♯s.

In the sixth movement (Figure 7.43) Gorton creates a reflection of an image of a conventional guitar soundscape through repeated arpeggios. The end of the movement resolves in the arpeggiated open-string set.

Figure 7.42 Gorton, *Six Miniatures* V. mm. 36–38. © Verlag Neue Musik, Berlin.

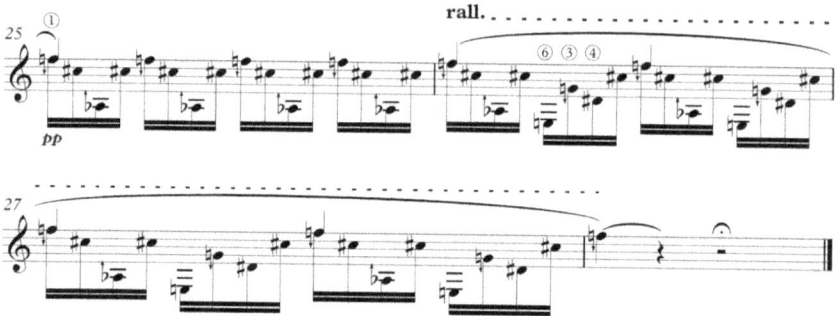

Figure 7.43 Gorton, *Six Miniatures* VI. mm. 25–28. © Verlag Neue Musik, Berlin.

Gorton composed the piece through experimenting on a guitar; however, he did not have magnet capos to work with. When referring to chords, he often describes 'finding them' on the guitar, although we can see that his composition is, in many ways, quite conceptual. Thus, the process interestingly combines improvisation and imagination. When I asked about the balance between the two, he described it as following:

> You've used this word affordances. And that's very interesting, because I often work out what may or may not be practically possible from an unusual setup, and that suggests material, and then ends up being refined, or selected or deselected depending on what I like to sound or what I'm interested in, but it's a very powerful way of generating ideas; the kind of instrumental setup, the practicalities of it, the haptic tactile quality of it, ends up suggesting ideas to me. (Gorton 2022)

Furthermore, we discussed the challenges and limitations of working with the Ligeti Guitar:

> It felt like the instrument was more locked down. Once you put it in a mode, once you put it into; 'okay, now we're doing this', it felt like it had locked it into a sort of state, a kind of type that then had its own quite wonderful and beautiful

affordances to explore as a composer. But it, it also felt like, I mean, maybe this isn't a reality, but in my mind, it felt like they were obstacles for the left hand. (Gorton 2022)

Although the capos liberate the instrument in a way, such as creating bridges between notes far away from each other on the fretboard, the higher fret the magnet capo is, the more string loss happens on the above part of the string. In a way the more radical the capo setting is, it results in locking the guitar down more, losing longer bits of the string. However, the fact that the capos can be moved very fast for Gorton means 'that it that makes it incredibly versatile, and with all these extra potentials and all these things that a guitar can't do and you can think harmonically, in these weird spacings' (Gorton 2022).

Gorton also relates this ambiguity of new affordances and the 'locked down' modes problem by choosing the form of his piece:

> that's one reason why I settled on these miniatures. Because I didn't want it to get to the point where that the material is so exhausted, [so I chose a form] very short: Bang, you've done it. Okay. Now, let's have the next one. (Gorton 2022)

The idea of locking musical sections into different instrumental modes is of course not extraordinary, we see something similar with harp pedals, and Gorton connects it to other examples such as

> putting a mute on and off or in and out. If you're taking a violin mute off or if you're a trombone player, putting a mute in. These are all things that are possible to do, but they need to be set up in a controlled way. (Gorton 2022)

Conclusion: Liberate or limitate?

In this chapter, I hoped to demonstrate how the transformed guitar space of the Ligeti Guitar expanded the idiomatic boundaries of the six-string 'classical' guitar in the 21st century. With the four arrangements of Bartók, Ligeti and Chopin's piano music and Gorton's composition, I aimed to provide, by using Gorton's words, a 'proof of concept'. We have seen that with the magnet capo system, we gained unlimited fret intervals, and in a way a kind of independence between layers, in other words, a connection between unconnected parts of the guitar space. For the theoretic mind, the described new affordances may suggest a very versatile, in a way, 'open' guitar idiom. However, as Gorton very precisely describes it, the system not only liberates the instrument but at the same time locks it down into different *modes*. While it provides a fertile world for conceptual compositional processes, it may also very rigidly enforce its soundscape. While in a certain arrangement, it creates a sense of 'everything possible' and provides great adaptability to compositional features. In other cases, the system is incapable of adjusting to the flow of transformation throughout a piece. When working with pitch sets, ostinatos, pedal notes and so on, the system is greatly adjustable but it proves to be rigid with compositions with less static tonal/pitch centre. In a way, I am looking at a system that prioritizes the role of open strings and that is ideal for composition with strong pitch centres or centre motifs. Understanding the potential of the Ligeti Guitar happens through experimenting with it. I also aim to expand the system to different types of guitars and combine it with other tools of music technology, such as the augmentation of loop pedals. Going back to the starting quote of this chapter, in the journey of the Ligeti Guitar, I see my position similar to the 'child at the piano searching for a chord never previously heard. This chord, however, was always there. . . . [T]he new is the longing for the new, not the new itself' (Adorno 1997: 32).

References

Adorno, T.W. (1997), *Aesthetic Theory*, London: Continuum.
Anderson, J. (2016), Interview, Available online: https://youtu.be/Ic4uyYNrbcY (accessed 25 April 2022).
Bartók, P. (2002), *My Father*, Homosassa, FL: Bartók Records.
Berlioz, H. (1948), *Treatise on Instrumentation*, T. Front (trans.), New York: Edwin F. Kalmus.
Boulez, P. (1976), *Conversations with Célestin Deliège*, London: Eulenburg.
Brouwer, L. (2018), 'Leo Brouwer Teaches "Estudios Sencillos"', *YouTube, Tonebase Guitar*, Available online: https://youtu.be/2IWN8NWflZA (accessed 25 April 2022).
Chang, H., F. Ngunjiri and K.A.C. Hernandez (2013), *Collaborative Autoethnography*, 1st ed., New York: Routledge.
Clarke, E. F., M. Doffman, D. Gorton and S. Östersjö (2017), 'Fluid Practices, Solid Roles? The Evolution of *Forlorn Hope*', in E.F. Clarke and M. Doffman (eds), *Distributed Creativity: Collaboration and Improvisation in Contemporary Music*, 1–22, Oxford: Oxford University Press.
Davies, C.A. (2007), *Reflexive Ethnography: A Guide to Researching Selves and Others*, 2nd ed., London: Routledge.

De Souza, J. (2017), *Music at Hand: Instruments, Bodies, and Cognition*, Oxford Studies in Music Theory, New York: Oxford University Press.

De Souza, J. (2018), 'Fretboard Transformations', *Journal of Music Theory*, 62 (1): 1–39.

De Souza, J. (2021), 'Guitar Thinking', *Soundboard Scholar*, 7 (1): 1–23, https://digitalcommons.du.edu/sbs/vol7/iss1/1/ (accessed 5 Sep 2022).

Galbraith, P. (2018), Interview, Available online: https://clevelandclassical.com/galbraith-returns-with-extra-strings-to-cleveland-classical-guitar-society/ (accessed 25 April 2022).

Gibson, J.J. (1966), *The Senses Considered as Perceptual Systems*, Boston, MA: Houghton Mifflin.

Gibson, J.J. (1977), 'The Theory of Affordances', in R. Shaw and J. Bransford (eds), *Perceiving, Acting, and Knowing: Toward an Ecological Psychology*, 67–82, Hillsdale, NJ: Lawrence Erlbaum Associates.

Gibson, J.J. (1979), *The Ecological Approach to Visual Perception*, Hillsdale, Boston, MA: Houghton Mifflin.

Gorton, D., S. Shaw-Miller and N. Heyde (2013), 'Instrumental Choreography: Gesture and Performance in Gorton's Capriccio for Solo Cello', in M. Castellengo and H. Genevois (eds), *La musique et ses instruments*, 485–96, Sampzon: Editions Delatour France.

Grunstein, S. (2005), *Improvisatory, Compositional and Performance Issues in Chopin's Berceuse, Op. 57*, Doctoral diss., City University of New York.

Hajdu, A. (2008), 'A Galaxy Called 'Mikrokosmos' – A Composer's View', *Tempo*, 62 (243): 16–35.

Hipkins, E.J., (1937), 'How Chopin Played', in E.J. Hipkins (ed.), *Contemporary Impressions Collected from the Diaries and Notebooks of the Late A.J. Hipkins*, London: J.M. Dent & Sons.

Hoppstock, T. (2021), A personal interview with K. Koltai carried out on 16 November.

Huron, D. and J. Berec (2009), 'Characterizing Idiomatic Organization in Music: A Theory and Case Study of Musical Affordances', *Empirical Musicology Review*, 4 (3): 103–22.

Kazandjian, F. (1992), *The Concept and Development of the Yepes Ten-String Guitar: A Preliminary Investigation*, Master's thesis, University of Cape Town.

Kirsh, D. (2013), 'Embodied Cognition and the Magical Future of Interaction Design', *ACM Transactions on Computer-Human Interaction*, 20 (1): 1–10.

Kerékfy, M. (2008), 'A "New Music" from Nothing': György Ligeti's Musica Ricercata', *Studia Musicologica*, 49 (3–4): 208.

Koltai, K. (2020), 'Breaking the Matrix: Transcribing Bartók and Ligeti for the Guitar Using a New Capo System', *Soundboard Scholar*, 6 (1), Available online: https://digitalcommons.du.edu/sbs/vol6/iss1/6.

Koozin, T. (2011), 'Guitar Voicing in Pop-Rock Music: A Performance-Based Analytical Approach', *Music Theory Online*, 17, Available online: www.mtosmt.org/issues/mto.11.17.3/mto.11.17.3.koozin.html.

Kurtág, Gy. (2021), Personal communication with K. Koltai, 19 August.
Leathwood, J. (2020), Personal communication with DeSousa, 26 October.
Lewin, D. (1987), *Generalized Musical Intervals and Transformations*, New Haven, CT: Yale University Press.
Merleau-Ponty, M. (2012), *Phenomenology of Perception*, trans. Donald A. Landes, London: Routledge.
Quinn, I. and C.W. White (2017), 'Corpus-derived key Profiles Are Not Transpositionally Equivalent', *Music Perception: An Interdisciplinary Journal*, 34 (5): 531–40.
Rehding, A. (2016), 'Instruments of Music Theory', *Music Theory Online*, 22 (4), Available online: http://mtosmt.org/issues/mto.16.22.4/mto.16.22.4.rehding.html.
Rink, J. (1989), *The Evolution of Chopin's "structural style" and its Relation to Improvisation*, Doctoral thesis, University of Cambridge.
Rosen, C. (1995), *The Romantic Generation*, Cambridge, MA: Harvard University Press.
Schiff, A. Available online: https://youtu.be/Ibbkz2FxI74 (accessed 23 April 2022).
Schneider, D.E. (2006), *Bartók, Hungary, and the Renewal of Tradition: Case Studies in the Intersection of Modernity and Nationality*, Berkeley: University of California Press.
Shea, N. (2020), *Ecological Models of Musical Structure in Pop-Rock, 1950–2019*, PhD diss., Ohio State University, Available online: https://search.proquest.com/docview/2489204736.
Steinitz, R. (2003), *György Ligeti: Music of the Imagination*, London: Faber & Faber.
Tallián, T. (1981), *Béla Bartók: The Man and His Work*, trans. Gy. Gulyás, Budapest: Corvina Kiado.
Treitler, L. (1997), 'Language and the Interpretation of Music', in, J. Robinson (ed.), *Music and Meaning*, 23–56, Ithaca, NY: Cornell University Press.
Tresch, J. and E.I. Dolan (2013), 'Toward a New Organology: Instruments of Music and Science: Music, Sound, and the Laboratory from 1750–1980', *Osiris*, 28 (1): 278–98.
Varga, B.A. (ed.) (2009), *György Kurtág: Three Interviews and Ligeti Homages*, Rochester: University of Rochester Press.
Vincens, G.C.L. (2009), *The Arrangements of Roland Dyens and Sergio Assad: Innovations in Adapting Jazz Standards and Jazz-Influenced Popular Works to the Solo Classical Guitar*, Doctoral diss., The University of Arizona.
Zaleski, B. (February 2,1844), 'From the Personal Diary of the Polish Poet Bohdan Zaleski (1 8 0 2 8 6)', qtd. in G. Anche (ed.), *Dans lesouvenir de Frederic Chopin*, 24–5, Paris: Mercure de France.
Zbikowski, L.M. (2017), *Foundations of Musical Grammar*, New York: Oxford University Press.

Media references

Bartok, B. (1926), [Composition] *Im Freien* [Out of Doors], Universal Edition, Vienna.

Brouwer, L. (1972), [Composition] *Estudios sencillos*, Eschig, Paris.
Galbraith, P. (2015), 'Paul Galbraith | Adagio Sonata K570 - Mozart | Allemande', YouTube, produced by GuitarCoop. 6 April 2017. https://www.youtube.com/watch?v=hqS66sXf1Bo&ab_channel=GuitarCoop (accessed 19 July 2022).
Gorton, D. ([2011] 2018), [Composition] *Forlorn Hope*, Verlag Neue Musik, Berlin.
Gorton, D. (2021), [Composition] *Six Miniatures*, Verlag Neue Musik, Berlin.
Gorton, D. (2022), A personal interview with K. Koltai carried out on 23 March.
Kurtág, Gy. (1989), [Composition] *Grabstein für Stephan*, op. 15/c, Editio Musica Budapest, Budapest.
Ligeti, Gy. ([1951–53] 1995), [Composition] *Musica ricercata*, Schott, Mainz.
Miró, J. (1924), [Painting] *Catalan Peasant with a Guitar*, Museo Nacional Thyssen-Bornemisza, Madrid.
Quartet, Kreutzer (2017), [Film] *Choreography: The Soundtrack*, Metier, Barnsley.
Sagreras, J.S. (1954), [Composition] *El Colibri*, Ricordi Americana, Buenos Aires.
Yepes, N. (1976), 'Narciso Yepes plays his composition on "Two Catalan Folksongs" | 10-string guitar | restored'. YouTube, uploaded by Viktor van Niekerk, 26 Nov 2021. https://www.youtube.com/watch?v=inepbELIVaE&ab_channel=ViktorvanNiekerk%7C10-stringguitar (accessed 19 July 2022).

8

Grains, glitches and infinite space

Guitar effects pedals, digitization and textural guitar aesthetics

Robert Strachan

This chapter is concerned with developments in the guitar effects pedal since the turn of the millennium. In particular, it examines how technological, cultural and aesthetic convergency during this period has led to the emergence of a distinct set of new sonic trajectories for the guitar in a distinct but significant niche in current guitar aesthetics. At the heart of these developments has been the latter stages of digitization which has simultaneously afforded a shift in the technological components of guitar pedals, the incorporation of digital aesthetics within guitar cultures and a freeing up of technical information (a central characteristic of digital culture) which has led to the democratization of pedal making and an experimentation afforded by 'free innovation' (Von Hippel 2017). The chapter traces how these elements of digitization intersect, with a specific focus on three digitally native types of time-based audio processing: so-called 'glitch' effects, granular delays and digital reverberation effects (see Figure 8.1.). It first outlines the parallel emergence of what has become known as the boutique effects pedal industry and changes in audio-focused digital signal processing (DSP) technology and design before placing these developments in the context of creative guitar practices in alternative rock and ambient/experimental music.

As such, the chapter also seeks to open up a broader discussion around historical and analytical approaches to the guitar. First, foregrounding the effects pedal goes towards a perspective which considers the guitar as part of a socio-technical assemblage in which creativity is a process in which the technological, social and individual all have agency. Second, this focus allows for the reading

Figure 8.1 Time-based DSP and glitch effects pedals. Clockwise: MWFX Judder Mk I, MWFX Judder Mk II, Electro-Harmonix Freeze, MASF Possessed, Strymon Night Sky, Author's own collection.

of the electric guitar as a textural instrument in whose aesthetics and creative practices are bound up with the technological manipulation of the instrument's resonances through the signal chain. I am using textural as a term as opposed to timbral as I want to foreground and give agency to the differing elements of the signal chain in the sounding process. It is not just the timbre of the instrument itself that is crucial here, neither are effects merely the 'staging' of a specific musical voice. Rather, the effects pedal is a sounding agent in itself and has the ability to affect all of the parameters (such as timbre, melody, harmony and time) that we find musically meaningful. Clearly, this is done in combination with the sounding properties of the instrument itself and of course the choices made by musicians. Thus, understanding this combination as textural considers these differing sounding agents in combination in a nonlinear and non-hierarchal way. This agency is apparent in the way in which musicians work with the particular sonic properties of audio effects as a key part of the creative process. Indeed, within the genre cultures discussed towards the end of the chapter, technique and musical structure cannot be separated from the effects pedal as a mediating technology.

Bruno Latour's (2005) formulation of actor network theory (ANT) suggests human and non-human agents (people, machinery, technologies and objects) combine to make achievable what each could not accomplish individually. For Latour, taking all these elements into account avoids a reductionist tendency within 'sociologism and technologism' by acknowledging that we are never just faced with 'objects or social relations, we are faced with chains which are associations of humans . . . and non-humans' adding that 'no one has ever seen a social [or technical] relation by itself' (Latour 1991: 110). As such, ANT has provided a useful framework for exploring music technology. As Nick Prior notes ANT 'alerts us to how the technical and the social are inextricably linked, in turn sensitizing us to the fact that instruments and associated devices are not passive intermediaries but active mediators' (Prior 2008: 315). This theoretical framing of dispersed agency is crucial for understanding both the historical trajectory of the effects pedal and in beginning to unpack their importance for contemporary creative guitar practices.

The effects pedal industry

Although audio effects had existed in some form since the 1940s and had been subject to several key innovations (such as the introduction of distortion, fuzz and overdrive pedals) in the 1960s, the market was dominated by a few small companies serving national markets and a small number of releases from established guitar companies (such as Gibson's Maestro Fuzz, Fender's standalone reverb units). From the 1970s a broader consumer market had been established by large Japanese companies and US start-ups. The introduction of Philips Research Lab's Bucket Brigade Chip in 1969 allowed these companies to add time-based and modulation effects such as delay, reverb, chorus, phase and flange into the smaller pedal format in addition to the distortion-based effects.[1] In the early 1970s Electro-Harmonix and MXR became the main players in the US market through the introduction of pedals which were widely adopted by well-known guitarists. Both had started as micro-businesses which quickly expanded through distribution deals with larger instrument manufacturers. In Japan Ibanez and BOSS (both part of larger technology corporations: Hoshino Gakki and Roland, respectively) both released a range of compact effects pedals in 1977. Both manufacturers benefit from significant research and development

---

[1] Previously, reverb and echo units had been relatively large and cumbersome as they needed to accommodate analogue tape loops or reverberation tanks.

budgets, access to investment in large-scale production and an artificially low valuation of the yen in the late 1970s and 1980s (Music Trades 2007), enabling them to reach a broad consumer market of international amateur and professional players. The BOSS range, in particular, became hugely successful, selling tens of millions of units over the coming decades. By the mid-1980s both EHX and MXR's pedal operations were essentially overtaken by the Japanese manufacturers (Roland and Ibanez were followed into the market by companies such as Yamaha, Aria, Guyatone, Pearl and Maxon) who had the economies of scale that the US companies could not compete against and both companies ceased pedal building to concentrate on other products. As Glukin (2020) notes, up until the 1990s the market was dominated by these big players 'plus a handful of outlier operations'.

Kim Bjorn and Scott Harper (2020: 362) note, the early 1990s saw a swing back towards analogue effects in the light of aesthetic shifts afforded by the popularity of grunge and indie rock in which older, non-digital gear became desirable. Trevor Pinch and David Reinecke's (2009) ethnographic study on the use of vintage equipment concludes that this type of 'technostalgia' is, rather than being purely backwards looking, serves multiple purposes for musicians, to achieve classic sounds but also in the creation of new sonic combinations and giving tactile engagement with sound in a way in which digital equipment could not. As a result of these shifts in guitar culture, the prices of vintage analogue pedals began to rise and new niche entrants to the market began to replicate well-known analogue effects and develop new circuits. The success of pedals now considered classic such as the Klon Centaur and the ZVex Fuzz Factory in the mid-1990s (see also interview with Nels Cline in this volume, Chapter 9) saw the visibility of boutique pedals rise and facilitated by several factors relating to digitization discussed as follows, the immediate period after the millennium saw a huge expansion of boutique companies with countless new startup businesses. The emergence of boutique companies provided competition which has clearly stimulated the market. The effects pedal market had increased by 56 per cent over a ten-year period from the mid-2000s in which the rest of the fretted instrument market had either stagnated or declined (NAMM 2016: 13). The sector continued to grow in the 2010s with an overall 88 per cent increase over the course of the decade (NAMM 2016: 13). While established companies such as the revived EHX, MXR and BOSS remain the top-selling brands, established boutique sellers can sell significant amounts of units (JHS, e.g. produced 100,000 pedals in 2020 see Roeder 2021) and the market has a significant long tail which sustains thousands of businesses of varying sizes.

Although the explosion in boutique pedals was initially driven by a rediscovery of analogue technologies, it was fuelled by a number of significant developments in digital technologies. First, the democratization of information facilitated through internet culture allowed many more hobbyists and small businesses to enter the market. Second, developments in computer hardware such as printed circuit boards (PCBs), DSP chips and their programming interfaces allowed for increased participation and experimentation with effects pedals than was hitherto possible. Third, there was the enculturation of particular signature sounds within popular music culture more broadly which became influential on the types of audio effects that pedal makers were trying to create.

The emergence of the 'boutique' pedal market can thus be understood as having two main strands. A major element of the trend has been through smaller manufacturers (usually small traders of micro-businesses) making hand-wired pedals that make effects within the existing set of classic effect types. The USP of these pedals is generally that they make small adjustments in familiar circuits in pursuit of 'tone' or resurrect a discontinued or hard-to-find circuit. This type of effect often uses premium components such as classic, new old stock (NOS) and rare transistors. The second strain in the boutique market is manufacturers who are engaged in producing more experimental circuits, often through the programming of specific audio-focused microchips in order to create more digitally coded sonic effects.

Democratization

Democratization has been a key feature of the way in which the various stages of digitization have impacted on music-making cultures (Théberge 1997; Ryan and Hughes 2006; Strachan 2017a), and a major factor in both these strands of the boutique explosion was a democratization of information about technology. In a large part, this was the expansion of the tradition of tinkering within guitar cultures (see Waksman 2004) and experiments with amateur electronics that had been part of the development of pedals throughout their history. DIY pedal builds had always existed for the engineering-minded musician but the information was limited to general hobbyist publications (Chris Carter of Throbbing Gristle for instance, famously created the band's signature Gristelizer pedal from a schematic in Practical Electronics in the late 1970s) or was tacitly acquired from a variety of electronic engineering sources. In addition, components would have to be obtained either from generic electrical retailers or mail order services aimed at hobbyist electronic engineers making some specialist components difficult to obtain (see for example Anderson 1975: 29). Another significant source of information was Anderson's *Electronic Projects for Musicians*, a how-to guide which clearly introduced elements of the theory of electronic engineering which were applied in a series of pedal projects. While as Tzvi Gluckin (2020) notes the book would be an influence on many early DIY pedal builders, any difficulties encountered in creating a circuit often led to dead ends. The 1990s saw this information opening up with initially Usenet groups, message boards and later, multiple forums including diystompboxes.com and freestompboxes.org which provided information and support (ibid.). Users not only had free access to a much larger number of schematics and build instructions but also could now receive instantaneous feedback as they were undertaking a project. These online spaces functioned as virtual communities of practice (Wenger 1998) or 'knowledge communities' (Salavuo 2006) in which learning is a social process in which engaged parties collectively develop solutions to given problems and progress their individual and collective knowledge. It is also significant that this democratization of knowledge coincided with early manifestations of the platform economy. By the late 1990s, eBay had become widely used in specialist interest and hobbyist communities[2] and provided a key market for the nascent boutique industry, providing many builders with the jumping-off point for going full-time (Gluckin 2020).

Such spaces became a key way in which technical knowledge is transmitted but they also allowed for major innovations in terms of the scope of what effects pedals could do. The culture of exploration, allied with low-outlay access to niche markets, allowed for the more left-field makers to experiment beyond the established classic effects. Mellis et al. (2016) point to an increased accessibility to information and construction with regard to the creation of electronic devices more generally. Following Neil Gershenfeld (2007) they refer to amateur engagement with the design of PCBs as 'personal fabrication'. In an empirical workshop-based study they identify that amateurs even 'in a world full of mass-produced electronic devices' (2016: 1279), clearly see a role for personal

---

[2] Indeed, the idea of eBay as a hobbyist company was central to the company's early branding strategy with a false story about eBay starting as a way for the founder's fiancé to trade Pez dispensers (Berkun 2010: 6).

fabrication in the creation of products that otherwise would not exist. For many amateur pedal makers, the push towards innovation is seen as a creative end in itself. Eric Von Hippel (2017) points to the rise of various types of maker culture and the dissemination of information across digital platforms as 'free innovation'. While some boutique manufacturers were established by professionals who had gained experience in larger companies before starting their own operations (Strymon for instance, was founded by ex-Alesis and Line 6 personnel),[3] most of the experimental digital pedal manufacturers started producing through this type of personal fabrication, some maintaining a very small production schedule while others mutated into full-time micro-businesses. Others brought knowledge from non-music related fields such as programming and electrical engineering which was applied in the search for new effects.

Printed circuit boards

The boutique pedal scene also benefitted from the rise of mass customization, a business strategy facilitated by advances in computer technologies 'that aims to provide customers with individualized products and services at near mass production efficiency' by merging craft and mass-production techniques (Blecker and Abdelkafi 2006: 2). In practice, this means that individuals and small businesses can avail of mass-production techniques by outsourcing the production of their product designs to larger specialist manufacturing companies. Developments in the 1990s saw significant advancements in computer-aided design (CAD) of schematics for PCBs and standardization of the file format outputs from such design tools which are utilized in the physical production of PCBs. This meant that PCBs could be easily made by third-party manufacturers specializing in small runs according to the design specifications of individuals and small-scale manufacturers. In addition, schematics can be shared with interested parties through online channels along with support through specialist forums before manufacture. As Anderson reflects:

> It's not hard to get circuit boards made [now] . . . You can get a couple hundred made in India or China for pretty cheap and they're not big to ship or anything. [It used to be] more complicated, because the circuit boards had to all be laid out by hand using tap and dots and things like that, and measuring them was

[3] See C (2020).

difficult. Nowadays, you can whip the stuff off on computers in a few minutes and send it off to get a bunch made. (qtd. in Gluckin 2020)

Being able to design and produce short-run circuit boards for pedals means that lone DIY pedal makers/hobbyists/tech communities/forums working with DSP such as Hexe, Montreal Assembly, MWFX, MASF and Sonic Crayon produced quite sonically radical time-based textural pedals in comparison with the traditional space/modulation/fuzz effects which had hitherto dominated the market. Without the need for investment, research and development from larger instrument manufacturers looking for a guaranteed market these sole producers were able to produce pedals which were experimental and esoteric, producing effects which sit uncomfortably with the mainstream of guitar playing styles. Hence practices of free innovation are central to the way in which these pedals developed. As Von Hippel notes, the self-rewarding nature of free innovation 'does not require compensated transactions' to reward the often amateur or part-time engineers for the money and labour they invest in developing new trajectories in technology and that 'free innovation therefore differs fundamentally from producer innovation, which has compensated transactions at its very core' (2017: 3).

These initial pedals were (and continue) to be produced in very small batches when and as the makers have the finances and time to produce a run of pedals. The economies of scale of this style of cottage production mean that the pedals themselves are sometimes quite rare and become highly valued albeit to a very small niche market. The pedals became valued for the individuality of the tone and some became very difficult to obtain. Even now most of these producers operate a waiting list for the production of their pedals or are even elusive about the dates of production and release limited runs online which sell out almost immediately. This has led to the fetishization of these pedals as cult items and early additions of pedals such as the sonic crayon Nautilus or the MWFX Judder Mark I sell for up to £700 in the used market through sites such as eBay and Reverb.com.

Integrated circuits

Another factor in the rise of more experimental effects was that the mid-2000s saw the release of a number of new microchips (or integrated circuits – ICs) specifically devised for audio processing which could be programmed by third-party engineers. In 2005 the US manufacturer Analog Devices (AD) had refined the handling of analogue audio in their DSP technology so that smaller and more powerful chips could process audio without interference to the signal; 'a problem that had plagued the audio industry and prevented major progress since the '90s' (C 2020). While this meant that AD's third-generation SHARC chip was targeted at affordable consumer focused audio technologies such as home theatre, external computer audio and hi-fi (Palenchar 2003,10, Business Wire 2005) it was also adaptable and small enough to be used in effects pedals. SHARC and other AD chips (such as Blackfin and Sigma) were both very powerful and adaptable opening up new programming possibilities. Pete Celi, co-founder and chief programmer of the high-end digital effects brand Strymon, highlights how, given the necessary programming knowledge, the process of designing new audio effects is opened up significantly.

In analogue, achieving a certain 'equation' for a specific sound might require very complicated and time-consuming circuitry. Whereas, in DSP, it's as easy as typing ab + cy and boom. Basically, DSP is this free-running process where we can take a signal and, within a set period of time, we can do whatever we want to it mathematically before converting it back to analogue. The sky is the limit.[4]

The SHARC chip is central to the full range of Strymon pedals and is essentially used as a blank canvas which is programmed according to the specific remit of the project. Dave Frueling of the company points to the ease of use being facilitated by the accompanying visual programming interface as opening up the creative possibilities of what can be achieved in pedal form.

The SHARC platform allows us to approach the design of signal processing as art rather than technology. The power of the SHARC processor, in combination with the VisualDSP++ tools, allows us to write code in 'C' rather than in assembly language. This allows us more freedom and creativity in the development of our algorithms. We're able to spend more time trying out new ideas rather than worrying about the low-level workings of the processor. (Rambo, Undated)

Another significant example of this technological shift was the FV-1 chip, developed and released by Spin Semiconductor in 2006 which has eight built-in time-based audio effects programmes but significantly has an external electrically erasable programmable ROM, or EEPROM which can be programmed to make new effects. Again, we can see visual means of programming as being key to the

---

[4] See, interview with Dave Frueling, https://www.strymon.net/dsp-anyway/ (accessed 2 May 2021).

widespread adoption of the chip among pedal makers. Using an open-source object-oriented design interface (SpinCad) individual patches can be created by combining signal-conditioning electronic components. In a similar way to the computer-based environment Max/MSP, modular effects can be built to create unique combinations. The FV-1 has been the basis of hundreds of boutique pedals as well as allowing amateur and small-scale pedal builders to create time-based DIY effects in a way that was not possible previously and to experiment through free innovation to create products that had not yet found a market. The chip was at the heart of perhaps the first granular delay pedal the Red Panda Particle (Figure 8.2) (as well as subsequent granular pedals such as Chase Bliss Mood) along with unnatural or 'atmospheric' reverbs from boutique companies such as Nuebauer, Keeley, Old Blood Noise Endeavours, Mr Black and Earthquaker Devices.

The result of these developments in DSP, allied with the democratization of engineering and programming meant that there was a significant opening up of the types of audio effects that could be placed within the signal chain through

Figure 8.2 Red Panda Particle Mk I. The first granular delay effects processor in pedal form. Author's own collection.

the guitar pedal. However, rather than being solely led by technology these developments are also intimately tied to cultural and aesthetic factors. As Jason Toynbee notes: 'technology and the social and cultural are always imbricated. Technology is never just selected, rather it is already a discursive formation . . . [musical] technologies take off because they are congruent with an emerging aesthetic among musicians: they must literally be imagined into existence' (Toynbee 2000: 99). The advances in technology and manufacturing described here occurred in a historical timeframe which was convergent with a series of aesthetic strands within guitar music that meant that small-scale pedal makers could make increasingly esoteric sounding pedals which made creative sense in terms of the creative practices of popular music. The concentration of the remainder of the chapter, therefore, is the effect of these developments in DSP on time-based pedals within their aesthetic context. More specifically it will examine three core time-based effects types which have developed significantly since the turn of the millennium: glitch pedals, extreme reverberation and granular delay and their use in alternative rock and post-ambient guitar genres.

Shoegaze and post-rock

First, there were strains in alternative rock which had been developing for some time. In the late 1980s shoegaze had foregrounded a 'textural approach to the . . . [guitar] which eschews traditional rock virtuosity in favor of the foregrounding of timbral qualities . . . [and its] heavy use of guitar effects [including] . . . large and often unnatural sounding reverb settings . . . and techniques (extended drones, extensive use of feedback, often discordant riffs, pronounced application of the tremolo arm)' (Strachan 2017b). As Bjorn and Harper note, for shoegaze artists pedals were 'used as the centrepiece of a record and not an enhancement' on recordings which would 'have a huge impact on the generation of guitarists who [would] fuel the boutique explosion' (2020: 362).

This textural approach would also be central to post-rock, which would become a defining alternative rock genre of the 1990s, again with a concentration on the exploration of texture and soundscape. The genre's 'renewed seriousness – a restoration of grandeur, beauty, and intensity' to indie rock culture (Hibbert 2005: 66) was often facilitated by the staging of the guitar in unnaturally long digital reverbs. For example, several scholars (Elsdon 2014; Mitchell 2009) have pointed to the use of foregrounded reverb in the work of Sigur Rós as being central in the creation of soundscapes which are read as reflective of the Icelandic landscape. For Elsden, reverb is central in the textural nature of Jónsi Birgisson's guitar work whereby 'the move from one harmony to another lacks definition' and parts 'float apparently unanchored to ... [the] underlying [rhythmic] foundation'. Storvold points to the fact that the length and depth of reverberation in Birgisson's work means that 'a chord will continue to sound after Jónsi has changed to the next harmony, thereby producing a clashing moment when the two chords sound together ... [using] long decay of the reverb to produce complex harmonic structures bordering on noisy, microtonal clusters' (2018: 384–5). These readings of Sigur Rós are indicative of a more textural foregrounding within post-rock in which musicians can be seen as part of a socio-technological network within their creative practices. Technology, in the form of effects, has agency. In this case, the reflective frequencies of reverberation become key parts of the composition for post-rock and shoegaze artists. In turn, these movements within alternative rock provided an aesthetic context which allowed pedal makers to utilize developments in DSP to experiment with ever more experimental time-based algorithms. Digital algorithms enable the effect of reverberation to be deliberately taken into what is described as imagined, unreal or 'ethereal' spaces.[5]

Often this is done through the combination of spatial modelling with other audio effects such as modulation, pitch shifting or granular delay which are often used to colour the reverb trail. As Pete Celi notes, the possibilities of DSP make effects designing very open and 'For many effects, like on the BigSky reverb, some of those reverbs have long abandoned the reality of any physical space. It's about creating resonances and pitches and feedback and ambient soundscapes that don't have any physical counterpart' (Piper 2015).

The pedal effect format for post-rock acts is significant as they were worked into the sonic distinctiveness of many bands' sounds from an early stage as opposed to the earlier development of experimental effects in shoegaze. Kevin Shield's signature sounds (which were central in defining the guitar conventions of shoegaze) were derived through a lengthy (and expensive) process of studio experimentation using digital rack effects alongside pedals. In contrast, from the beginning of their careers, bands such as Mogwai and Explosions in the Sky utilized pedals such as the 1994 BOSS RV-3 (one of the first pedals to utilize

---

[5] The semiotic associations of otherworldliness are clearly reflected in the marketing of many of these boutique reverberation pedals which evoke space 'Black Hole', 'Dark Sky', religiosity, transcendence and altered states 'Trinity', Cathedral, 'TrancePortal', etc.

digital reverb algorithms that had previously been solely available in rack form) as a core of their sound. For both bands, effects pedals have always been a central part of the creative process, with the textural possibilities they afford being part of the trial-and-error experimentation of the writing process. For example, Michael James of Explosions in the Sky acknowledges the agency of technology to the writing process in harnessing the sonic possibilities of new pedals as a spur to creativity:

> We all . . . experiment with new pedals during the writing process and it was usually a case of finding something to achieve a sound we hadn't made before . . . I still get a giddy feeling unboxing a new pedal and spending hours trying to find that special sound that I haven't heard before. (Baines 2019)

Indeed, the genre's aesthetic core of sonic experimentation has meant that post-rock acts have tended to integrate new effects into their sounds as they developed and brought to market. For example, Mogwai's Stuart Braithwaite describes how the Electro-Harmonix Superego, a 'sound retainer' effect which uses DSP to hold audio information indefinitely, became central to the band's sound in their later work: 'We use [it] on pretty much everything these days. The sound capture, the kind of drone thing, that works amazingly well [for the band's sound]' (Lynham 2018). While a non-virtuosic textural foregrounding is a strain within art-rock traditions that can be traced through from the Velvet Underground and Krautrock to Post-Punk, the democratization facilitated by technology at this time is significant as it allowed for rapid development in technologies which had an immediate aesthetic context.

Digital aesthetics

In addition to the influence of these developments in rock genres, electronica has also served as a template for new guitar trajectories facilitated through the signal chain. For instance, the glitch aesthetic that emerged in electronic music in the late 1990s resulted in a series of pedals that would be significant in textural guitar modalities. The glitch became a signature sound of post-digital culture, a defining sonic gesture often read on the one hand as signalling the aesthetics of failure and on the other as indicative of our increasingly close relationship to digital technologies. In the early 2000s, the glitch moved from electronic artists (often with fine art/philosophy backgrounds who were interested in post-structuralist theory) into a much broader range of creative applications. Ragnhild Brøvig-Hanssen (2013: 172) points out that glitch techniques could be heard in a diversity of music from hip-hop to Madonna during this period. In these contexts, glitch sounds were employed towards a variety of affective and expressive ends: funky, beautiful, relaxing, transcendent, hypnotic and so on. This range of signification is indicative of the way in which glitch was part of a wider incorporation of natively digital sonic palette inexorably linked the personal computer into electronic music of the time.

The incorporation of glitch into guitar-based music is simultaneously a continuation of the textural foregrounding in art-rock traditions, a kind of digital transcendence, and a reflective use of digital technologies which mirror a broader digital aesthetic within electronic music. The turn of the millennium saw the release of a number of influential albums (such as Fennesz *Hotel Paral.lel* (1997) and *Endless Summer* (2001), Tim Hecker *Haunt Me, Haunt Me Do It Again* (2001), Keith Fullerton Whitman *Playthroughs* (2002)) that were key in establishing new digital trajectories for the guitar. These formative digital guitar albums were composed with the guitar being processed through extensive pedal boards and laptops. All three of these artists used the granular processing capabilities of Max/MSP patches or similar computer-based applications as a key element of their sound. These applications of computer processing saw a further abstraction of the guitar as a source in an aesthetic where the textural becomes the focal point of attention. At points, the signal chain takes over to an extent where it is often difficult to recognize the 'original' sound source as a guitar in which the effect elements of the signal chain become dominant of the timbral character. Part of Fullerton Whitman's system, for instance, used processing to convert the pitch and amplitude information generated from the guitar to trigger the pitch, envelope and dynamics of pure sign waves. In the track 'Fib01a' for example, one can hear the generated sine waves being processed through a buffer shuffler (which samples slices from the audio information and reorders them) to create the rhythmic characteristics of the track. Here, the tone of the guitar is subsumed by the computer creating an entirely digital soundworld. In other instances, the signal chain is used to play with the semiotic conventions of the guitar refracted through digital processing. The title track to Fennesz's *Endless Summer* for instance is based around a repeated two-chord acoustic guitar strum which is processed through the signal chain, gradually emerging from digital crackle to a recognizable form, the nostalgic affordances of the acoustic layered with a digital patina, a recognizable glitch acting an episodic marker into the conclusion of the track. In a tradition of certain types of art rock, repetition is at the heart of the aesthetic but it is layered with the material interruptions of the glitch and the grain. Both of these examples are indicative of a yielding to technological agency and an embrace of the sometimes-disruptive effects of processing through the digital signal chain. Fullerton Whitman, for instance, talks about the major part of the creative process leading to the recording of *Playthroughs* as being experimentation with the signal chain. This allowed him to set up an individualized system through which he could feed material. He is explicit about the way in which his system becomes generative in and of itself.

> In time I became familiar with the system enough that I could feed notes into it in an almost subconscious level. . . . I intrinsically knew what note needed to be played next, almost a sort of 'automatic music' with only one stage of human interaction, and a few tweaks of the plugin parameters for slight variation and formic buildup.[6]

One of the key features of these recordings is the use of micro-sampling to create a glitch or stutter effect whereby a programmed patch momentarily records and replays audio creating a staccato loop of the captured audio or continually records audio into a buffer, before chopping and reordering the subsequent slices. This glitch/stutter effect would come to prominence in the mainstream guitar world through the use of Max/MSP patches by Radiohead guitarist Jonny Greenwood, initially on the extended guitar outro of the band's 2003 track 'Go To Sleep' and on live versions of 'Airbag', '2+2=5' and Feral among others. Greenwood's use of the effect was widely debated in online guitar communities with discussions on how the effect was achieved and how it could be replicated in pedal form.[7] These performances would also have an influence on pedal makers. Matthew Warren creator of the MWFX Judder, produced in 2009 and one of the first glitch pedals, cites Jonny Greenwood as an influence in its creation.[8] More recently the Radiohead gear fansite The King of Gear raised over $9,000 in 2018 through a crowdfunding drive to produce a series of pedals (the Miniglitch and the Feral Glitch) specifically to reproduce the randomness in Greenwoood's use of the Max patch.

---

[6] https://keithfullertonwhitman.com/playthroughs (accessed 31 March 2021).
[7] See for example the 2008 discussion on the subject on the Gear Page forum: https://www.thegearpage.net/board/index.php?threads/what-glitch-effect-is-being-used-in-this-radiohead-song.368194/ (accessed 17 July 2021).
[8] See: http://www.effectsdatabase.com/interviews/brands/mwfx# (accessed 20 May 2021).

The glitch effect is indicative of the way in which digitization has facilitated new trajectories for the guitar and has accelerated the textural approach to the instrument.[9] In terms of processing, effects such as granular delay, unnatural or incredibly long reverbs, drones, glitches are part of a different form of musicality/aesthetics for the instrument. Drones hold time, extend it and suspend us in a sense of stasis. Glitches interrupt the natural flow reverberation of sound waves from sound source to reverberant surface. In pedal form, the glitch has a physicality in the holding process. Many pedals such as the MWFX Judder and the Drolo Molecular Disruptor have momentary as well as latch modes in which pressing the pedal itself holds the audio signal and thus time. The glitches and grains produced by these pedals interrupt, rather than stage, the flow of melodic and harmonic lines of the musematic units of the riff, the lick and the solo providing direct structural interventions into their linearity. The effects produced by these pedals are not just part of the tone of the instrumental voice, they produce musematic information in terms of structure, timing, melody and harmony. The musical unfolding of time when using these effects thus has to be a two-way flow between the guitar and the audio effect in which both elements of the signal chain have agency. This agency is sometimes articulated as a combination of effects as being central to both the creative process and the signature sound of an artist or a conceptualization of the pedalboard as being an instrument within itself. For example, Sarah Lipstate (who performs as Noveller) points out that her signal chain is fundamental to the creative process and her own sense of musicality:

> I like to think of my A channel as being my very unpredictable but awesome ambient foundation that I'm going to send to a separate amp. So when I'm building loops through the B output, with my main looper which is Boomerang Phrase III Sampler undulating ever shifting and permutating [sic] bed of sound to compliment that.[10]

In this instance, the pedal board becomes a way of understanding and compartmentalizing the differing aspects of her compositions. The signal chain is understood as a designed system through which music is realized but with an understanding of the differing aspects of her music as being facilitated by separate parts of her signal chain.

---

[9] See also McGrath's Chapter 10 of this volume.
[10] Swiss Things First Impression – Sarah Lipstate (Noveller) | EarthQuaker Devices https://www.youtube.com/watch?v=nR4Bay4-jUY (accessed 20 May 2021).

Conclusion

This chapter has outlined how the influence of textural experiments within alternative rock and late 1990s ambient guitarists' use of computer-based digital processing within the signal chain lead to experiments with guitar pedals. The audio effects facilitated by environments such as Max/MSP and time-based studio digital hardware effects were reproduced and developed in pedal form, making them more user-friendly for live performance and available to a wider community of guitarists. This was largely facilitated by the democratization of digital technologies by allowing small-scale producers to experiment with reproducing and expanding the types of audio processing facilitated by computer-based applications. The way in which this area of pedal development has been led is in keeping with the trends that Von Hippel (2005) identifies in wider processes of innovation in both computer software and physical products. He argues that digitization has produced democratization of production through 'user-centered innovation processes' which have shifted patterns of 'manufacturer-centric development systems' that was the dominant mode of technological change and product development from the industrial revolution onwards. Because of the free sharing of information via the internet, 'lead users' of a given field can develop technologies in very distinct ways for niche markets or specific uses rather than being dependent upon manufacturers to act as 'their (often very imperfect) agents' (2005: 2). These innovations are in some ways developed collectively in that they are often derived 'from innovations developed and freely shared by others' (ibid.) and respond to emergent patterns in user need.

The tangibility and the physicality in the placement of these digital technologies into the stomp box form are also highly significant. The digital algorithms that make up the core functions are remediated into the conventions of the analogue pedal, the affordances of which invite physical manipulation through the act of 'knob twiddling'. They are physical analogues to the parameters of the algorithm which invite the instability and imprecision that comes with the turning of an unscaled rotary controller which often introduces an element of randomness and experimentation. A sense of randomness is perhaps in contrast or even opposition to the predominant aesthetic of digital perfection that's been noted within contemporary the mainstream of contemporary pop production. Indeed, the historical account outlined in this chapter demonstrates the way in which guitar culture can be understood as a heterogeneous cultural space which simultaneously integrates and values both analogue and digital technologies. Contemporary guitar culture simultaneously encompasses the search for authentic (and elusive tone) through 'pure' analogue signal paths (see Herbst and Menze 2020) and sonic exploration through the endless possibilities of DSP, and most modern effects pedals are in fact digital/analogue hybrids in terms of components. In many accounts of the cultural repercussions and meanings of the digital turn, there has often been a tendency to understand the analogue and the digital in a polarized way. Within music cultures the analogue has been ascribed with a sense of authenticity pitted against a perceived digital inauthentic other. Pat O'Grady's (2019) discussions of recording techniques, for example, position discourses around analogue and digital as a matter of Bordieuan identity play in which the analogue and knowledge about it, represents a form of cultural capital among music produces. While there are undeniably authenticity debates around the analogue–digital split, what this account shows is the way in which often within music-making cultures, innovation and new developments entail the overlapping of analogue and digital technologies in which both types of technology are used according to use value rather than symbolic capital.

References

Anderson, C. (1975), *Electronic Projects for Musicians*, New York: Amsco Publications.

Baines, H. (2019), 'Explosions in the Sky Guitarist Michael James Revisits the Band's Formative Records', *Guitar.com*, Available online: https://guitar.com/features/interviews/explosions-in-the-sky-how-strange-innocence-the-rescue-reissues/ (accessed 24 June 2021).

Berkun, S. (2010), *The Myths of Innovation*, California: O'Reilly Media.

Bjorn, K. and S. Harper (2020), *Pedal Crush: Stompbox Effects for Creative Music Making*, Copenhagen: Bjooks.

Blecker, T. and A. Nizar (2006), 'Mass Customization: State-of-the-art and Challenges', in T. Blecker and A. Nizar (eds), *Mass Customization: Challenges and Solutions*, 1–26, New York: Springer.

Business Wire (2005), 'Analog Devices SHARC Processor Powers the World's First Standalone DTS Interactive Solution from Creative Labs', *Business Wire*, Available online: link.gale.com/apps/doc/A138445343/ITOF?u=livuni&sid=bookmark-ITOF&xid=a905cb55 (accessed 9 June 2021).

Brøvig-Hanssen, R. (2013), 'Opaque Mediation: The Cut-And-Paste Groove in DJ Food 's " Break "', in A. Danielsen (ed.), *Musical Rhythm in the Age of Digital Reproduction*, 159–76, Farnham: Ashgate.

C, M. (2020), 'Guitar Pedal DSP 101: A Look at the Chips Being Put to Work in Modern Digital FX Pedals', Available online: https://noisegate.com.au/guitar-pedal-dsp-101-a-look-at-the-chips-being-put-to-work-in-modern-digital-fx-pedals/ (accessed 2 May 2021).

Elsdon, P. (2014), 'Embodied Listening and the Music of Sigur Rós', *Popular Musicology Online*, 2 (l): 75–88.

Gershenfeld, N. (2007), *Fab: The Coming Revolution on Your Desktop–from Personal Computers to Personal Fabrication*, New York: Basic Books.

Gluckin, T. (2020), 'When Exactly Did Boutique-Pedals Become a Thing?', *Premier Guitar*, 17 September, Available online: https://www.premierguitar.com/gear/when-exactly-did-boutique-pedals-become-a-thing (accessed 24 May 2021).

Herbst, J.P. and J. Menze (2020), *Gear Acquisition Syndrome: Consumption of Instruments and Technology in Popular Music*, Huddersfield: Huddersfield University Press.

Hibbett, R. (2005), 'What Is Indie Rock?', *Popular Music and Society*, 28 (1): 55–77.

Latour, B. (1991), 'Technology is Society Made Durable', in J. Law (ed.), *A Sociology of Monsters: Essays on Power, Technology and Domination*, 103–31, London: Routledge.

Latour, B. (2005), *Reassembling the Social: An Introduction to Actor Network*, Oxford: Oxford University Press.

Lynham, A. (2018), 'Mogwai's Career in Gear: "We've got drawers full of pedals and we'll just try them until something sounds good"', *MusicRadar.com*, 9 November, Available online: https://www.musicradar.com/news/mogwais-career-in-gear-weve-got-drawers-full-of-pedals-and-well-just-try-them-until-something-sounds-good (accessed 24 June 2021).

Mellis, D. A., L. Buechley, M. Resnick and B. Hartmann (2016), 'Engaging Amateurs in the Design, Fabrication, and Assembly of Electronic Devices', in *Human Factors in Computing Systems*, 542–9, New York: ACM.

Mitchell, T. (2009), 'Sigur Ros's *Heima*: An Icelandic Psychogeography', *Transforming Cultures eJournal*, 4 (1): 172–98.

Music Trades (2007), '30 Years 10 Million Pedals! From a Humble Garage in Osaka, Boss has Emerged as a Global Leader in Electronics for the Guitar. How the Division of Roland Effectively Blends the Soul of Rock 'n' Roll with Precision Engineering to Deliver a Steady Stream of Hit Products', *Music Trades*, 155 (1), Available online: https://link.gale.com/apps/doc/A158623366/ITOF?u=livuni&sid=ITOF&xid=0cd6c782 (accessed 24 May 2021).

NAMM (2016), *The 2016 NAMM Global Report*, Carlsbad: NAMM.

O'Grady, P. (2019), 'The Analogue Divide: Interpreting Attitudes Towards Recording Media in Pop Music Practice', *Continuum Journal of Media and Cultural Studies*, 33 (4): 446–59.

Palenchar, J. (2003), 'Analog Device's SHARC will Get a Q1 Ramp-up', *This Week in Consumer Electronics*, December: 10.

Pinch, T. and D. Reinecke (2009), 'Technostalgia: How Old Gear Lives On in New Music', in K. Bijsterveld and J. van Dijck (eds), *Sound Souvenirs: Audio Technology, Memory and Cultural Practices*, 152–66, Amsterdam: Amsterdam University Press.

Piper, M. (2015), 'The Sound of Strymon: Sound Designer Pete Celi', Available online: styrmon.net (accessed 24 April 2022).

Prior, N. (2008), 'Putting a Glitch in the Field: Bourdieu, Actor Network Theory and Contemporary Music', *Cultural Sociology*, 2 (3): 301–19.

Rambo, N. (Undated), 'There Is No Brand: An Interview with Strymon Engineering', originally featured in *Tone Report Weekly*, Available online: https://www.thegearconfessions.com/post/strymon (accessed 2 May 2021).

Roeder, J. (2021), 'The Market for Musical Gear Is Amping Up Like Never Before', *Bloomberg*, Available online: https://www.bloomberg.com/news/articles/2021-03-17/musicians-are-hoarding-musical-gear-like-never-before (accessed 1 July 2021).

Ryan, J. and M. Hughes (2006), 'Breaking the Decision Chain: The Fate of Creativity in the Age of Self-Production', in M. D. Ayers (ed.), *Cybersounds: Essays on Virtual Music Culture*, 239–53, New York: Peter Lang.

Salavuo, M. (2006), 'Open and Informal Online Communities as Forums of Collaborative Musical Activities and Learning', *British Journal of Music Education* 23 (3): 253–71.

Storvold, T. (2018), 'Sigur Rós: Reception, Borealism, and Musical Style', *Popular Music*, 37 (3): 371–91.

Strachan, R. (2017a), *Sonic Technologies: Popular Music, Digital Culture and the Creative Process*, New York: Bloomsbury Academic.

Strachan, R. (2017b) 'Shoegaze', in Paolo Prato and David Horn (eds), *Bloomsbury Encyclopedia of Popular Music of the World, Volume XI : Genres: Europe*, 715–16, New York: Bloomsbury.

Théberge, P. (1997), *Any Sound You Can Imagine: Making Music/Consuming Technology*, Hanover, NH: Wesleyan University Press.

Toynbee, J. (2000), *Making Popular Music*, London: Arnold.

Von Hippel, E. (2005), *Democratizing Innovation*, Cambridge, MA. MIT Press.

Von Hippel, E. (2017), *Free Innovation*, Cambridge, MA: MIT Press.

Waksman, S. (2004), 'Tinkering with Hardcore and Heavy Metal in Southern California', *Social Studies of Science*, 34 (5): 675–702.

Wenger, E. (1998), *Communities of Practice: Learning, Meaning, and Doing*, New York: Cambridge University Press.

Media references

Endless Summer (2001), [Album] Fennesz, Mego.
Haunt Me, Haunt Me Do It Again (2001), [Album] Tim Hecker, Substractif.
Hotel Paral.lel (1997), [Album] Fennesz, Mego.
Playthroughs (2002), [Album] Keith Fullerton Whitman, Kranky.

9

The sonic maelstrom

Interview with Nels Cline

John McGrath

Nels Cline is an American guitarist and composer. He has been the lead guitarist for the band Wilco since 2004 and has performed on over 200 albums in jazz, pop, rock, country and experimental music. Cline's innovative and influential use of effect pedals and his early adoption of devices such as the Kaoss Pad has expanded the affordances of the augmented 21st Century Guitar. He leads the Nels Cline Singers, Nels Cline Trio and the Nels Cline 4. *Rolling Stone* listed him as both one of twenty 'new guitar gods' and among the top hundred guitarists of all time. He has recorded with some of the most exciting guitar players of recent times including Henry Kaiser, Lee Ronaldo and Thurston Moore, Julian Lage, Jim Campilongo and Elliott Sharp. His latest album with the Nels Cline Singers, *Share the Wealth*, came out in 2020 on Blue Note.

JMcG: I'd love to chat about the particular affordances of things like the Jazzmaster, offset guitars. What are your thoughts on that particular instrument and what it might enable?

NC: My interest in what are now called offset guitars – nobody called them that anybody heard this term till about five years ago so I don't know where it came from – but my interest in them came from Sonic Youth specifically and also from Tom Verlaine on the first two Television records before he switched to his Stratocaster with the lipstick pickups.

JMcG: The ability to play behind the bridge that Sonic Youth made use of for instance?

NC: It had to do with what the guitar's properties had for a specific song and tuning and those textures and sonorities. It's still so intoxicating and inspiring to me so I think that I then began, this was in the 1980s, that I began, reconsidering my instruments of choice because I wanted to get some of these sounds when I was in high school. Nobody played a Jazzmaster except this guy who I learned to play normal sort of rock guitar, a little bit by standing next to him in our band. This guy named Bill Watts. But he was always buying and trading his guitars away. So, he had a Jazzmaster for about, maybe not even a year, and I remember thinking like why do you have this guitar? And they were, along with Jaguars, quite derided, and then dismissed out of hand in those days. So, the first guitar I played that was now what we would say an offset was, and I still have it, was a 1966 Jaguar, which I got out of the Recycler which was a newspaper that was sort of like pre-Craigslist. And this guy brought it over. I bought it for $325. It was the first guitar of this sort I'd ever really picked up and played so I just bought it. But I didn't know the difference between the Jaguar and Jazzmaster. But it felt really, really comfortable immediately. This became my main guitar for years and all the early trio records I did when I started my own band The Nels Cline Trio and moving forward. That was the guitar I played all the time and yeah, I had my strings behind the bridge. I had a multiplicity of tones and a really comfortable body and neck profile. It just felt really natural and good for me.

But ultimately, I see the Sonic Youth methodology as being far more about sound, which is to say whatever works. They were just using the cheapest guitars they could find so it doesn't have to be any kind of name-brand guitar or familiar guitar or popular guitar. Yeah, just a matter of what works and in my case what works is certainly more string length, which the Jazzmaster has, because I like more string tension as I play hard. I also like a guitar that doesn't break, as I play hard. And it's very hard to break a Fender as you'll know, the old bolt on neck is a real boon to brute force individuals. Yep, how many times have I seen Thurston Moore smash his guitar into his amplifier and my friend Eric have to fix it? Yeah, back in those days, I mean that's why Eric for a while was my guitar tech in Wilco. The only guitar tech at that point that I had ever had after Sonic Youth disbanded because he has fixed more Jazzmasters than any human being on the planet so he's an expert – it's hard to break. As you know if you saw Jimi Hendrix at Monterey Pop, you know, I mean he just couldn't do a Pete Townsend on that thing he had to set it on fire because they're really, really hard to break, so the combination of these things and then Jazzmaster pickups certainly have a

Figure 9.1 Nels Cline with pedal rig, taken on tour with Wilco 2022. (Photo: Charles Harris, used with permission.)

lot more depth than the Jaguar pickups, more output. P90s offer so much tonal variation so I love them. But you know, I still love the Jaguar (Figure 9.1).

JMcG: So, you got your main Jazzmaster from Mike Watt (Stooges)?

NC: The '59 I bought from him, I bought it at the end of our first tour together. Yeah, for $800 you know, I remember thinking that was really expensive, but that's what he had paid for it. I wanted the Jazzmaster when I went out with him in 1995 because I felt that my Jaguar was not quite cutting it to be honest, and this was before bridges were made where the strings didn't move around and what not. I knew I needed to play harder and have a beefier sound and when I saw Joe Baiza play this guitar of Watts at my old concert series that I had on Monday nights at this place in Santa Monica called the Alligator Lounge I was stunned, and it turned out that he was just borrowing it from Watt because his Strat was being refretted. You know Baiza is definitely somebody who has I think classic Strat tone in his own unique approach with Saccharine Trust and

Universal Congress Of. A remarkable personal voice on the guitar. but anyway, Watt just said 'I don't need this guitar, you can buy it at the end of the tour', so that's my main guitar, but that guitar is living in Chicago in the Wilco loft now and, I don't know, waiting for us to finally play a gig again. But yeah, playing the Jazzmaster definitely was like the big aha experience for me in terms of its relative feeling of strength compared to the Jaguar. But I also have a deep love for guitars without strings behind the bridge like old Silvertones and Danelectros, which have unique personalities and I just like to sort of bring out the personality. I have way too many guitars. But as Jeff Tweedy (Wilco) once asked me, I was standing next to my desk at the Wilco loft and he just happened to be standing there and he turned to me and he said: 'Nels, be honest. If you had to, you could just play a Jazzmaster right?' and I said: 'Yeah, yeah, I think so.' I do have a Jazzmaster that is a fake one that I play a lot and it's here right now. That's kind of my main one for New York. You know it's something that John Woodland [Mastery Bridges] put together that has PAFs that are Seymour Duncan pickups so they're not single coil pickups.

JMcG: I read an interview recently in which you describe today as a 'great time for sound'?

NC: Oh yeah, yeah, it is yeah, I mean, imagine, like there was a moment back in whatever the year was that Henry [Kaiser] made the record *Yo Miles!* [2005]. So, we had a little meeting and then he invited me to play on the record. And Henry being Henry he walked into the session with an entire crate of wah pedals he just threw together to try out because he had never used a wah pedal before until that session – to try to get some of that Miles stuff. I mean, literally a pile of wahs. Wah pedals new and used, vintage and current, and then, I don't even know, at least two crates of effects. Pedals just piled up, he just puts them in like US Mail plastic crates or the equivalent, and they were just piled up in there. And one of the pedals in there that he brought over to me to try was the Klon Centaur.

JMcG: That's what got you onto it initially was it?

NC: Yeah, yeah, and so that was a life changer. I still don't use it when I'm playing in New York because it's too big. I know it's very valuable now but that's kind of not my motivation. It's really more about the fact that it takes up tons of room on my board and it uses a different type of power and then I have to have a Pedal

Power or have to use batteries anyway. I do love it. It's like my favourite overdrive for sure. It has a cult around it that I'm sure is half crap and half sincerity you know but anyway, yeah, I don't really read chat rooms about pedals and, I don't know, there's scuttlebutt about all kinds of stuff out there that I'm not paying attention to. The other pedal that Henry showed me that day was the Zvex Fuzz Factory. I remember hearing it and thinking – come on Henry. I can't use this thing? What is this? You know it's completely out of control and it was a little later that I was playing a duo gig in San Francisco, with Carla Bozulich and a duo called Scarnella when a guy walked up to me that I didn't even know and said 'you need to get a Zvex Fuzz Factory. I know you could really do something with it', and so I just thought back on Henry and went over to what is the name of that store in San Francisco, bought one and the rest is history you know, very important. It's usually somewhere on my board, particularly in improvised settings like we were talking about at the beginning of the interview because it has the potential for madness. And it started I think what is now quite a renaissance of not just boutique noise, but innovation wherein one can attain almost previously unimaginable sounds. The combination of this granular world, which is less of interest to me personally, but I know is having an amazing effect on timbre and just all kinds of flavour you can get with these incredibly advanced but still small and affordable pedals. And then way too many fuzz boxes and overdrive pedals and what not, and all kinds of delays that now can model the old Tel-Ray Oil Can Delay or whatever.

And this is all a good thing. Even if there are too many fuzz boxes. I'd rather have that situation than when I used to experience it even in the early 1990s when there was only a handful on the market. And if you wanted to get like a really nasally vintage sounding fuzz you had to go find one in a pawn shop or something – there were very few vintage pedals available. When I was growing up there was no vintage guitar market. It was just new or used. And there was no internet to search for things on so it took a lot of intrepid energy to find things and mostly when you found old pedals back then they were broken and I don't have any expertise in pedal repair. Yeah, so not having to do all that and have it be almost good certainly is not as good as having way too many fuzz boxes out there, you know.

JMcG: Yeah, we have a chapter on the boom of boutique pedal makers [see Chapter 8]. Well, actually there's some nice wah stuff on the new record that you reminded mind me of there.

NC: Oh, the wah yeah. But the thing is about wah. I mean, I really like using it. I do know that it is kind of like a very specific thing for people when they hear it or a lot of people are going to have an association with it. I've never used it with Wilco. There's never been a wah moment with Wilco. I've rarely use it in my own music because then I'm going to have to bring it out on tour and it's heavy and big and I can't tour with all this heavy crap when I'm out by myself, you know. Yeah, I can, but it's a pain as I already have too much other stuff, but when I played for example, with Medeski, Martin and Wood and we were playing completely improvised music I brought along a wah because I thought it would be useful. There's something that might work, and I was really happy that I did in the case of the new record. Certainly, the use of the wah on that piece called 'Princess Phone' is a blatant Miles Davis homage and all. An homage to that era in a way and even Skerik is playing wah saxophone. So, it has a beautiful application in all kinds of groove music.

And it's something that was kind of invented when I was cutting my teeth on, well, not cutting my teeth when I was just being exposed to rock 'n' roll with all kinds of innovative sounds. The experience of growing up and getting exposed to rock 'n' roll in the mid- to late 1960s as a boy and a young teen changed me forever. And I'm amazed sometimes that I'll start kind of channelling these Hendrix kinds of things once in a while. Because I never tried to play like that back then. Even though my initial inspiration to play guitar for the rest of my life was Jimi Hendrix and the song 'Manic Depression' specifically, as described in *Arcana* [Cline 2009]. I had no desire to play that way, and thought no one could, you know. I had this more modest idea of what I was going to do but I also didn't even know chords. I didn't know anything back then. I just knew I wanted to participate in something musical.

JMcG: Sound itself is of such importance in what we call or what we understand is or generally just classify as 'pop music'. Not that I particularly like genre classifications but there's a theory that the text of pop music is the record you know [Gracyk 1997], that the score cannot capture all of the timbral data in any inadequate way, and sound is so important, and there's also this idea of the studio as virtual environment. You know it's not always trying to, since things like *Electric Ladyland* or The Beatles, not trying to portray actual spaces but kind of virtual spaces, which is interesting. And I think you touched on this earlier, the whole dialogic aspect of music, and guitar playing, guitar sounds. There's now this vocabulary of sounds and tones that operate like episodic markers.

Sounds that are talking to other sounds, other music all the time, I guess. This goes back to the affordance thing a little bit, too, like we get the ability of guitar sounds to talk to the history of guitar. You know, like you said. You're bringing in the wah thing and you know it was kind of signalling this moment in a way, this kind of this influence and so there's an interesting dialogic aspect to guitar playing isn't there?

NC: Well, I think it comes from what you were talking about before which is recorded media. Yeah, in our general emphasis or insatiable love of songs that are recorded we can cart them around with us and listen to them anywhere, and it also has to do with the guitar being so incredibly ubiquitous. And at this point, probably overanalysed by other guitarists like me and holding a kind of iconic place in the culture whether justified or not. It's too late. It's just already happened and it's certainly part of what attracted me to the instrument; its sway over the sonic landscape. You mentioned *Electric Ladyland* and *Sergeant Pepper's* and you know all these kind of sonically adventurous recordings of a certain era that used the recording studio as an instrument in a way.

There's a way to create something, not unlike a pop song or blues version of *musique concrète*, or something of Varese, where you're using the medium of tape and any kind of outboard gear to change sound and now we have this ability with the effects pedal world, and the multiplicity of such with the boutique pedal world that we were discussing, to recreate sounds on stage that were previously only heard in studio recordings or on studio recordings and that to me was what excited me probably the most about effects pedals.

Even though it was an accident in my case, I went out and thought I was going to be a jazz guitar player and then went out and bought a little Polytone Mini Brute amp. And the next thing I did with it was improvise with my brother and his friend of ours named Brian Horner playing synths and flutes into an Echoplex that my friend Vinny Golia had left in my bedroom. We had the thing turned up all the way up and were doing complete space noise, and this was the probably the first moment where we went to a level of, in this trio called Spiral, where he went to a level of sonic overwhelm that sometimes scared the hell out of us, like we would get to this threshold, and we'd back down in almost terror of the sort of sonic maelstrom that we could create.[1]

---

[1] Follow-up email from NC to JMcG, 22 November 2020: 'For years I have attributed my shift in consciousness/awareness to Vinny Golia leaving his old Echoplex in my bedroom, and while this

And I think this was also the moment when I first realized that I'd heard some of these sounds on recordings. You know the sound of an Echoplex and Echoplex feedback.

Something I do now, with the Kaoss Pad 2. I don't have to cart around a tape delay but I used to take tape delay with me everywhere you know trying to emulate not only just what we heard on *Electric Ladyland*, which has got an incredible amount of tape delay, but also Tommy Bolin, like his recording with Zephyr or on the Billy Cobham album *Spectrum* used a tape delay, so these were the first inklings of I think electronic manipulation of the guitar sound that made sense to me, or that were inspiring to me and it had to do I think with getting these studio effects live because the studio effects made you feel so wild you know. The psychedelic sounds of 1966–7 and beyond are still exciting to me so the possibly of having them at my fingertips was irresistible.

did foster a rather dramatic gravitation to sonic exploration, a much earlier encounter with a friend's Maestro phase shifter – almost forgotten – had a telling effect as well.

In High School – 1971–74 – my brother and I became friends with two remarkable musicians who had managed, through what must have been quite a great effort, to matriculate from their high school in Watts – Locke High School – to our high school – University High School – all the way across town. Their names were Glenn Jeffery and Shasta Harville. Glenn was a superb guitarist and a phenomenally dignified, meticulous young man. He also owned the car that drove them the many miles to and from school five days a week. Shasta was a drummer and a very colorful, more outgoing fellow, and a fantastic drummer. Both these guys were into much of the same music that my brother Alex and I were getting into on the jazz and jazz/rock front, and they quickly became close friends of ours and also inspired us and exposed us to much of the music coming out of their neighborhood, which had some seriously deep musical talent. Anyway, Glenn had a Maestro phase shifter, that oversized thing that was the first non-studio version. The phase shifter was, in a more extreme studio application, the mind-bending sound of tracks like "Bold As Love" and "And The Gods Made Love" by The Jimi Hendrix Experience. The Maestro was the sound of dozens of players in the jazz/rock world, primarily electric guitarists and electric piano players such as John Abercrombie, Joe Zawinul, both of whom made the sound identifiable and, hence, enticing and sought after. Glenn brought his to a jam one day – a 2 guitarists/2 drummers jam with himself, Alex, Shasta, and me. Two nights ago, after being asked by a good friend to attempt some 70s-era Ernie Isley on a kind of disco song he was had written and recorded, I plugged in a phase shifter he had and this memory returned! The memory of all of us standing there in my bedroom (it was in a separate space behind my parents' house and where innumerable jams and rehearsals took place for many years) with Glenn, Shasta, and Alex as we switched the rocker switches back and forth to change the speed feeling, with great exhilaration, the magic of this sound "in person". How I could have shunted this memory so far back in my consciousness is a mystery.

Straight out of high school Glenn toured with Deniece Williams, then with The Jacksons – this despite his basic focus on jazz music. He had played in Locke High's justifiably lauded Msingi (probably misspelled) Jazz Workshop and played briefly with Freddie Hubbard. But the pop world was not for this dignified, straight-edge young man, and he quit music professionally in his early 20s. Shasta moved to songwriting and keyboards, inspired primarily by Stevie Wonder's remarkable records from that period, and drifted away from his Alphonse Mouzon/Eric Gravatt-style jazz drumming. Where they are now I do not know. But these two young men were two of the mere handful of things about my high school experiences that I recall with fondness and deep appreciation'.

JMcG: Yeah, and the kind of the passion just comes across so much in that stuff as well. You know that kind of soulfulness of the thing. Were you aware of frippertronics in the 1970s and things like that?

NC: Right absolutely, yeah, yeah that's another example. You know, and thank God I didn't have to go out and get a bunch of Revox tape machines yeah. But yeah, that's a perfect example of a very cool idea done with great eloquence. So-called progressive rock took it to another level in this in the case of someone like [Robert] Fripp. Steve Howe is hugely important and seeing that guy play multiple guitars with you know a bunch of different pedals and a bunch of different styles with amazing mastery, but also originality. Steve Howe became this kind of icon to me as did Fripp and it was only later that somebody like Steve Hackett became of interest. He was always orchestrating he was creating amazing sounds, but he had subtlety. And so, my appreciation for him grew later. I was definitely much more into heavy finger wiggling as a teenager. You know because we're talking now about high school for me. You know, and I've been listening to Ralph Towner play nylon string and John Abercrombie and John McLaughlin. George Benson and people like that, they're playing a lot of crazy amazing guitar ideas.

Around the same time a friend, Lee Kaplan, bought just for the cover and the title, *Topography of the Lungs*. I believe it's the first Incus record with Han Bennink, Derek Bailey and Evan Parker and it was on sale and in the import bin at this record store called Vogue Music in Westwood Village in West Los Angeles, and he played it for me and my brother over the phone and it sounded like I mean, it doesn't even sound like music. You know, we just thought: what is this coming over right now? And that along with Fred Frith *Guitar Solos*, the first record, became my first introduction to what we now call extended techniques, you know on the guitar. And thus, highly influential, though the intrepid decision on Derek Bailey's part with all convenient and conventional language on the guitar is far more uncompromising than I could ever be in life, you know.

JMcG: I've heard you play some non-idiomatic kinds of stuff.

NC: Touristic and tiny, but I did have an opportunity to thank him for his intrepid exploration and discoveries but and he was very nice and very humble but you know, people like Derek are so rare. And also, I'm kind of sentimental guy. I mean, emotional guy, so I do like conventional harmony and music, when it makes me feel a certain way, and I just try to go after that.

JMcG: You seem very open to different kinds of relationships, different chemistries with different people, like, as you were saying, that with Elliott Sharp it can be a bit more folky, a bit more bluesy.

NC: You know, he's an amazing blues player, so the fact that that can emerge from somebody who's mind is truly that of an avant-gardist, an innovator, is so heart-warming to me and that we can find common ground there without talking about it, it just kind of happens.

JMcG: Yeah. Not going in there with an agenda that 'This is going to sound like this, or I have to play this kind of thing'.

NC: Yeah, yeah, and also, I'm not I mean, I'm personally not especially doctrinaire, which I know is not exactly true of Derek and a lot of people in his scene who are phenomenally opinionated and even dismissive. At least to hear them talk or write – to read them.

Which I also attribute to a certain kind of intrepid iconoclastic personality that I am not.

But these are the people who push the culture forward and blow our minds. So, you know they can be grumpy and dismissive, it's OK.

JMcG: It might be too broad a question but what do you see as kind of interesting developments so far this century in terms of guitar, where do you see guitar going generally?

NC: So, you know, I have no sage or visionary idea about this, I'm just amused. I remember when, would have been maybe the late '80s, that there was this whole idea that the guitar is dead and it had to do with synth pop, and had to do with a lot of what was coming out of the UK. This attitude, and I remember thinking well how can you have rock 'n' roll without guitar? Well, I mean you can have all kinds of music without guitar if you listen to hip-hop. If you listen to what's going on with club music there's no guitar. You know it's interestingly in Japan, a lot of this J-pop or what not has a lot of heavy shredding guitar, but that's, I think, very specific to the Asian world. This idea that the guitar was dead because of synth pop, I thought, was at the time a fatuous, almost insulting idea. I had this kind of weird, defensive feeling about it, particularly because I was so enamoured with Sonic Youth and all these very guitar-based sounds. In what I guess wasn't pop, It was a kind of underground rock. But then grunge happened. And it was all about guitar or you know the heavy guitar. And Led Zeppelin-style riffs and what not that everyone was basically thinking were the most passe thing ever. Yeah, so what I see now and if you follow the trajectory of like The White Stripes and Black Keys, this recycling of riffs kind of thing. It kind of leads one to believe that you're maybe inching forward but is that the language kind of always coming back and being either honoured or just imitated or recycled in some way that it must be kind of timeless. As far as what the guitar can do in the future or even right now, I just see it as inching forward in sort of like baby steps, mostly relating to the world of effects pedals that we talked about and maybe getting away from identifiable guitar sounds, but I think that there will always be a reaction to that that will bring things back to this kind of basic power and bluster of guitar that comes I think from blues. Electric blues probably mostly because we go back to this sort of Chicago blues thing again and again.

And, you know, the guitar of say Django Reinhardt when he started playing electric guitar in the 1950s, which is very underrated, but also related to Charlie Christian's guitar and I think that this direct sound of guitar in that regard, as in the blues style, is forever, and it has nothing to do with going forward. It has to do with I don't know if it's going to be like slavishly traditional but it's the sound of an instrument that just like a trombone or a clarinet or a snare drum that doesn't just go away. And I remember that it wasn't that long ago that you had somebody like Annette Krebs doing you know, taking guitar and scraping it across the stage for performances or whatnot on the chair. All that seems to have at least abated in my consciousness. I'm not aware of people doing things quite that avant-garde with the guitar, but ultimately somebody has to do it. You know somebody has to take it to some new extreme so that we can all sort of have our own version of that and have our minds opened, but I have no idea where it's going, none whatsoever, right now in this so-called pandemic or Covid-19 period. I read an article recently that guitar sales for I guess primarily new guitars, but guitar sales in general are way up and they're calling it six-string therapy like people who thought maybe I'd like to play guitar someday are. They have time, they're at home and they think this is my moment, maybe to try to learn guitar and that there is now a 45 per cent increase in female guitar purchasers and for me, this is like the best news. Because who knows what people are going to do with the guitar at this point whether they just get on YouTube and learn how to play just like somebody else. Well, that's always been the case. You know whether they were using YouTube tutorials or not you know, we just used to play along with our records and imitate them, but somebody else might do something completely different.

And hopefully it'll be a female guitar player and it will be in a completely different tuning. And it will change music forever. I don't know if you know my directive for guitarists when they ask me for advice? Sounds glib, but it's not meant to be, it's: pick the number of strings that work for you because obviously, five strings work for the Melvins and for Keith Richards. Pick the tuning that works for you, and have a guitar that works like if it's electric you should be able to plug it in and have sound come out and the amp should work.

But if you want to play other people's music, you're probably going to have to tune to standard tuning and learn all the normal stuff and in that case, I think learning harmony is job one, learn chords and how songs are put together but if you don't want to do all that, take your own route, it'll be a hard road but do whatever you want with the instrument, it is extremely malleable, in particularly electric guitar. Just changing the string gauge changes the sound, so do pickup selections, effects/no effects, distortion or no distortion you know.

The possibilities are almost infinite so it's always going to be an intriguing future for the guitar, and possiblyw unpredictable. I don't think it's going away.

Editors' Choice – Recommended Listening:

Share the Wealth (2020), Nels Cline Singers, Blue Note.
Ode to Joy (2019), Wilco, dBpm.
Currents, Constellations (2018), Nels Cline 4, Blue Note.
Lovers (2016), Nels Cline, Blue Note.
Website: www.nelscline.com

References

Cline, N. (2009), 'A Weakness for Sound', in John Zorn (ed.), *Arcana IV: Musicians on Music*, New York: Hips Road.
Gracyk, T. (1997), 'Listening to Music: Performances and Recordings', *The Journal of Aesthetics and Art Criticism*, 55 (2): 139–50.

10

'Something seems wrong, should that be happening?'

Avantfolk guitar and glitch aesthetics, a practice-based perspective

John McGrath

Much like the archetypal protagonist in folk-horror tales – I, like a lamb to the slaughter, brandished my pedalboard before discovering the rituals of a dogmatic cult and experiencing the ensuing blood sacrifice (or look of disdain/confusion). I jest of course, employing, in medias res, Michael Newton's depiction of conventional folk-horror narrative structure:

> the arrival of a stranger, the discovery of a secret cult, then a vicious murder, perhaps a sacrifice, designed to propitiate pagan gods. The metropolitan visitor, the outsider from the mainland, comes into a situation strange to them and to us. (2017)

The occasion in question was a soundcheck for a UK folk festival which involved the sound technician asking me: 'Something seems wrong, should that be happening?'

In this chapter, I relate the concept of hauntology to glitch aesthetics in contemporary 'avantfolk' guitar practice, by way of folk horror and Mark Fisher's concept of 'the weird' (2016). The specific affordances (Gibson 1966; 1977; 1979) of glitch pedal technological augmentations will be explored later in such a theoretical context.[1] Drawing on the experimentation of John Fahey (1939–2001) with acoustic and electronic textures, his sonic palette and revoicing of acoustic guitar styles, I here formulate a theory of *avantfolk*. More of an aesthetic

---

[1] For a detailed discussion of 'affordance', see Perks's Chapter 3 in this volume.

than a genre per se, avantfolk takes on Fahey's risk-taking, progressive approach rather than simply appropriating his early form of acoustic instrumentals and the ideology of what Peter Narváez calls the 'myth of acousticity' (2001).

Avantfolk has emerged as a form of a *living* tradition that is neither concerned with nebulous notions of *authenticity* nor a retrogressive ideological clinging to particular instruments and acoustic technology.[2] In my practice, I respond to this living, ahistorical form of musicking (Small 1998) through live 'glitch looping' and experimental music video work. Pursuing a transformative kind of repetition – both sonic and audiovisual – I seek to refresh preservationist conservatism through hauntological and 'weird' critical and sonic frameworks. My use of the modernist terms 'experimental', 'avant-garde' and the prefix 'avant' here refers to the employment of innovative technological developments that press at the supposed boundaries of 'folk' instrumentals. 'Folk' itself is a term with multiple ontologies (Bohlman 1999) yet remains useful for present purposes in drawing attention to the salient dialectics of tradition/innovation and past/present at play. The binary oppositional nature of the semi-oxymoronic closed compound 'avantfolk' serves my purposes precisely, highlighting the inherent contradictions of both classifications. Here, I invoke Bill Martin's justification for his use of the prefix 'avant' in a compound with 'rock' (2002) where he posits:

> To talk about an avant-garde in rock music involves one in all sorts of contradictions and confusions. But it might be said that all good art and all good thinking is a matter of grappling with contradictions, because they are there to be dealt with in the world. (243)

Fahey is an important precursor to this approach. Although it is important to problematize the potentially retrogressive connotations of the label 'American primitive', which has become attached to his style. Fahey coined the term in the 1950s to playfully describe his own kind of solo untutored or outsider minimalist guitar instrumentals (or *guitar soli*) based on country-blues fingerpicking technique and the dissonance of composers like Charles Ives. He referred to himself as a 'classical guitarist' and while he avoided the term 'folk', Fahey's music evokes a lost America, one haunted by its past and one steeped in the crackle and texture of 78 rpm records.[3] As both an academic and performing

---

[2] I employ the term 'living' here less in regard to oral cultural transmission but as opposed to Goehr's depiction of a reified 'imaginary museum of musical works' – see Goehr (1994).
[3] 'I consider myself a classical guitar player, but I'm categorized as a folk musician', see: https://pitchfork.com/features/starter/9314-john-fahey/ (accessed 6 February 2022). Fahey played Carnegie Hall in 1973 (21 September), sharing the stage with Laurindo Almeida and Gabor Szabo

musician, his musicological/ethnomusicological interests led to his UCLA MA thesis on Charley Patton's music (1966).

And yet, while he was a blues scholar, and did much to promote the work of Patton, Son House and others, he was sceptical of the revival movement and the politicization of music for an imagined 'folk'.[4] In his MA thesis, for instance, he is critical of such readings of artists; on Patton, he writes: '[l]east of all did he try to express the "aspirations of a folk"'(1966: 29). Primitivism itself, and the collecting of indigenous folklore and art was part of the American modernist movement in the 1920s, something that Fahey often critiques, and distances himself from.[5] In fact, Fahey deconstructed the ideology of the revivalists in his humorous, satirical and often loquacious liner notes and in the deliberate blatant inauthenticity of the assumed persona, 'Blind Joe Death', under the name of whom he released his early compositions.[6] This embrace of the inauthentic, a recognition of the fact that 'authenticity' is itself a nebulous term often signifying little more than an 'ascribed' (Moore 2002) marketing ploy, together with Fahey's skills in critical and historical scholarship, encourages a new reading of his 'American primitive' style/genre (Fahey 2000: 222-3). Did he really embrace its regressive nature, or does this term in fact harbour self-reflexive, even ironic, stylistic and cultural connotations? Fahey might instead be viewed as a modernist composer in a number of senses: he straddled the divide between old and new, experimented with collage, *musique concrète*, noise and quotation; and he collected and archived lost materials in a manner similar to the composers whom he admired: Béla Bartók, Antonín Dvořák, Igor Stravinsky and Ives.[7] Brian Jones has described other figures of the folk-revival in this way, negotiating 'individual expression without severing oneself from

---

and relished the opportunity to be billed as such, if approaching it in a somewhat subversive manner (see Lowenthal: 112).
[4] Fahey notoriously admonished Pete Seeger, while the later was at the height of his folksong protest endeavours (see Lowenthal: 39).
[5] See Mancini (2004).
[6] For more on self-mythology among blues artists see *Fictional Blues* (Mack); Fahey had previously used the pseudonym Blind Thomas (Fontome Records), note also that Charley Patton used earlier pseudonyms like The Masked Marvel. A brief liner note example: 'Unfortunately, when we played the tape for Mr. Fahey in order to determine what it was in fact he, Mr. Fahey was unable to state without qualification that it was in fact he on the tape. He said that he thought it probably was, but "you know there were quite a few musicians around then that sounded just like that." Examination of the mineral-oxide constituents of the paper-based tape reveals that the recording was probably made in 1948 or 1949. Mr. Fahey was also unable to identify the triangle player' – liner notes to *Voice of the Turtle* (1968, Takoma).
[7] See: Carpenter (2017); See also: *Days Have Gone By* (1967), John Fahey, Takoma; *Requia* (1967), John Fahey, Vanguard.

the wellspring of artistic tradition' (2010: 427). George Henderson describes Fahey well when he writes:

> [Fahey's] unusually strong intellectual appetites hell-bent on the implosion of traditional forms and settled content, and a driving interest in what can be done with the pieces left lying on the ground.... Fahey could be regarded as an eager heir to American novelists of the 1930s who exposed the political underpinnings of the national obsession with 'folk' by narrating it through hybridized genres. (2021: 9)

It is these 'pieces left lying on the ground' that are the building-blocks of avantfolk. While the term 'avantfolk' is relatively fluid, a brief primer of artists who might be associated with it display an apposite interest in fragmentation and openness:[8] Richard Dawson's work juxtaposes folk song collecting and raw and enthralling solo vocal performances with improvised guitar noise; Laura Cannell experiments with fragments of medieval scores to form improvised folk textures with deconstructed bow and double recorders; John Martyn created rhythmic waves of folk experimentalism using an Echoplex with an acoustic guitar in the 1970s; Jim O'Rourke's avantrock background brought him to John Fahey in the 1990s as it did Thurston Moore, and *Bad Timing* (1997, Drag City) merges solo fingerstyle instrumentals with sprawling instrumentation and electronics; Sandy Bull wasn't afraid of combining electronics with fingerstyle guitar instrumentals on his debut record *Fantasias for Guitar and Banjo* (1963, Vanguard), a key early folk fusion record, best known for its opening improvised track 'Blend'; and one might even include Fennesz's *Endless Summer* (2001, Mego) in this list, with its mix of acoustic guitar and Max/MSP glitches. [9]

Here, I theorize that hauntology works to destabilize the one-way flow of folk revivalism. Rather than look back through a nostalgic lens, we can refresh the past through remediated, dialogic soundscapes that revoice extant textures. Hauntology points to impossible futures, but avantfolk looks to impossible, imagined pasts; fragmentary glimpses of landscapes that superimpose upon our own present setting. Now, I'll provide a theoretical framework of hauntology,

---

[8] Here, avant/experimental folk is not directly associated with 'Old, Weird America' (Marcus 2011), the more nebulous and predominantly American sub-genre 'Freak-Folk', 'Free Folk', the derivative 'New Weird America', or even what John Doran has recently labelled 'New Weird Britain' (2019), though there is of course some crossover. Doran's focus on outsider experimentation rather than on idealized pasts and nostalgia for instance (2019).

[9] See for instance: *Peasant* (2017), Richard Dawson, Weird World; *Quick Sparrows Over the Black Earth* (2014), Laura Cannell, Brawl; *Solid Air* (1973), John Martyn, Island Records.

folk horror and 'the weird' before undergoing a case study of the composition and multimodal collaborative output 'Four Hills'.

Hauntology

Hauntology has been a buzzword in popular music studies over the last fifteen years or so, having originally been coined as a kind of pun on 'ontology' by Jacques Derrida in his 1994 book *Specters of Marx*. Part of his wider philosophical project, Derrida's concept refers to the traces of history that linger in and around everything from politics to artwork and music; according to him, we can never escape the shadows of the past nor those of the future. Taken up and extensively developed by Fisher, Simon Reynolds, Adam Harper and others, the idea became more focused, referring more commonly to futures that have failed to fully manifest, or that never came to happen – what Fisher calls 'lost futures' (2014). Fisher and Reynolds initially applied the term hauntology to a group of musicians that shared certain affinities – including William Basinski, Burial, Philip Jeck and the UK label Ghost Box.[10] Many of these artists use sound, music, film and technology to explore the peculiar resonances and absences of hauntological affordances, noting that common tropes include foregrounding the medium (the crackle of vinyl, the hiss of tape and analogue gear), nostalgic TV from the 1970s, folk, psychedelia, and sci-fi and horror films that depict imagined alternate futures that never materialized.[11] The analogue decay and lo-fi fetishization of Scottish electronic duo Boards of Canada is seen as pioneering the movement, and hauntology is most often seen as a particularly British genre; its American counterpart being hypnagogic pop with subsequent offshoots like vaporwave. Reynolds writes: '[h]auntology is all about memory's power (to linger, pop up unbidden, prey on your mind) and memory's fragility (destined to become distorted, to fade, then finally disappear' (2011: 335)). In a similar way, many folk-horror stories revolve around entities popping up 'unbidden', an ill-advised unearthing or disinterring of 'things' and the subsequent fall out – M.R. James's 'Oh, Whistle, and I'll Come to You, My Lad' (1904) for instance, resonates with this idea of hauntological memories 'preying on the mind' as the protagonist

---

[10] See for instance Fisher (2014).
[11] See also Sexton (2012).

unearths a whistle that he really shouldn't have, and terror ensues. Whether it is Cannell de-contextualizing motifs, borrowing fragments from medieval tunes to form a basis for recomposed improvisations or my own disjointing of musical fragments via glitch-pedal technology, avantfolk embraces hauntology in the sense that 'memory's fragility' – and as we'll see next, folk horror and glitch aesthetics – provides an ideal metaphor to evoke a fragmentary and dislocated past, a non-place (Augé 1992) and a non-time (Fisher 2014).

Folk horror

If hauntology positions avantfolk within an imaginary historical timeline, in which 'lost' materials are reimagined as soundworlds they never were, through the foregrounding of technology, physicality and posthuman affordances, folk horror's depiction of the sinister further suggests a darker subtext for avantfolk. Is this imagined atemporality a safe place to inhabit? We've mentioned already the problems of assuming an 'imagined folk' above and this very issue is what folk horror as a genre critiques best.

Some context here is important to the avantfolk aesthetic that I explore. The original boom of folk-horror movies in the late 1960s and early 1970s revolved around the so-called 'unholy trinity' of films: Michael Reeves's *Witchfinder General* (1968), Piers Haggard's *The Blood on Satan's Claw* (1971) and Robin Hardy's *The Wicker Man* (1973). As Adam Scovell proposes in his analysis of these films: '[t]hough their imagery has since defined all things "olde" and "wyrd" about Britain . . . The trilogy follows an alternative vision of Albion, unearthing a darker past often kept on its little-visited, uncanny copse-ways' (2021). These films express a strange tribal community, sometimes rooted in historical fact, or deep-set ideology and myth. The scores are interesting for their play with historical time and the juxtaposition of nineteenth-century Romanticism, folk tunes and modernist experimentalism. In the case of Marc Wilkinson's score for *Blood on Satan's Claw*, for instance, we have an orchestra that includes an *ondes martenot* and folk melodies that are skewed by chromaticism into what I would call avantfolk textures. Wilkinson's score creates a 'cognitive dissonance', to use Sergei Eisenstein's audiovisual term ([1949] 1977), with the seventeenth-century rural backdrop, while at the same time the anachronisms are strangely apt for the narrative. 'Time is out of joint' here and the 'strange simultaneities' in the music adumbrate the spectral action of the horror.[12]

These films follow similar archetypes to those that Newton describes above, an outsider enters a secret 'folk' community and things turn bad, quickly. The recent 'folk-horror revival' may be read as a comment on something not being quite right in contemporary Britain and beyond. While the first wave from 1968–73 might have reflected the darker side of psychedelia, the Altamont, the bad trip, the eventual failure of the hippie movement, perhaps the current revival of the genre provides a mirror on contemporary society. Examples include Ben Wheatley's *Kill List* (2011), *A Field in England* (2013), *In the Earth* (2021); Felix Barrett and Dennis Kelly's miniseries *The Third Day* (2020); and Paul Wright's *For Those in Peril* (2013), while international echoes include films like Robert Eggers's *The Witch* (2015) and Ari Aster's *Hereditary* (2018) and *Midsommar* (2019). In *Kill List*, the main character is haunted by his past, and reviving it feeds this trauma in a Freudian compulsively repetitive manner. The events of the past are dug up by the job he takes on as a hired killer, just as the trapped demonic forces are unleashed from the ground in *Blood on Satan's Claw* or in James's *Whistle and I'll Come To You* (see Jonathan Miller's BBC production, 1968). Reviving the past or forgotten figures in folk horror is clearly discouraged. Avantfolk's transgression of the revival paradigm resonates with this scepticism for disinterment and the reification of idealized pasts in addition to recognizing the fallibility of memory; instead, it welcomes a 'strange simultaneity'.

The weird, technostalgia and glitch looping

Fisher's concept of 'the weird' further chimes with the idea of 'strange simultaneity', an atemporality and a disinterring of the past. He writes: '[m]odernist and experimental work often strikes us as weird when we first encounter it. The sense of *wrongness* associated with the weird – the conviction that *this does not belong* – is often a sign that we are in the presence of the new' (2016: 13). Here too we are back to 'modernism'. So, we can view the incorporation of glitch aesthetics in avantfolk as a form of *weirding* in opposition to the 'nostalgia mode' (Jameson 1991) of conservative folk. There

---

[12] Fisher is fond of this Hamlet quote 'time is out of joint' when discussing hauntology (see 2012). See also his essay on Philip K. Dick's novel *Time Out of Joint* (1959) in Fisher (2016: 45–52).

is sometimes a backlash to avantfolk from folk conservatives; the intrusion of newer technology into 'their' folk deemed unwelcome. There is no better example of such a phenomenon as the infamous moment when Bob Dylan was proclaimed a 'judas' for going electric.[13] Such an invasion might be read as a weirding of dominant culture. For Fisher, the weird involves that which arises through the intrusion of the 'outside' into the 'inside' (10). This disturbance invokes 'a sensation of *wrongness*: a weird entity or object is so strange that it makes us feel that it should not exist, or at least it should not exist here' (15). In relation to H.P. Lovecraft, Fisher writes that 'the weird is constituted by a presence – the presence of *that which does not belong*. In some cases of the weird . . . the weird is marked by an exorbitant presence, a teeming which exceeds our capacity to represent it' (61). As the 'exorbitant presence' of Dylan's 1965 stage volume exceeded some audience members' capacity to grasp the new artistic direction, so experimental folk pushes the boundaries of what folk means today. What might this weirding of folk represent, what does it reflect culturally and what insights might it provide into contemporary society?

Nick Srnicek and Alex Williams chart what they call leftist 'folk politics' which have developed in opposition to musical innovation, an approach that 'chooses the familiarities of the past over the unknowns of the future' (2015). As Harper writes:

> Countercultural popular music has often been mistrustful of technology . . . Even electronic dance music, which as it first developed was seen as a locus of futurist and utopian practice, is insisting upon its roots at every turn, either positively and insipidly (Daft Punk) or with a self-awareness that typically results in deconstructive melancholy (Burial, Actress). Analogue and classic are for the true believers, while digital, ridden into town by the internet, is seen as a corruption. (2015)

These so-called 'true believers' are echoed when Robert Strachan points out in Chapter 8 of this volume, that there has often been an imagined Bordieuan polarization of tech/analogue in popular music aesthetics (page 170). While lo-fi and grunge promulgated a fetishization of the analogue in the 1990s (Bjorn and Harper 2020: 362), what Trevor Pinch and David Reinecke' (2009) term

---

[13] 17 May 1966 at Manchester Free Trade Hall. The heckler was later identified as one Keith Butler – a second-year Keele University student, see: https://mail.expectingrain.com/dok/who/b/butlerkeith.html (accessed 27 April 2022).

'technostalgia' soon became widespread in the industry, from The White Stripes to James Ferraro.[14]

Strachan's *Sonic Technologies* charts the rise of glitch aesthetics in the 1990s through the deliberate scratching of CDs and the foregrounding of previously unwanted pops and blips from the production process (2017). Glitch was founded on an aesthetic of failure.[15] In glitch, the mistakes become the content, the unwanted is foregrounded. Paul Hegarty has spoken of noise aesthetics in a similar way, and indeed there is much overlap in their modernist oppositional nature (2007). But what do I mean by the term 'glitch looping'? Early pioneers of tape looping including Les Paul, Robert Fripp, Terry Riley, Steve Reich and so on had to go to considerable lengths to achieve the effect that now can be easily obtained with any digital audio workstation.[16] Loopers began sweeping the market from the 1980s onwards and made it to the mainstream in pedal form as part of pop live performance with the one man/woman band style of Ed Sheeran and KT Tunstall – a phenomenon that Dale Chapman (2013) sees as a product of late capitalist, neo-liberalist and post-Fordist entrepreneurship. By contrast, what I term *glitch looping* involves the employment of loops not as direct repetitions of supposed parts (bass lines, percussion and so forth) but instead in a musematic and live improvised manner that welcomes a certain degree of unpredictability. Glitch looping illuminates the short pops and blips, the disjecta of electronic failure. Bill Frisell and Nels Cline (see Chapter 9 in this volume) were early exponents of a mode of looping that is more concerned with effect and affect than with being a building block for structuring conventional song, a novel performance gimmick, an accompaniment for soloing or as a way of keeping all the cash without having a band to pay. Repetition can be transformative. Gilles Deleuze (1968) famously discussed how at the moment of reception a repeat is never the same; its very reiteration changes with every utterance, as the past and future become present in the mind of the listener. For Derrida, the present is always haunted by the past but repetition can be a positive

---

[14] Of course, new technology often incites a moral panic; sometimes a period of acclimatization is needed before the device or instrument is destigmatized in particular contexts. An example is the laptop being eventually accepted *as an instrument* in the mainstream. it is worth noting that, alongside general ignorance of the intricacies of style or genre, social order and economic accessibility also play a part in such prejudice. The ubiquity of the laptop in homes appeared to initially feed the idea / stigma that anyone could make electronic music – 'just press a button, right?'– but access to *Microsoft Word* doesn't mean one can write *Ulysses* or that anyone with access to a guitar in the house (more common than an expensive piano situated in a Victorian upper-class salon) can play like Jimi Hendrix or Fernando Sor.
[15] There are resonances here with the work of Samuel Beckett (see: Tereszewski for instance).
[16] For more on this see: McGrath (2018).

force. As Adrian Parr writes: 'Deleuze encourages us to repeat because he sees in it the possibility of reinvention, that is to say, repetition dissolves identities as it changes them, giving rise to something unrecognisable and productive' (2005: 225). Where Freud saw only negative connotations, the compulsive repetition of trauma, Deleuze found positive protean creativity in the repeat.[17]

So, what might the use of technology, glitch looping, mean in avantfolk guitar practice, and how does this relate to hauntology, folk horror and the weird? As we revive the past, as we mechanically reproduce motifs and figures, is trauma (Freud) emphasized or can this process be more transformative (Deleuze)?

'Four Hills' – A practice-based case study

As a professional guitarist since the age of seventeen, I have worked in various scenarios, spanning jazz, blues, free improvisation, avantrock and scratch orchestras (including collaborations with Dustin Wong, Sharon Gal, Cavalier Song, Rhys Chatham, Howard Skempton and the aPAtT Orchestra). Within all these styles is a commonality of approach. No one genre or aesthetic is deemed to be overly fixed, restrictive or hierarchical; each allowing a playful openness and experimentalism. By 2013, however, I started to explore ways to combine and recontextualize these disparate practices, taking the improvisatory looseness of jazz, the structures and technology of electronica, the driving rhythms of blues and the noisy DIY, chance aesthetics of scratch orchestras and mixing them all into an instrumental fingerpicking style that loudly echoed John Fahey. Hauntologically different eras are echoed simultaneously in combinations that never previously came to pass. Like how T.S. Eliot described the role of the modernist poet, avantfolk 'lives in what is not merely the present, but the present moment of the past' ([1919] 2005: 155). This 'present moment of the past' embraces dark undertones and doesn't shy away from the dissonances of folk horror nor the beauty of melody. Fundamentally, this dichotomy is modernist in a very real sense, and such a position is itself atemporal in that its foundational aesthetic is over a hundred years old. On a personal level, I struggled for many years with what Lisa Carpenter calls the 'modernist dilemma' of chasing the new while at the same time seeking out the past, and rather than view this position as modernist 'baggage' as opposed to a more archival process through which

[17] Ibid.

popular music canonizes itself, or the more pessimistic perspective whereby modern music rehashes, replays and imitates (Reynolds's retromania) – I found this atemporal modernist approach very fruitful in fact.

'Four Hills' was one of my earliest explorations of this avantfolk space. Appearing first on my *Lanterns EP* (Crooked Stem Recordings, 2013) the track is a simple two-part fingerstyle improvisation exemplifying this contemporary experimental folk and folk-horror style by way of my invocation of glitch looping technology in a single-take recording with no overdubs.[18] The composition for solo guitar explored these themes of hauntology, folk horror and glitch aesthetics, as I'll now explore multimodally. A short film, an experimental music video, that Scovell later made for 'Four Hills' in 2014[19] was included in an exhibition at FACT Liverpool entitled 'Science Fiction: New Death'.[20] The instrumentation, landscape and stop-motion texture of Scovell's video directly reflect the folk horror and hauntological aesthetic of the composition, as blues structure, D A D G A D (6–1) tuning (reminiscent of Bert Jansch and Davey Graham), and the use of drones and quick glitches created via pedal technology, together evoke a 'time out of joint'.[21] Scovell was a key theorist in the folk-horror revival of the mid-2010s, in fact; having written numerous primers for *BFI* and *Sight & Sound* he authored the seminal *Folk Horror: Hours Dreadful and Things Strange* in 2017. In short, we shared a keen interest in the movement and aesthetics at this point.[22] Reynolds's notion of hauntological memories popping up 'unbidden' and 'preying on the mind' is exemplified by the insistent

---

[18] The track also appeared on the *Liverpool International Music Festival Fringe CD* (2013). The work came about initially as part of a call out for site-specific live recordings by the magazine Bido Lito! for another compilation, for whom I agreed to record a take of the track 'Lanterns' in a small chapel in Liverpool, St Stephens, on 26 March. The engineer (Bjorn David Bancel) and I decided to keep going and record enough for a full EP then and there. 'Four Hills' thus went on to appear on said EP. Subsequently, 'Four Hills' was featured in *Wire* magazine's *Tapper 33* compilation: https://www.thewire.co.uk/audio/the-wire-tapper/the-wire-tapper-33/8 (accessed 6 February 2022).

[19] Video available on YouTube: https://www.youtube.com/watch?v=eSm-XdcCabI&ab_channel=AdamScovell (accessed 6 February 2022).

[20] 'Opening in March 2014, *Science Fiction: New Death* seeks to provoke the question – have the Sci Fi visions we once imagined of the future since become a reality? The exhibition presents works of art that explore these questions and considers how technology has created new ways of living, fashioning new identities, forms of intimacy and desire. This has occurred in tandem with the growth of cult-like communities both online and in physical space, the conceit of social media, and the hyperrealist architecture of computer screens. Arguably, our everyday lives have increasingly become a form of science fiction': https://www.fact.co.uk/event/science-fiction-new-death?token=5bluLutuCMYExY2w0ao7XKZD9LVBrPiw (accessed 6 February 2022).

[21] See Williams's Chapter 5 in this volume for more on the 'extended acoustic guitar'.

[22] A later folk-horror collaboration with sound-artist Make Flames would further explore such spectral areas, fuelled by the fact that we never met in person and only exchanged folk-horror literature, film and found-sound material virtually (see: 'Lady into Fox' CRSTEM003 https://crookedstemrecordings.com/track/lady-into-fox).

repetition of the motifs alongside the build-up of drones and glitches in 'Four Hills'. 'Strange simultaneities' in the music adumbrate the spectral visual action. Directorially, Scovell pays homage to James – in particular, Miller's TV adaptation *Whistle and I'll Come to You* mentioned earlier – as a disinterred watch leads the protagonist of the music video to experience a psychedelic transformation of reality (Figure 10.1).

In Chapter 8 of this volume, Strachan outlines some of the affordances of pedal/stompbox technology and augmentations. He writes concerning glitch pedals:

> In pedal form the glitch has a physicality in the holding process. Many pedals such as the MWFX Judder and the Drolo Molecular Disruptor have momentary as well as latch modes in which pressing the pedal itself holds the audio signal and thus time. (page 168)

Two pedals afforded the glitching in the composition 'Four Hills'. The recording was a one-take solo live performance and so the glitches were to be physically manipulated in real time. The BOSS DD-6 Digital Delay (sold from July 2002 to 2008) included a 'hold' mode that allowed a loop/recording time of over five seconds (5,200 ms). Though the pedal was quickly made obsolete in terms of looper functionality (this wasn't even its initial selling point, it was the first BOSS pedal to offer stereo delay inputs and outputs), its very limitations afforded unique opportunities. I realized that by very quickly tapping the hold function

Figure 10.1 Still from Adam Scovell's video for 'Four Hills' – the protagonist disinters a watch from the soil and unleashes its forces.

the pedal would grab very small segments of sound and produce a glitching effect. The physical process of engaging minute foot movements meant that the glitches were extremely arbitrary, any miniscule fluctuation in activation time resulted in very different effects, 'embracing . . . the glitch aesthetics of chance and disturbance' as Janne Vanhanen (2003) puts it. I immediately liked this inherent capability of the device and began exploring the affordance of this as a glitch pedal. Various complex rhythmic patterns could be achieved (see Figure 10.2) through developing a vocabulary of movements, the pedal almost acting as collaborator or co-composer/improviser rather than servile machine; it had agency in its unpredictability (Latour 2005).

The second pedal that I employed was the Electro-Harmonix Freeze. Released in 2010, the Freeze offered a new way of sustaining a single note or chord in real time via a momentary footswitch. Again, I enjoyed the fact that this didn't work perfectly and that there were glitchy residues included if used in a particular way – the aesthetic of failure – especially if you deliberately struck the pedal slightly 'out of time' with the sounded notes. You could either keep your foot on the pedal to hold the single sound or select the 'latch mode', which would hold the sound infinitely until you disengaged the footswitch. Strachan goes on:

> [t]he glitches and grains produced by these pedals interrupt, rather than stage, the flow of melodic and harmonic lines of the musematic units of the riff, the lick and the solo providing direct structural interventions into their linearity. The effects produced by these pedals are not just part of the tone of the instrumental voice, they produce musematic information in terms of structure, timing, melody and harmony. (page 168)

Like 'cracked media' (Kelly 2009), an unconventional use of these pedals enables a method of holding time, a desired sense of randomness, and an expression of temporal incongruity – a time that is literally 'out of joint'. The present coexists with a fragmented past. Built in affordances of manufacture (though likely unintentional; i.e. not included as features in the user manual) render new aesthetic possibilities. The musematic motifs produced through the physical

Figure 10.2 Transcribed excerpt of BOSS DD6 hold function glitch effect in 'Four Hills'.

bodily engagement of stompbox and the capture of acoustic sound are digitally manipulated and thus weirded via the technological affordances of the devices. An excess residue is manifested by this augmentation of the instrument. It is the very mistakes, the limitations and failures of the particular technology that renders the desired effect. The machine strives to carry out a task and its failure becomes the very thing that the human responds to.[23] In a sense, they 'fail better' than if they succeeded in capturing the recorded fragment in a more faithful, neutral way.[24] More than 'extensions' of the human (McLuhan 1964), these 'desiring machines' possess a certain agency of their own (Deleuze and Guattari 1988). Returning to Reynolds' discussion of hauntology and 'memory's power (to linger, pop up unbidden, prey on your mind) and memory's fragility (destined to become distorted, to fade, then finally disappear' (2011: 335)), this is exactly what 'Four Hills' is doing. Through glitching, the musematic motifs pop up unbidden, they distort, fade and disappear. Scovell's visual glitches mirror that of the sonic material, as the B-section becomes more experimental and psychedelic in nature.

The process developed in 'Four Hills' yielded an innovative new vocabulary for me as a composer/performer and a number of subsequent pieces utilized this glitch aesthetic including 'Lanterns', 'Breath', 'Moreover, the Moon' and even a more subtly glitched version of the traditional tune 'Si Bheag Si Mhor', originally composed by blind Irish harper Turlough O' Carolan.[25] As Bill Meyer discussing the arrangement in a review for Dusted Magazine put it: 'there's just a candle's wattage of digital sound processing flickering in the background, which makes this writer hope that somewhere on the auld sod there's a bartender who slips it on late at night to mess with pub-closers who can't tell if it's the music or the pours of Redbreast that are messing with their senses.'[26] Something is weirded, that doesn't quite fit the normal expectations, as the glitched material affords a level of listener alienation.[27]

---

[23] Obsolescence has often gone hand in hand with fetishization. The valves that remain in high-end guitar amplifiers, for instance, are the result of the failure of a once dominant technology in practice. Their perceived 'natural, warm overdrive' is the result of overheating, and what were initially unintended results become the taste, as newer more efficient and cheaper options like transistors are avoided.
[24] The famous Beckett quote – 'Ever tried. Ever failed. No matter. Try Again. Fail again. Fail better' – occurs in *Worstward Ho* (1983).
[25] See: crookedstemrecordings.com for these releases.
[26] https://dustedmagazine.tumblr.com/post/187031437771/john-mcgrath-wake-and-whisper-crooked-stem (accessed 23 April 2022).
[27] When I was commissioned by the Immix Ensemble (Erased Tapes) to write some new material for the group and to rework some extant original work, the live recording of which (performed at Static Gallery, Liverpool) was later released on my solo album *Wake & Whisper* (Crooked Stem

Conclusion

Conservationism often imbues performance reception with a pedantic pigeonholing and an unimaginative reification of a living tradition.[28] Historically, the concretization of idealized pasts has even led to divisive forms of nationalism and we have witnessed the far-right usurping folk music to further their own ends.[29] There has even been a recent appropriation of folk horror and folk music more generally by right-wing groups and neo-fascists. Kelly Weill writes, for instance, that 'neo-folk music – along with a handful of other genres like black metal, industrial music, and some spheres of the punk scene – has a white supremacist problem' (2019). Cecil Sharp's own ideology is somewhat to blame here as nationalism and idealist nostalgia played what some view as a sinister role in his form of preservationism (see Harker 1985 and Boyes 1993).[30] We must acknowledge the larger ideology and commodification of imagined authenticity at play here and recognize the historical dominance of nostalgia in times of political and cultural upheaval (Cohen).

Deleuze viewed repetition as positive transformation, with the repeat of every note our perception is altered. We are in a moment of transformative technological repetitive culture and we are operating in different times and realities all at once – non-places and non-times, imagined cannons and constructed authenticities, hauntology and nostalgia. The false dichotomy of folk and technology presents an outdated construction; instead, the binary oppositional closed compound 'avantfolk' affords creative play and critique.[31] In this chapter, I have related the concept of hauntology to glitch technology in contemporary avantfolk guitar performance, by way of a discussion of folk horror, the weird and its resonances in the context of contemporary society. In doing so, I've explored how one example – a music video of solo avantfolk guitar – can both disinter the past and seek out transformative future developments by way of ghost guitars in the

---

Recordings, 2019), this glitch folk experimentation provided a basis for expanded instrumental arrangement.

[28] See also Wilson (1973) and Hobsbawm (1992).
[29] Of course, both left and right of the political divide have conservative aesthetics when it comes to folk, the nostalgia industry infiltrates in a non-partisan fashion. Cohen writes: 'The belief that the past was better than the present, and the only way forward is back, can be found in the corners of any society at any time. But when nostalgia grows to dominate Britain and much of the West it is as sure a symptom of decay as the stink of dry rot' (Cohen 2021).
[30] See also Bearman (2000) and Anderson (2006). Though such direct critique has also been read as historical revisionism (Gregory 2009).
[31] Avantfolk is also 'weird' in the sense of it being 'the conjoining of two or more things which do not belong together' (Fisher 2016: 11).

machine (those fragmentary musematic motifs electronically decaying).[32] Rather than idealizing the past, we can begin to see the present folk-horror revival and avantfolk more broadly in a very hauntological light, as phenomena that express a critical attitude towards nostalgia, sometimes evoking a lost Utopianism but fundamentally deconstructing cultural narratives of what 'folk' means. This opens up further questions outside the scope of this chapter such as: Does 'folk' music still connect or refer to a group of people in the same way that revivalist scholars once discussed, be this group mythologized or not (Boyes 1993)? What is clear is that the guitar plays a key role in such developments, its augmented voice is changing/informing the aesthetic of the avantfolk genre/music culture. Through weirding dominant ideological narratives and aesthetic criteria through the employment of new technology and the abandonment of nebulous notions of authenticity alongside problematic imagined pasts, avantfolk thus offers a unique window into, and critique of, the political and cultural landscape of modern Britain and beyond: '[t]he weird thing is not wrong, after all: it is our conceptions that must be inadequate' (Fisher 2016: 15).

References

Anderson, B. (2006), *Imagined Communities: Reflections on the Origin and Spread of Nationalism*, Rev. ed., London: Verso.

Augé, M. (1992), *Non-Places: Introduction to an Anthropology of Supermodernity*, Le Seuil: Verso.

Bearman, C.J. (2000), 'Who Were the Folk? The Demography of Cecil Sharp's Somerset Folk Singers', *The Historical Journal*, 43 (3): 751–75.

Bjorn, K. and S. Harper (2020), *Pedal Crush: Stompbox Effects for Creative Music Making*, Copenhagen: Bjooks.

Bohlman, P.V. (1999), 'Ontologies of Music', in N. Cook and M. Everist (eds), *Rethinking Music*, 17–34, Oxford: Oxford University Press.

Boyes, G. (1993), *The Imagined Village: Culture, Ideology and the English Folk Revival*, Manchester: Manchester University Press.

Carpenter, L. (2017), *Folk into Art: John Fahey, Modernism and the American Folk Revival*, MA diss., College of William and Mary.

Chapman, D. (2013), 'The "One-Man Band" and Entrepreneurial Selfhood in Neoliberal Culture', *Popular Music*, 32 (3): 451–70.

---

[32] A play on Ryle's 'Ghost in the Machine' (*The Concept of Mind*, 1949).

Cohen, N. (2021), Available online: https://www.theguardian.com/commentisfree/2021/jun/26/our-politics-of-nostalgia-is-a-sure-sign-of-present-day-decay (accessed 4 February 2022).

Deleuze, G. (1968), *Différence Et Répétition*, Bibliothèque De Philosophie Contemporaine, Paris: Presses Universitaires de France.

Deleuze, G. and F. Guattari (1988), *A Thousand Plateaus: Capitalism and Schizophrenia*, London: Athlone Press.

Derrida, J. ([1994] 2006), *Specters of Marx: The State of the Debt, the Work of Mourning, and the New International*, London: Routledge.

Doran, J. (2019), *New Weird Britain*, [Radio Series] BBC, 4, Available online: https://www.bbc.co.uk/programmes/m0005mr0 (accessed 4 February 2022).

Eisenstein, S. ([1949] 1977), *Film Form: Essays in Film Form*, ed. and trans. J. Leyda, New York: Harcourt Brace & Company.

Eliot, T.S. ([1919] 2005), 'Tradition and the Individual Talent', in L. Rainey (ed.), *Modernism: An Anthology*, 152–5, Oxford: Blackwell.

Fahey, J. (1966), *A Textual and Musicological Analysis of the Repertoire of Charley Patton*, MA diss., UCLA, Los Angeles.

Fahey, J. (1968), 'Liner Notes to *Voice of the Turtle*', Takoma, Available online: https://www.johnfahey.com/pages/the-voice-of-the-turtle-liner-notes.php (accessed 27 April 2022).

Fahey, J. (2000), *How Bluegrass Music Destroyed My Life*, Chicago: Drag City.

Fisher, M. (2012), 'What is Hauntology', *Film Quarterly*, 66 (1): 16–24.

Fisher, M. (2014), *Ghosts of My Life: Writings on Depression, Hauntology and Lost Futures*, Winchester: Zero Books.

Fisher, M. (2016), *The Weird and the Eerie*, London: Repeater Books.

Gibson, J.J. (1966), *The Senses Considered as Perceptual Systems*, Boston, MA: Houghton Mifflin.

Gibson, J.J. (1977), 'The Theory of Affordances', in R. Shaw and J. Bransford (eds), *Perceiving, Acting, and Knowing: Toward an Ecological Psychology*, 67–82, Hillsdale, NJ: Lawrence Erlbaum Associates.

Gibson, J.J. (1979), *The Ecological Approach to Visual Perception*, Hillsdale, Boston, MA: Houghton Mifflin.

Goehr, L. ([1994] 2007), *The Imaginary Museum of Musical Works: An Essay in the Philosophy of Music*, Oxford: Oxford University Press.

Gregory, D. (2009), 'Fakesong in an Imagined Village? A Critique of the Harker-Boyes Thesis', *Canadian Folk Music Bulletin*, 43 (3): 18–26.

Harker, D. (1985), *Fakesong: The Manufacture of British 'Folksong' 1700 to the Present Day*, Milton Keynes: Open University Press.

Harper, A. (2015), 'On Music and Folk Politics', Available online: https://www.versobooks.com/blogs/2367-adam-harper-on-music-and-folk-politics (accessed 28 January 2022).

Hegarty, P. (2007), *Noise/Music: A History*, New York: Continuum.
Henderson, G. (2021), *Blind Joe Death's America: John Fahey, the Blues, and Writing White Discontent*, Chapel Hill: The University of North Carolina Press.
Hobsbawm, E. (1992), *The Invention of Tradition*, Cambridge: Cambridge University Press.
James, M.R. (1904), 'Oh, Whistle, and I'll Come to You, My Lad', in *Ghost Stories of an Antiquary*, London: Edward Arnold.
Jameson, F. (1991), *Postmodernism: Or, the Cultural Logic of Late Capitalism*, Durham, NC: Duke University Press.
Jones, B. (2010), 'Finding the Avant-Garde in the Old-Time: John Cohen in the American Folk Revival', *American Music*, 28 (4): 427.
Kelly, C. (2009), *Cracked Media: The Sound of Malfunction*, Cambridge, MA: MIT Press.
Latour, B. (2005), *Reassembling the Social: An Introduction to Actor Network*, Oxford: Oxford University Press.
Lowenthal, S. (2014), *Dance of Death: The Life of John Fahey, American Guitarist*, Chicago, IL: Chicago Review Press.
Mack, K. (2020), *Fictional Blues: Narrative Self-Invention from Bessie Smith to Jack White*, Amherst: University of Massachusetts Press.
Mancini, J.M. (2004), '"Messin; with the Furniture Man": Early Country Music, Regional Culture, and the Search for an Anthological Modernism', *American Literary History*, 16 (2): 208–37.
Marcus, G. (2011), *The Old, Weird America: The World of Bob Dylan's Basement Tapes*, Updated ed., New York: Picador.
Martin, B. (2002), *Avant Rock: Experimental Music from the Beatles to Björk*, with a foreword by Robert Fripp, Chicago, IL and LA Salle: Open Court.
McGrath, J. (2018), *Samuel Beckett, Repetition and Modern Music*, Abingdon and New York: Routledge.
McLuhan, M. (1964), 'The Medium is the Message', in *Understanding Media: The Extensions of Man*, 23–35, New York: Signet Books.
Moore, A. (2002), 'Authenticity as Authentication', *Popular Music*, 2 (2): 209–23.
Narváez, P. (2001), 'Unplugged: Blues Guitarists and the Myth of Acousticity', in A. Bennett and K. Dawe (eds), *Guitar Cultures*, 27–44, Oxford: Berg.
Newton, M. (2017), 'Cults, Human Sacrifice and Pagan Sex: How Folk Horror is Flowering Again in Brexit Britain', Available online: https://www.theguardian.com/film/2017/apr/30/folk-horror-cults-sacrifice-pagan-sex-kill-list (accessed 28 January 2022).
Parr, A. (2005), *The Deleuze Dictionary*, New York: Columbia University Press.
Reynolds, S. (2011), *Retromania: Pop Culture's Addiction to Its Own Past*, 1st American ed., London and New York: Faber & Faber.
Scovell, A. (2017), *Folk Horror: Hours Dreadful and Things Strange*, Leighton Buzzard: Auteur.

Scovell, A. (2021), 'Where to Begin with Folk Horror', Available online: https://www.bfi.org.uk/features/where-begin-with-folk-horror (accessed 28 January 2022).

Sexton, J. (2012), 'Weird Britain in Exile: Ghost Box, Hauntology, and Alternative Heritage', *Popular Music and Society*, 35 (4): 561–84.

Small, C. (1998), *Musicking: The Meanings of Performing and Listening*, Hanover and London: Wesleyan University Press.

Srnicek, N. and A. Williams (2015), *Inventing the Future: Postcapitalism and a World Without Work*, Brooklyn, NY: Verso Books.

Strachan, R. (2017), *Sonic Technologies: Popular Music, Digital Culture and the Creative Process*, New York: Bloomsbury Academic.

Tereszewski, M. (2013), *The Aesthetics of Failure: Inexpressibility in Samuel Beckett's Fiction*, Newcastle: Cambridge Scholars Publishing.

Vanhanen, J. (2003), 'Virtual Sound: Examining Glitch and Production', *Contemporary Music Review*, 22 (4): 45–52.

Weill, K. (2019), 'Neo-Folk Has a Nazi Problem', Available online: https://www.thedailybeast.com/neo-folk-music-folks-futuristic-cousin-has-a-nazi-problem. (accessed 4 February 2022).

Wilson, W.A. (1973), 'Herder, Folklore and Romantic Nationalism', *The Journal of Popular Culture*, 6 (4): 819–35.

Filmography

A Field in England (2013), [Film] Dir. Ben Wheatley.
Blood on Satan's Claw (1971), [Film] Dir. Piers Haggard.
For Those in Peril (2013), [Film] Dir. Paul Wright.
Four Hills (2014), [Music Video] Dir. Adam Scovell.
Hereditary (2018), [Film] Dir. Ari Aster.
In the Earth (2021), [Film] Dir. Ben Wheatley.
Kill List (2011), [Film] Dir. Ben Wheatley.
Midsommar (2019), [Film] Dir. Ari Aster.
The Third Day (2020), [TV Miniseries] Dir. Felix Barrett and Dennis Kelly.
The Wicker Man (1973), [Film] Dir. Robin Hardy.
The Witch (2015), [Film] Dir. Robert Eggers.
Whistle and I'll Come To You (1968), [Film] Dir. Jonathan Miller.
Witchfinder General (1968), [Film] Dir. Michael Reeves.

11

A field of reactivity: Moog guitar and experimental systems

Interview with Bill Thompson

John McGrath

Bill Thompson is a sound artist and composer. He performs regularly as a soloist as well as in a number of groups, including The Seen, Zerøspace and Airfield (with Ian Spink), and duos with Phil Durrant, Phil Maguire, Richard Sanderson and Yoni Silver. Past collaborations include performances with Keith Rowe, Faust, EXAUDI and others. Although originally trained as a guitarist, Thompson has worked with live electronics for the better part of fifteen years. Recently, he has returned to guitar using one built by Moog combining it with electronics with miscellaneous tabletop devices, found objects, flashing lights and the occasional vibrator. He has earned numerous awards and commissions, including the PRS for New Music ATOM award, the GAVAA visual arts award, a PRS for New Music Three Festival commission, the 2010 Aberdeen Visual Arts Award, and was nominated for the Paul Hamlyn Award.

JMcG: So, tell me about the Moog guitar, when did you come across that?

BT: Yes – that was amazing. It turned out that it was in Milton Mermikides's office just next to mine. Matt Sansom, who was head of CMT at the time (BA Creative Music Technology, Surrey), told me I needed to see this guitar that Milton had. So, we headed over and he gave us a demonstration – which amounted to something like 'you just turn that knob and it starts to resonate'. I didn't quite understand so he repeated 'you turn that knob and the strings start to vibrate'. So, I did and the strings started to hum as though they had been strummed but continued to sustain. I was like, 'holy **** man, that's got my name written all over it – I can work with that!'

It was basically the instrumental realization of what I do as an artist. I knew, regardless of anything else that it did, that it was something I could use. I mean, I never intended to become a 'drone artist', but I do a lot of long-tone pieces. Everything is predicated on sustaining tones that interact with each other, that play in relation to the room and time and people's perceptions (including mine). I'm interested in how all of these elements interact and shift and change over time. And here was a guitar, something physical that I could interact with, that does that! I just thought there's a lot of potential in this thing for me. It has a few other functions as well including one I particularly like called blend which affects the harmonic spectrum between the two pickups. That's how I understand it anyway – it's a weird instrument with only a one-page manual.

Basically, the Moog runs through a foot pedal that can be set to control either the harmonic blend or a Moog filter. Unfortunately, as nothing is going through the filter of any complexity it just becomes a kind of anaemic volume/tone pedal. The harmonic blend, though, is absolutely genius because you can use the pedal to shift the harmonic spectra between the two pickups as you play. Depending on what you're doing I've found this to be pretty incredible. As we had access to two Moog guitars in the Moog Soundlab, Matt and I individually worked up our ability to play it, and then we recorded a set.

JMcG: Were you playing in a more conventional position, like in a guitar position, or was it tabletop by then?

BT: It was tabletop – playing conventionally wouldn't work for what I was doing. I think Matt played it horizontally too but on his lap. Basically, only rock stars and psychopaths bought it and they stopped making it after about five years so I've never met anyone who plays it conventionally.

JMcG: How many did they make? Do you know if there was much distribution of them?

BT: I don't know. I did look into it but I couldn't find a final number. They made several versions and I think we've got two of the late prototypes. I actually realized after that first gig that this was something I wanted to continue using. I could have continued to borrow one as a staff member but I really don't like the idea of being dependent on equipment that I don't own.

So, I was fortunate that when I started looking (they're super rare) that I amazingly – and this never happens to me – found a brand new one in the States that a music shop had stored in their backroom for ten years! They put it on eBay and although it was expensive it was still cheaper than when it was new (i.e. in production) and this *was* new, so new that when I actually got it was still considered under warranty.

JMcG: Excellent. It's got kind of a banjo setting as well, doesn't it?

BT: Yeah, exactly right. I use that sometimes – basically instead of resonating the strings it dampens them. It's very clicky and it gives you another timbral playground to use, almost like a drum machine. By laying the guitar flat on a table I can approach it almost like a found object to combine different settings and explore it physically to discover different timbres. It helps to use preparations and other objects too.

This relates somewhat to my laptop setup that always included lots of additional gear. I used to be terrified that my laptop would crash and I wouldn't be able to do the gig so by default I always brought extra kit. As a result, I developed a lot of techniques around found objects and different devices like light-to-sound sensors or electromagnetic pickups, anything that could translate 'non-sonic' activity into sound – light, electromagnetic or vibration using contact mics.

So, I took that half of my laptop set up, plus all of the tricks from my previous conventional guitar practice, and applied them to the Moog guitar. I found some interesting combinations but not all of them worked of course. The EBow, for instance, doesn't work on the Moog guitar at all. I mean, you can place it way up on the neck and it'll do what's expected but if you put it anywhere near the pickups it completely interferes with them and creates this horrendous noise.

JMcG: Yeah, I didn't even think of that. It must interact with the field.

BT: It creates distortion, but not in a good way. I was really disappointed. Then I stopped myself and sort of had a Cageian moment – you know, 'if you don't like a sound, listen to it for ten minutes', etc. So, I worked with it some more and came to the conclusion that I could use it – it's sort of become my signature sound.

What I discovered was that if you held the EBow at a certain angle you could 'surf' over the pickups and create different types of distortion. It becomes almost like a handheld feedback device that allows you to bring out different tones or depending on where your pedal is at and what you're doing with your other hand (dampening strings), you can create a kind of 'field of reactivity' where all kinds of interesting interactions occur.

That was magical for me – sort of like a really dirty theremin but with much more timbral variety. I realized that my other 'sound sensors' would interact with the Moog's pickups in interesting ways too. For example, I have these really cheap bicycle lights – so cheap they actually emit a magnetic pulse, and if you put them near the pickups, you hear different pulsating sounds that you can manipulate. Because they have different settings, you can change the duration between pulses and they even seem to affect the strings. If you have a couple of them (which I do), you can get a nice beating effect which is not worlds apart from the gate effect that I used to use with Ableton. So, you can get all kinds of interference patterns with just the pickups.

JMcG: I've seen you use fans too.

BT: Yeah, that's the one thing (besides using a table) that I stole from Keith Rowe's approach. He's a good friend and also a huge inspiration.

JMcG: Yeah, I wanted to ask you about Keith Rowe and that kind of tabletop influence?

BT: Yeah, I know – it's funny because when I first started out, I played guitar on the floor with found objects and had never actually heard about Keith Rowe. I was quite naive and everything I did I learned just by experimenting or being inspired by reading books, magazines or liner notes. At that time, I really only knew about the New York School. I think I'd read a guitar player magazine featuring Derek Bailey and I think something about prepared guitars and Fred Frith but I don't remember if they even mentioned Keith.

So, I went through this huge phase of playing unconventionally and preparing and screwing up my guitar, putting things on it to try to get different sounds. Eventually, I reached the point where I abandoned the guitar altogether and just started using my guitar pedals and a microphone shoved in a shoe to get feedback and resampling that to make pieces. I felt like I had exhausted this 'found guitar business', like 'It's done, it's dead. There's nothing left in this'. And then I heard Keith perform in Austin.

JMcG: Oh really? OK.

BT: Yeah, it was organized by the Austin New Music Co-op that I was a member of and he gave a performance and a workshop. I'd really didn't know anything about him and so, at the gig I saw this guy – you know, probably thirty to forty years older than me who I'd never even heard of doing way more things with the guitar than I had ever imagined. I mean, he had taken it so much further. Holy **** I was completely floored.

JMcG: Well, that's a real serendipitous thing, isn't it? He just turned up in Austin.

BT: It was organized by the co-op but I had somehow missed the meeting about booking him. So, it was quite the eye opener for sure. But the thing is, I didn't feel any need to rush out and return to guitar, because I had kind of done it by then and moved on. I didn't want to ape Keith Rowe's style. When I eventually moved to Aberdeen years later in 2004, I did play guitar in a composition that I'd written using found objects I'd collected from an eight-hour soundwalk. Basically, I prepared the guitar with the objects and then hit, scraped or bowed it while holding it like a cello or on my lap. But it was relevant to the piece I'd written and I didn't feel like I needed to repeat what I'd done before (or what I'd seen Keith do).

Eventually I was invited to play with Keith in Nottingham. I'd never properly met him at that point even though I'd seen him perform in Austin. He was doing his guitar-based setup and I was doing my laptop-based setup and that's how we met and became friends. A couple of years later we did a tour based on a piece I'd written using induction mics. I'd conceived of it for a specific trio between myself, Keith and a mutual friend of ours from Austin, Rick Reed. I performed with laptop, hacked electronics and found objects, Rick was using a VCS3 and guitar effects and Keith was performing with tabletop guitar and objects, of course.

Sometime later I realized that I was probably going to go back to guitar eventually but it felt tricky as I'd toured with Keith and he is kind of the father of that (tabletop) style. I just had to get over it and stop worrying that I'd be seen as aping someone else's style.

JMcG: Like a disciple or something?

BT: Yeah, because I mean I have deep respect for Keith, you know, deep. I've actually never seen him perform where he didn't just wipe the floor with his set. He's so strong as an improviser. But even so, I don't want to be anyone else, you know. Fortunately, it turns out that what I do with the guitar is quite different anyway, especially with how the Moog guitar works – it's a very different instrument in a lot of ways.

JMcG: Well, he's definitely not a drone artist.

BT: No, he's not. And although my stuff can be quite aggressive when I get into the noisier territory, I don't think I've ever achieved that raw quality that Keith is so good at. He could be exceptionally abrasive in a very beautiful way because he's not inhibited by sounds that might be considered ugly, you know. And I find myself, over the years, going through periods where I have to shed kinds of training that I've had as a composer. It's like being more open to any sound. It took me a long time to kind of 'un-indoctrinate' myself about what was musical – you know, am I pulling my punches and why am I pulling my punches? And why am I not more open to these sounds?

JMcG: Yeah, like that EBow you mentioned.

BT: Yeah, exactly, it rears its head even now. But there were things that I did borrow from Keith, like the fan thing because with the guitar the only way that you can get it to sustain is to have something constantly agitating it. And it was Keith who showed me that and how he did it, how he came up with it and so on. The irony is that it doesn't work the same on the Moog guitar anyway because it doesn't need that to sustain. So, the way that I use it is not to make the guitar sustain, but to interrupt it, to break up the sustain. And if you get two or three fans going at the same time, you can get these kind of weird aleatoric polyrhythmic textures that are really lovely.

JMcG: So, you're always on the lookout for weird kinds of gizmos and stuff like that? (Figures 11.1 and 11.2)

BT: Exactly, I just kind of approach the guitar as a found object. Actually, I kind of treat any gear like a found object, I'm not that interested in using things the way you're supposed to be used. I sort of think everything that we buy is quite

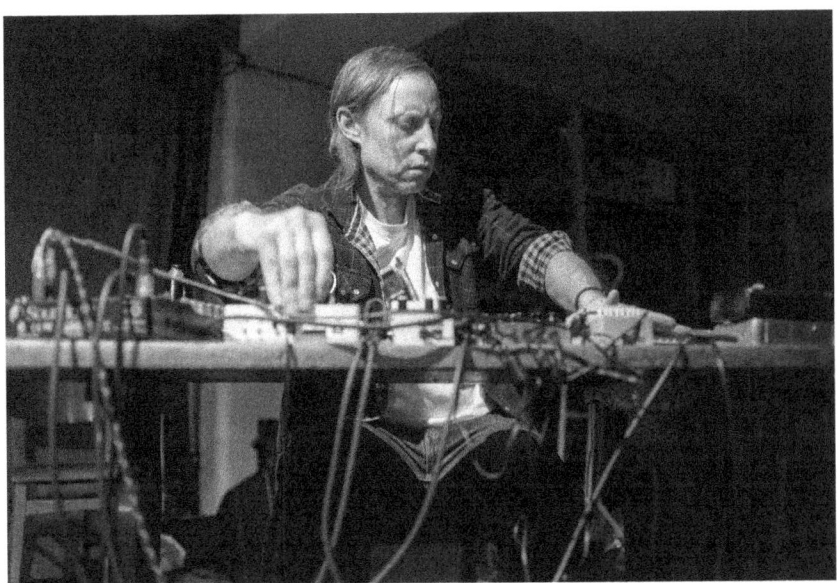

Figure 11.1 Bill Thompson, Cafe Oto, London 2022. (Photo: Dawid Laskowski, used with permission.)

Figure 11.2 Bill Thompson's Moog guitar setup. (Photo: Bill Thompson, used with permission.)

over-determined by the market and what will sell, and I'm not that interested in doing things the way that somebody in some office thinks I should be doing it.

JMcG: Yeah, that's what I love about the what you said about the Moog guitar, like the instruction manual. Basically, there wasn't one. You know, it's like here you go, play with this, see what you can do.

What are the affordances of this? What's the market in terms of what people are going to play with it, you know?

BT: That's the funny thing, right? And this is, uh, I don't know if it was Matt [Samson] that said this – they didn't really realize what they had made, I mean God bless Moog, you know they're great, but if you look at the promo videos for it, they're really trying to sell it to guitarists.

JMcG: It's like a shredder thing or something?

BT: Yeah, it's like you could play it and do this infinite sustain and they've got people doing this kind of like really, you know, quite cheesy stuff. And also, for five grand. Right? It's heavy, doesn't sound that great, is super expensive and it basically does one thing. How many songs can you write with ultimate sustain in a conventional context, you know? But as an electronic drone string machine? Brilliant.

JMcG: The most interesting stuff is often created when using something in a way it isn't designed for or outside of what the intended outcomes of it are, like that 'cracked media' [Kelly 2009] kind of stuff.

BT: Totally, it's exactly like cracked media. A writer that I'm really enamoured with at the moment is Hans-Jörg Rheinberger [1997] who talks about experimental systems and taking objects or devices or ideas and putting them in new contexts and seeing what develops (that's my understanding anyway). When this is productive you can create conditions where unexpected results come up. He writes that this is how new knowledge actually arrives – you get this unexpected result and then it's your job to make sense of it. So, for me it was like taking two separate systems and connecting it to this new system and seeing what happens and then new things developed.

JMcG: New perspectives, yeah.

BT: It was quite a remarkable experience as it developed into a whole new kind of practice. Or borrowing ideas from other people and using them in different contexts, like the idea about the fan that turned out to have the opposite effect with the Moog guitar but with really interesting results. I think that's why it's important that we're encouraged to work against the grain of whatever device we have, but also to borrow from each other, because the way we implement different ideas in our own system is going to reveal new things. I think this entire process, how we relate to each other, how ideas and practices move around and mutate and function differently in different contexts is fascinating.

Editors' Choice – Recommended Listening:

Live at the Brunswick (2017), Bill Thompson, Touchradio.
Mouthful of Silence (2017), Bill Thompson, Burning Harpsichord Records.
Improfest (2022), Bill Thompson, https://youtu.be/QSwtA1BxPEo
Live at Sound Festival Aberdeen (2019), Bill Thompson, https://youtu.be/bQM-JYZ6B-_M
Website: www.billthompson.org

References

Kelly, C. (2009), *Cracked Media: The Sound of Malfunction*, Cambridge, MA: MIT Press.
Rheinberger, H. (1997), *Toward a History of Epistemic Things*, Stanford, CA: Stanford University Press.

12

The digital fretboard

Remapping and relearning the guitar's pitch matrix with MIDI and Max/MSP

Milton Mermikides

For Pat Martino, a fretboard pioneer

Encountering the fretboard

The act of manipulating – through constraint, reordering and remapping – the pitch profile of guitar strings and their fret positions, intersects with a swathe of research fields within and beyond guitar scholarship. These include (1) *guitar cognition* – how guitarists conceptualize, absorb and negotiate the idiosyncrasies of the instrument (see Brandon and Westwood 2019; De Souza 2021; Dean 2014); (2) *fretboard pedagogy* – where the fretboard (rather than stave or abstract space) is the central interface for the (usually improvisational) engagement, manipulation and understanding of musical objects (see Willmott 1994; Goodrick 1987; Martino 2016; Capuzzo 2006; Damian 2001; Leathwood 2014; De Souza 2018); (3) *fix-and-vary improvisational pedagogy* of the 'Berklee school' of jazz pedagogy (see Crook 1991); (4) *instrument design* and *organology* (Paine 2011; Magnussen 2019); (5) *computer performance* and *human–machine interaction* (Fell 2013; Emmerson 2011; Butler 2014); and (6) *Pitch surface* representations where pitches, rather than arranged linearly or cyclically, are organized in two (and higher) dimensional arrays such as the dual-interval spaces of Stephen Brown (2003).

While I can now point to such neatly defined – if diverse – reference points, the initial and ongoing motivations of the project are a sprawling web of whimsical tinkering, solutions to performance objectives, digital teaching tools and other by-products of my activities as a jazz guitarist (with a history of hand injury), electronic musician, performer and programmer. In addition, a deep interest in music theory, analysis and diverse musical representations predates – and usually extends beyond – any fluency of notation reading I have gathered. While there was no clear starting point of this project, a series of experience and insights in my guitar learning are perhaps useful vignettes in framing some relevant themes:

(a) My adolescent first encounter with the 'Hendrix chord' (a dominant seventh chord with a sharpened ninth and omitted fifth) and the indescribably satisfying blended experience of the feel of the idiomatic zig-zag fretboard shape and its acoustic intervallic richness. Years later I uncovered – through improvising with MIDI programming rather than theoretical reasoning – that these four notes (and not their usually simplified '7#9' spelling) are in fact an inversion of the all-interval tetrachord 4-z15 – an optimally efficient realization of all-interval classes, in some part explaining and validating that first impression.

(b) As a music student, the painful struggle to sight-read the sort of musical material I was routinely improvising, absorbing aurally and 'storing' on the fretboard rather than stave. While reading guitar transcriptions with tablature I would feel guilty when my eyes flicked to the tablature as if the staff notation was a more pure – and real – representation of the music.

(c) After months of deep jazz guitar practise at Berklee, I would often experience the 'Tetris effect' of visualizing fretboard shapes (particularly with audio cues) and could practise and retain fretboard knowledge during a period of a hand injury. MRI scans years later with colleagues at UCL neuroscience would reveal these 'neural fingerprints', a deeply engrained connection between abstract musical objects and their physical realization.

(d) On occasion, I might hear a recording of a guitar phrase and know instantly its shape on the fretboard. This 'fretboard transcription' occurred before knowing the note names or notational representation.

(e) The use of the fretboard as an analytical tool. First as a simple calculator (e.g. 'What is a minor sixth up from E♭?') but also as a way of providing theoretical insight. For example, discovering that an augmented triad shape can be made into any of six major and minor triads by moving any note up or down a fret. Similarly, by adjusting any one note of a diminished seventh triad down or up one fret, any of four dominant seventh, or four half-diminished seventh (or minor sixth if one prefers) chords may be produced. Such fretboard insights can be found in the pedagogy (and playing) of Pat Martino (see Martino 2016, and Capuzzo 2006). However, the fretboard is also an excellent workbench for visualizing and calculating other voice-led transformations including those found in Neo-Riemannian theory (for an introduction to the field, see Cohn 1998). Some examples of such pluripotent 'fretboard stem-cells' are presented in Figure 12.1. These transformations are of course not exclusive to the fretboard and can be realized on any pitched instrument. However, the inbuilt structure of the fretboard with its strict voice-per-string constraint, shape-based cognition and chromatic parallelism of frets, I suggest illuminates such transformations with particular clarity.

(f) In addition to this pluripotency, I discovered – with varied levels of joy and confusion – that the same fretboard shapes could have multiple harmonic implications. Some exercises at Berklee (see Willmott 1994) invite the student to find the (many) valid harmonic readings of a single fretboard shape. The limited polyphony of the fretboard, its inconsistent string tuning and the flexible nature of jazz harmony would create situations where a handful of (sometimes just one) fretboard shapes could negotiate an extended progression.

(g) Performing in big band settings, I discovered that rarely were the chord symbols in chart notation a complete or correct prescription of what to play harmonically. It was often impossible to include all extensions and the chord symbols were often fussily prescriptive. Effective comping involved a real-time analysis of the written notation (and aural context) and translation to a musical, idiomatic and often simpler solution on the fretboard. This is exemplified in the playing of Count Basie rhythm guitarist Freddie Green who used very succinct fretboard shapes to produce elaborate, sophisticated and deceptively simple fretboard strategies in the elegant negotiation of complex harmonic progressions, notably his use of 'one-note chords' (see Dickert 1994 and Buttermann 2009).

(h) The embarrassment of finding myself 'improvising' the exact comping or soloing strategy on repeated choruses of a jazz tune, demonstrating that I had forged near-Pavlovian responses to notational and theoretical

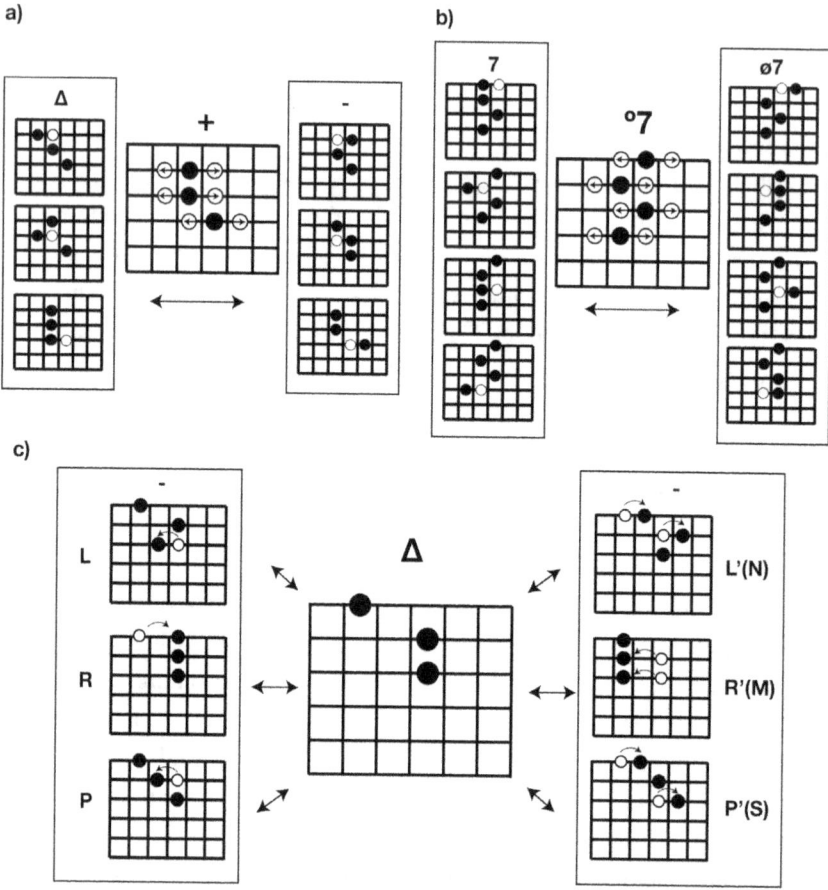

Figure 12.1 Some fretboard 'stem cells'. By adjusting one note up or down a fret of (a) an augmented triad (b) a diminished seventh chord, produces three major and three minor triads, and four dominant seventh and four half-diminished (or minor sixth) chords, respectively. The archetypal Neo-Riemannian transformations of L, R, P and their prime counterparts L', R', P' (also known as N, M and S) in this case transforming a major triad into six minor chords are also shown.

stimuli. These unhelpfully 'fluent' links from chord symbol/theory to fretboard realization were only effectively mitigated by the active enforcing of constraints such as Hal Crook's *How to Improvise* fix/vary improvisational challenges (Crook 1991), and from a fretboard perspective, Jon Damian's palette studies (Damian 2001) and Mick Goodrick's 'disadvantage exercises' (Goodrick 1987: 11).

(i) When jamming with the virtuosic (and left-handed) guitarist John Wheatcroft, he mischievously suggested swapping guitars, so we were each playing 'upside-down' reversing the orientation of the strings. It is hard to articulate the liberating sense of joy this silly and simple act afforded. Attempting, variously failing but unexpectedly succeeding to play familiar jazz tunes with this conceptually similar but orientationally and tactiley alien configuration, allowed me to reconnect with the naive joy of my 'first chords' and for them to be re-heard with a naive clarity that was somehow lost in the process of deep fretboard training.

(j) As an electronic musician and performer, I often use a range of MIDI controllers including the Ableton Push. This device includes an 8 × 8 grid of velocity-sensitive pads which – among other functions – can act as a two-dimensional keyboard. The lowest pitch occurs in the lower left-hand corner, and ascends from left to right chromatically (or – if you choose – diatonically in a number of scales). Pitches also rise vertically from each pad in fourths (although this interval can be altered). This chromatic horizontal/vertical fourths configuration (what Brown (2003) would term an ic1/ic5 dual-interval space) closely mimics an eight-string eight-fret fretboard, tuned in perfect fourths. This similarity to the guitar immediately allowed a level of inherited proficiency. However, I also discovered two significant hindrances to complete virtuosity on the instrument. First, when playing melodies that moved from the lower half to the upper half of the grid, I experienced a hesitation as I tried to accommodate the 'missing' major third fretboard anomaly between strings 3 and 2. Although the Push's layout is consistent, and chord patterns can be transposed vertically without modification, my intense fretboard training in fact inhibited the full potential of fluency. This gap still somewhat lingers despite repeated practice. Second – and what was only noticed after hours of play time – I discovered that I avoided playing simultaneous notes *on the same row*. While this was perfectly allowable on the Push, the limited note-per-string polyphony blinded me to this most obvious affordance of the Push.

The preceding vignettes suggest that a broad range of guitar activity (such as performance, pedagogy, theory, improvisation and composition) occurs in – and between – various conceptual 'spaces' – ways of knowing. I find it helpful – and illuminating – to consider such spaces to be: (1) *Fretboard space (F-Space)* – guitar fretboard 'objects' (e.g. the Hendrix chord shape) where musical objects are visualized, manipulated and technically realized; (2) *Acoustic space (A-Space)* – acoustic sounding – and/or 'internally heard' events (e.g. the sound produced by playing the Hendrix chord); (3) *M-Space* (see Mermikides 2010) – abstracted theoretical (both declarative and intuitive) knowledge and their representational structures (e.g. understanding the Hendrix chord as a [0, 1, 4, 6] PC-set, an <1 1 1 1 1 1> interval vector, a shape in a chromatic circle, a subset of an octatonic scale, etc.) – these objects can be used in composition, performance, improvisation and analysis; and (4) *N-Space* – representations of musical objects in conventional notation (e.g. E, G♯, D, G on a treble clef). These spaces are represented in Figure 12.2, using the Hendrix chord as an illustration. Fluency in translation between these spaces may be gained, such as sight-reading (N-Space to F-Space) or recognizing a mode in a recording (an 'aural analysis' from A-Space to M-Space), and so on.

This representation allows us to see the missing connection from N-Space in the old – and anachronistic – joke: '*how do you make an electric guitarist shut*

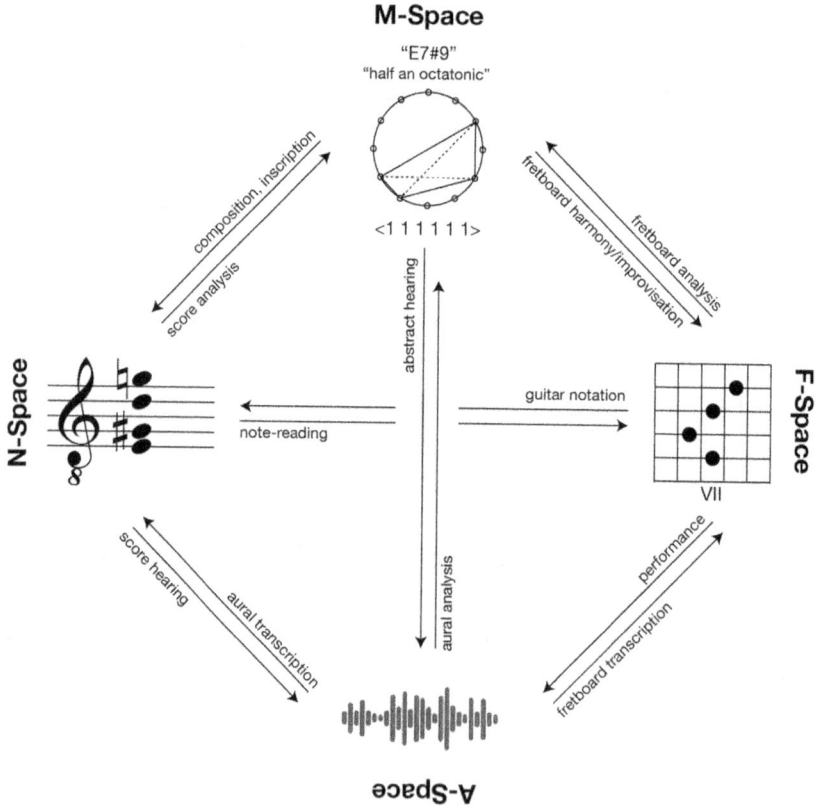

Figure 12.2 Four spaces or 'ways of knowing' the guitar and their interactions, using the Hendrix chord as an example.

up? – put sheet music in front of them', but also in its counter: '*how do you make a classical guitarist shut up – take the sheet music away*' – where presumably all activity is reliant on N-Space. This view also gives a more nuanced concept of 'literacy'. For example, Wes Montgomery is often described – not without agenda – as a 'natural gifted guitarist' despite that (or even because) he 'couldn't read music, or know theory' (Stolzenburg 2022). However, recently circulated footage of Wes rehearsing a new composition with the Pim Jacobs Trio (All That Jazz 2017) reveals a wholly different perspective. Wes teaches the piece's harmonic structure to the ensemble by both playing and saying chord names and modulation intervals. He notices immediately – by ear – the pianist's misplayed chords, correcting him through verbal direction and demonstration. Here, almost all connections in Figure 12.2 are fluent and active, except for those coming to or from N-Space. Given that the ensemble memorized the piece in minutes through this instruction (and any sheet music prepared would probably also be memorized and then abandoned), it's hard to see here any inefficiency or deficiency of 'literacy' – nor the musical experience for all involved.

From the examples of my personal experience, we might see that translation between these spaces can be stronger than others, for example 'fretboard harmony' (M-Space to F-Space) and 'fretboard transcription' (A-Space to F-Space) are more robust than sight-reading (N-Space to F-Space). Translations can also be indirect such as the 'sight analysis' of big band guitar playing (N-Space to F-Space via M-Space) or 'working out' M-Space objects ('a minor sixth up from E♭') on the fretboard. Practice can increase fluency between spaces in sight-reading, aural analysis, playing by ear and so on. However, repetition might also contribute to unhelpful automated mannerisms (the same solo/chords on every chorus), and 'fluency myopia' where we can become blind to opportunity (as in the Push example). As Jonathan De Souza clearly presents in the context of Kurt Rosenwinkel, a level of learning – knowing exactly what to play and how it will sound – can lead to an 'overly schematic' and 'unsurprising' musical act (De Souza 2017: 9), and a 'redundant' musical experience. My suggestion here is that there is a keen benefit to challenging, disrupting, resetting, unlearning, relearning, turning upside-down and sabotaging these links between spaces. In this project, I do so by manipulating – through technology – the pitch matrix of the fretboard; rewiring the connections between the fretboard (F-Space), theoretical systems (M-Space) and the resulting sound objects (A-Space). The motivation is to strengthen and extend existing practice, but also to reconnect to a naive but profound sense of joy and discovery. In the spirit of 'resetting', let's take a first principles look at the guitar fretboard and its affordances.

Surveying the fretboard

How musical pitches are represented in score notation, abstracted theoretical systems and instrumental interfaces varies widely, including left-right linear keyboard presentations, woodwind fingerings, circle of fifths, chromatic circles, the string-per-note layout of the harp, the bilateral symmetry of the *mbira* and *kora*,[1] 'pitch surface' representations in two (and more) dimensions, the 8 × 8 layout of the Ableton Push, logarithmic distance to the theremin's antenna and countless others including the standard guitar fretboard and the vertical layout of the stave. As it happens, these latter two exist in a somewhat awkward relationship. The layout of pitches on the standard guitar's fretboard, echoes the stave's horizontal lines and pitch ascension, but distorts them. But we should reject the bias in implying that the fretboard is the 'distortion' of the 'correct' stave – rather they are two of countless equally valid pitch representations. In any case, this unhelpfully proximal similarity between stave and fretboard might explain the guitar's relationship – and associated jokes about guitarists – with standard notation. These 'deviations' and idiosyncrasies of the guitar I suggest are useful and wonderful constraints, giving the instrument its melodic and harmonic character and rich repertoire. These include *pitch-repetition*, *pitch-spacing* and *polyphonic* characteristics. Each of these is explored as follows.

Pitch repetition

Goodrick's observation that on the guitar, 'the average note has 2.8 locations and 9.2 possible fingerings' (Goodrick 1987: 93) is a useful proxy for the guitar's idiosyncratic pitch complexity, but is worthy of some exploration. Unlike keyboard instruments, this *pitch repetition* – being able to find the same note in different parts of the instrument – is a combined function of how close the open strings are tuned, the number of strings and fretboard length. We can, for example, maximize pitch repetition by tuning all strings identically (each note would have

---

[1] The *kora* incidentally is one of the few instruments naming high-frequency notes are described as 'low' and vice versa, a valid but starkly rare perspective (Titon et al. 2016)

six locations). Conversely, if we wanted a guitar with zero pitch repetition, the interval between each string would have to be wider than the interval between the open string and top fret (one would need a very short fretboard to achieve this acoustically, but it's possible digitally). Tuning systems exist between these two extremes, and this '*Goodrick number*' – the average number of locations for each note – is a useful comparative tool. To calculate this, we need the number of fretboard locations – which is the number of strings multiplied by the number of 'fret-spaces' (that is, the number of frets and the open string). We divide this number by the number of unique pitches or *continuous range*. In most cases, this is the number of semitones between its highest and lowest note, but I use this clumsier term for the rare cases when there are gaps. Here is its calculation:

$$Gn = \frac{strings * (frets + 1)}{continuous\ range}$$

A twenty-fret six-string guitar in standard tuning would have (6 × 21) = 126 locations, and a continuous range of 45 semitones, and so a Goodrick of 126/45 = 2.8.

Any extension of the instrument's continuous range by – for example – dropping the lowest string, or sharpening the highest string, would decrease the Goodrick number subtly (a twenty-fret guitar in drop D and Ant Law's perfect fourths tuning have a *Gn* of about 2.68 and 2.74 respectively, compared to standard tuning's 2.8).[2] Conversely, we could increase pitch repetition by 'clustering' the strings as in Nashville Tuning where the lowest 4 (E, A, D and G) strings are tuned up an octave, and *Gn* = 3.5.

This pitch repetition may complicate sight-reading but we are compensated by a broader range of timbral options as well as the possibility of note doubling in chords. There are also registral affordances to this repetition: a note can be the top of a chord in open position, or the bottom of a chord in eighth position, extending its voicing possibilities. What isn't addressed in the Goodrick calculations is *where* on the fretboard such repetition lies. It is not evenly distributed. In standard tuning, there is a peak of repetition around E3[3] which appears six times (one for every string) on a twenty-four-fret guitar. The amount of repetition falls away either side from this apex (see Figure 12.3, top right).

---

[2] See interview with Ant Law in Chapter 5 of this volume.
[3] In this chapter I use the MIDI convention of middle C (MIDI note 60) as C3. This is the concert pitch so E3 (a third above middle C) is the top string of standard tuning.

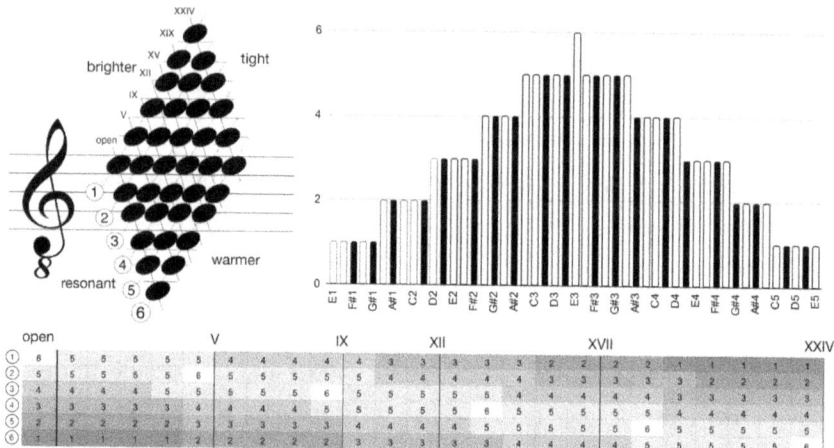

Figure 12.3 Three representations of the pitch repetition profile of a twenty-four-fret guitar in standard tuning. Clockwise from left, (1) The *fretboard diamond* showing selected repeated (but timbrally varied) pitches on the stave intersecting with their string and fret location, (2) the distribution curve of pitches and (3) *Repetition ridge* – the distinctive pattern of repetition across the fretboard.

On the fretboard itself, we see the lowest amount of pitch repetition towards the nut in the low strings, and in the high register of the top strings. Conversely, the highest level of repetition runs from the open top string to the high position of the sixth string. If we visualize the amount of repetition as altitude, like contour lines on a map, the fretboard has a diagonal 'repetition ridge' running through its length (see Figure 12.3, bottom[4]). The complex – but rather beautiful – relationship of the fretboard with the stave (see Figure 12.3, top left). This *fretboard diamond* shows some selected pitches and their level of repetition on the stave, intersecting with a representation of the string and fret numbers (note that repeated notes are varied in terms of timbre). These three perspectives reveal some of the intricately complex relationships between N-Space and F-Space, a relationship that shifts as we explore a wider range of tunings.

Pitch spacing

The stave has an implicit diatonic bias, in that every note *name* (E, F, G, etc.) rather than chromatic pitch is given an equal visual distance; for instance, the

---

[4] I have tried as much as possible to minimize the right-hand guitarist bias of diagrammatic representations, but space and the nature of the concepts made this challenge. Left-handed versions of diagrams are however available on my site www.miltonline.com

line-to-line distance on a treble clef stave can represent a minor third (E to G) or major third (G to B). Chromaticism, keys and further disruptions to this spacing are introduced through key signatures and accidentals. Some instruments – like the pedal harp replicate this closely: each string is tuned to a diatonic note name and is equally spaced to an adjacent one regardless of its semitone distance. The pedals – like accidentals or key signatures – chromatically shift the pitch of these note names but not their physical position. The keyboard is a little more subtle in its diatonic bias – while chromatic notes are inserted between five of the seven notes, the gaps between E and F, and B and C, take the same physical distance as their whole-tone counterparts. The guitar fretboard does not bend to this diatonic edict in either of its pitch dimensions. The steps of the fret are equally spaced (at least logarithmically) based on chromatic, not diatonic distance, so the vertical distance on the stave does not map neatly to the horizontal distance of frets. The strict chromaticism of the frets allows easy parallelism, favouring the shape of patterns over pitch content. Neither do the strings' tuning pattern match the horizontal lines of the stave, employing fourths over the mixed third intervals of the stave. The only concession to diatonicism is the major third interval between the third and second strings, interrupting the cycle of fourths to prematurely close the two-octave distance between E1 and E3. This small anomaly in the tuning pattern of the strings has profound effects on vertical guitar learning in contrast to its 'easy' horizontal parallelism. To unpack this further let's take again the Hendrix chord as an illustration of the horizontal-vertical distinction. Let's consider the Hendrix chord from two perspectives: (1) as an intervallic structure (represented for example as a prime form pitch-class set [0, 1, 4, 6] and interval vector <1 1 1 1 1 1>) – an object in M-Space, and (2) A zig-zag shape in the middle of the fretboard, an object in F-Space. Moving the object in either direction horizontally along the fretboard makes no difference to its intervallic structure. However vertical movement against the strings reveals the mismatch between M-Space and F-Space, if we want to keep the fretboard shape, the intervallic structure changes (a different chord name suggestion, pitch-class set and interval vector); if we want to retain the intervallic structure, then the fretboard shape has to adjust to accommodate the tuning inconsistency. This is illustrated in Figure 12.4.

This observation may be self-evident to most guitarists, but looking at the issue closely raises some helpful questions and perspectives. For example, we can see that the Hendrix four-string block needed three different shapes to retain its intervallic structure across the strings (conversely the one shape produced

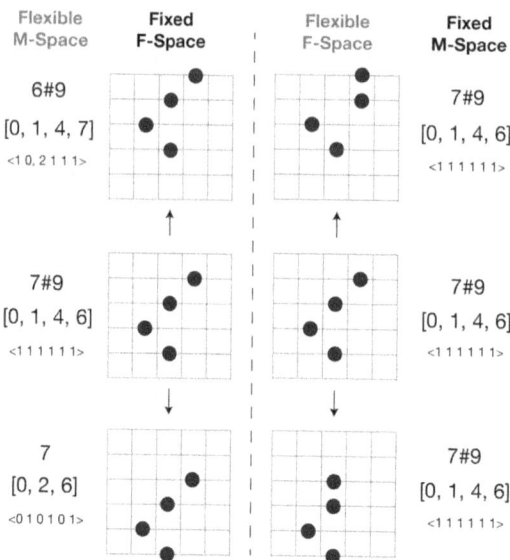

Figure 12.4 M-Space versus F-Space: the Hendrix chord as fixed fretboard shape (left) and as a fixed intervallic structure, moved vertically across the standard tuning fretboard. An illustrative chord symbol, prime form pitch-class set and interval vector are shown for each object.

three different intervallic structures). We can consider this a measure of *shape consistency* of the fretboard object in a specific tuning. For two-note string blocks (two notes on an adjacent strings) we only need two shapes as some are 'reusable'. The three possible four-note string blocks are all different, as are the two possible five-note blocks. The number of chord shapes needed to retain intervallic structure for one, two, three, four, five and six-note chord blocks, respectively, are <1 2 3 3 2 1> – a sort of *shape consistency vector*[5] of standard tuning. This complexity needn't be the case: Law's perfect fourths tuning (Law 2011) has a shape consistency vector of <1 1 1 1 1 1> – all chord blocks can be transposed vertically without alteration. This – and other uniform and altered tunings – comes with the cost of breaking the pitch-class connection between the sixth and first string, a much relied upon resource in standard tuning practice. The top F against the low E would – from a standard practice – be seen as a type of *barré drift* of +1 semitone, as compared to 0 in standard tuning and D A D G A D, -2 in drop D and +5 in Rosenwinkel's *Zhivago* tuning and so on.

[5] The outer two numbers of a shape consistency vector will always be 1, but are included for completion, as well as a simple indication of the number of strings on the instrument. For example, vectors for the standard tuning of the bass guitar, ukulele, charango and 7-string guitar are <1 1 1 1>, <1 2 2 1>, <1 3 3 2 1> and <1 2 3 3 3 2 1> respectively.

There are other implications to string tuning, of course, the intervals between the strings not only impact the overall range of the instrument but also what range is available in a fixed position. If we take the fifth fret of the lowest tuned string and the eighth fret of the highest tuned string (excluding open strings) to represent a comfortable *underhand range*, then standard tuning comes out at twenty-eight semitones, perfect fourth tuning at twenty-nine semitones, Nashville Tuning a constrained nineteen semitones and Fripp's New Standard Tuning a sizeable thirty-five semitones. Again, with the fretboard, there are trade-offs involved with such in-position range. The wider the range (that is the wider the tuning between strings) the more 'stretchy' the fingering is between strings (think of playing a chromatic scale in position). In this model, the ideally un-stretchy fingering for a guitarist with four fretting fingers is augmented tuning (strings a major third apart), which would allow four notes per string in a chromatic scale. We can imagine a four fret by six block of twenty-four 'underhand frets'. If strings are tuned any wider then we break out of the ergonomic finger-per-fret layout, if the strings are tuned narrow then we waste fingers (and range). We can quantify this stretchiness by counting the number of 'chromatic gaps' in position.[6] Four for standard tuning, five for perfect fourth tuning and eleven for 'New Standard Tuning'. 'Negative gaps' would imply an overall 'scrunchiness' to the tuning. From these gaps, we can generalize *stretchiness* as the average number of gaps between strings.

As we construct and explore common (and uncommon) tuning systems, *Goodrick numbers*, repetition profiles, *shape consistency vectors* and *stretchiness*, alongside the established scordatura terms tuning *consistency* and *displacement* (see De Souza 2017: 10), are simple but helpful measures of a tuning system's particular character, challenges and affordances.

Polyphony

The construction of the guitar only allows as many (conventional produced) melodic voices as there are strings. As seen in Figure 12.1, this six-voice polyphony is a useful constraint in the engagement with contrapuntal transformations. The challenge comes not only in the voice limit but also (in standard tuning) a restriction on close voicing possibilities – diatonic seventh chords (in close

---

[6] We can generalize the number of gaps for any number of strings and fretting hand fingers on conventional tuning systems as (highest note in position – lowest note in position +1) - *(strings * fretting hand fingers)*.

voicings) are far more technically challenging than their theoretical simplicity would suggest. A keyboardist would have little trouble learning the concept and the execution of close position seventh chords, while the advancing guitarist is obliged to either gain a higher level of theoretical sophistication or fracture the link between understanding a chord's construction and its fretboard realization.

The polyphony of the instrument is also used in guitar pedagogy as a mechanism for technical development, fretboard knowledge and improvisational development. Goodrick's 'unitar' exercise (Goodrick 1987: 10–11) a single-string exercise is introduced to the 'advancing guitarist' to hear the 'the direct relationship between interval and distance and movement in space', to encourage horizontal movement and exploration of higher frets, to engage with the intervallic construction (rather than shape) of arpeggios and chords, and focus on specific technical challenges including legato and position shifts. He encourages this 'unitar' exploration on every string, before moving on to the five pairs of adjacent strings, exploring permutations of fingerings and slowly earning the privilege and revealing the potential of all string access. Martino's pedagogy (Martino 2016) engages with this string limit concept comprehensively by presenting all sixty-four possible combinations of string use, as improvisational strategies to explore. He relates them with – with stunning insight – to the hexagrams of the *I Ching,* an ancient Chinese divination text (see Adler 2002) in which hexagrams (made of two three-line *trigrams*) are presented in every combination of broken ('*yin*') and unbroken ('*yang*') lines. A perfect representation of all possible patterns of string activation. I've recreated the concept in Figure 12.5 with the first eight hexagrams,[7] annotating each with their *I Ching* sequence number, Chinese and English names, string labels and additional fretboard information. I've named the hexagrams by their binary spelling (the first is 111111 in binary 63, the Hendrix chord would be 0111110 = 30). However, I've used the elegant 12th-century BC *King Wen* sequence, where each pair of hexagrams are upside-down versions of each other or – if vertically symmetrical – 'shadows', with played strings turning silent and vice versa. I have also linked these hexagrams to the *shape consistency* concept of the previous section. Two numbers represent how many positions the pattern could be shifted in a vertical position, and how many shapes would be required to maintain intervallic structure, respectively. In other words < 4 3 > is a hexagram that – if shifted – has four vertical positions, and in so doing creates

---

[7] All sixty-four annotated hexagrams are available at: www.miltonline.com/hexagrams

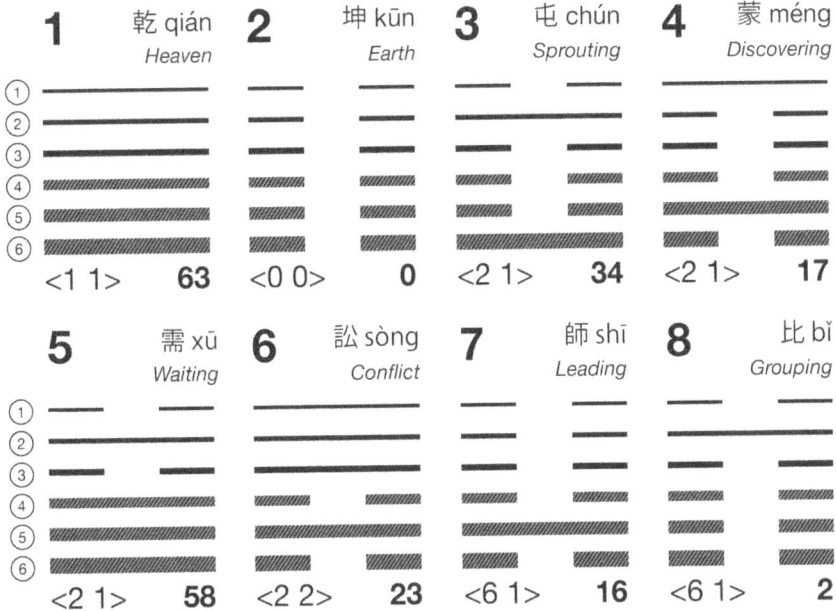

Figure 12.5 An illustration of Pat Martino's concept (Martino 2016) of linking the *I Ching* hexagrams to the sixty-four possible combinations of string use (of which the first eight are shown here). I have added at the bottom right of each hexagram its *binary value*. The vector in the lower left contains two integers, the first showing the number of available vertical positions of each shape, and the second its *shape consistency* – the number of intervallic structures these would produce in standard tuning.

three different interval structures (or would need three shapes to maintain an intervallic structure) in standard tuning. This allows the hexagrams to be used not just as useful constraints, but as mechanisms to learn and develop chord and scale structures.

These hexagram constraints connect neatly with the fix-and-vary jazz pedagogical approach (see Mermikides 2010), notably Hal Crook's *How to Improvise* (Crook 1991) and Goodrick's 'disadvantage exercises' (Goodrick 1987: 10–11). Representative exercises might include 'improvise in A Lydian using only strings 2 and 5' or ascribing a random hexagram to each chorus of a blues solo. As we will see this combinatorial completion can not only be used in practice, but also as a digitally executed mechanism. When working on the documentary of Martino (*Martino Unstrung* 2007), I used MIDI technology so he could visualize the hexagrams as he improvised. But later in this chapter, we will see how digital technology can reverse this relationship and enforce – not just respond to – such inspiring constraints.

The *Fretboard Remapper*

Intercepting the MIDI guitar

A MIDI guitar pickup and interface converts audio signals into discrete MIDI messages, allowing the guitarist to play any MIDI-compatible hardware or software instrument, while still functioning as a conventional guitar. These MIDI messages are relatively simple, they can communicate the pitch of a note (any of 0–127 chromatic notes, with middle C at 60), and indicate when a particular note starts and ends (a 'Note on' message is sent when the amplitude incoming signal exceeds a customizable threshold, and a 'Note off' message when it drops below it). In addition, a note can be associated with a range of velocity levels (0–127) as well as pitch bend and other data. Crucially for this project – and what sets it apart from completely software-based real-time audio to MIDI converters (like Jam Origins *MIDI Guitar* plug on) – the system here uses the Roland GK hexaphonic system[8] which has a pickup for each individual string, assignable to distinct MIDI channels. That way each string has its own discrete series of notes, and so we can identify the originating string for any note and even assign each string to a different instrument. This ability to recognize the source of a note would not be necessary without the pitch repetition aspect of the guitar, but the ability to identify its string origin is essential to the project: if we know what pitch is played, and on what string, then (given we know the guitar's tuning), we can identify the fret also.

While MIDI guitar is conventionally used to set up the fretboard interface (rather than say the MIDI keyboard) to perform hardware and virtual MIDI instruments, my aim here was to intercept the MIDI messages before they reached their instrument. By doing so I could digitally visualize and manipulate those messages before (if desired) sending them on to be sounded in A-Space. To achieve this interception, I use Cycling 74's Max/MSP, a very well-known graphical programming language that allows – among many other things – the capture, generation and manipulation of MIDI data.

The patch *Fretboard Remapper* (aka *'the DeSouzaphone'*) first started as a tool to teach composition and guitar online during lockdown.[9] I built a simple visualizer which created live fingerings, so I could demonstrate on the guitar and

---

[8] For this project I used a Brian Moore i7 electric guitar with an inbuilt hexaphonic GK pickup connected to a Roland GI-20 which sent MIDI messages to an Apple Mac running Max/MSP 8 and Ableton Live Suite 11.
[9] Reference to lockdown during 2020 coronavirus pandemic.

The Digital Fretboard 231

have the fretboard clearly seen by students. The patch would listen on each of the six MIDI channels, if it appeared on channel 1 (string 1) it would place an oval on the top row, its horizontal position would represent the fret number which was simply calculated as *fret number = (incoming note on string n) – (pitch of open string n)*. For example, the high E string of standard tuning is MIDI note 64. If the patch receives MIDI note 68 (G♯) on channel 1, we know that it originated from fret 4 (68 – 64 = 4). This logic is repeated for every string so that with an image of a fretboard as a backdrop the live guitar's fretboard activity can be clearly visualized (see Figure 12.6, top-middle of image).

I could, and often do, use the system – in parallel with the conventional audio output of the guitar – as a passive fretboard visualizer. In addition, since I had the MIDI data it could also be used to trigger a keyboard display, stave notation, a

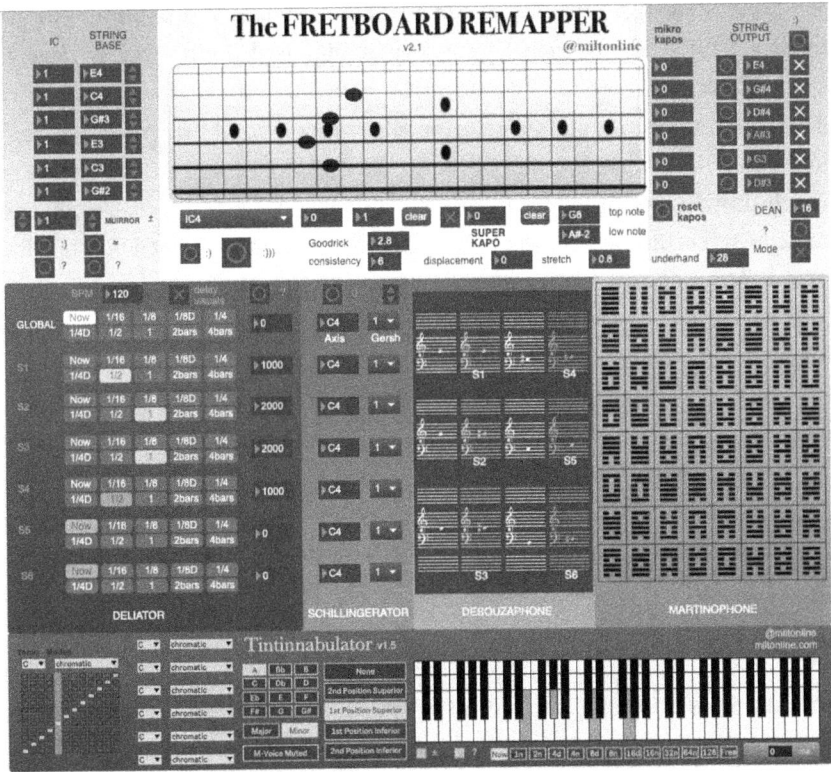

Figure 12.6 The *Fretboard Remapper* built in Max/MSP allowing the visualization and manipulation of real-time fretboard data. Several modules are available including a library of tunings, delays of individual strings (left), hexagram constraint (right), geometric expansions (centre) and automated tintinnabulation (bottom right).

pc-set calculator or shapes on a chromatic circle and *tonnetz*, deepening the level of real-time analysis and musical (F-Space, M-Space and N-Space) display. As it happens, this is how I discovered the all-interval property of the Hendrix chord.

Virtual string sets

Having the MIDI input, and thus fretboard data of the incoming signal also allows its *manipulation* before it is passed on to a sounding instrument. Consider it this way, using the process above (for each string n: *fret number = (incoming note on string n) − (pitch of open string n)* we are converting the incoming MIDI pitch data to simply a (fret, string) coordinate in F-Space): (3, 1) is fret 3 of string 1, (6, 0) the open sixth string and so on. If we want to pass this data on unaltered we – for each string – add back the open string value to the fret number. For example, for (3, 1) – third fret of top string we would add 3 semitones to the top string pitch of our virtual fretboard (in standard tuning the top note is E3 = MIDI note 64), so sending out MIDI note 67, returns us with the G3 we played on the physical guitar. We use the same process on all strings – in standard tuning the MIDI notes for strings one to six are (64 59 55 50 45 40). However, by substituting this virtual tuning set we can quickly construct, save, recall and implement instantly any tuning system for our virtual instrument. Drop D is the set (64 59 55 50 45 38), Law's perfect fourths is (65 60 55 50 45 40), Joni Mitchell's *Magdalene Laundries* reentrant tuning is (59 54 47 52 45 40), John Wheatcroft's upside-down guitar is (40 45 50 55 59 64) among the literal billions[10] of tuning systems. These can be immediately edited, stored in and recalled from a library. New tunings can be created by rotating, reordering, editing and randomizing pre-existing string sets, allowing an exploration of all possible combinations of Goodrick number, stretchiness, shape consistency and so on. A selection of such data is presented in section 'Appendix: Tuning system sampler'.

Virtual frets

Emulation of (and extension beyond) physical capos is also possible. A virtual *super capo* can raise the pitch of all strings to implausible heights, and also lower it below the nut to the limit of human hearing. In addition, each string has its

---

[10] Given six strings chosen from a three octave range (with twelve divisions of the octave), there are over 2.17 billion possible tunings.

own individual *mikro-kapo* to emulate Koltai's magnetic capo inventions and 'radically altered open-string sets' (Koltai 2020).

Since we are processing notes by adding back a fret number to a virtual open string, we can also change the behaviour of the frets themselves, with a *fret multiplier*. By default, frets add one chromatic note to the open string, but I introduced the ability to enable the user to make them act in whole tones, minor thirds, perfect fifths and so on. This allows engagement with the fifteen dual-interval spaces[11] (a two-dimensional array of two different interval classes) which Brown uses to analyse and illuminate the music of Arnold Schoenberg, Anton Webern and Carl Ruggles (Brown 2003). By playing on – and improvising in – these dual-interval spaces directly, fretboard shapes (and their inversions, transpositions and 'flips') are used as primary musical objects, centralizing the fretboard – not the keyboard or stave – in this otherwise distant tonal language.

We can extend beyond physically plausible systems by creating 'negative frets' so the pitch descends as we ascend the fingerboard. And of course, each string can have different fret multipliers, with some ascending in different intervals while others descend and others staying still. Frets can also adopt Joseph Schillinger's concept of 'geometric expansions' by increasing in size the further they are from an 'axis' fret, emulating precisely the opening of George Gershwins's *I Got Rhythm* variations (see Adler 2002). These axis frets also allow mirrored fretboards that radiate notes upwards (or downwards) from a fret in both directions. Again, globally or on any number of strings. This allows convincing improvisations with reflected material, particularly when made to produce responses in the same key, such as C Dorian, F♯ Dorian, C Aeolian Dominant, F♯ Aeolian Dominant, and all their modes: twenty-eight modes from one C axis. It is possible (and disarmingly effective) to use the guitar's audio, and have these mirror harmony responses – at the sweet spot between familiarity and surprise – return and interact (see Mermikides 2021).

Constraints and augmentations

MIDI notes can also be further processed: the right middle portion of Figure 12.6 shows that the system can enforce any of Martino's sixty-four hexagrams (by muting particular strings), or extend the 'disadvantage exercise' to paint out

---

[11] There are six interval classes, Brown's dual-interval spaces use two different interval classes creating fifteen unordered pairs. I engage however with all thirty so that, for example ic2 can be assigned to frets and ic3 to strings or vice versa.

parts of the fretboard and enforce activity on the 'dustier' zones.[12] The tool can also quantize notes (on any string) to particular scales or collection of pitches, allowing for example, a real-time implementation of Arvo Pärt's tintinnabulation technique (see Shenton 2012).

With the *Deliator* (middle left of Figure 12.6) any or all strings can be delayed by adjustable millisecond (or synchronized musical time) values, engaging with Simon Emmerson's *variant/clone* paradigm of electronic performance (2011). Familiarity can be further thwarted by randomizing string and fret values automatically, so that performing becomes an act of ear training, and a healthy invitation to rely on gesture, shape and time-feel.

I came to realize that the fretboard could be seen not as the complete collection of available pitches, but as a 21 × 6 window of a larger pitch surface, so I allowed the player to effectively scroll up, down, left and right through a virtual instrument of any string or fret number. Practically this allows playing virtual theorbos, harps and other real or imagined multi-string chordophones. The ability to assign different instruments to string sets, extends the possibilities further.

So far in this chapter, we have considered twelve divisions of the octave as the only possible pitch material. Microtonality however, can readily be engaged on a number of levels: (a) *Instrument level*: MIDI instruments – particularly those equipped with MPE (MIDI polyphonic expression) can be set to any static or dynamic temperament, so for example every G♯ can be tuned down 14 cents. (b) *String level*: since the system receives, and can transmit, pitch data on different MIDI channels we can effectively tune any string to any microtonal position, allowing a virtual microtuning of each string. (c) *Fret Level*: fret multipliers need not be integers and can be set to quarter tones (0.5), eighth tones (0.25) or any harmonic or non-harmonic ratio. Again, this is possible on any number of strings and irregular fret multipliers similar to Tolgahan Çoğulu's Adjustable Microtonal Guitars can be constructed.[13]

Despite this cluster of ideas, it is only very recently that I noticed a hidden bias in my design and musical conception. I – naturally enough – built the *Fretboard Remapper* in the image of a physical guitar in that an open string (or particular fret) would act as a marker from which frets would 'count up', adding pitch values using whatever method I'd like. I now realize that the system need not be linear. Essentially we can consider the fretboard as a table of pitches with no obligation to emulate the broad concept of pitch ordering, and have started

---

[12] If the guitarist plays in a blocked-out string or zone, the instrument is silenced. Early experiments triggering a loud klaxon alarm proved too stressful for effective practice.

[13] See Chapter 2 of this volume for an in-depth interview with Tolgahan Çoğulu

reprogramming it as such. This nonlinear system would of course include every conventional and unconventional tuning system so far discussed, with an identical interface for their construction, but it could allow any imaginable – or unimaginable – pattern of notes including – as arbitrary examples – a fretboard profile with a *repetition basin* – the most repeated notes at its edges – or one with augmented tuning from frets 1–5 (to eliminate stretchiness), perfect fourths from frets 6–12, and Tōru Takemitsu's *Equinox* (1993)– down an octave – at the top of the instrument. This nonlinear approach – even with just twelve notes in the octave – would produce a staggering number of configurations,[14] but highly precise microtonal notes could be placed in any or all fret spaces if desired, exhausting the pitch possibilities within the fretboard's constraints.

Summary and reflections

While I have explored and presented only a sample of applications, I hope that it is clear the extent of possibilities and fresh perspectives such an approach affords, and how it can help reset, augment and revitalize existing practice and connections between the 'guitar spaces'. Even as a guitarist who – other than in these experiments – almost exclusively plays in standard tuning on a six-string guitar, my conventional fretboard knowledge has become far stronger and fluid through this process, as has my general theoretical knowledge, and – strangely – sight-reading ability. Indeed, instead of confusing or distracting from 'normal' literacy, this digital self-sabotage has been an invigorating addition to my practice, in terms of fretboard development, composition, improvisation and analytical insight. As such, the aims of this chapter were not only to present the *Fretboard Remapper* as one example of the use of digital technology in guitar pedagogy and creative practice but also to offer the potential benefits of continually unlearning, reconfiguring and relearning our knowledge and connections to the guitar fretboard. Like a martial arts student who progresses slowly to the black belt, not through pride but by wearing daily – and slowly darkening with sweat – the white belt, this repeated humility and novice's mindset can help reconnect the guitarist to the instrument, and the naive but profound sense of discovery we felt at its first encounter.

---

[14] Considering a range of a grand piano, with twelve notes per octave, this nonlinear fretboard library would include over 10^{245} tuning systems. There are, for reference, fewer than 10^{80} atoms in the universe.

Appendix: Tuning system sampler

A small sample of tuning systems and their characteristics are presented in Figure 12.7. For each tuning system, the following are shown:

- Open strings in standard notation
- Open strings as MIDI note numbers (strings 1 to 6)
- *Underhand Range*. The range from low string fifth fret to top string eighth fret
- *String Interval*. The average number of semitones between adjacent strings with standard deviation
- *Stretchiness*. The average number of 'chromatic gaps' between strings

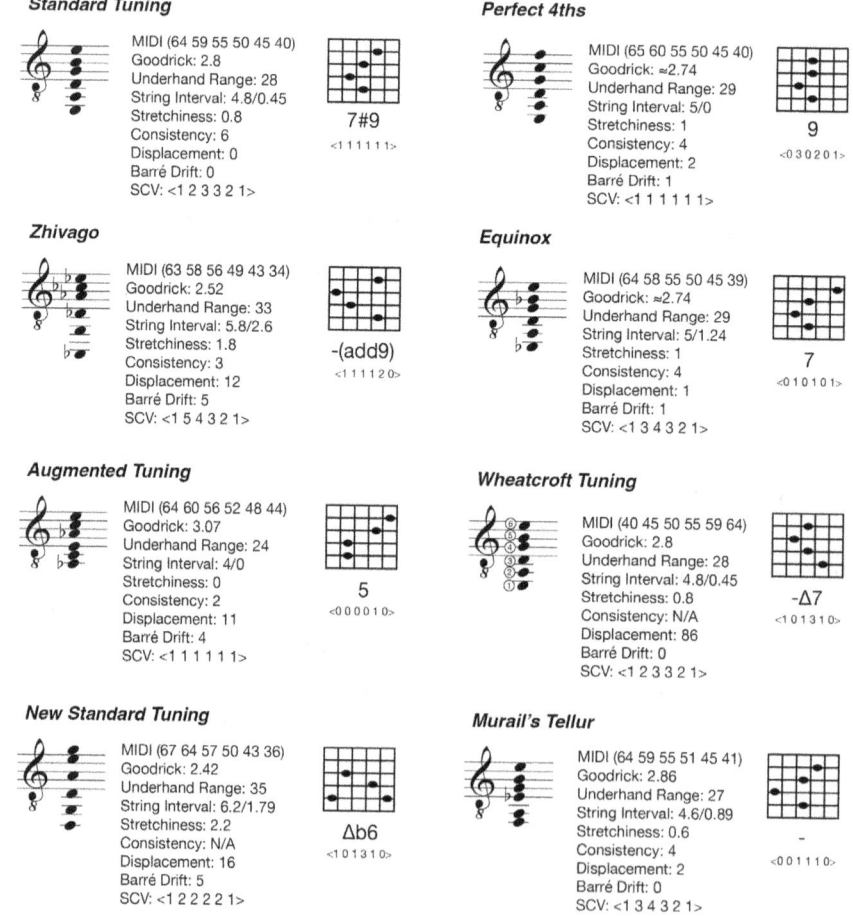

Figure 12.7 A sample of tuning systems with their characteristics.

- *Consistency.* The number of strings that move the same distance from standard tuning (See DeSouza 2017: 10)
- *Displacement.* The number of chromatic shifts from standard tuning. (See DeSouza 2017: 10)
- *Barré Drift.* The offset from an octave between fret 5 on the lowest and fret 5 on the highest string
- *Shape Consistency Vector* (SCV). The number of interval structures created by moving vertically one, two, three, four, five and six 'chord blocks' (see section 'Pitch spacing')
- The final column of each shows the fretboard shape of the Hendrix all-interval tetrachord, together with its 'reciprocal' – its intervallic identity (as a simplified chord symbol and an interval vector) when played back in standard tuning, a sort of fretboard 'Rosetta Stone'.

References

Adler, J. (trans.) (2002), *Introduction to the Study of the Classic of Change*, Provo: Global Scholarly Publications.

All About Jazz (2017), *Wes Montgomery & Trio Pim Jacobs*. Rehearsal footage 2 April 1965, Concordia: Bussum Netherland, Available online: https://www.youtube.com/watch?v=itcuDggJY_Y.

Arden, J. (2008), *Keys to the Schillinger System*, Nottingham: Clock & Rose Press.

Brandon, A. and D. Westwood (2019), 'How the Guitar Shapes us.' Two-Part Article on Motor Control and Guitar Performance', *Soundboard*, 45: 39–45.

Brown, S.C. (2003), 'Dual Interval Space in Twentieth-Century Music', *Music Theory Spectrum*, 25 (1): 35–57.

Butler, M. (2014), *Playing with Something That Runs: Technology, Improvisation, and Composition in DJ and Laptop Performance*, Oxford: Oxford University Press.

Buttermann, M. (2009), *Freddie Green: A Musical Analysis of the Guitar in the Count Basie Rhythm Section*, MA Thesis, College of Arts and Communication, William Paterson University.

Capuzzo, G. (2006), *Pat Martino's The Nature of the Guitar: An Intersection of Jazz Theory and Neo-Riemannian Theory*, Music Theory Online.

Cohn, R. (1998), 'Introduction to Neo-Riemannian Theory: A Survey and a Historical Perspective', *Journal of Music Theory*, 42 (2): 167.

Crook, H. (1991), *How to Improvise*, Advance Music.

Damian, J. (2001), *The Guitarist's Guide to Composing and Improvising*, Distributed by H. Leonard Corp, Berklee Press.

De Souza, J. (2017), Chapter 4 'Voluntary Self Sabotage', in *Music at Hand*, Oxford: Oxford University Press.

De Souza, J. (2018), 'Fretboard Transformations', *Journal of Music Theory*, 62 (1): 1–39.

De Souza, J. (2021), 'Guitar Thinking', *Soundboard Scholar*, 7 (1): 1–23, https://digitalcommons.du.edu/sbs/vol7/iss1/1/ (accessed 5 Sep 2022).

Dean, J. (2014), 'Pat Metheny's Finger Routes: The Role of Muscle Memory in Guitar Improvisation', *Jazz Perspectives*, 8 (1): 45–71.

Emmerson, S. (2011), 'Combining the Acoustic and the Digital: Music for Instruments and Computers or Prerecorded Sound', in R.T. Dean (ed.), *The Oxford Handbook of Computer Music*, 167–88, Oxford: Oxford University Press.

Dickert, L.H. (1994), *An Analysis of Freddie Green's Style and His Importance in the History of Jazz Guitar*, PhD Thesis, University of Memphis.

Fell, M. (2013), *Works in Sound and Pattern Synthesis ~ Folio of Works*, PhD Thesis, University of Surrey.

Goodrick, M. (1987), *The Advancing Guitarist: Applying Guitar Concepts & Techniques*, Wisconsin: Hal Leonard.

Koltai, K. (2020), 'Breaking the Matrix: Transcribing Bartók and Ligeti for the Guitar Using a New Capo System', *Soundboard Scholar*, 6 (1): 1–36, https://digitalcommons.du.edu/sbs/vol6/iss1/6.

Law, A. (2011), *3rd Millenium Guitar: An Introduction to Perfect 4ths Tuning*, Fenton, MO: Mel Bay.

Leathwood, J. (2019), 'Improvisation as a Way of Knowing', IGRC Conference Lecture Recital.

Magnusson, T. (2019), *Sonic Writing: Technologies of Material, Symbolic and Signal Inscriptions*, London: Bloomsbury.

Martino, P. (2016), *The Nature of the Guitar*, Online video course, Truefire, Available online: https://truefire.com/pat-martino/the-nature-of-guitar/c1002.

Martino Unstrung (2007), Video Documentary dir. Ian Knox. DVD. Sixteen Films, London.

Mermikides, M. (2010), *Changes over Time*, PhD thesis, University of Surrey.

Mermikides, M. (2021), 'Digital Self-Sabotage', Online lecture recital, 21st Century Guitar Conference, Lisbon, March, Available online: https://youtu.be/mHs8BhU0EiQ.

Paine, G. (2011), 'Gesture and Morphology in Laptop Music Performance', in R.T. Dean (ed.), *The Oxford Handbook of Computer Music*, 214–32, Oxford: Oxford University Press.

Shenton, A. (2012), *The Cambridge Companion to Arvo Pärt*, Cambridge: Cambridge University Press.

Stolzenburg, M. (2022), *Wes Montgomery - The Great Jazz Improviser*. Online article. Available at https://jbonamassa.com/wes-montgomery-the-great-jazz-improviser/.

Titon, J.T., and T.J. Cooley (eds.) (2016), *Worlds of Music: An Introduction to the Music of the World's Peoples*, 6th ed., Boston, MA: Cengage Learning.

Willmott, B. (1994), *The Complete Book of Harmony, Theory & Voicing*, Fenton, MO: Mel Bay.

13

Augmented reality guitars

Extended instruments and notation for a 21st-century practice

Amy Brandon

The guitar takes many different physical forms. Body-size, scale-length, materials, design, fret patterning, number of strings and specialized augmentations are all physical elements that have been modified in the contemporary guitar.[1] In the 21st century, guitars and their notation can also be extended beyond their physical form into digital space. XR technologies, in particular, augmented reality controlled by gesture, allow the instrument to be performable in both the real and digital worlds simultaneously. XR is a term which encompasses a broad cross-section of 3D digital technologies such as 360, virtual and augmented reality.[2] Using specialized headsets, or mobile devices, XR technology can create digital objects and immersive environments that users can inhabit and/or interact with (see Figure 13.1).

Augmented reality (AR) is the placement of 3D digital objects within real environments. By using hand and gesture recognition, in AR the hands themselves become controllers, triggering sonic events, effects and visuals (see Figure 13.2).

While used primarily for gaming, XR technologies have also been used in music composition and performance. Works from the last half-decade have included pieces using 360 visuals (Prestini 2016), VR scores (Masu et al. 2020; Cotter and Packham 2019), sound installations (Chroma Mixed Media 2019), VR compositional platforms (Magnusen 2019), and VR instruments (Mäki-Patola

---

[1] 20th and 21st-century guitar alterations range from simple amplification of acoustic guitars and electric solid-body guitars, to fanned-fret guitars (Novax Guitars 1989), microtonal fretboards (Çoğulu, 2008), and alterations for moveable capo systems (Koltai 2020) among other innovations.
[2] For an overview of current XR technology, see Chuah, S. (2019).

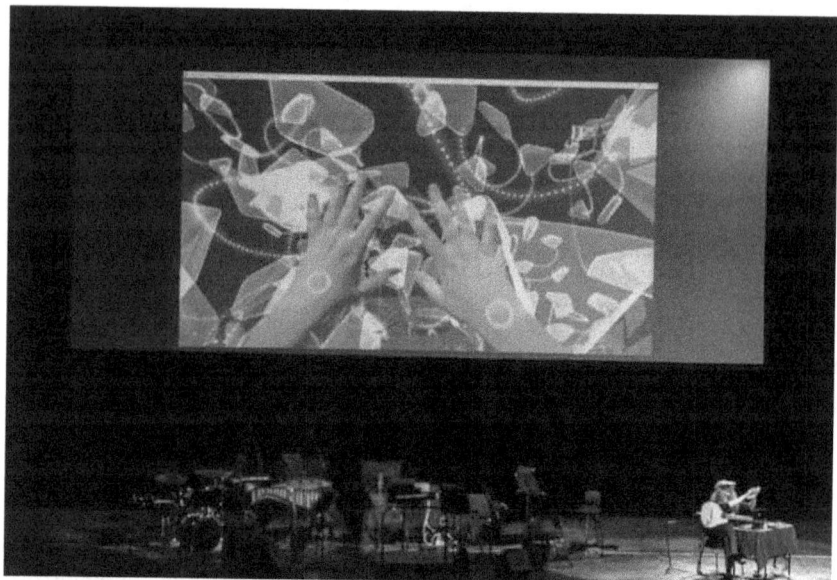

Figure 13.1 Performance of *flesh projektor II* at Winnipeg New Music Festival, 26 January 2020. (Photo: Matt Duboff, used with permission).

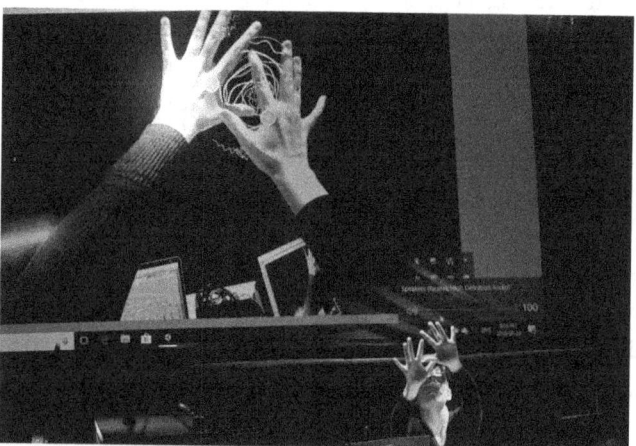

Figure 13.2 Kristina Warren performing *Hidden Motive III* in NYC, September 29, 2018. (Photo: Moon Young Ha, used with permission.)

et al. 2005; Hamilton 2021). AR has also been used in composing and improvising with acoustic instruments – for piano and chamber ensemble (Santini 2021), as well as percussion, laptop improvisation and guitar (Brandon 2018b; 2019a and 2019c), and improvised telemetic works (Hein 2021).

From my perspective as a guitarist, a composer of XR and guitar works, and a researcher in motor control and guitar notation, I see the guitar as uniquely placed as an AR instrument in the 21st century. AR is able to extend both the physical guitar and its notation into digital performative space. Notation and 3D scores can be mapped onto the fretboard itself, and gesture-reactive digital sculptures can be embedded into the body and fretboard of the guitar, which can trigger electronics or other sonic parameters. The characteristics and affordances of the guitar and its performance practice allow for these extensions in a way that is somewhat unique among instruments. The spatial aspects of guitar notation and performance (Brandon 2019e; 2019f) lend itself well to fretboard-embedded notation. Guitaristic gestures can also be harnessed by the composer to trigger digital objects embedded in the instrument, making a playable 'hyper-guitar'. The ability of the fretboard to be custom inlaid with markers of AR image recognition (the technology that fixes digital objects in position relative to real-world objects) creates unique possibilities with AR development in guitar composition (Visser 2020).

This chapter explores the capacities of the guitar as an AR instrument through my work as a composer creating XR and guitar works. This multi-year project has impacted what I perceive to be the compositional and performance possibilities for AR guitar, and the potential impact of AR technology on 21st-century guitar development, notation, composition and performance practice. I also explore the drawbacks of AR technology as it relates to guitar performance, and how my research in motor control and guitar notation feeds into this concept of the guitar as an AR instrument. The table in Figure 13.3 shows the development of my compositional approach to AR over the last four years from simple 360 graphic scores to mobile development.

Immersive graphic notation in XR (2017–18)

AR is often seen as very futuristic, but its development in the last decade into a fully realized technology has been more gradual than expected (Chuah 2019). AR technology companies like Hololens (2021), Metavision (2021) and Magic Leap (2021) have developed headsets to bring AR to the commercial market, but it remains a niche technology that has not always fulfilled the promises of its press releases (Robertson 2020). However, the technology continues to develop, particularly with AR using mobile device technology (AR Foundation 2021).

Table 1: XR works 2017–2021 by Amy Brandon			
Title	Collaborator / Performer	Year	Instrumentation
-	Fernando Bravo	2017	Improvising guitarist and 360 video score
-	RJ Brandon and Laura Brandon	2017	Improvising guitarist and 360 graphic score
Bicinium	Shannon Novak	2017	Installation
Hidden Motive I	Kevin Davis	2018	HTC Vive, telemetic graphic score
Hidden Motive II	Kristina Warren	2018	Metavision AR and elec.
Hidden Motive III	Amy Brandon	2018	Metavision AR and elec.
7 Malagueña Fragments for Augmented Guitar	Emma Rush	2019	Metavision AR, guitar and elec.
flesh projector I	Amy Brandon	2019	Metavision AR, improvised guitar and elec.
flesh projector II	Amy Brandon	2020	Metavision AR, guitar and elec.
Augmented Percussions	Mélissa Labbé	2019	Metavision AR, percussion and elec.
WNMF x AR installation	-	2020	MetaVision sound installation
WNMF xAR	-	2020	AR app
Boundary	Sara Constant	2020	AR app sound installation
points of light	Emily Visser	2021	Custom-built AR fretless guitar and AR app

Figure 13.3 Table of XR works 2017–21 by Amy Brandon.

My own early guitar compositions and performances using XR[3] were very simple, often simply 3D iterations of typical elements of new music composition like static and video graphic scores (scores using imagery and visuals instead of traditional music notation) viewed in 360. The 360 technology forms a 2D image or video into a sphere, and the viewer is 'placed' within that sphere using a headset, and can view the graphic score from any angle. The image is not interactive.

My primary motivation for beginning to create XR graphic scores was the capacity to place the performer and the notation in the same immersive performance space. This theoretically creates a more direct connection between the notation and the physical gestures creating the music. As researcher and composer Giovanni Santini writes about his own work with AR graphic notation 'we can now have an analogic notation of gestures, rather than a symbolic one' (Santini 2018: 1). In other words, the performer is surrounded by the score, and immersed within it, and both the performer and the score occupy the same physical–digital environment, potentially leading to a more direct connection between the graphic score and the performance gestures.

With developments in AR technology, this 'analogic notation of gestures' begins to extend beyond a static immersive environment to the instrument itself. Gesture recognition allows the elements of the score to not only be seen by the performer in digital space but also interacted with using the hands as

---

[3] See Bravo and Brandon (2017a), Brandon et al. (2017b) and Brandon (2018a).

controllers. In 2018 I began experimenting with holographic AR graphic scores that were also sound controllers,[4] using a headset called the Metavision (2021) (See Figure 13.2). Gesture-reactivity allowed interactive electronics to form part of the score, where touching or moving the digital objects triggered electronic sounds or effects (Brandon 2018d). This ability to incorporate gesture-reactivity into AR graphic scores led me to consider the concept of an augmented reality guitar, an acoustic instrument that is 'extended' into digital space and performable in both simultaneously.

Extending acoustic instruments into digital space (2019–present)

Physical guitars are often 'extended' using technology and electronics. The simplest example would be amplified acoustic guitars, or electric guitars, where the natural acoustic sound is modified electronically in volume and timbre. This capturing and manipulating of the natural sound and performance practice of the guitar exists along a continuum from simple to complex. On one side of the continuum, amplification and effects processing can morph the acoustic sound of the instrument through pedals, or processing using live and fixed electronics. Further along the continuum, performative physical electronics such as embedded sensors in the instrument (Meneses et al. 2018), or plectrum (Morreale et al. 2019), can gather and manipulate non-sonic elements of guitar performance. External motion capture devices (Bartos 2019) can also track performance gestures and use them to control sonic parameters beyond the intended sound of the instrument. Entirely digital instruments can also be made in VR (Hamilton 2021) which can be 'performed' using similar movements as acoustic instruments. The main delineation of this continuum of 'extended guitar' is that the extensions are connected in some way either to the body of the guitar, or the movement of the hands or both, and are therefore *performable* just as an acoustic instrument is – and so the technological enhancement is connected to the natural performance practice of the instrument (Tanaka 2000).

As my ability to programme AR improved, and the technology progressed, I started exploring ways to adapt the Metavision headset to merge these

---

[4] See Brandon (2018b; 2018c; 2019b and 2020a). See also concert performances Brandon (2018d) and Labbé (2019).

Figure 13.4 Amy Brandon – improvised performance in Halifax, May 2019. (Photo: Jennifer Thiessen, used with permission.)

gesture-reactive digital objects with the guitar, creating a prototype of an AR guitar whose digital objects would react naturally to a performer's movements. My first piece in this line of thought was *7 Malagueña Fragments for Augmented Guitar* (Brandon 2019a) for guitarist Emma Rush, which premiered at the Sound and Music Computing Conference in Málaga, Spain, in May 2019 (Rush 2019). In order to come close to the effect that I wanted, I first experimented by using the Metavision headset unworn, positioned in front of the performer (see Figure 13.4).

This allowed the performer to maintain a natural performance practice, unencumbered by wearing an awkward and uncomfortable headset. It also allowed me to place digital objects extremely closely to the fretboard, soundhole and bridge. This presented some technical challenges, in that the performative range of the Metavision headset favours head-mounting (see Figure 13.8), making the exact placement of the digital objects in relation to the acoustic guitar difficult when used unworn. When Emma performed the work, several digital objects were placed in front of the soundhole of the guitar (see Figure 13.5) so

Figure 13.5 Emma Rush performing *7 Malagueña Fragments for Augmented Guitar* at the SMC Conference, 28 May 2019 in Málaga, Spain (Photo: author).

as she performed tambour and other guitaristic gestures from the written score, her hand would travel through the digital objects and trigger electronics.

One advantage to this system was that to perform the piece she required no additional training on how to manipulate the system, it was designed primarily with her own performance practice in mind, which was consistent with the philosophy that extended instruments should not alter or impede a performer's natural performance practice.[5]

While the piece worked, the technological limitations of the time prevented me from fully realizing the concept of an AR guitar. While the Metavision had a certain capacity for occlusion (how well AR objects merge with the real world)

---

[5] Morreale et al. (2019) emphasize that extended and augmented instruments like the Magpick should prioritize existing guitar technique, saying on p. 70: ' that the locus of augmentation corresponds to the traditional locus of actuation (i.e. the plucking hand) forces an integration of gestural language between traditional and extended techniques, while the sound design that modifies the guitar signal and maintains the status of the augmented guitar as a single instrument rather than the first step towards a theme park one-man band'. See also Tanaka (2000).

(see Figure 13.6) its limitations meant that the digital objects were never really 'embedded' or 'merged' with the physical instrument, only placed in front of it. As well, they retained a typical early AR 'cartoonish' look that seemed out of place with the real environment being augmented, contributing to the sense of 'separation' from the instrument.

While it reacted fairly consistently to natural performance gestures when positioned correctly, because it was never directly merged with the guitar, and any change of position meant the digital objects would be out-of-sync with the performance gestures.

I also created a second work at about the same time, *flesh projektor I* (Brandon 2019d) with the aim of working on merging the guitar and digital objects into an improvisatory piece for solo guitar. I was slightly more successful in the visual merging of the AR objects with the instrument (see Figure 13.7) but navigating the digital objects again remained an issue using the headset unworn.

The Metavision headset is designed specifically to be worn, and the performative space is calibrated to work primarily within arm's length of the user (Metavision 2018) (see Figure 13.8).

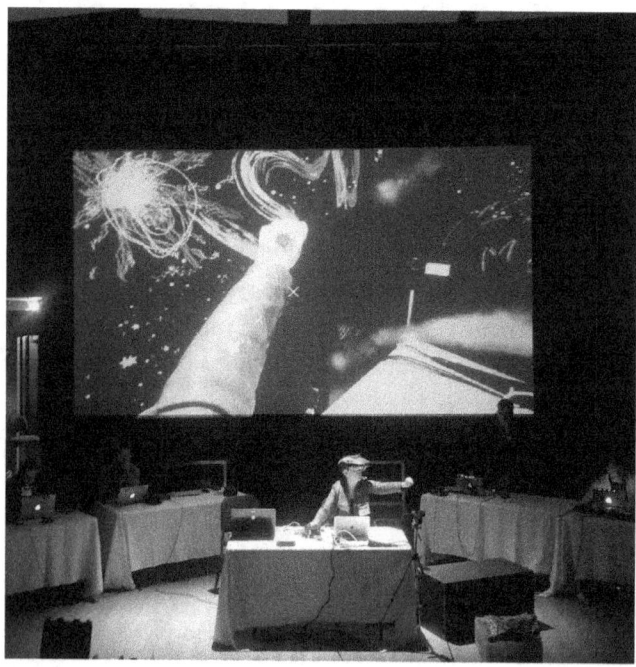

Figure 13.6 Kristina Warren performing *Hidden Motive II* at the TENOR Conference, Montreal, 2018 (Photo: author).

Augmented Reality Guitars 247

Figure 13.7 Amy Brandon with *flesh projektor I* at New Music Edmonton in Edmonton, Alberta, 4 May 2019 (Photo: author).

Using the headset unworn meant that it was difficult for an improvisatory performer to locate and activate the objects in space. This, in addition to the lack of visual feedback, meant that interacting with the objects was hit or miss, and the digital objects could be activated by a gesture by accident.[6]

Fortunately, technological advancements in the following year allowed me to bring my concept a little closer to fruition. First, advancements in mobile AR removed the need for headset-based technology, as gesture recognition was available for mobile applications via the third-party gesture-recognition software ManoMotion. I used this software in the creation of my gesturally reactive mobile AR work *Boundary* (Brandon 2020c), for the Gaudeamus Festival in 2020. For future guitar works, this meant that instead of placing a headset the wrong way round in front of a performer, all that was needed was a smartphone or tablet which could be placed in front of the performer. In the fall of 2020, mobile AR technology from Google (ARCore 2021), Apple (ARKit 2021) and

---

[6] See Brandon (2019d). See 02:55–03:05 for an example of accidentally triggering AR electronics in performance using the headset unworn.

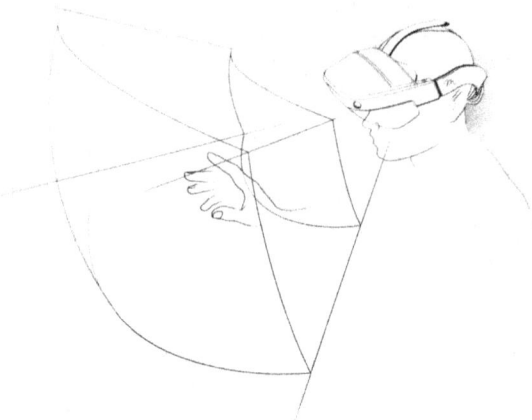

Field of View

The Meta 2 device enables you to interact with holograms within a 90° field of view.

However, gestures outside of the virtual area represented in the figure above might not be detected by your device.

Figure 13.8 Image of the field-of-view and performative space using the Metavision headset. (Image Source: Metavision 2018: 16).

AR Foundation (2021) improved aspects of mobile AR development including depth-sensing and occlusion. This meant that AR objects could be seen more in perspective with surrounding real objects, as well as 'merge' or 'sink into' planar objects like floors, tables and fretboards.[7] Finally, additional advancements such as environment probes (which can create reflections in AR objects of the real surroundings) and light estimation (which measures real-life light levels and applies it to AR objects) meant that objects could have a fair degree of realness, removing the cartoonish, uncanny valley effect of earlier AR visuals, as you can see in the comparison between an earlier AR work, *WNMF x AR* (Brandon 2020b) and *Boundary* (Brandon 2020c).[8]

One issue that remained was permanently pairing digital objects with the guitar. In *7 Malagueña Fragments for Augmented Guitar* (Brandon 2019a) and *flesh projektor I* (Brandon 2019b) I could manually place objects close to the

---

[7] A video of the fretboard and depth test is available here: https://drive.google.com/file/d/1XLCNqqbL1y9Vxfr7y8sRmMyNCs0TCbcc/view?usp=sharing

[8] Videos of these works are available in the citations.

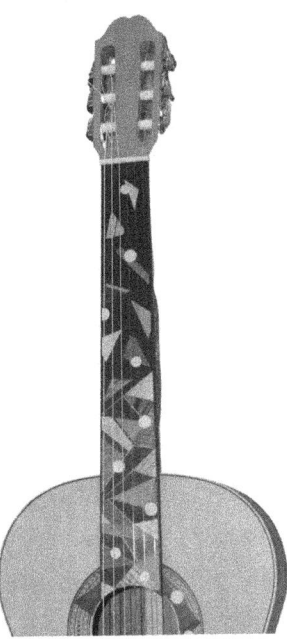

Figure 13.9 Custom image-tracking fretboard (Visser 2020) (Image: courtesy of the luthier, used with permission).

guitar, but if the guitar moved, the digital objects did not. The solution for this came from older technologies, image-tracking paired with custom lutherie. Image-tracking is a consistent means of pairing digital objects with real ones, and one of the earliest AR technologies. With image-tracking, digital objects can be paired with a 2D image, such as a fretboard inlay design, so that as the image moves in the real world, the digital object does as well. Guided by image-tracking optimization principles (Vuforia 2021), luthier Emily Visser created a custom AR fretboard that would allow me to create embeddable objects that would consistently pair with her guitar neck (Visser 2020) (see Figure 13.9).

The piece I wrote for her and this new guitar is called *points of light*, and will feature AR sculptures that grow from her guitar (Brandon, forthcoming).[9] When touched by audience members, the sculptures play manipulated versions of the same piece. This new methodology solves certain previous issues: it allows for gesture-reactivity without a headset, and it also allows for precise placement of the digital objects in reference to the guitar body and fretboard.

[9] An early test video of the augmentations for this work is available here: https://www.dropbox.com/s/11ly3sdor7npmav/RPReplay_Final1619788805.MP4?dl=0

AR performance practice: Challenges for performers and audiences

With each technological change and development this project underwent, the performance practice for XR and guitar works changed. For example, in my initial 360 scores and works with the VR system HTC Vive, the vision occlusion of the headsets was a significant difficulty to performing because performers could not see their instruments or hands (see Figure 13.10).

Furthermore, the occluded headset created a sense of alienation between the performer and the audience. My own experiences in this feeling of separation from the audience due to headset occlusion in VR works from 2017 to 2018 are echoed by guitarist David Cotter, who in a conversation with the author describes a similar performance experience in playing guitar using VR headsets in 2020–1.[10] This discomfort is not just limited to guitarists. While performing my 2018 telematic 360 score work *Hidden Motive I* using an Oculus Go, cellist

Figure 13.10 Improvised performance with 360 video score. (Photo: Rita Taylor, Banff Centre, 2017, used with permission).

---

[10] David Cotter, interview by Amy Brandon. Conducted in person / via correspondence on 11 April 2021.

Figure 13.11 Projected 360 graphic score at Nocturne Festival, Halifax NS, 14 October 2017 (Photo: author).

Kevin Davis removed his headset halfway through, citing that it was too difficult to perform with it on (Davis 2018).

Besides the discomfort and alienating nature of the headset, the second major difficulty in XR and acoustic performances is in translating the 3D nature of the XR environment to the audience. Simply projecting a screen capture essentially 'flattens' the 3D world, nullifying the impact of the score. In my earlier works, I tried a number of techniques to translate 3D scores to audiences, with minimal success, including projecting 2D 360 scores in performance (see Figure 13.11) and experimenting with green screens and split video live capture (see Figure 13.12).

These twin problems: the occlusion of vision in VR, and the difficulty in bringing audiences into the XR experience were the main reasons I chose to work exclusively in AR in 2018. The clear visor of the Metavision headset allowed me to perform guitar and XR works in a less alienated way (see Figure 13.13) and also allowed for a first-person perspective to be projected to the audience, bringing them partially into the XR environment along with the performer.

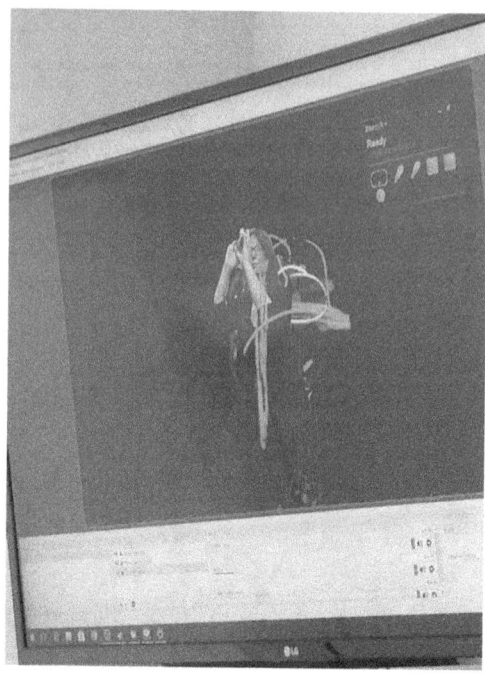

Figure 13.12 Amy Brandon experimenting with split video capture using HTC Vive, Halifax 2018 (Photo: author).

Figure 13.13 Amy Brandon performing using the Metavision headset, Winnipeg New Music Festival, 26 January 2020 (Photo: Matt Duboff, used with permission).

However, while the audience could witness a first-person perspective of the 3D environment in the Metavision works, it was still rendered in 2D on the projector screen, lessening its magic and impact. Other performative difficulties with the Metavision headset remained. The headset was still clunky and uncomfortable, and the gesture recognition of the Metavision, although advanced, was not seamless, meaning that the performativity of the gesture-reactive digital objects was limited. Ultimately, this meant that in addition to a guitar performance practice, a second set of gestures had to be learned by the performer in order to activate digital objects in compositions using the Metavision. Moving from the Metavision to mobile AR solved some issues, but not all. Mobile AR allows the audience to 'walk around' the augmentations using a smartphone or tablet,[11] and view them in a truly 3D way, which is an improvement over viewing the augmentations projected on a screen. However, there is still a gap in technology that allows both the performer and the audience to perceive the augmentations simultaneously in performance. In addition, the performativity of digital objects has to be baked into the piece, as with *7 Malagueña Fragments for Augmented Guitar*, otherwise, an entirely new set of movements must be learned by the performer.

Guitar notation in augmented reality

As my AR guitar compositions developed, I became particularly interested in how AR notation embedded in the fretboard might connect with previous research I had done on notation and motor control in guitar performance. Primarily, the idea of the guitar as a spatially navigated instrument inhabiting a dual-notation environment, and how guitar notation, specifically tablature, tends to reflect the spatial aspects of guitar performance that are less common to the performance practices of other instruments.[12]

The guitar holds a unique place among musical instruments, in that more than one notational system is typically used. In addition to traditional notation, which primarily consists of musical symbols (pitch, rhythm and articulation), the guitar also has a second language of *spatial notation* such as chord charts,

---

[11] See Brandon (2020c) for a video of *Boundary* where this is demonstrated.
[12] See Brandon (2019c; 2019f), and also De Souza (2018) and Baily and Driver (1992).

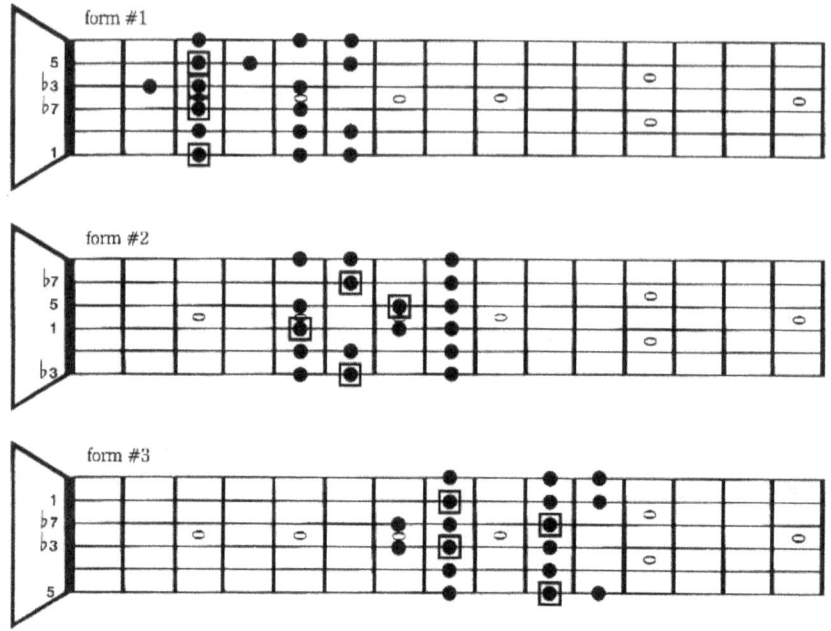

Figure 13.14 Example of guitar scale charts (Image source: Martino, 1989: 7).

scale patterns and tablature that indicate finger positioning on the fretboard in a highly visual and graphic manner (see Figure 13.14).[13]

The persistent popularity of tablature, chord and scale charts in common pedagogical materials (Beaumont 2015) remains a key feature of guitar culture, and it is not well understood exactly why the guitar uniquely retains multiple notational systems in pedagogical and performance practice, and how this may relate to the inherent cognitive or motor control processes of guitar performance.

The relative popularity of traditional notation and tablature has waxed and waned since the origins of the modern guitar in the mid-18th century. Initially, tablature was the only notation for both lute and early guitar prior to 1750, when it transitioned through several types of single-stemmed and multi-stemmed traditional notation (Stenstadvold 2006: 11–29, and Tyler and Sparks 2002: 200–1) with the advent of the modern guitar until the mid-19th century. A return to tablature began in the 20th century, primarily in jazz and popular music (Lang and Berend 1936). Moving into the 21st century, the debate has not concluded in any way, with many guitarists, researchers and pedagogues of all

---

[13] See, for example, Eddie Lang and Dave Berend's *Fingerboard Harmony,* one of the earliest jazz guitar method books.

guitar styles having strong opinions on which one works best for themselves and their students,[14] and with each argument following similar lines as in the 18th century, positing that tablature helps with spatial navigation of the fretboard, while traditional notation leads to more musical performance for instance.

Spatial navigation and the unique complexity of the fretboard

What is interesting that the persistence of tablature is the apparent need to communicate the spatial navigation aspects of guitar performance. It begs the question: What is it about the guitar, specifically, that results in the need or desire for a *spatial* movement notation? After all, like Giacomo Merchi indicated in the 18th century,[15] there are other instruments that are navigated spatially (piano, harp and strings) that do not employ spatial notation. So, why? It's not clear, however; it could be argued that the uniquely complex layout of the guitar fretboard is a possible genesis point for why spatial movement notation remains persistent. The 'labyrinthine' (McFadden 2010: 52) layout of the fretboard may present unique cognitive challenges to learning and executing complex motor sequences, and graphically expressed spatial navigation may ease this complexity by encouraging perceptuomotor patternings with which to bind or encode complex fine motor sequences. In essence, a spatial notation that represents the fretboard may reduce cognitive load, by removing the effort of translating traditional notation (which includes less spatial information) into complex, spatially oriented movements (Brandon 2019e, 2019f).

As jazz guitarist Mick Goodrick wrote in his method The Advancing Guitarist, on the guitar 'the average note has 2.8 locations and 9.2 possible fingerings' (Goodrick 1987: 93). So, in order to sight-read traditional notation, the guitarist must first memorize (or partially memorize) the locations of seventy-two

---

[14] See Elmer (2009). Other examples include Ward (2011: 59–60), Beaumont (2015: 45–6), Balistreri (1995: 3) and Berard (1998: 31).
[15] The 18th-century Italian musician and composer Giacomo Merchi was vociferous in his condemnation of tablature, writing in 'Le Guide des ecoliers de guitarre, oeuvre VII of 1761': 'I believe that it is an abuse, and I shall prove it by the following reasons. Those who only know tablature cannot truly play, and accompany only by routine and without balance. Those who use tablature successfully were good musicians before they learned it, and had no need of it. These reasons have led me to suppress its use in this work. If someone objects that it is necessary to mark the [left hand] positions, I would respond that the violin, the cello, etc. never use tablature, and that the guitar has less need [to do so] than them because it has frets. As with other instruments, all that is necessary for success is the application of a good method; I have neglected nothing to render mine easy, clear, and agreeable' ((Merchi 1761) as quoted in Tyler and Sparks 2002: 201).

individual notes, some of which are doubled or tripled, and whose layout does not conform to any simple pattern or layout for ease of memorization. The guitar tuning system of fourths and thirds was initially designed to allow chords to be played with ease, which results in a non-symmetrical layout unlike that of the harp, piano or strings. With this layout, the finger mechanics of which of the four fingers plays which note in any given context (often there are multiple options) is almost exclusively left to the performer, compounding the difficulty (Matone 2005: 1). So, efficient movement for fast sequences must be planned in advance to ensure proper finger placement, making sight-reading a series of rapid decision-making tasks which may be particularly challenging for beginners. The fretboard is also a blank grid – not colour-coded and directional, as is the piano. The language used to describe guitar navigation is also biomechanically counterintuitive, as notes ascend and descend in pitch counterintuitively to the direction of hand motion. As your hand moves 'up' the fretboard, not only is your hand actually moving towards the floor, but the pitches can ascend or descend depending on string choice. As James Sallis notes in his book *The Guitar Players*: 'The guitar is, physically, a difficult instrument; to get past its cumbersomeness to the music inside requires considerable application. Things other musicians take for granted – legato playing, dynamics, even simple reading – can become awesome problems on the guitar' (Sallis 1982 as quoted in Matone 2005: 1–2). The non-sequential nature of the guitar fretboard could be significant from a music cognition perspective as well, as some studies indicate that our brains process melodic information better when it is mapped sequentially or congruently to the physical device being used, where keys or buttons are mapped as left to right equals low to high (Stephan et al. 2015: 318). Therefore, it could be argued that the guitar fretboard, with its doubled notes, irregular layout of pitches, multiple fingering options and blank-grid appearance, presents a unique cognitive challenge to performers, which may encourage or invite a spatial approach in both conception and notation.

Spatial navigation and the affordances of augmented reality with the fretboard

The tendency of the guitar towards spatial navigation had already led researchers to animate or augment the physical guitar fretboard for pedagogical purposes, using a variety of technologies from as early as 2003. Animated tablature in online videos,[16] LED guitars such as the FretLight (2021) and Yamaha EZ AG (Yamaha 2003), and early AR such as the GuitAR (Liarokapis 2005) are some of the systems developed to augment the guitar fretboard directly with visuals reflecting spatial notation. Notating music in VR has also been explored for other spatially navigated instruments such as drumkit (Ham 2017), and in AR for graphic notation for percussion (Santini 2018). This combined history of augmenting the guitar fretboard, and the presence of XR spatial notations, takes the concept of the AR notation for guitar out of the realm of gimmickry or novelty by virtue of the guitar's historic tendency to prioritize spatial types of notation, and the historical presence of AR notations for guitar and other spatially navigated instruments.

The forms that future AR guitar notation may take are multiple. They may simply represent specific note locales, as with the FretLight (2021) or GuitAR (Liarokapis, 2005), or animated sequences of note locations as with animated fretboard tutorials (i.e. Lorange 2017). In keeping with current AR notations such as the percussion works of Giovanni Santini (2018), they may also reflect the 'analogic notation of gesture' over an instrument. Non-digital notation graphically representing playing area on an instrument is not uncommon either, seen, for example, in the use of 'bridge clef' in the compositions of Helmut Lachenmann, such as *Pression* (1969). Graphic notation representing gestural information can be seen in a number of guitar works such as Pierluigi Billone's *Sgorgo Y* (2012), which depicts gestural information for the tremolo arm (Babb 2020), and Clemens Gadenstätter's *Studies for a portrait for electric guitar* (2018).[17] Animated graphic notations unfolding over time, similar to the works of Cat Hope,[18] are also possible, and their relationship to fretboard location may be linked to spatial or gestural information, or simply to sonic result or representation. Skeletal mapping of the hand (ManoMotion) may allow for notation to be linked with specific finger movements, leaving 'traces' on the fretboard where the LH fingers have been placed. As well, as with *points of light* (Brandon, forthcoming), a sculptural graphic representation of sound is possible, connected with the fretboard as a point of emergence, freezing the results of the performance in time using electroacoustic triggers.

[16] There are many animated fretboard guitar tutorials available online, for an example see Lorange (2017).
[17] For an overview of guitar notation practices, see Babb (2021) and Josel and Tsao (2014).
[18] A list of animated notation works by Cat Hope are available at https://www.cathope.com/compositions (accessed 3 April 2021).

Conclusion

AR technology continues to develop, and with it, artistic possibilities for extending the guitar into digital performative space. While challenges remain, significant strides have allowed for pieces to be created which merge the guitar with interactive digital objects and notation. AR technology embedded in the guitar and fretboard can bridge the boundary between performative real and digital space at the locus of the instrument, creating a 'hyper-guitar' playable in both worlds simultaneously, which may expand possibilities for contemporary guitar composition in the 21st century.

Works cited

Bartos, D. (2019), *Motion Origami Guitars Using Leap Motion.* [Online performance]. Video available online: https://danielbartos.com/portfolio/motion-origami-guitar/ (accessed 4 April 2021).

Billone, P. (2012), *Sgorgo Y*, Self-published. Score excerpt available online: https://www.pierluigibillone.com/pdf/sgorgo_y_example.pdf (accessed 31 May 2021).

Brandon, A. (2017a), *Untitled A*, by F. Bravo and A. Brandon, [Concert performance], February 2017, Concert in the 21st Century, Banff Centre for the Arts, Banff, Alberta.

Brandon, A. (2017b), *Untitled B*, by A. Brandon et al., [Concert performance], 14 October 2017, Nocturne Festival, Fort Massey Church, Halifax, NS, Video available online: https://www.youtube.com/watch?v=QlUAKcH0ghc (accessed 31 May 2021).

Brandon, A. (2018a), *Hidden Motive I* [telemetic *HTC Vive* graphic score].

Brandon, A. (2018b), *Hidden Motive II* [Metavision interactive graphic score].

Brandon, A. (2018c), *Hidden Motive III* [Metavision interactive graphic score].

Brandon, A. (2018d), *Hidden Motive III*, by A. Brandon, [Concert performance], 18 November 2018, MINT Conference, Dalhousie University, Halifax, NS, Video available online: https://vimeo.com/303991623 (accessed 4 April 2021).

Brandon, A. (2019a), *7 Malagueña Fragments for Augmented Guitar* [Metavision and classical guitar].

Brandon, A. (2019b), *flesh projektor I*, [Metavision and guitar score].

Brandon, A. (2019c), *Augmented Percussions* [Metavision and percussion score].

Brandon, A. (2019d), *flesh projektor I*, by A. Brandon [Concert performance], 3 May 2019, New Music Edmonton, Edmonton, Alberta, Video available online: https://youtu.be/l6vD6lWIeA4 (accessed 4 April 2021).

Brandon, A. (2020a), *flesh projektor II* [Metavision and guitar score].

Brandon, A. (2020b), *WNMF x AR* [Mobile AR app]. Presented at the Winnipeg New Music Festival, Winnipeg, Manitoba, 26–31 January 2020, Video available online: https://www.youtube.com/watch?v=hJO7Mqr4oOo (accessed 4 April 2021).

Brandon, A. (2020c), *Boundary* [AR app sound installation]. Presented at the Gaudeamus Festival (Screen Dive), 9–20 September 2020, Video available online: https://www.youtube.com/watch?v=ALlPCj1evpY (accessed 4 April 2021).

Brandon, A. (2020d), *flesh projektor II*, by A. Brandon, [Concert performance], 26 January 2020. Centennial Hall, Winnipeg New Music Festival, Winnipeg, Alberta.

Brandon, A. (2021), *points of light* [Mobile AR and classical guitar score]. Forthcoming.

Brandon, A., R. Brandon and L. Brandon (2017), *Untitled B* [360 Graphic Score]. Unpublished.

Bravo, F. and A. Brandon (2017), *Untitled A* [360 Video Score]. Unpublished.

Chroma Mixed Media. (2019), *NaonaVR* [VR installation], Available online: http://www.chromamixedmedia.com/naona.html (accessed 4 April 2021).

Davis, K. (2018), *Hidden Motive I*, by A. Brandon, [Concert performance], 13 March 2018, Interactive Traces, Open Circuit Festival, University of Liverpool, Liverpool.

Gadenstätter, C. (2018), *Studies for a Portrait for Electric Guitar*. Unpublished. Score example available online: https://www.youtube.com/watch?v=T6C6-zN2sWs (accessed 31 May 2021).

Hein, N. and C. Schmitz (2021), *UNSTUMM – Conversation of Moving Image and Sound*. [Mobile AR work], Available online: https://unstumm.com/augmented-voyage-ar-vr-platform (accessed 17 April 2021).

Labbé, M. (2019), *Augmented Percussions*, by A. Brandon. [Concert performance], 6 December 2019, Centre d'Expérimentation Musicale, Chicoutimi, Québec, Video available online: https://www.youtube.com/watch?v=UqnW-KdkQRY (accessed 30 May 2021).

Lachenmann, H. (1969), *Pression*, Breitkopf & Härtel, Leipzig, Video score available online: https://issuu.com/breitkopf/docs/eb_9221_issuu (accessed 31 May 2021).

Magnusen, R. (2019), *solsticeVR* [VR composition work], Available online: http://www.solsticevr.net (accessed 4 April 2021).

Novak, S., and A. Brandon, (2017), *Bicinium* [AR sound installation].

Prestini, P. (2016), *The Hubble Cantata* [Concert and VR work]. 360 VR visuals by Eliza McNitt, Available online: https://www.paolaprestini.com/compositions/the-hubble-cantata (accessed 4 April 2021).

Rush, E. (2019), *7 Malagueña Fragments for Augmented Guitar*, by A. Brandon [Concert performance], 29 May 2019, SMC Conference, Málaga, Spain, Video available online: https://youtu.be/uHDFBw1LRCE (accessed 30 May 2021).

Visser, E. (2020), *Custom Inlaid Fretboard for Classical Guitar* [Musical instrument].

Warren, K. (2018), *Hidden Motive II*, by A. Brandon [Concert performance] 24 May 2018, TENOR Conference, Tanna Schulich Hall, Montreal, Video available online: https://www.youtube.com/watch?v=LgXGZOSeszU (accessed 4 April 2021).

Reference list

AR Foundation (2021), [AR software profile], Available online: https://unity.com/unity/features/arfoundation (accessed 31 May 2021).

ARCore (2021), [AR software profile], Available online: https://developers.google.com/ar (accessed 31 May 2021).

ARKit (2021), [AR software profile], Available online: https://developer.apple.com/augmented-reality (accessed 31 May 2021).

Babb, T. (2021), 'New Compositional Potential in Free Improvisation', The 21st Century Guitar Conference, 22–26 March, Universidade NOVA de Lisboa, Portugal.

Baily, J. and P. Driver (1992), 'Spatio-motor Thinking in Playing Folk Blues Guitar', *The World of Music*, 34 (3): 57–71.

Balistreri, D. (1995), *Intuition and Fretboard Intimacy: Approaching Improvisation on the Guitar*, MA diss., San Jose State University, San Jose.

Beaumont, W. (2015), *Bringing it all Together: Formal and Informal Learning in a University Guitar Class*, PhD diss., Boston University College of Fine Arts, Boston.

Berard, M. (1998), *Production and Evaluation of a Self-Instructional Method for Teaching Jazz Guitar*, PhD diss., Concordia University, Montreal.

Brandon, A. (2019e), 'How the Guitar Shapes Us: Part 1', *Soundboard*, 45 (1): 39–45.

Brandon, A. (2019f), 'How the Guitar Shapes Us: Part 2', *Soundboard*, 45 (2): 44–8.

Chuah, S. H. W., (2019), 'Wearable XR-Technology: Literature Review, Conceptual Framework and Future Research Directions', *International Journal of Technology Marketing*, 13 (3–4): 205–59.

Çoğulu, T. (2008), *Adjustable Microtonal Guitar*. [Instrument] As referenced in Schneider, John (2015), 'The Contemporary Guitar', Rowman & Littlefield: 63.

Cotter, D. and J. Packham (2019), 'BREKEKEKEX (2019): A New Collaborative Work for Classical Guitar, Live Electronics, & VR Headset Score'. [Conference lecture], presented at The Classical Musician in the 21st Century Conference, 23 May, University of Cambridge, UK.

De Souza, J. (2018), 'Fretboard Transformations', *Journal of Music Theory*, 62 (1): 1–39.

Elmer, C. (2009), *Replacing Patterns: Towards a Revision of Guitar Fretboard Pedagogy*, PhD diss., University of Adelaide, Australia.

Fretlight (2021), [Instrument], Available online: https://fretlight.com (accessed 16 April, 2021).

Goodrick, M. (1987), *The Advancing Guitarist*, New York: Hal Leonard.

Ham, J. J. (2017), 'An Architectural Approach to 3D Spatial Drum Notation', [Proceedings]. International Conference on Technologies for Music Notation and Representation (TENOR), 24–26 May, University of A Coruña, A Coruña, Spain.

Hamilton, R. (2021), 'Composing (and Designing) Trois Machins de la Grâce Aimante: A Virtual Reality String Quartet', in M. Ciciliani, B. Lüneburg and A. Pirchner (eds), *Ludified: Artistic Research in Audiovisual Composition, Performance & Perception*, 77–96, Berlin: The Green Box.

Josel, S. and M. Tsao (2014), *The Techniques of Guitar Playing*, Kassel: Bärenreiter.

Koltai, K. (2020), 'Breaking the Matrix: Transcribing Bartók and Ligeti for the Guitar Using a New Capo System', *Soundboard Scholar*, 6 (1): 1–36, https://digitalcommons.du.edu/sbs/vol6/iss1/6.

Lang, E. and D. Berend (1936), *Eddie Lang's Fingerboard Harmony for Guitar*, New York: Robbins Music.

Liarokapis, F. (2005), 'Augmented Reality Scenarios for Guitar Learning. Theory and Practice of Computer Graphics', [Proceedings], PCG 2005, Eurographics UK Chapter.

Lorange, K. (2017), 'Heatwave Blues - A Guitar Lesson with Animated Fretboard', Available online: https://www.youtube.com/watch?v=gBQy-KnoT_E (accessed 16 April 2021).

Mäki-Patola, T., A. Kanerva, J. Laitinen and T. Takala, (2005), 'Experiments with Virtual Reality Instruments', [Proceedings], New Interfaces for Musical Expression, 26–28 May 2005, Vancouver, Canada.

Martino, P. (1989), *Linear Expressions*, New York: REH Books.

Masu, R., P. Bala, M. A. Ahmad, N. N. Correia, V. Nisi, N. J. Nunes and T. Romão (2020), 'VR Open Scores: Scores as Inspiration for VR Scenarios', [Proceedings], New Interfaces for Musical Expression, 21–25 July, Birmingham, UK.

Matone, R. (2005), *An Integral Concept for Jazz Guitar Improvisation*, M.M diss., Rutgers College, Rutgers University, New Brunswick, New Jersey.

McFadden, J. (2010), *Fretboard Harmony for University Study: Method and Historical Context*, PhD diss., University of Toronto, Canada.

Meneses, E., S. Freire and M. Wanderley (2018), 'GuitarAMI and GuiaRT: Two Independent yet Complementary Augmented Nylon Guitar Projects', [Proceedings], New Interfaces for Musical Expression, 3–6 June, Blacksburg, Virginia, USA.

Merchi, Giacomo (2007), 'Le Guide des ecoliers de guitarre, oeuvre VII de 1761', as quoted in Tyler, J. and P. Sparks (2007), *The Guitar and its Music: From The Renaissance to the Classical Era*, Oxford: Oxford University Press.

Metavision (2018), Meta 2 Developer Kit Quick Start Guide, Redwood City, San Francisco: 16.

Metavision (2021), [Company profile], Available online: https://www.metavision.com (accessed on 31 May 2021).

Microsoft Hololens (2021), [AR headset profile], Available online: https://www.microsoft.com/en-us/hololens (accessed 31 May 2021).

Morreale, F., A. Guidi and A. Mcpherson (2019), 'Magpick: an Augmented Guitar Pick for Nuanced Control', [Proceedings], New Interfaces for Musical Expression, 3–6 June, Federal University of Rio Grande do Sul, Porto Alegre, Brazil.

Novax Guitars (1989), [Instrument], Available online: http://novaxguitars.com/info/concept.hstml (accessed 31 May 2021).

Robertson, A. (2020), 'What's Left of Magic Leap? The Dream of Mixed Reality is on Life Support', [News article], Available online: https://www.theverge.com/2020/6/16/21274638/magic-leap-app-store-partnerships-update (accessed 4 April 2021).

Sallis, J. (1982), *The Guitar Players: One Instrument and Its Masters in American Music*, New York: William Morrow, as quoted in Matone, R. (2005), *An Integral Concept for Jazz Guitar Improvisation*, M.M diss., Rutgers College, Rutgers University, New Brunswick, New Jersey: 1–2.

Santini, G. (2018), 'Composition as an Embodied Act: A Framework for the Gesture-based Creation of Augmented Reality Action Scores', [Proceedings], Sound and Music Computing Conference, 24–26 June 2020, Torino, Italy.

Santini, G. (2021), *Explorations in Augmented Reality for Interactive Gesture-based Musical Notation*, PhD diss., Hong Kong Baptist University, Hong Kong.

Stenstadvold, E. (2006), 'The Evolution of Guitar Notation, 1750–1830', *Soundboard*, 31: 11–29.

Stephan, M. A., B. Heckel, S. Song, and L. G. Cohen (2015), 'Crossmodal Encoding of Motor Sequence Memories', *Psychological Research*, 79 (2): 318.

Tanaka, A. (2000), 'Musical Performance Practice on Sensor-Based Instruments', *Trends in Gestural Control of Music*, 13 (389–405): 284.

Vuforia (2021), 'Vuforia: Best Practices for Designing and Developing Image-Based Targets', [Software instruction], Available online: https://library.vuforia.com/features/images/image-targets/best-practices-for-designing-and-developing-image-based-targets.html (accessed 16 April 2021).

Ward, S. M. (2011), *Attitudes and Perspectives of Pre-College Guitar Students: A Study To Help Explain Difficulty with Note-Reading in Class Guitar*, PhD diss., Arizona State University, USA.

Yamaha EZ-AG (2003), 'No Strings Attached: Yamaha EZ-AG Goes Acoustic', [Press release], Available online: https://usa.yamaha.com/news_events/2003/20030818_no-strings-attached-yamaha-ez-ag-goes-acoustic_us (accessed 16 April 2021).

Index

'2+2=5' (song)   167
3D design   32
3D technologies   239
360 scores   241, 250–2
7 Malagueña Fragments for Augmented Guitar (musical composition)   244–8, 253

Abasi, Tosin   77
Abercrombie, John   181
Aberdeen, UK   209
Ableton   208, 219, 222
Acet, Ruşen Can   32
Actress   192
Adams, John Luther
  Athabascan Dances (musical composition)   16
  Yup'ik Dances (musical composition)   16
Adapted Guitar   15–16, 47. *See also* Partch, Harry
Adjustable Microtonal Guitar   3, 21, 25–35, 97, 234
Adorno, Theodor   111, 148
affordance
  of augmented reality   256–8
  hauntological affordances   189–90
  of musical instruments/within performance practice   3, 5, 54–62, 77–8, 80, 87–8, 94, 97–8, 111–48, 166, 169, 173–84, 196–8, 212, 219, 222–3, 227, 241, 256–8
  theory of   4, 39, 51–62, 111–12, 116, 185 (*see also* Gibson, James J.)
'Airbag' (song)   167
Airfield   205
Alden, Howard   87, 88
Alien Love Secrets (website)   93
Altamira Guitar Foundation   123
Altamira Guitars (company)   51
alternative (genre)   153, 163–9

Alves, Bill
  American Gamelan (musical composition)   18
  Concerto for Guitar (musical composition)   18
ambient music   153, 163–4, 168–9
American Gamelan (musical composition)   18
American primitive (guitar/genre)   186–7
Amsterdam (Netherlands)   26
Anatolia. *See also* Turkey
  music of the region   26, 29, 31, 34, 38, 44–5, 67, 69, 74
Anderson, Julian   114–16
animated graphic notation   257
Antalya, Turkey   67
aPAtT Orchestra   194
Apple (company)   247
Arabic traditional music   31, 45, 58
AR Foundation (company)   241, 248
Aria (company)   156
Aristocrats, The   41
Armstrong Pickups (company)   108
Asia   44
assemblage   153
Aster, Ari
  Hereditary (film)   191
  Midsommar (film)   191
Athabascan Dances (musical composition)   16
augmented reality
  instrument   6, 239–58
  instrument, via outboard technologies   5, 62, 98
  performance practice   250–8
  other   1, 6, 239–58
Austin, Texas (USA)   209
Austin New Music Cooperative   209
autoethnography   4, 39, 121, 124
automation
  automated (moving) frets   27–8, 32, 34, 234

Automatic Microtonal Guitar   3, 25, 27–8, 32, 34
tintinnabulation, automated   *231*
avant
    avantfolk, theory of   5, 185–200
    avant-garde   7, 182, 186
    avant rock (/avantrock)   188, 194
    prefix definition (Martin)   186
Awake (album)   90
Ayyıldız, Sinan   29, 34

Bach, Johann Sebastian
    Cello Suite No. 5 (musical composition)   120
    other   9, 11, 26, 31, 85
Bad Timing (album)   188
bağlama   3, 26, 28, 29, 35, 38, 44 n.26, 46 n.37, 58–9, 69, 70. *See also* saz
Bailey, Derek
    Topography of the Lungs, The (album)   181
    other   182, 208
Baiza, Joe   175
Bali
    folk music of the region   31–2
banjo   3, 51, 87, 188, 207
baroque music   26, 31, 112
Barstow: 8 Hitchhiker's Inscriptions (musical composition)   14
Bartell (company)
    fretless guitar   39–40
Bartók, Béla
    'Night Music' (style)   125
    Night Music, The (movement IV of *Out of Doors*)   125–6
    Out of Doors (musical composition)   125
    Wedding Dance (musical composition)   126
    other   5, 124–8, 147, 187
Basie, Count   217
Basinski, William   189
bass
    bass guitar (lines/parts), emulation of   5, 34, 43, 87–8, 91, 95, 101–4, 107–8, 136, 193
    lines, compositional device   108, 136–8, 140, 142, 145
    register   87–8, 90–1, 95

resonance, of body/strings   85, 119
slap, technique   91
strings   4, 71, 88, 91, 102, 108, 119, 121, 123 n.17
Bates, Eliot   44
Batio, Michael Angelo   93
Beatles, The
    Beatles, The ('White Album') (album)   40 n.5
    Sgt. Pepper's Lonely Hearts Club Band (album)   179
    studio as virtual space   178
Belew, Adrian   40
Bellamy, Matt   40
Bennett, Andy   51
Bennink, Han
    Topography of the Lungs, The (album)   181
Benson, George   181
Berceuse (musical composition)   137–42
Berg, Jeff   48
Berklee College of Music   46 n.36, 215–17
Berlioz, Hector   111
Billone, Pierluigi
    Sgorgo Y (musical composition)   257
Birgisson, Jónsi   164
Bir Ömürlük Misafir (album)   67. *See also Fretless* (album); Oğur, Erkan
Black Keys, The   183
Blackwood, Easley
    Suite for guitar (musical composition)   19
'Blend' (song)   188
Blind Joe Death   187
Blood on Satan's Claw, The (film)   190, 191
Blue Note (record label)   88, 106, 173
blues music   42, 74, 82, 179, 182, 183, 186, 187, 194, 229
Boards of Canada   189
Bolin, Tommy   180
BOSS (company)   155–6, 164, 196–7
Boulez, Pierre   111
Boundary (musical composition)   247, 248
Bourdieu, Pierre   170, 192
Braithwaite, Stuart   165

Brandon, Amy
  7 Malagueña Fragments for Augmented Guitar (musical composition) 244–8, 253
  Boundary (musical composition) 247, 248
  flesh projektor I (musical composition) 242, 246, *247*, 248
  flesh projektor II (musical composition) *240*, 242
  Hidden Motive I (musical composition) 250
  points of light (musical composition) 249, 257
  WNMF x AR (musical composition) 248
  other 6, 239–58
Brar, Lucas 33
Bream, Julian 114
'Breath' (musical composition) 198
Breau, Lenny 83, 87
Bristol (UK) 30
British Film Institute (publication) 195
Brouwer, Leo
  interview with 116
  Simple Studies (musical score) 113
Budapest (Hungary) 130
Bull, Sandy
  'Blend' (song) 188
  Fantasias for Guitar and Banjo (album) 188
Burial 189, 192
Byrnes, Brendan 31

Cage, John
  indeterminacy 58
  other 14
California (USA) 10
Cambridge University (UK) 32
Campilongo, Jim 173
Canada 47
Cannell, Laura 188, 190
Cardiff University 9
çarpma, technique 68–70
Carrillo, Julián 9, 19
Carter, Chris 157
Catalan Peasant with Guitar (Artwork) 114

Cello Suite No. 5 (musical composition) 120
chamber music 31
Charlie Hunter Quartet 108
Chatham, Rhys 194
Chicago, Illinois (USA)
  blues 183
  other 176
China 159
Chopin, Frédéric
  Berceuse (musical composition) 137–42
  Valse op.69. no. 2 (musical composition) 117
  other 6
choreography, instrumental 113, 125
Christian, Charlie 183
cithara 82
classical guitar
  arrangements 5, 26, 30
  fretless classical guitar 26, 28, 38, 44, 46, 49–51, 59, 67–75 (see also *perdesiz*)
  guitarists/musicians 3, 9–16, 25–35, 44, 49–51, 68–75, 85
  microtonal classical guitar 25–35
  other 3, 5, 9–22, 25–35, 38, 51, 68–75, 82, 84, 85, 111–48
clavinet keyboard 19
Cline, Nels
  interview with 173–84
  'Princess Phone' (song) 178
  other 5, 156, 193
Cobham, Billy
  Spectrum (album) 180
Çoğulu, Tolgahan
  Adjustable Microtonal Guitar 3, 21, 25–35, 97, 234
  Automatic Microtonal Guitar 3, 25, 27–8, 32, 34
  interview with 25–35
  LEGO Microtonal Guitar 3, 25, 32–3
  other 3
Colchester Arts Centre (UK) 57
collage technique 187
Cologne (Germany) 28
computer aided design (CAD) 159
Concerto for Guitar (musical composition) 18

contemporary music   26, 47, 62, 77, 114
Costa, Yamandu   77, 83, 85
Cotter, David   250
counterpoint   102-7, 140
country music
  fingerpicking techniques   42, 173, 186
Covid-19 (coronavirus)   101, 142 n.22, 183, 230
cracked media, theory of   197, 212.
  See also Kelly, Caleb
Cuban music   109. *See also* montuno; tres; tumbao
custom-made/built, instruments   1, 25-35, 41, 42 n.18, 44 n.24, 45, 46 n.36-7, 51, 87-8, 91-2, 111-48, 241, 249

Daft Punk   192
Darreg, Ivor   19
Davis, Kevin   251
Davis, Miles   178
Dawe, Kevin. *See also* 'guitarscape'; new guitarscape, concept of
  New Guitarscape in Critical Theory, The   6, 37, 77-8
Dawes, Mike   86
Dawson, Richard   188
'Deep Down Into the Pain' (song)   92
Deftones   90
Delap, Bill   91
Deleuze, Gilles   193-4, 197, 199
Denver, Colorado (USA)   20
Derrida, Jacques
  Specters of Marx   189, 193
De Souza, Jonathan
  guitar thinking, theory of   5, 111-13, 117
  instrumental affordances   111-13, 117, 121
  other   77, 215, 221, 227
Diaspora Arts Connection (San Francisco)   58
digital
  aesthetics   153, 165-9
  digital audio workstation (DAW)   193
  digitisation   153, 156
  effects   98, 153-9, 161, 163-5, 196-8, 239, 243 (*see also* effects)

instrument(s)   98, 173, 180, 215-35, 241, 243, 253, 257
  mobile device technology   242, 246-8, 253
  signal processing (DSP)   153, 164, 166-9
  space   239-58
  teaching tools   215, 219, 235
  tools   173, 180, 230, 239-58
dildo (vibrator)   98, 205
Dines, Jared   92
Diystompboxes (website)   158
djent   90, 92
Donahue, Tim   46
Dream Theater
  Awake (album)   90
Dresden guitar   85
drone   5, 40, 86, 93, 168, 195-6, 205, 212
Dsilton   19
Dufour, Antoine   85, 86
Dunlop (company)   43
Duoist   26
Durrant, Phil   205
Dusted (magazine)   198
Dvořák, Antonín   187
Dyens, Roland   117
Dylan, Bob   192

'An Earth Dweller's Return' (song)   40
eBay   15, 160, 206
EBow   1, 43-4, 52, 55, 57, 70, 98, 207, 208, 210
Echoplex   179, 180, 188
ecological psychology   111-12
effectivity, concept of   53-60
effects
  analogue effects (pedals)   156-7, 169
  BOSS (company)   155-6, 162, 164, 196-7
  Electro-Harmonix (EHX) (company)   *154*, 155, 165, 197
  granular delay   153, 162-4, 166, 168
  pedals (various)   5, 30, 44-6, 52, 55, 57 n.59, 62, 71, 98, 108, 110, 148, 153-70, 173, *175*, 176-7, 179, 181, 183, 185, 190, 193, 195-8, 205-6, 208-9, 225, 243
  studio technology   164, 169-70, 178-80

Eggers, Robert
  Witch, The (film)   191
Eisenstein, Sergei
  cognitive dissonance, theory of   190
El Colibri (musical compositions/score)   113
Electro-Harmonix (EHX). *See under* effects
electronic music   165, 166, 194, 216, 219
Electronic Projects for Musicians   158
electronics
  amateur electronics   156–7, 160
  components/machine parts   9, 25–35, 43–60, 243–58
  integrated circuits (ICs)   160–3
  live electronics (performance)   58, 205, 209, 215, 234
  printed circuit boards (PCBs)   157–60
Ellison, Michael   25
embodiment   5, 53–5, 58, 113
Endless Summer (album)   166, 188
England (UK)   73
Eps, George Van   83, 87
equal divisions of the octave (EDO). *See under* tuning systems (general)
equal temperament (TET). *See under* tuning systems (general)
Equinox (musical composition)   235
Erdoğan, Cenk
  interview with   67–75
  other   4, 44, 45, 63
Eroğlu, Sinan Cem   44
Escheté, Ron   87
Europe   28, 48
Evans, Bill   88
Evett, Ned
  interview with   41–2
  other   47, 63
EXAUDI   205
experimental music   5, 41, 46–7, 153, 173, 193, 205–13
Explosions in the Sky   164–5
extended range (guitar/instruments)
  by fretting   10, 80, 83, 85, 97
  by neck   83, 85, 97
  by strings   78, 80, 83, 85–7, 90, 92, 97
  by technique   62, 83, 93, 97
  by technology   62, 80, 97–8, 230–5, 243–58
  by tuning   83, 86, 90, 97
  other   4, 77–98
extended reality (XR)   6, 239–58
Eyes Wide Shut (film)   135

Facebook   39
FACT Liverpool (UK)   195
Fahey, John   185–8, 194
failure, aesthetic of   165, 193, 197–8
Fantasias for Guitar and Banjo (album)   188
Farinelli   112
Faust   205
Fear Factory   90
Fellowship, The   41
Fender (company)
  Jaguar   174–6
  Jazzmaster   173–6
  Stratocaster   31, 42 n.18, 52, *59*, 173, 175
  Telecaster   20
  other   155
Fennesz, Christian
  Endless Summer (album)   166, 188
  Hotel Paral.lel (album)   166
'Feral' (song)   167
Ferraro, James   193
'Fib01a' (song)   166
A Field in England (film)   191
fingerboard. *See* fretboard; fretless; frets
Fisher, Mark   185, 189–92. *See also* hauntology and weird, the
Fiuczynski, David 'Fuze'   31, 46–7
flamenco   30, 72–4
flesh projektor I (musical composition)   242, 246, *247*, 248
flesh projektor II (musical composition)   240, 242
folk
  avantfolk, theory of   5, 185–200
  experimental folk   182, 188, 188 n.8, 192, 195
  horror   5, 185, 189, 190, 194–200
  other   82, 84–6, 96, 199
  taxonomies   81
Fongaard, Bjørn   19

Forcione, Antonio 46
Forlorn Hope (musical score) 143
For Those in Peril (film) 191
found objects 208–9
'Four Hills' (multi-modal composition) 189, 194–200
Frankfurt (Germany) 71
Freestompboxes (website) 158
Fretboard. *See also* fretless; frets
 Adjustable Microtonal Guitar 3, 21, 25–35, 97, 234
 augmented reality fretboard 239–58
 automated 27–8, 32, *34*
 Automatic Microtonal Guitar 3, 25, 27–8, 32, 34
 digital fretboard 6, 215–37, 239–58
 digital manipulation of fretboard 221, 230–5
 fretboard pedagogy 3, 33–4, 43, 215–16, 228, 235
 interchangeable fretboard/fingerboard 10, 14, 19, 22, 27–8, 45 (*see also* tuning systems (general))
 LEGO Microtonal Guitar 3, 25, 32–3
 moveable/adjustable frets 3, 11, 14, 21, 25–35, 97, 234, 239 n.1
 non-octave fretting 19 (*see also* tuning systems (general))
 transformation(s) of 112, 122–3, 241
Fretless (album) 44, 67. *See also* Oğur, Erkan
fretless
 fingerboard materials 15, 41–2, 68
 fretless baritone guitar 44 n.25, 47 n.41, 67, 71–2
 fretless classical guitar 26, 28, 38, 44, 46, 49–51, 59, 67–75 (*see also* perdesiz)
 fretless electric guitar 4, 15–16, 38–41, 44 n.28, 45 n.33, 46–63, 70
 fretless guitar (general) 1, 4, 15–16, 26, 28–9, 31–3, 35, 37–63, 67–75, 92, 93 n.8, 98
 fretless guitar, composition/s for 43, 44, 50, 57–8, 58 n.60, 72, 75
 fretless guitar festivals 38, 42 n.19, 48

 fretless guitar performance (approaches to) 37–63, 67–75
 fretless guitar videos 48–51, 74–5
 fretlessness, concept of 4, 39, 59–62
Fretless Architecture (music project) 57
Fretless Guitar Lessons (website) 74
Fretless Guitar Masters (album) 48
fretlet. *See under* frets
frets. *See also* fretboard
 automated (moving) 27–8, 32, *34*
 de-fretted instruments 15, 37, 51 n.1 (*see also* fretless)
 fretlet 14, 31
 moveable/adjustable 3, 11, 14, 21, 25–35, 97, 234, 239 n.1
 non-octave fretting 19 (*see also* tuning systems (general))
 positioning (alternative systems) 1, 3, 9–22, 25–35, 45, 47 n.40, 91–3, 97, 234 (*see also* fretboard; microtonal; tuning systems (general))
 re-fretted instruments 11, 14–15, 18–20, 26
 virtual 232–5
fretting. *See* frets
Freud, Sigmund 191, 194
Fripp, Robert
 frippertronics 181
 other 181, 193
Frisell, Bill 193
Frith, Fred
 Guitar Solos (album) 181
 other 208
Frohberger, Johann Jakob
 Suite No. 19 (musical composition) 120
Frusciante, John 40
funk 4, 101, 107
fusion music 45, 46, 74

G&G Guitars (company) 51
Gadenstätter, Clemens
 Studies for a portrait for electric guitar (musical compositions) 257
Gal, Sharon 194
Galbraith, Paul
 Brahms Guitar 83, 85, 118
Gamba 11

gamelan   18
Gerritsen, Stefan   31
Gershwin, George
    I Got Rhythm   233
Ghostbox (record label)   189
Gibson
    J-2000   86
    Maestro Fuzz pedal   155, 180 n.1
Gibson, James J.   4, 39, 51–62, 111–12, 116, 185. *See also* affordance, theory of
glass–slide capo technique   42–3
gliss/glissandi (articulation). *See under* slides
glissentar   47 n.41, 51, 59
glitch
    aesthetic   5, 165–9, 185–200
    effect   153, 163, 166–7, 185, 188, 190
    looping/micro-sampling   167, 186, 191, (theory of)   193–5
globalization   79
Goodrick, Mick
    disadvantage exercise   229
    Goodrick number, the   223–7, 232
    unitar exercise   228
    other   255
Google (company)   48, 247
Gorton, David
    Forlorn Hope (musical score)   143
    Six Miniatures (musical score)   143
    other   5, 142–7
'Go To Sleep' (song)   167
Govan, Guthrie   41, 48, 49, 73
Grabstein für Stephan (musical composition)   115
Graham, Davey (/Davy)   86, 195
Gravelle, Buzz
    interview with   49–51
    other   63
Green, Freddie   109, 217
Greenwood, Johnny   167
Gretch (company)   87, 89
Grgić, Mak   31
Grove Oxford Music Online (website)   25
guitar communities   38, 77–98. *See also* intercultural (collaboration/exchange); virtual, scene(s)

guitar festivals
    Dutch Fretless Guitar Festival   48
    Microtonal Guitar Festival   22
    NYC Fretless Guitar Festival   42 n.19, 48
    other   28, 38
Guitar Interactive (magazine)   48
Guitar Player (magazine)   19, 208
'guitarscape'   4, 6, 37–63, 77, 92, 97. *See also* Dawe, Kevin; new guitarscape
guitar soli   186
Guitar Solos (album)   181
'guitar space'   111–48, 235
Guthman People's Choice Award   33
Guyatone (company)   156
gypsy guitar   83

Hába, Alois   19
Hackett, Steve   181
Haggard, Piers
    Blood on Satan's Claw, The (film)   190, 191
Hammond organ   108
Han, Ali   31
Hardy, Robin
    Wicker Man, The (film)   190
harp   13–14, 16, 29, 46, 82, 93 n.8, 97, 147, 225, 234
Harper, Adam   189, 192
harp guitar   44 n.27, 46, 46 n.38, 86, 93 n.8, 97
Harrison, George   39
Harrison, Lou
    Serenade for guitar (with optional percussion) (musical composition)   12
    Serenado por Gitaro (album)   11
    other   11, 12, 14, 20
Harvard University (USA)   32
Hasse, Johann Adolph   112
Haunt Me, Haunt Me Do It Again (album)   166
hauntology   5, 185–6, 188–91, 194–200
Haverstick, Neil   47
Hawaii (USA)
    music of the region   20
    Oahu Hawaiian guitar   16

Hecker, Tim
  Haunt Me, Haunt Me Do It Again (album) 166
Hedges, Michael 85
Hegarty, Paul
  noise aesthetics 193
Hendrix, Jimi 174, 178, 180 n.1
  Electric Ladyland (album) 178–80
  Hendrix chord, the 216, 219–20, 225–6, 228, 232
Hereditary (film) 191
Hidden Motive I (musical composition) 250
hip-hop 166, 182
HLK 88
Holdsworth, Allan 91–2
Hololens (Microsoft) 241
Hope, Cat 257
Hoppstock, Tilman 120
Hornbostel-Sachs classification system 79
Hoshino Gakki (company) 155
Hotel Paral.lel (album) 166
House, Son 187
Howe, Steve 181
Hungary
  Budapest 130
  music of the region 115
Hunter, Charlie
  Charlie Hunter Quartet 108
  interview with 101–9
  'Run for It' (song) 108
  Songs From the Analog Playground (album) 108
  other 4, 5, 77, 88–9, 91
Hutchins, Gary 93
hybrid
  guitar (object) 4, 101–9
  guitar (performance approach) 88, 101–9
  instrument 47, 51, 101–9
  music(s) 58, 188
Hybrid Guitars (company) *102*, 108
'Hydra' (Ibanez guitar) 40 n.9, 93. *See also* Vai, Steve
Hygens-Fokker Foundation, The (Amsterdam) 2, 6
hyper-guitar 241, 258
hypnagogic pop 189

Ibanez (company) 88, 89, 95, 155–6
identity
  cultural 4, 45, 62, 72–3
  of the guitar 1, 6, 109
  as performer 4, 30, 43, 59–60, 62, 72–3, 86, 101–3
  other 194, 195 n.20
'I Know You're Here' (song) 40
Imposition (album) 51 n.53
improvisation
  in composition 19, 50, 51, 57, 137–9, 146, 188, 190, 197, 240
  fingerstyle improvisation 74, 195
  free improvisation 44, 47, 58, 62, 194, 210
  with noise/drones 5, 57, 177–8, 188, 205–13, 215–17
  pedagogy 215–20, 228–9, 233, 235
  in performance 19, 40, 45–7, 57, 87, 104, 193–5, 215, 219, 235, 246–7
  with technology 46, 179, 216, 233, 239–40, 246–7
Improweb MMXIX (musical composition) 58 n.60
India
  folk music of the region 31
  other 159
industrial music 199
Instagram 39, 49, 50, 75
intercultural (collaboration/exchange) 37–9, 51–2, 58–62
interdependence 103
International Guitar Research Centre (IGRC) 58 n.60, 123
In the Earth (film) 191
Intonation Systems (company) 10–11, 14. *See also* Novatone
Iran 50
Israel 45
Istanbul (Turkey) 21, 30, 67
Istanbul Technical University 25, 32
Ives, Charles 186

James, M.R.
  Oh, Whistle, and I'll Come to You, My Lad (Story) 189
James, Michael 165
Jameson, Fredric
  'nostalgia mode' 191

Jam Track Central (YouTube channel) 84
Jansch, Bert 195
Japan
   electronics, general 155
   music of the region 183
jazz
   extended guitar in 84, 87–9, 93–5, 216
   fusion 41, 45, 46, 101
   harmony 44, 74, 89, 96, 217–18
   microtonal guitars in 19, 35
   modern jazz 4
   straight-ahead 72, 74, 87
   other 45, 46, 77, 83, 173, 194, 229, 254
Jeck, Philip 189
Johnston, Ben
   'Tavern, The' (Song) 18, 20
Jones, Elvin 103
Jordan, Stanley 91
Just (pure) intonation. *See under* tuning systems (general)
Just Strings 16

Kaiser, Henry 173, 176–7
Kansas, Missouri (USA) 11
kanun 28
Kaoss pad (Korg) 93, 173, 180
Kaplan, Lee 181
Kelly, Caleb
   'cracked media' 197, 212
Kill List (film) 191
King, Kaki 33, 86
King Gizzard & the Lizard Wizard 31, 34
King of Gear, The (website) 167
Klon Centaur 156, 176
Koltai, Katalin 5, 233
Koozin, Timothy
   relative system of fret intervals 112
kora 222
Korn
   Korn (album) 90
krautrock 165
Krebs, Annette 183
Kubrick, Stanley
   Eyes Wide Shut (film) 135
Kudirka, Michael 27, 35
Kurdistan
   music of the region 58

Kurtág, György
   Grabstein für Stephan (musical composition) 115
   other 5, 115–16

Labella (company) 87
Lachenmann, Helmut
   Pression (musical composition) 257
Lacôte, Réne 27
Lage, Julian 173
Lang, Eddie 87
Lanterns (EP) 195
'Lanterns' (musical composition) 198
Last Testament 19
Latour, Bruno
   actor network theory (ANT) 5, 154–5, 197
Lattice İşi (musical composition) 26, 28
Law, Ant
   interview with 4, 93–6
   other 83, 88–9, 91
LED guitars
   FretLight 257
   guitar 57
   Yamaha EZ AG 257
Led Zeppelin 183
LEGO Microtonal Guitar 3, 25, 32–3
Lennon, John 40
Lewin, David 112
Lick Library (website) 48, 84
Ligeti, György 5, 147
   Musica Ricercata (musical composition) 122, 130–7
   other 5, 147
Ligeti Guitar 5, 111–48
Lindley, Mark 25
Line 6 POD 30
Los Angeles, California (USA) 49, 181
Lovecraft, Howard Philips 192
lute 3, 11, 82, 85, 121, 254

McGrath, John
   avantfolk, theory of 5, 185–200
   'Breath' (musical composition) 198
   'Four Hills' (multi-modal composition) 189, 194–200
   glitch looping, theory of 193–5
   Lanterns (EP) 195
   'Lanterns' (musical composition) 198

'Moreover, the Moon' (musical composition)   198
'Si Bheag Si Mhor' (musical arrangement)   198
Wake & Whisper (album)   198 n.26–7
other   5, 173
McKee, Andy   85, 86
Mackenzie, Stu   31
McLaughlin, John   85, 86, 181
Madonna   166
'Magdalene Laundries' (song)   232
Magic Leap (company)   241
Magnet Capo System (Koltai)   5, 121–4, 137, 143, 233
Maguire, Phil   205
MAKAM (magazine)   45
makam/maqam   3, 21, 25–9, 33, 34, 44, 47
ManoMotion (company)   247, 257
Manring, Michael   93
Marchione Guitars (company)   73
marimba   57
Marin, Gabriel   46
Martino, Pat   217, 228–9, 233
Martyn, John   188
Mathieu, William Allaudin
  Lattice İşi (musical composition)   26, 28
Max/MSP   6, 166–7, 169, 188, 215, 230
Maxon Effects (company)   156
Mayr, Ernst   80
mbira   222
meantone temperament   3, 10, 11, 26, 32
Mercury Tree, The   31
Merleau-Ponty, Maurice
  phenomenology   5, 111
Mermikides, Milton   5, 205
Meshuggah   90
Messiaen, Olivier   94–5
Metavision headsets (AR)   241–53
Metheny, Pat   46, 85, 86
Meyer, Bill   198
MicroFest (festival)   20
MicroFest (record label)   20
MicroStock (festival)   20
microtonal
  Adjustable Microtonal Guitar   3, 21, 25–35, 97, 234
  Automatic Microtonal Guitar   3, 25, 27–8, 32, 34
  LEGO Microtonal Guitar   3, 25, 32–3
microtonal classical guitar   25–35
microtonal electric guitar   30–1
microtonal harmonization   28, 46
microtonality   3, 9–22, 25–35, 44, 46–7, 56, 58, 60–2, 69, 72, 85, 92, 94, 97, 143–5, 164, 234–5, 239 n.1
microtonal music festivals   20, 22, 48 n.45
microtonal music theory   33
scordatura/tuning   143, 234
world microtonalities/ microtonal traditions   20, 25–35, 38, 44, 46–7, 58, 69 (*see also* makam/maqam; tuning systems (general))
Microtonal Guitar Competition   21, 30–1
Microtonal Guitar Duo   29
Microtonal Guitar Festival   22
Microtonal Guitars (company)   22
MIDI   6, 46, 62, 215–37
Midsommar (film)   191
Miller, Johnathan
  Whistle, and I'll Come to You (BBC production)   191, 196
Miner, Gregg   86
Mirarab, Mahan   45
Miró, Joan
  Catalan Peasant with Guitar (artwork)   114
Mitchell, Joni
  'Magdalene Laundries' (song)   232
Mizrap   70
Mogwai   164, 165
Monda, Tom   40
Mongrain, Erik   86
Montgomery, Wes   221
montuno   104
Moog (company)
  guitar   5, 205–13
  soundlab   206
Moore, Thurston   173, 174, 188
'Moreover, the Moon' (musical composition)   198
motion capture devices   241–4
Mraihi, Amine   45

multi-neck   40 n.9, 41, 44 n.24, 45, 46 n.36–7, 51, 83, 86, 93
Muse   40
Musica Ricercata (musical composition)   122, 130–7
music cognition   111, 215, 256
musicking, theory of (Small)   186
Musikmesse (Frankfurt)   71
musique concrète   179, 187
MXR Innovations Inc. (company)   155–6
Myers, Oren   123

Nanotechnologies   32
Naples (Italy)   81
Nashville tuning. *See under* tuning/s
National (company)
    'New Yorker' electric Spanish guitar   15
    Tricone Resophonic   20
Nels Cline Singers
    Share the Wealth (album)   173
Nels Cline Trio   174
Neo-Riemannian theory   217
new guitarscape, concept of   6, 37, 77–8
New Guitarscape in Critical Theory, The   37, 77, 78
New Standard Tuning. *See under* tuning/s
New York City, New York (USA)
    NYC Fretless Guitar Festival   42 n.19, 48
    other   33, 48, 72, 176
New York School, the   208
New York Times (newspaper)   34
niche, concept of   52, 54, 58, 60. *See also* affordance, theory of
Niehorster, Willem   48 n.45. *See also* fretless, fretless guitar festivals
Night Music, The (musical composition)   125–6
noise
    aesthetics   193, 194
    (s) in music   56, 57, 125–6, 177, 179
    noise music (genre)   62, 187–8
North American Rock Guitar Competition   42
North Carolina, USA   108
notation
    animated graphic notation   257
    digital   239 43, 253 8

guitar (conventional)   216–17, 220–2, 231, 236, 253–4
guitar (non-conventional/alternative)   6, 19, 52, 128, 239–58
    spatial notation   255–8
    tablature   123, 128, 216, 253–6
Nottingham (UK)   209
Novatone (company)   14. *See also* Intonation Systems

Oahu Hawaiian guitar   16
Oğur, Erkan
    Bir Ömürlük Misafir (album)   67
    Fretless (album)   44, 67
    other   26, 28, 44, 67, 72–4
'Oh, Whistle, and I'll Come to You, My Lad' (story)   189
Ohana, Maurice   9
on-board processing units   1, 43–6
open tuning. *See under* tuning/s
organ
    emulation of   108
    Fokker organ   26
    Hammond organ   108
organology   4, 77–98, 111, 215
Ormsby Guitars (company)   92
O'Rourke, Jim
    Bad Timing (album)   188
Östersjö, Stefan   143
oud   38, 44, 45, 58, 60, 69, 71, 82
Out of Doors (musical composition)   125

Paris (France)   115
Parker, Evan
    Topography of the Lungs, The (album)   181
Partch, Harry
    Barstow: 8 Hitchhiker's Inscriptions (musical composition)   14
    other   9, 11, 14–18, 20–2, 37, 47
PARTCH Ensemble   16–17
Pasieczny, Marek   31
Patton, Charley   187
Paul, Les   193
Pearl (company)   156
Pearl Jam   70
pedal (effects). *See under* effects
Peker, Salih Kortut   **44**

pelog (tuning) 18
perdesiz (*gitar*) 44, 51 n.52, 67-75. *See also* fretless
Perez, Fernando 31
Perks, Richard
   Fretless Architecture (music project) 57
   fretlessness, concept of 4, 39, 59-62
   Imposition (album) 51 n.53
   Improweb MMXIX (musical composition) 58 n.60
   Strung Together (music project) 58-9
   other 4
Persia
   classical music (dastgāh) 44 n.22, 58
   folk music 31, 45, 58
Peterson, Richard A. 51
Philips Research Lab
   bucket brigade chip 155
piano music 88, 95, 111-48
Pim Jacobs Trio 221
pitch
   class/sets 130, 136, 148, 215, 225-6
   comprehension of 56, 106, 113, 122, 130, 216-36, 253, 256
   manipulation devices 98
   matrix 6, 215, 221
   microtonal pitches (*see* fretboard; frets; microtonal)
   polyphony 28, 217, 219, 222, 227-30
   repetition 222-4, 230
   spacing 222, 224-7
   surface 215, 222, 234
Pizzarelli, Bucky 87
platform economy 158
Playthroughs (album) 166-7
points of light (musical composition) 242, 249, 257
Polansky, Larry 20
ponticello 9
popular music 4, 39-40, 96, 163, 169, 173, 178, 192, 194, 254
post-punk 165
post-structuralist theory 166
Powell, Edward 47
Practical Electronics (magazine) 157
prepared guitar 208-13

Pression (musical composition) 257
primitivism 186, 187
'Princess Phone' (song) 178
psychedelia 189, 191
Pythagorean (tuning) 3, 10, 12

Quartet #7 (musical composition) 18
Quayle, Tom 91

Radiohead 167
   '2+2=5' (song) 167
   'Airbag' (song) 167
   'Feral' (song) 167
   'Go to Sleep' (song) 167
raga 42, 47
ragmakamtar 47
range, (extended)
   by fretting 10, 80, 83, 85, 97 (*see also* tuning systems (general))
   by neck 83, 85, 97
   by strings 78, 80, 83, 85-7, 90, 92, 97
   by technique 62, 83, 93, 97, 205-14
   by technology 62, 80, 97, 98, 230-5, 243-58
   other 4, 77
Rascal, Dizzee 41
Ravel, Maurice 112
Recycler (magazine) 174
Reeves, Michael
   Witchfinder General (film) 190
Reich, Steve 193
Reinhardt, Django 183
remediation 188
renaissance music 26, 31, 32
'Resistance' (song) 40
resonance
   cultural 189, 193 n.15, 199
   effects, use of 154, 164
   guitar (body/physical) 85, 102, 111, 115, 117-20, 143, 154 (*see also* Yepes, Narciso)
   sympathetic 82, 85, 135 (*see also* Yepes, Narciso)
Reverb (website) 160
Revox (company) 181
Reynolds, Simon 189, 194, 195, 198
Rheinberger, Hans-Jörg 0212
rhythm 95, 102, 104, 107, 166

rhythm section
   guitarist's role   5, 101–7
Richards, Keith   184
Riley, Terry   20, 193
Roche, Eric   86
rock music
   alternative rock   153, 163–9
   commercial   19, 35
   djent   90, 92
   experimental/ progressive   5, 40, 41, 84, 90, 181
   general   38, 39, 41, 43, 50, 70, 73–4, 77, 89–91, 173, 183
   grunge   156, 192
   indie rock   156
   metal   19, 78, 83–4, 89–91, 199
   nu-metal   90
   post-punk   165
   post-rock   163–5
   punk   199
   rock 'n' Roll   178, 182
   stadium   5
Rodgers, Nile   109
Roland Corporation (company). See also BOSS
   Roland GK hexaphonic system   230
   other   155–6
role
   in performance/ensemble   5, 101–9
Rolling Stone (magazine)   173
Ronaldo, Lee   173
Roos, Randy   46
Rós, Sigur   163–4
Rosenwinkel, Kurt   221, 226
Ross, Don   86
Roth, Uli Jon   91, 95
Rowe, Keith   205, 208–10
Rowman & Littlefield (publisher)   22
   Contemporary Guitar, The   22
Royal Academy of Music (London)   142
Ruck, Jürgen   31
Ruggles, Carl   233
'Run for It' (song)   108
Rush, Emma   244–5
Rypdal, Terje   46

Saccharine Trust   175
Sagreras, Julio Salvador

El Colibri (musical compositions/ score)   113
Sanderson, Richard   205
San Diego, California (USA)   11
San Francisco, California (USA)   58, 59, 177
Santa Monica, California (USA)   175
Santini, Giovanni   242, 257
sarod   60
saz   44 n.26, 46 n.37, 58–9. *See also* bağlama
Schenkerian analysis   113
Schneider, John
   Contemporary Guitar, The   22, 26
   other   3, 31
Schoenberg, Arnold
   Serenade   9
   Serialism   9
   other   233
'Science Fiction: New Death' (exhibition)   195
scordatura. *See under* tuning/s
Scovell, Adam   195–7
scratch orchestras   194
Seen, The   205
Serenade for guitar (with optional percussion) (musical composition)   12
Serenado por Gitaro (album)   11
Sex and Religion (album)   40
Sgorgo Y (musical composition)   257
Sgt. Pepper's Lonely Hearts Club Band (album)   179
Share the Wealth (album)   173
Sharp, Elliott   47, 173, 182
Shaw, Robert E.   52. *See also* effectivity, concept of
Shea, Nicholas
   'enactive landscapes'   113
Sheeran, Ed   193
Shields, Kevin   164
Shillinger, Joseph
   geometric expansions   233
shoegaze music   163–5
'Si Bheag Si Mhor' (musical arrangement)   198
Sight & Sound (magazine)   195
Silver, Yoni   205

Simple Studies (musical score)   113
Six Miniatures (musical score)   143
Skempton, Howard   194
slide (device)   9, 42–3, 98
slides (articulation)
   fretless guitar (characteristic to)   28–9, 33, 38, 40, 57, 69
   gliss/glissandi   28–9, 33, 40, 69
   types of   28–9, 38, 40, 42, 57, 60, 69
Slip of the Tongue (album)   89
Small, Christopher
   musicking, theory of   186
Social media   4, 39, 48–50, 58, 62. *See also* Facebook; Instagram; YouTube
Song, Cavalier   194
Songs From the Analog Playground (album)   108
Sonic Youth   173, 174, 183
Sons of Apollo   41
soul music   101
Sound and Music Computing Conference (Malaga, Spain, 2019)   244
Spain   72, 244
Specters of Marx   189, 193
Spectrum (album)   180
Spink, Ian   205
standard tuning. *See under* tuning/s
Stone, Tom   10–12, 27
Stooges, The   175
Stowell, John   46
Strachan, Robert   5, 192–3, 196
Stravinsky, Igor   9, 187
Strung Together (music project)   58–9
Studies for a portrait for electric guitar (musical compositions)   257
Suite for guitar (musical composition)   19
Suite No. 19 (musical composition)   120
sul tasto   90
Summers, Andy   40
switchboard guitar   11
Sword, Ron   19
synth pop   182, 183

tablature   254–5
tabletop guitar   208–9
Takemitsu, Tōru
   Equinox (musical composition)   235

tanbur   28, 38, 44, 67, 69–70
'Tavern, The' (Song)   18, 20
taxonomy
   of guitar   80, 97
   macrotaxonomy   80
   microtaxonomy   80
technostalgia   156, 191, 193
Tehran   45
Temperament. *See* tuning systems (general)
Tenney, James   20
Thal, Ron 'Bumblefoot'   41, 98
Thames, Michael   83
Thank You Scientist   40
theramin   57, 208, 222
Third Day, The (TV series)   191
Thompson, Bill
   interview with   205–13
   other   5
Throbbing Gristle   157
timbre
   development/exploration of   9, 11, 26, 51, 78, 115, 120, 154, 177, 207
   innovation/originality in   163, 166
tintinnabulation   *231*, 234
Topography of the Lungs, The (album)   181
Torres, Antonio de   82
'Torture Never Stops, The' (song)   40
Toto   70
Towner, Ralph   181
Townsend, Devin   83
Treehouse   43
tres   109
Truefire (website)   84
tumbao   104
tuning/s (guitar)
   alternative   5, 9, 20, 86, 106–7, 115, 117, 120–2, 133, 136, 143, 195, 226–7
   approaches to   4, 71, 77–8, 80–4, 86–90, 92–4, 96–7, 102, 106–7, 120–2, 136, 143, 174, 184, 195, 217, 222–37, 256
   augmented/digital   215–35
   DADGAD   20, 86, 195, 226
   microtonal   143, 234

Nashville tuning   223, 227
New Standard Tuning   227
open tuning   16, 20, 82–3, 86, 195
scordatura (specific use of term)   5, 9, 115, 117, 120–2, 133, 136, 143, 227
standard tuning   82, 90, 93–4, 97, 184, 223, 224, 226–9, 231–2, 235, 237
zhivago   226
tuning systems (general)
   approaches to   9–22, 26, 28, 31, 56, 58, 61, 62, 69, 71, 77–8, 80–2, 96–7, 222–7, 230–2, 235
   equal divisions of the octave (EDO)   3, 19–20, 47 n.40, 92, 94 (*see also* fretboard; frets; microtonal)
   equal temperament (TET)   3, 10–12, 14, 19, 22, 26, 29–32, 44 n.22, 44 n.24, 47 n.40, 56 (*see also* fretboard; frets)
   guitar tuning/s (by string) (*see* tuning/s (guitar))
   Just (pure) intonation   3, 10, 12, 16, 18–19, 26, 27, 29, 32, 39, 47 n.39, 48 n.45 (*see also* microtonal; fretboard; frets)
   meantone temperament   3, 10–11, 26, 32 (*see also* fretboard; frets; microtonal)
   microtonal   3, 9–22, 25–35, 38, 44, 46, 47, 56, 58, 60–2, 69, 72, 85, 94, 97, 143–5, 234–5, 239 n.1 (*see also* fretboard; frets; microtonal)
   pelog   18
   Pythagorean   3, 10, 12
   Well   26
   xenharmonic   19
Tunisia (Africa)   45
Tunstall, KT   193
Turkey. *See also* Anatolia
   audiences   50
   identity as Turkish performer   44, 72–3
   music of the region   29, 31, 33, 34, 38, 44, 45, 67–70, 74
   türkü   45
Turkish Scientific Council   31
türkü   45

Turvey, Michael T. *See* effectivity, concept of
Tweedy, Jeff   176
Twining, Toby   20

U2   70
UK-grime   41
Unfretted.com (website)   48
United Kingdom (UK)   30, 32, 41, 57, 185, 209
United States of America   10, 11, 20, 33, 46, 48, 49, 72, 108, 175–7, 181, 183, 186
Universal Congress of   176
University College London
   Neuroscience department   216
University of California, Los Angeles (UCLA)   187
University of California Press (publisher)   11
University of Surrey   205. *See also* International Guitar Research Centre (IGRC)
Ünlenen, Emre   31
'Uprising' (song)   40

Vai, Steve
   'Deep Down Into the Pain' (song)   92
   'An Earth Dweller's Return' (song)   40
   'I Know You're Here' (song)   40
   Sex and Religion (album)   40, 92 n.7
   other   19, 40, 89–90, 92–4
Valse op.69. no. 2 (musical composition)   117
vaporwave   189
Varèse, Edgard   179
Velvet Underground, The   165
Venezuelan music
   cuatro   109
Verlag Neue Musik (publisher)   143
Verlaine, Tom   173
Vic, Michael 'Atonal'   48
Vicentino, Nicola   26
Vigier (company)   41, 46 n.37, 48
Vigroux, Franck   47
Village of the Unfretted (album)   48
Vinaccia, Gaetano   81
virtual

instruments   230, 232–5, 239–58
networks   4, 39, 47, 51
reality   239–58
scene(s)   39, 50–1, 62, 84, 89, 158
spaces   6, 158, 178, 219, 239–58
Visser, Emily   249
vLookup Trio   52, 57
Vogt, Walter
   Fine-Tuneable Precision Fretboard system   14
   guitar design   16, 27
Vogue Music (record shop, Los Angeles)   181

Warren, Matthew   167
Watt, Mike   175
Webb, Michelle   46
Webern, Anton   233
Wedding Dance (musical composition)   126
weird
   weird, the (Fisher)   185–200
   weirding, theory of   191
Weiss, Gilad   45
Well-temperament   26. *See also* tuning systems (general)
Well-Tuned guitar   3, 9–22
Western art music   9, 82, 96, 111–48
whammy bar (tremelo)   40, 60
Wheatcroft, John   218, 232
Wheatley, Ben
   A Field in England (film)   191
   In the Earth (film)   191
   Kill List (film)   191
Whistle and I'll Come to You (1968 BBC production)   191, 196
Whitesnake   89
White Stripes, The   183, 193

Whitman, Keith Fullerton
   'Fib01a' (song)   166
   Playthroughs (album)   166–7
Wicker Man, The (film)   190
Wilco   173, 174, 176–8
Williams, Tom   4
Wire, The (magazine)   195 n.18
Witch, The (film)   191
Witchfinder General (film)   190
Wittgenstein, Paul   112
Wizard of Oz, The (film)   11
WNMF x AR (musical composition)   248
Wong, Dustin   194
Worldwide Music Exposition (WOMEX)   35
Wright, Paul
   For Those in Peril (film)   191

xenharmonic   19

Yamaha (company)   156, 257
Yepes, Narciso   82, 85, 86, 119
Yo Miles! (album)   176
Young, LaMonte   14
Young, Larry   104
YouTube   33, 39, 48, 49, 84, 92, 184
Yup'ik Dances (musical composition)   16

Zaleski, József Bohdan   139
Zappa, Frank
   'Torture Never Stops, The' (song)   40
   other   40
Zbikowski, Lawrence   113, 125
Zephyr   180
Zerøspace   205
zhivago   226
Zimmer, Hans   49
ZVex Fuzz Factory   156, 177

www.ingramcontent.com/pod-product-compliance
Lightning Source LLC
Chambersburg PA
CBHW052215300426
44115CB00011B/1697